S0-CYE-285

Paperback Trade Inn
145 East Fourteen Mile Rd
Clawson, MI 48017
✆ (248) 307-0226

Deliberate Speed

■ *W. T. Lhamon, Jr.*

Deliberate Speed

THE ORIGINS

OF A

CULTURAL STYLE

IN THE

AMERICAN 1950s

Smithsonian Institution Press
Washington and London

© 1990 by the Smithsonian Institution
All rights reserved

Editor: Nancy Dutro
Production Editor: Jennifer Lorenzo
Designer: Alan Carter

The author takes full responsibility for documenting sources for song lyrics and gratefully acknowledges permission to reprint excerpts from the following copyrighted works. From *Howl*, by Allen Ginsberg, reprinted by permission of Harper & Row Publishers, Inc. From "Tutti-Frutti," in *Life and Times of Little Richard*, by Charles White, Richard Wayne Penniman and Robert Blackwell, copyright 1984, by Harmony Books. From "Good Golly Miss Molly," written by Robert Blackwell and John Marascalco, courtesy of Jondora Music. From "Radio Radio," by Elvis Costello, copyright 1978, Plangent Visions Music Limited.

Library of Congress Cataloging-in-Publication Data

Lhamon, W. T., Jr.
  Deliberate speed : the origins of a cultural style
  in the American 1950s / W. T. Lhamon, Jr.
     p.   cm.
  Includes bibliographical references.
  ISBN 0-87474-379-6 (alk. paper)
     1. United States — Popular culture — History — 20th century.
  2. United States — Civilization — 1945–   I. Title.
  E169.12.L49   1990
  973.921 — dc20   89-26197

British Library Cataloguing-in-Publication Data is available

∞ The paper used in this publication meets the minimum requirements of the American National Standard for Permanence of Paper for Printed Library Materials Z39.48-1984

Manufactured in the United States of America
97 96 95 94 93 92 91 90   5 4 3 2 1

For the memory
of my mother,
Dorothy Kearton Lhamon,
who fostered libraries
and worked for
civil rights,

AND

To Dan Lhamon
and Catherine Lhamon

CONTENTS

ACKNOWLEDGMENTS

During the years I have been trying out these ideas, many people pointed the way. Gene Bluestein laughed at crazy authority early and encouraged specific ideas later. First Reed Whittemore then Doris Grumbach gave me wonderful assignments over the years at *The New Republic,* as did Jonathan Yardley at the *Miami Herald.* Specific conversations with Robert Silberman showed me lodes of information I would never have mined on my own and he later read hundreds of pages of my manuscript. Jerry Stern listened patiently to prototypes of many of these ideas. George Fleming helped an early draft of my first chapter. Michel Fabre tried to minimize mistakes in my second and third chapters. For years now I have relied on David Hagen's friendship and heeded his advice about rhythm 'n' blues. Martin Williams spurred my writing and improved it with his advice and information. I had important correspondence or talks with Greil Marcus, Chris Farrell, Edward Mendelson, Allen Ginsberg, Houston Baker, Peter Ripley, Geneviève Fabre, Jeff Todd Titon, David Evans, James Guetti, Philip Brookman, Charles White, and Norman Malcolm.

During our term in London, my son Dan helped me in many ways, not least by teaching me word-processing skills to tame my tangle of drafts and notes. My father's keenness for intellectual byways and latenight driving started me on this road in the first place. My sorrow is that I did not finish in time for my mother to read *Deliberate Speed.*

Thanks to Hunt Hawkins for years of good conversation and for arranging my research semester. Thanks to the Graduate School at Florida

State University for awarding me a summer writing grant. Thanks to *Studies in Popular Culture* for permission to reincorporate here "Little Richard as a Folk Performer."

Thanks most of all to Fita for her congenial scrutiny and always being there.

PREFACE

Style and decision quickened in American life during the 1950s. Citizens put the Second World War behind them by tuning their daily practices to fit the jumped pulse of information, manufacture, and Cold War competition. Government, business, and education likewise strove to match the excitements of electronic speed, face down nuclear anxiety, and incorporate newly aggressive demands and examples from black and youth cultures. Singly and collectively, people converted their crises to opportunities.

Deliberate Speed concerns this conversion, its existence and its methods. In governance and the arts, as well as in looser forms of work and play during the fifties, there was a sometimes conscious, usually subliminal attempt to catch, cash in, and affirm real chances. People were coming out of hibernation, like Ralph Ellison's invisible man at the end of his novel (1952), to the feeling of "infinite possibilities" (435). They were using—and enhancing in the use—a newly supportive body of lore. Although they could hardly know it at the time, they were borne on a new lore cycle.

Deliberate Speed is about this concerted cultural cycle that was in place by the mid-fifties and still continues. This cycle came into being to wrestle the intense divisions troubling people at the time—the new cast of delinquency, the rights and suffrage struggles, the fears of communism and radioactive fallout, the uprootings of career and postwar migration, and the startling technologies spawning portable radios, televisions, and high-fidelity record players. Across their chasms of regional, racial, class, gender, and age differences, quite various groups were crafting quite similar practices to accommodate the new social challenges and material conditions in their lives.

Their nascent repertoire of shared gestures bonded their burgeoning alliance, but hardly made it universal. In showing the origins of a cultural style, therefore, I imagine no miraculous moment when everyone saw the light. For instance, I enjoy but do not share the obligatory fantasy at the end of fifties rock 'n' roll movies. In many of these films, after parents, high school principal, and police have resisted the music and its performers for an hour and a half, they somehow *hear the beat*. Grinning, tapping toes, and popping fingers, they are soon united with their youths, students, and delinquents, all jitterbugging arms-over-shoulders at the center of a climactic sockhop. This happy cementing of all the social groups is a significant conclusion as useful for matinee-grade films as for Shakespeare's festive comedies, but it is a dream too good to be true.

In real cultural struggle, fractional alliances win compromised victories. Bound together by their common lore in the fifties, a newly congenial alliance cleared cultural territory and began to hold it against the persistent forays of time and opponents. Shorn of the details that compose this book, that was the origin of the deliberately speeding cultural style. But to speak of such origins is hardly to mean *the* cultural style. There are always others. *Deliberate Speed* studies just one widely held way of being in the world, one cultural style that is partly conscious, mostly subliminal, and continually adjusting its mediations among its clients, their competitors, and the material world. The deliberately speeding style has shown its significance by largely prevailing — though, again, never wholly. During and since the fifties, it has cleared and held more and more of the cultural terrain. Its assumptions generated surface phenomena from freedom rides to Jackson Pollock's painting, rock 'n' roll to inclusive aesthetics for all the arts.

Such reworking of the root form extended from the most vernacular to the most cloistered level, from Elvis Presley to Earl Warren. The Chief Justice's concept of "deliberate speed," decreed in the middle of the year 1955, specially conjured for the time's troubles a responsiveness that hovered at the threshold of consciousness. Part of the institutional top of the society pronounced and enforced the phrase, but it is immediately clear that this elite was choosing and codifying cues from impulses moiling at the vernacular bottom.

The multifold significance in the phrase "deliberate speed" showed that the Supreme Court, an agency of conservation, affirmed the radical changes already ongoing in the casual life of the populace. Here in this phrase was rare adaptiveness for an institution, with rare carrythrough.

The term indicated the ripeness of the moment. Had circumstances not been just the way they were, neither the phrase nor the style it epitomized would have prevailed. The end of the war, the lapse of European prestige, the technological revolution, the recognition of the baby boom, the extraordinary surge of black culture, a climate of improvisation in art and mores, the presence of courageous individuals to formulate, argue, and pursue policies, to compose and daily deepen artistic practice — these and more were necessary together.

Because it involves an oxymoron, the concept of deliberate speed was difficult for people to conceive, hard to hold together, and remains difficult to analyze. Just as ordinary living pushes people to one rate or the other, so writers and philosophers have promoted one or the other of its moods. Samuel Johnson favored the slow aspect when, in his *Preface to Shakespeare* (1765), he prided himself on speaking "not dogmatically but deliberately."[1] Charles Olson preferred the fast aspect when he declared, in "Projective Verse" (1950), "fast. . . there's the dogma." Institutions and cautious individuals associate with deliberation; rebels, impetuous lovers, and bebop musicians associate with speed. Fools rush in where justices fear to tread. Thus, when judges appeal to speed they do so in grave circumstances. In addition to the difficult bridge American justice obliged itself to construct, therefore, the phrase "deliberate speed" indicates the alarm the Court felt in the middle of the fifties.

Well beyond the Supreme Court, significant moments of the fifties joined deliberation to speed. In each such nexus, both strands crossed and recrossed to knot together an apparently rickety web. In the sequences of Robert Frank's photographs, in Vladimir Nabokov's prose, in Thelonious Monk's music, in Chuck Berry's performances, in Jack Kerouac's prose sketching, and in Martin Luther King's voice there is this yoking of opposites into the prevailing form of deliberate speed. Important to see in these examples is how they meld their contrarieties. They seem always on the verge of vibrating apart. Nevertheless, they continue to cohere because they grow out of a body of lore that agrees to understand its contributing elements as complementary. These yoked artifacts are *cultural* objects. Particular circumstances conspired to create and continue to acclaim them.

You might say that the contemporary period has earlier dates than *Deliberate Speed* identifies. You might argue that the fifties began in the late forties with the invention of the transistor, the marketing of the first televisions and tape recorders, with Jackson Pollock's first clutch of flung paintings, with Jack Kerouac's initial cross-country experiences. You might claim that the fifties began in 1940 when Hans Hofmann painted

Spring, probably the first avant-garde drip painting. You might say that as early as the twenties the Jazz Age anticipated what was important in the fifties by setting white feet dancing to black rhythms.

If you proposed those points, you would be more an ally than an opponent of the arguments of *Deliberate Speed.* But I would reply that the mid-fifties was when those separate ingredients, and many more, cooked down into a recognizable aesthetic. They became then a set of strategies for cultural action. The focus here is on the fifties, particularly the middle of that decade, because then all the elements of contemporary American culture were in the pot, swapping around, and affecting each other. My disagreement is with those sixties chauvinists who believe countercultures, radical artistic experimentation, and the civil rights movement all began under President Kennedy, with Woodstock, or because of some cosmic consciousness which the moon walk evoked. Not true — in the sixties and after, people ratified the insights of fifties cultural life, popularizing them into mass movements. Contemporary circumstances became conceptual as a usable present about 1955, not much sooner, not much later.

People did have early glimpses of speeding culture in the saxophone excitements of Lester Young and the tumultuous sentences of William Faulkner. They felt vernacular deliberation in the grainy dependencies of William Carlos Williams's poems, the homegrown paintings and photographs of Charles Sheeler. But a form that sustained itself, that was both constant and constantly varied, that extended from the highest Court in Washington to the lowly Dew Drop Inn in New Orleans (where Little Richard surfaced with "Tutti Frutti") — such a form took time to fashion, first, and discover, second.

If deliberate speed was to be found abroad in Ludwig Wittgenstein's later philosophy as well as at home in Benoit Mandelbrot's mathematics of Chaos, it would take time to foment and formulate. The horrors of the Second World War surely delayed and complicated this formation, as did the anxious readjustment to the shortages and intelligence migrations from Europe to America for ten years after the war. The very foraging among the separate ingredients of fifties life for the complements of a satisfying cultural gumbo itself took place with deliberate speed. The contemporary era could not begin immediately after V-day if only because no one invents a congenial lore overnight. It took ten years.

The eventual precipitate at the center of the fifties was culture strong and rich enough to nurture an era. It may not be "good to eat a thousand years," as Allen Ginsberg hoped in "Howl" (131), but it has already served more than one generation. The moves performers devised to remark the hopes and fears of the fifties became and remain the common culture of deliberate speed.

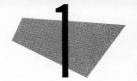

Material Differences

The usual theory about the 1950s is that the decade lacked serious culture. This curious judgment asks people to imagine they had no useful heritage to guide their choices. It contends gestures and actions had no useful context in the fifties, and that no fruitful echoes reassured men and women of their value. The consensus judgment is nonsense at the literal level, because every people has deeply etched structures of feeling to mold its actions and responses. And the consensus is possible to hold at the cultural level only by ignoring or repressing the pesky upstart practices of the era.

Because they diminish complexity, consensus agreements about an era are themselves serious problems. Like any other time, the decade of the fifties had many parts, all of them flowing, none of them dammed for long. The main current into the fifties was a relatively calm stream of canonical culture — tired of doctrinal struggle after the thirties, further exhausted in the rigor of war and its aftermath in the forties, but confident of its course. Yet the fifties were the years of the great expansion of mass and popular culture. This expansion pumped the calm flow that had entered the decade to flood heights by mid-decade. This cultural freshet whorled into side-streams, splashed into turbulent eddies, diverged into puddles. People previously excluded from cultural representation peered then into those diverted cultural reflectors and often enough found themselves imaged there, sometimes for the first time. Other people found clarifications of themselves quite different from their mainstream interpretations. The side-streams provided supportive, shifting, complex pictures of people's lives.

Although many or most of those reflections have been lost, finally some of them are being saved—as with the reissuing of rhythm 'n' blues and rockabilly disks in formats finely enough presented that auditors can decode them. Researchers are turning up old issues of small-circulation magazines with remarkable constellations of talent—like *New World Writing*, no. 7 (1955). In this seventh issue appeared the first excerpts of both Jack Kerouac's *On the Road* and Joseph Heller's *Catch-22*, a sampling of then-new English poets that included Thom Gunn and A. Alvarez, a short story by Evelyn Thompson Riesman, and a review by Donald Hall of "The New Poetry" that called attention not only to Robert Lowell and Theodore Roethke, but also to Adrienne Rich and Elizabeth Bishop. Hall finished his piece—and his words were the last of the issue—wondering if "we are only at the beginning, and not at the end, of a poetic golden age" (247).

Donald Hall's wonder at beginnings and endings in the middle of the fifties aptly answers the consensual agreement that there was no culture in the decade. As the price of democracy is eternal vigilance, so the cost of vital culture is its continual re-creation. People never find out who they are, or their value, by looking into someone else's mirror, nor by accepting cultural judgments from an earlier time. Those reflections are necessary correctives. They guide people toward goals and around pitfalls. But a living culture constantly adapts the usable past to present pressures. Not the other way around. When critics measure the present only with past yardsticks, or when they fail to search widely enough for an era's authentic gestures, then it appears to them that no usable present culture exists.

Concerning the fifties, participant observers made both mistakes. The early critics during the decade generally judged it by the past. Later critics generally refused to see the value in their midst. If they were trying to be sympathetic, appraisers argued that Americans were recoiling from the stress of war when they opted to conceive families and careers rather than new artifacts. According to this apparently sympathetic excuse, American achievement in the fifties was political and social, not cultural. Americans survived and beat back Senator McCarthy with his lists of communists in high places. They survived but sustained the Cold War. They encouraged their President's golf game and forgave his spy planes over Russia. They fought more or less willingly in Korea. They chuckled at the sounds of Beatnik bongos syncopating poetry in the San Franciscan night. They smiled at teenagers revving hotrods over the babble of their car radios. All this, and much more, was quaint and sometimes interesting, but it produced no symphony, no cathedral, no *Moby Dick*. Intellectual convention has it that the fifties amounted to a hole in cultural history.

This consensual hole-in-history is itself an artifact imposed on the times during and continually after it. It has become as much an association of the fifties as pastel coffee tables with wire legs, domed toasters, and the wonder of white wobble bread. It is as fetishized as a Maidenform ad, as constant in discussion of the period as a Zippo cigarette lighter. At the end of the forties, observers agree, the lines of cultural development were clear, canonical, and content. As the fifties came on, culture turned out the lights, settled into its deep torpor, and woke up when a windblown Robert Frost recited "The Gift Outright" at the Kennedy inaugural in 1961.[1] The sixties seemed all the more stunning because the hole-in-history consensus encouraged people to misunderstand how those crucible years had forged the succeeding decades.

How then did this conventional idea of the fifties arise and survive? It served a trade-off purpose. If there was no serious culture, if balm was everywhere in the land, if everyman might happily oscillate between job and hearth, then Americans had successfully turned the corner from the discipline, privations, and social commitment of the war. This agreement, and its survival as a convention, shows how narrowly shrunken was the documented domain at the end of the modern era. The agreement's ethnocentrism left out the grass roots organizing and culture of black people, for instance, as well as the segregation that set them in motion. The agreement's certainty of superiority inhibited its seeking out or understanding the quality in popular culture. As a convention, its autonomous momentum rolled right past the bases for contemporary culture; it excluded and ignored the budding rock 'n' roll, fiction, poetry, sculpture, photography, jazz, and cinema extant at the time. The trade-off was that ignoring and suppressing these pests prolonged the calm contentment of the national host.

When in the early sixties the host culture began to notice that a threatening, difficult culture had been growing under its feet, then would-be sympathizers were at a loss to explain it. Because they, too, had subscribed to the convention that the fifties were a cultural vacuum, these liberals tried to blame the vacuum on the resentments of cultural Yahoos. Murray Kempton wrote this wrinkle on the conventional idea of the previous decade in his *New York Post* column (13 November 1962). The "fifties were not the Eisenhower years but the Nixon years," said Kempton: "That was the decade when the American lower middle class in the person of [Nixon] moved to engrave into the history of the United States, as the voice of America, its own faltering spirit, its self-pity and its envy, its continual anxiety about what the wrong people might think, its whole peevish, resentful whine. The Nixon years belonged to all the young men who had been to the schools which instructed them that they could not be too careful."

How miraculous the surprises of the sixties must have seemed to people who believed the fifties consensus. The aggressive movements for social justice, the new literary styles and forms of painting, the surprising music of rock 'n' roll and reinvigorated jazz syntheses, the multiple excitements of popular culture, the bottom-up political action to muzzle American imperialism — all these phenomena surely seemed a series of immaculate conceptions arising from the orthodox understanding of the fifties. Caught as they were in the consensus agreement, it was inconceivable to contemporary observers that there might have been vitality where they assumed a vacuum.

If the conventional view were a simple misunderstanding set straight in the best cultural accounts, this historical hole would not be so alarming. Most of the best books dig the hole deeper, however, confirming and causing the popular view. Histories such as Godfrey Hodgson's *America in Our Time* celebrate the Kennedy Camelot years and regret those which came before and after. William Manchester's history terms the mid-fifties the "Eisenhower Siesta" (772). Tony Tanner's otherwise thorough study, *City of Words: American Fiction 1950–1970,* in fact tilts sharply toward the sixties. And, until David Garfield's *A Player's Place* (1980), no book dealt with the evolution of American method acting — which, after all, greatly altered theater and film in the postwar period. Not until Taylor Branch's *Parting the Waters: America in the King Years 1954–63,* did the sifted-out political movements begin to receive their due. Nor has the nostalgic haze which the popular media lavished on the fifties helped people notice and understand the significant forces already coalescing in those days. From TV's Dick Clark revivals and reruns of the Fonz to the lists of fifties pleasantries that newspapers continue to publish, the media reinforce the consensus vacuum.

What has always attracted everyone's attention, then as now, was the baby boom growing adolescent and spending its pocket money. The youth domain, that most seething area of fifties culture, was so visible to orthodox critics, in fact, that their labeling placements of it are still influential. Early critics divided adolescent behavior of the fifties into delinquency or apathy, or, as Benjamin DeMott was still lecturing in 1982, "corner boys" and "college boys." By this illusory division pundits severed experience from its expression and set up their own aghast wonder when it turned out, in the sixties, that the two poles were not asunder. The Beatles and Rolling Stones and SDS and the activists of Mississippi Freedom Summer — all these varying types voiced corner experiences in vivid ways that made college men and women attend passionately. As always, the actual people, the actual times, clamber out of the cubbyholes in which observers place them.

By not seeing how the decade's differences were setting new standards and adding up to a new paradigm, even well-wishing commentators contributed to the idea of the hole in the fifties. The hole has as little connection to what really happened then as did *Ozzie and Harriet*. In fact, the fifties were alive with vital art, new codes of behavior, and strong patterns of shape and energy that still survive without conventional acclaim. Films and novels and paintings and songs had to stand on their own. Their composers had to clarify to themselves what their aims were, at least question their own biases, because the popular view, liberal through conservative, correctly states how chilly was the Cold War climate. Those years did not spoil art. The consequence was a period with an uncommonly high proportion of embattled and daring works. It is odd to think of Robert Rauschenberg assemblages, the apparently haphazard sequences of Robert Frank's photos, or the verbose improvisations of Jack Kerouac as pared down, fit for a fight, and aggressive. But they were fit because of the hostility they faced at conception and during their nurture. Their makers had each shed from their deliberately speeding artifacts as many inherited assumptions as they could. Instead, these artists consciously indulged oppositional ideas.

The indulgence was expensive. Even established writers had difficulty publishing their new work. After his well-received first novel, *The Town and the City* (1950), Jack Kerouac accumulated fourteen separate book manuscripts in his duffel before Viking finally realized there were profits to reap from vagabond romance and published in 1957 his now-famous six-year-old roll of typescript, *On the Road*. From among those fourteen titles would come at least three important volumes: *On the Road*, an iconographic celebration of consuming energy on vanishing two-lane blacktops; *Dr. Sax*, in which Kerouac does for a child's vision of good and evil what Joyce did for Molly Bloom's; and *Visions of Cody*, Kerouac's wedding of America's experimental prose tradition with the outcast excitements of male bonding and popular culture. Neither could Vladimir Nabokov find a publisher in the United States for his novel, *Lolita*, so it appeared first in Paris in 1955 with the green leather binding of a pornographic publishing house, before coming home to controversy and ultimate acclaim in 1958.

Norman Mailer has similarly written of his agony while placing and reworking *Deer Park*, the 1955 novel in which he forged his stylistic signature. Already acclaimed as the best writer of his generation, Mailer was trying to slough off the naturalism that linked him to Dreiser and Dos Passos. But because they liked the link which Mailer wished to renounce, the first seven houses that read his novel turned it down. Significantly, it was Walter Minton, the same editor who welcomed home *Lolita* three years later, who finally took *Deer Park* at G. P. Putnam's Sons. When Putnam's accepted his typescript, Mailer rewrote it yet again. Somehow calling up remarkable confidence, he ultimately achieved his new antic style that undercut the bureaucratese and authoritarian spirit then blacklisting the Hollywood he took as his topic. He has embellished such gestures since 1955, often falling into self-parody, but the elements were all fixed then, during the struggle with *Deer Park*.

Tennessee Williams's *Cat on a Hot Tin Roof*, the first excerpts of Joseph Heller's *Catch-22* and Jack Kerouac's *On the Road* (appearing as "Catch-18" and "Jazz of the Beat Generation"), Allen Ginsberg's "Howl," Flannery O'Connor's *A Good Man Is Hard to Find*, and much more originated in 1955. It is, however, not so much the literary surge of the fifties that is important by itself. Rather, what is important is that the same telling denominators that ran through books also ran through politics and everything else that was cultural. Even authors who hardly classify as political in any usual sense—Flannery O'Connor being one and Chuck Berry another—wrote about disenfranchised, displaced, and thus disordered people struggling to fix or simply understand their own place in a hostile or indifferent context. The quality uniting so many of these apparently disparate and subsequently important works is that they were born fighting the forces ignoring and suppressing them. And most important: insofar as art can win anything, this insurgent culture won. Its styles, attitudes, and icons more deeply shaped the styles, attitudes, and art of subsequent decades than have other fifties strains, or even the Cold War authorities themselves.

Despite the orthodox hole in history, the fifties were less the Nixon and McCarthy years, less the years of the whining, lower-middle class, than they were the years of deliberate speed. They were the years when a new cultural style rose from practices people were using to encompass experiences that felt new. Their moves were much more complex and unruly than either Joe McCarthy or Richard Nixon could hope to govern—as each discovered, sooner and later. It was a widespread culture establishing the era's eventual strategies because many separate cables in American life and art, high through low, kinked together, displayed a unified sensitivity and intent, and expressed a congenial awareness of their shared possibilities and impediments.

☐ ☐ ☐ ☐ ☐

Here, then, is an orienting glimpse at chief characteristics of the sudden bend culture and life took together at mid-decade.

Without denying or forgetting their recent agonies, Americans were distinctly more optimistic following World War II, after taking a decade to think it all over, than during the wallows of despair that followed the trench warfare of the first war and the dislocation of the Depression. In spite of the overwhelming impact of Belsen and Nagasaki, and their warning demonstration of human capacity — mass genocide and world incineration — contemporary American culture has tried to find alternatives rather than bewail the obvious. It has tried therefore to escape the modern feeling of confinement, of complete determination, which Jean-Paul Sartre's title *No Exit* so succinctly epitomized. Indeed, many of the central contemporary artifacts — *Catch-22,* Elvis Presley's "Mystery Train," Robert Rauschenberg's combine paintings, for instance — are about this process of finding new ways to overcome despair, reassembling old feelings in new ways so to feel possibility again in the world. These examples provide images also of rapidity, which was doubtless both tied up with the feeling of the fifties and one of its primary behests to contemporary life.

After 1955, the culture became demonstrably speedier in style, delivery, and cycles because it was inevitably starting to represent the megapolitan, geographic, and demographic development of the postwar period. Each of the several reasons for the new deliberate speed in culture is deeply connected to the illusion of what came to be known as "post-scarcity state"[2] energy and the arrogance of its consumption. The implicit aesthetic of a deliberately speedy style matches the consumer economics of the period.

In literary work, as in postwar life, new accents and dialects proliferated. Women, ethnic minorities, and Western and Southern voices capitalized on the beachheads Katherine Anne Porter, Langston Hughes, and William Faulkner had established in the previous generation. This expanded sociology evident in literature was part of a larger awareness of voices and forms in general — "new journalism," Ed Murrow's burrowing documentaries, theme parks such as the newly opened Disneyland, the music of rock 'n' roll, and the mass civil rights movement.

In the fifties occurred a major welling up of confessional and personal expression. Improvisation and emotional volubility became hallmarks of culture from song and poetry to painting and theater. Perhaps the urge to turn oneself inside out on the couch, page, and stage has been an attempt to colonize interior space to avoid the invasive sensory overload which electronic culture amplified on the outside. Perhaps the increasing urgency of personal details was an intuitive assertion of private parts against the public facelessness of a mass society. In any case, artists as disparate as the philosopher Herbert Marcuse and Leroy Griffin of the Nutmegs, a New Haven rhythm 'n' blues quintet, were saying respectively in 1955 that it was a political act simply for a person "to be for himself," and "deep in my heart, there's a story untold."

Culture tilted toward youth. The magnitude and staying power of the youth culture was of course not evident at first but gradually its scope and longevity both proved that the existence of rock films and music, of *Bildungsromane* and denim dishabille were not simply a case of relaxed ambitions on the part of artists, nor only of young faces and expressions, nor of producers flogging unrelated fads—as its critics have variously insisted. So many people, so many films, novels, plays, movies, ministers, mayors, and mothers were angry at the manners and values of the youth culture that for a while it seemed the ideal of Eternal Youth was the most obsessively threatening theme of our time. Clearly this perceived threat militated against calm appraisal. Otherwise, critics would have seen that a culture living under the fear of nuclear annihilation could be expected to fetishize cartoons of vitality. A consumer society without precedent could be expected to celebrate among its members those with the readiest energy for fulfilling its values. After all, much of the art made in service of the youth culture was promising and vital by anyone's standards—*Catch-22,* for example, and Little Richard's songs.

In short, there were structural reasons, material differences, that explained the existence of a youth culture (and the civil rights movement, and the culture of deliberate speed in general). It was foolish then—and irresponsible today—not to search out those reasons, to attack Elvis for his pelvis, Little Richard for his frenzy, Kerouac for his dislocations, without looking at the mutually generating matrix of their effects. Not that any of its opponents slowed down the youth culture, however. Neither the ethical tone of complaint about his songs, nor filming Elvis only above the belt (as Ed Sullivan did), hindered the impact of rock 'n' roll. So totally did youth culture come to integrate itself into contemporary consciousness that citizens now rarely even notice its presence. Taking occupation of the land, youth culture became largely the main culture; it became the atmosphere of American life.

That atmosphere is charged, and wanton squandering of energy—in decibels, pace, and unstable motion—always accompanies it. The best artists, of course, realized that unregulated energy, like any explosion, soon expends itself. After the orgiastic jazz descriptions and the stoned cross-country car rides in *On the Road,* Kerouac delivered both his most remonstrative and unremembered prose. In Part Four of the novel, Sal describes how he and Dean drove south among the Mexican Indians, who held "forth their hands for something they thought civilization could offer, and they never dreamed the sadness and the poor broken delusion of it. They didn't know that a bomb had come that could crack all our bridges and roads and reduce them to jumbles, and we would be as poor as they someday, and stretching out our hands in the same, same way" (246). In a few short years, youth culture became a complete idea of a culture, knowing its beginning, projecting its end, and believing it would choose when that time came whether to explode or consume itself. Jack Kerouac did both, but the youth culture really did neither. It has just lived on and on. Like the English rock group, the Who, the youth culture hoped it would die before it grew old. But it has not yet learned how to die.

After a muted moment between the two world wars, the classic American theme of male bonding, which Walt Whitman called "fervent comradeship," again found its voices. Along with Huck and Jim, Ishmael and Queequeg, Uncle Remus and the blond boy on his knee, now appeared Leslie Fiedler's provocative mid-fifties account of these literary instances ("Come Back to the Raft Ag'in, Huck Honey!"). And there were also instances simultaneous with his account that he did not remark: Dean and Sal on the road, Allen Ginsberg and Neal Cassady and Carl Solomon howling, Skipper and Brick outside Maggie's hot tin roof, Marty and Angie on TV, Yossarian rushing off to join Orr in Sweden, Elvis and the Guys tamped in pink Cadillacs and sleeping on each other's shoulders as they sped to the next town where they would fondle those long guitar necks and incite more frenzy.

Folk or oral culture completed its changes during the fifties to popular or mediated culture. Long produced anonymously at the local level, folklore had been *collected* in urban centers. People *make* popular culture in urban centers, however, and distribute it to the local level, where it usually dissipates uncollected. This was an important reversal of cultural vector. Lore, which previous generations had absorbed at Grandpa's or Uncle Remus's knee or on the store porch, was now absorbed basking in the blue glow of the TV, from the car radio, from comics and theme parks. Instead of producing and participating in their own lore, fifties people began buying it ready-made, became its recipients. Since lore is a substratum of culture — one resource from which all art is created — this basic change in

lore's nature deeply affected, and sometimes seemed to threaten, the creation of art in the postfifties epoch. One of the most substantial achievements of the early contemporary era was the quiet working out of a new
recognition of its own lore.

Around 1955, American culture rapidly moved toward promiscuity, of
which the sexual dimension is only the most obvious. The word's pro-mix
etymology refers to a tendency to blend surprising forms, which is precisely what one finds everywhere on the current cultural scene. "Queen for
a Day" began on TV in 1955, taking viewers into the tabloid lives of others
every afternoon. Rock 'n' roll is a promiscuous mix of previously discrete
musics made by whites and blacks. In the mid-fifties, Miles Davis, Art
Blakey, and Cannonball Adderley began playing soul music which fused
the previously exclusive strands of bop and cool jazz. Most of the exciting
literature of the decade refueled by looking outside literary tradition for
new paradigms. Painting, sculpture, and dance also searched beyond the
parameters of their own respective autonomies. The attempted reassembly
of culture from the scrambled refuse of the old order is what observers
witness in the fifties. Thomas Pynchon, in *Gravity's Rainbow* (1973), stated
this idea most succinctly: "Somewhere, among the wastes of the World, is
the key that will bring us back, restore us to our Earth and to our freedom"
(525).

Postwar changes in material caused the elaboration of all the electric
musics (from rock to synthesizer appendages on the classical tradition), the
new format of radio, and the new documentary. In the more numerous and
elusive cases of the tilt toward youth, speedy style, male bonding, multiplying accents and forms, these new material differences "fixed" — in the sense
of *taped, recorded, caught* — and thus amplified extant impulses or trends that
had not found their happiest medium until the fifties. These amplified
trends became the strategies that have unified first American — then much
of Western — culture since.

Countering the conventional consensus about the vacancy of the
fifties, deliberately speeding culture caught on not only in America, but
also abroad. The sense of a new epoch or cultural generation cropped up in
the developed industrial economies of Europe, in Japan, even in Russia, as
each sought its next stage. Angry young men were seizing London stages
while New Wave films were flooding Paris. But the seizing and flooding
erupted about a year earlier, and were both more widespread and consolidated, in the United States, where conditions created a rich medium for the
new strategies. America did most of the hybridizing, then exported the
seeds for sowing across both the Atlantic and Pacific.

□ □ □ □ □

American fifties culture developed in struggle against the McCarthyite xenophobia, against the increasing institutionalization of life outside traditional family structures, and against the postwar anxieties and ambitions that clamped down on its energies. But such a psychological and political explanation—although necessary—remains insufficient to explain the magnitude of its growth.

All history (not least American) indicates a push and pull for control. Histories of the arts, of the individual's personality, or of the state's domains all show a struggle for control of their field. Indeed, although there are intrinsic reasons for a topic's importance, its historical impact always adds a measure of interest. Did X win? Did X control its field? Did X change the direction of the field's development? For instance, Marcel Duchamp, Man Ray, and Francis Picabia—each of them European—during the halcyon days of New York Dada in the teen years of this century, anticipated almost all the activities of fifties youth. They proposed urinals as sculpted fountains, shaved their hair into stubby stars, and issued at least as many manifestos as any of the fifties avant garde. Duchamp's readymades and Man Ray's photograph of Duchamp's haircut are neither benchmarks of sublimity nor manifestly beautiful in their complexity. Their importance hangs instead on the bravado by which they shocked and shifted the autonomies of the art world, primarily, for they initially altered public taste hardly at all. Their beauty has been a function of their historical potency. As such, however, Dada and its successive Surrealism remained minority phenomena. They were interesting in themselves and in the ideas spinning off them. The widest significance of Dada and Surrealism, however, was to seed the main crops that grew as their progeny—rock 'n' roll, Pop and Abstract Expressionist art, confessional literature. There they had their widest effects, wildly altering public aesthetics. Dada grew out of social and cultural rebellion, influenced subsequent art, but remained largely unable to change life as most people lived it—until the 1950s. Until the fifties, Dada was not a mass movement. Only then did many people eat Dada's fruits. How did that happen?

A major difference between the versions of youth, black, women's, and avant-garde cultures at the beginning of the century and then at the middle of the century is that new broadcasting methods coincided with the mid-century versions. That shocking growth of a new culture in the mid-fifties is explicable only in the observation that material differences during the era swelled the cultural momentum well beyond individual genius and psychopolitical resistance.

The consumer electronic revolution caused the most significant changes in the way culture has felt during the postwar period. American industry introduced three major new appliances in the late forties and set them in American living rooms by the mid-fifties: tape recorders, hi-fidelity systems based on the long-playing record, and television. Moreover, the process of miniaturization, which transistors spawned, hastened the consumer end of this revolution. Transistors made both new and old appliances cheap, convenient, and portable. Furthermore, one leading recording tape manufacturer advertised stereo tapes available to the American public for the first time in 1955. By 1958, when stereo records were generally available, the movement to stereo was firmly entrenched (Gellatt 314–15). There would be no turning back of the electronic clock. From the living room, electronics spread to the bedroom, to the car, and on to the beach, to the jogger and bicyclist.

Much of this new technology derived from war-stimulated research, originally and in subsequent advances. During the Second World War, Germans developed the tape recorder especially to broadcast propaganda. It became available to the Allies only when they captured German equipment (along with rockets) in 1945. The tape recorder, first for audio then for visual playback, has gradually increased in importance ever since and in many ways now supersedes record players as a consumer convenience.

The tape recorder's earlier, pre-consumer, role was also significant. It enabled the documentation of diverse folk styles, thus giving access (among much else) to more models from which Elvis Presley, Chuck Berry, and Little Richard might soon synthesize their new music. And when that time came, from 1954 through about 1956, provincial taping capacities helped preserve rock's local, largely sunbelt sound. The tape recorder thus helped break down the concentration of culture production in its established locations. Finally, as time passed and sophistication increased, the recorder encouraged the manipulation, distortion, and processing of sound that are diagnostic in the current music industry.

Also a product of this era is the 33⅓-rpm long-playing record (LP), which Columbia Records introduced only in 1948, at the same time RCA provided the 45-rpm "single." Both these intended to supplant the 78-rpm recordings of the time, and, after a while, they did. (78s held on, though, until 1959 in the black rhythm 'n' blues market.) It was not at first clear that there was a place for both formats, however, and the so-called Battle of the Speeds began. Not until the mid-fifties did the outcome become evident:

the LP was the device for longer programs and anthologies, Beethoven's symphonies, and Chuck Berry's greatest hits (including "Roll Over, Beethoven"); the single was for individual pop songs; and the 78 "sides" withered away, like rulers no longer needed. Once that battle resolved into a complementary relationship, then the technology was ready to market the new miscegenated music of rock 'n' roll that the tape recorder (plus many factors beyond technology) had permitted. When rock then traveled north from southern cities in 1955, the record industry suddenly scored a $277 million market, $205 million of which was for LPs. So large was this increased market that RCA, then the other major labels, dropped the cost of an LP by as much as 40 percent (Chapple and Garofalo, and *Newsweek,* 1/10/55).

The same year Columbia introduced the LP in 1948, three scientists working in the Bell Lab invented the transistor. John Bardeen, Walter H. Brattain, and William B. Shockley, who together received the Nobel Prize for physics in 1956, thus started the necessary process of miniaturization that allowed hoisting computers into outer space and propelling ethnic voices into America's most private inner spaces. Lagging only seven years after the transistor's invention, Philco introduced the world's first transistorized, battery-powered phonograph, weighing in at seven pounds, for 45-rpm singles only, and costing some $60. And Raytheon introduced an all-transistor portable radio, claiming it cut "battery costs from 'dollars to dimes'" (*Newsweek,* 5/23/55).

This making-small of electronic appliances vastly changed the way people experienced life, from toys to defense, Simon to Sidewinder, toddler to pensioner. Integrated into aerospace, defense, and education, as well as into its initially intended communications, the transistor and then the microchip quickened the demographic flow from the Northeast to the South and Southwest, where the new jobs were. Indeed, the Sunbelt and so-called cowboy culture derive from the postwar invention, population shift, new industry, consumer culture cluster of change—which was all falling in place by the mid-fifties.

This southwestern migration of money, professionals, and entrepreneurs reversed the earlier migrations to northern cities which the South had suffered between the two wars. Between 1945 and 1975, the southern half of the country "underwent the most massive population expansion in history from about forty million people to nearly eighty million people in just three decades, giving the area . . . a population greater than all but seven foreign countries" (Sale 18). Moreover, with the new arrivals came can-do technique, risk capital, and Northern racial attitudes. The integration of the transistor chip had therefore much more than an incidental relationship to American social integration.

Another aspect of these demographics' influence is that they determined much of the content of fifties TV programming. The important growth region of the Sunbelt contained nearly all the "principal battlegrounds of the American frontier, from the Tennessee of Davy Crockett to the Texas of Sam Houston to the Arizona of Wyatt Earp" (Sale 10). Television told the Southern Rim whence it came. Reinforcing the Sunbelt's usable past, TV also provided myths for the wider America, indeed for the bemused contemporary world. Southern Rim culture, therefore, was an important target audience as well as production source for the new art forms of the fifties, from TV to rock 'n' roll, hula hoops to fast-food architecture in the sun.

The most immediately salient and important part of the consumer electronics revolution, at first surpassing even the process of miniaturization, was the concussion of TV's sudden prominence. So intricate and communal were the phases of its development and marketing stretching back through corporate secrecy into the twenties, that to isolate TV's inventors would entail a separate volume. Here, one can only chart its presence: the first TV sets went on sale in 1946; movie attendance was consequently dropping sharply in cities by 1951, when movie houses began folding in droves; commercial television had spread to Britain and Japan by 1955. In less than a decade, the presence of TV had become global.

It is necessary to remember that TV's presence was not always there, that the fifties was the decade of the TV takeover. In 1950, less than 10 percent of the homes in America knew the blue glow. By 1955, the percentage had leapt to 64.5 percent—30,700,000 American households with 42,893,550 TV sets operating. By the end of the decade, 86 percent of American homes had television. Since then, the process has simply completed itself. Now more homes in the U.S. have TV than have indoor plumbing. Televisions are on wrists, in desk drawers and bathroom cabinets, in cars and buses. The middle of the decade was also the moment when television's gross earnings first surpassed those of radio (Karmatz 21).

The penetration of TV into American life furthered a profound shift from time spent producing goods to time spent consuming them. There were implications for state governance. Television developed in the private sector in the U.S., citizens experiencing it almost wholly as a toy, and business treating it as a boon. It enjoyed virtual independence from state control. But European countries held tight the reins of TV's development, and the delivery of its messages, with purchase taxes, annual license fees, and appliance registration. Thus, the U.S. eagerly grasped TV's advertising potential while Europe (and Asia) feared its power of political propaganda. This fundamental difference indicates not only postwar Europe's understandable wariness of ideological amplification, but also partially explains the way America leapfrogged her parent nations into a consumer culture.

By the middle of the fifties, when England's first independent network (ITV) began tentative broadcasting, the U.S. pattern of deluging the airwaves with snowy, fleeting visions of consumer goods was not only rampant and secure, but ideologically conscious. No one needed to wait for Marshall McLuhan's sixties edicts for an adequate analysis. The essential details were extant a decade earlier, evident in the *Art Directors Club Annual 34* for 1955. In the introduction to their anthology of award-winning graphics, these commercial artists knew all about the "transition from word thinking to visual thinking," recognized the epoch as a "period of technical development unprecedented in history," claimed that such technology not only allowed but forced "publication for the fast, comprehensive communication of ideas," and linked it all to the business of creating consumption. Already in the fifties, that part of McLuhan's theory which has not since become risible — books are dead, for example — was simply working knowledge for the layout trade. They must have wondered what the hullabaloo over McLuhan was all about.

The same *Art Directors Club Annual 34* cited a Young & Rubicam ad for ads, "Answer to Automation," which congratulated advertising for solving all of America's problems, helping "American business move all the goods automation can turn out — and have people asking for more." The anonymous commentator for the Art Directors Club then continued in that marvelous *entre nous* tone so revealing in hindsight, "In the new impersonal mass selling era, the burden to manufacture customers will not be limited to . . . the actual point where a product is sold" (Section Five). American TV, this ad crowed, could now "manufacture customers" in their own living rooms. Advertising saw itself as a full partner in the burgeoning new economy. People had begun being advertising's raw material and consumers were already advertising's finished product. Only advertisements could create the hyped need to consume that was an absolutely necessary part of the rapidly expanding economy. As advertising's speediest and most-dimensional force, TV became advertising's chief tool for the processing of people into consumers.

Leisure was what Americans suddenly had plenty to consume. Alvin Toffler reports in *The Third Wave* that during the decade beginning in 1955 there came to be in the United States — for the first time in history, anywhere — more white-collar than blue-collar workers, more middle- than working-class people. Despite Toffler's breathless optimism about the shift, clearly a white collar does not a manager make, nor middle-class attire provide middle-class power. Expanding white-collar employment was cosmetic. It did not address basic powerlessness any more than did the ability to buy goods previously out of reach. Although the attire and affluence helped compensate the continued impotence, their hollowness also sped the cycle of consumption still inflating the economy today. In 1955, however, the syndrome of people spending more than they earned was a fresh enough horror to be news. Here was the burgeoning of the installment plan. In the year's first half, millions of American families "borrowed half a million dollars a month to pay for new cars and appliances on the installment plan. They borrowed a billion dollars a month for new homes. For six consecutive months the consumer debt of the United States reached an all-time high" (Hansen II-I2).

The middle of the fifties was when it became clear that the problem of production, at least in the United States, was yielding to the problem of consumption. Consumption of leisure, consumption of goods, consumption of all the planned and unplanned pollutants that came with charge-account prosperity and manufactured consumers and visual thinking: all these proved that problems accompanied possibilities. Few people were prepared for either. Most people muddled through at first, looking for ways to cope with the tangible differences in their lives. Their deliberately speeding culture was how Americans accommodated themselves in the fifties to their new world.

While deliberately speeding culture helped some citizens, it angered others. Much of the speed, style, slapdash improvisation, and rushing instability in poems, songs, films, and fiction offended keepers of maturing traditions. These characteristics were adjustments artists made to altered material conditions. Many times, however, the offense or delight people took from fifties art was due to changes larger than stylistic adjustments. People in the fifties were facing changes in the structural vectors of society. And their art showed it. As the industrial economy became postindustrial after the war and the modern prudential ethic modulated into a contemporary consumer creed, so were there corresponding changes in directions characters moved in stories.

During the heyday of the industrial economy in the first half of this century, for instance, modern American novelists celebrated people dying to build and impose designs. Fitzgerald's Jay Gatsby, Dreiser's Clyde Griffiths, Faulkner's Thomas Sutpen, and Hemingway's Robert Jordan all die in would-be heroic efforts to stencil the world with their plans. Quentin Anderson has termed such characters "imperial selves." The tragedy for these industrial heroes is their failure to stencil their will lastingly on the world. Their imperial wills fail. But that day is past. During the postindustrial economy of the century's second half, fictional characters in novel after current novel have died taking it all in, speeding on the road, incorporating inanimate matter, enjoying and ingesting their options. The problem now is to deal with this barrage of possibility.

Modern heroes died trying to produce. Contemporary protagonists live and sometimes die trying to consume. Who in serious Western fiction dies of overwork anymore, even in these latter days of workaholics? If the term *tragedy* still has contemporary meaning it is attached to Allen Ginsberg's narrator in "Howl" looking for his "angry fix." Contemporary tragedy is in Flannery O'Connor's Tarwater, in Pynchon's Victoria Wren, in Mailer's Stephen Rojack, in Heller's Bob Slocum, in Kerouac's Dean Moriarty, in DeLillo's Jack Gladney — postindustrial characters who flounder and fail trying to consume the plethoric possibilities jamming them all. Such characters indicate gross changes in American culture from before and after the middle of the twentieth century. Vladimir Nabokov's *Lolita* is an apt example, worth pausing over.

Lolita is a twelve-year-old "nymphet" when fortyish Humbert Humbert first sees her lolling on her mother's patio. He rents a room in her house, eventually marrying the mother in order to steal the daughter's surreptitious squeezes and sneak his own unilateral orgasms. However, Lolita's tastes are less for this ex-French teacher, this bundle of European *partis pris* and psychoses, than for the immediate gratification her era permits. "She it was," Humbert says, "to whom ads were dedicated: the ideal consumer, the subject and object of every poster" (136). The girl ultimately escapes, like some of the Little Red Riding Hoods before her, this wolf in her way. What particularly finishes Lolita is that she strays off the path not into the forest but onto the fast lane. Used up by the time she is seventeen, dead in frontier childbirth before she is eighteen, Lolita's life coincides with the fulcrum years of the country's tip from pre- into full-consumption economy, late forties to mid-fifties, about which Nabokov is carefully precise.

Humbert's pursuit of Lolita is at the beginning of the consumer electronic revolution. He pursues her at the moment of the marketing of

TV and tape recorders and the invention of the transistor. Such hardware and its new popular culture, with their attendant icons and dalliances and possibilities, permitted and began to encourage substantial deviation from traditional Euroculture. The inchoate American pop world is what separates Lolita from Humbert; Lolita's pop world allows her indifference. Those "luminous globules of gonadal glow that travel up the opalescent sides of jukeboxes" (124) in America—that's the incessant competition which ultimately beats Humbert at his gamining. "To the wonderland I had to offer," he laments, "my fool preferred the corniest movies, the most cloying fudge" (152).

In short, Lolita prefers the fast-food hamburger to Humbert's "Humburger" (152): and that is precisely the material difference the novel importantly recorded. Popular culture was there with enough presence, now, to set America off. The year *Lolita* appeared in Paris, 1955, was the year McDonald's raised its golden arches in America, the year *Playboy* first printed nude photos.

When not even many American intellectuals saw they had their own independent culture, when it was still (or again) commonplace to insist that America had no usable past,[3] no tradition of her own, no sense of an independent being, Nabokov demurred. He played his hand when he showed Humbert Humbert overestimating Lolita's dependency. That is, Humbert Humbert clearly tried to colonize Lolita. But, at novel's end, when Humbert remembers an overheard remark Lolita delivered to one of her friends, then Nabokov displayed his private sense of American independence:

> I simply did not know a thing about my darling's mind [said
> Humbert] and . . . behind the awful juvenile clichés, there was in her
> a garden and a twilight and a palace gate—dim and adorable
> regions which happened to be lucidly and absolutely forbidden to
> me. (259)

In plain words, Lolita and the innocent America for which she stands have their own cultures "absolutely forbidden" even to the loving voyeur. Correct in this insight, Nabokov was among the first to put it so articulately.

He was hardly alone, however. Artists in nearly every American form were making quite similar statements. Ralph Ellison, for instance, was describing the independent strength of black lore even transplanted, especially transplanted, to the cities. Elia Kazan and Nicholas Ray and Lee Strasberg were putting such an American spin to method acting that audiences now associated it more with Broadway and Hollywood than with the Moscow Art Theater and Constantin Stanislavski, its actual originator. American painting was by now in its second generation of independence and leadership. Improvisational art from jazz to poetry was flowering in New York and San Francisco as it had not often done since the coming of the Gutenberg galaxy. To have this independent art, Americans had had to discover their separation from dependency on earlier traditions.

In *The Americans,* Robert Frank recorded the precise moment of Americans discovering their difference: acknowledging and finding the means to step away from their colonized selves.[4] It is the moment that Nabokov and company rendered. Over and over, the participants in Frank's photos gesture in at least one of two ways. They put their hands to their faces in vernacular versions of "The Thinker." And they *look away,* memorializing moments which, according to Jack Kerouac talking about an outtake from this series, showed "man recognizing his own mind's essence, no matter what."[5] In both signals, their real gaze is inward, often with their eyes closed in public. These seeming signature gestures characterize not Frank's work as a whole, but this volume, these subjects at this time, ordinary citizens of the mid-fifties. They are a striking confirmation of provincials acknowledging the onset of their capital consciousness, for they enact it. And men like Frank and Nabokov—women like O'Connor and, later, Sontag—were there to fix the images. These were differences of consciousness that had material effects.

Matériel affecting consciousness might be the real contemplation of *The Americans, On the Road, Lolita,* Chuck Berry's songs, and, among many others from mid-decade, Agee's *A Death in the Family.* These works all have an elegiac cast to them in their attitude toward old ways, particularly about the road as they sense it becoming the superhighway, not to mention the Interstate, for which until 1968 there was no name.[6] These books, songs, films, and plays also puzzle over the new electronics, worrying about the differences they will make, as in Frank's images of television sets blabbing to blank cafés and studios, and jukeboxes gathering their environs round them at least as authoritatively as any Wallace Stevens jar taking dominion in Tennessee. In his stage directions for *Cat on a Hot Tin Roof,* Tennessee Williams bulks up this presence of media appliances:

Against the wall space between the two huge double doors upstage: a monumental monstrosity peculiar to our times, a *huge* console combination of radio-phonograph (Hi-Fi with three speakers) TV set *and* liquor cabinet . . . all in one piece. . . . This piece of furniture (?!), this monument, is a very complete and compact little shrine to

virtually all the comforts and illusions behind which we hide from
such things as the characters in the play are faced with. (xiv)

This anxiety about the new media which writers felt in the fifties was
real but predictable. Modern writers in the twenties and thirties had feared
film in the same way. Cecilia Brady in F. Scott Fitzgerald's *The Last Tycoon*
(published posthumously, 1941) opened her story of Hollywood in the early
thirties with memories of how much her English teachers at Bennington
College had "really *hated*" Hollywood "way down deep as a threat to their
existence" (3). Perhaps the new media are in every epoch convenient whipping boys for associated clusters of problems. Or, the media make opportunities. Whichever view observers take, the media of the fifties amounted
to a large portion of the new culture's material differences.

Beyond all that it did to create new customers for business, TV's
penetration into American life coincided with surprising prosperity. At
$375 billion, the GNP in the first half of 1955 reached higher than any such
period ever before in war or peace and up $10 billion over the most closely
competitive period, in 1953. Americans were spending $12 billion a year for
recreation, up $750 million over 1954, and another $55 billion for meals and
beverages outside the home, up $3 billion from the previous year. These
figures underscore *Lolita's* indication that all was not well with families in
Babylon. Parents were spending much money to enforce the home as the
center of leisure, but much money was also financing flight from the family.
This tension, to and fro the family, already pronounced in 1955 statistics, is
confirmed in and confirms the songs and novels of the time. It grew only
tenser as the decade passed, in the art as well as in the material statistics.

The fast-food industry, the new TV dinners that appeared at mid-
decade, the realization that the TV was a useful babysitter — these all testify
that the culture was adjusting to the burgeoning but then still unacknowledged women's movement. Employment shortages during the
war had drawn women from the distaff domain to the factory and office,
establishing a pattern that continues still, a pattern that contributes its bit to
the expanding possibilities of postwar life. A growing economy, better
roads and cars, mushrooming advertising, a culture starting to service
youth needs in addition to adult needs — all these directly or indirectly
squeezed attachments to the family. It wasn't just Junior, but also Mother
and Father, who were feeling tugged away from the conventional home,
even while other aspects of the culture pulled home toward the family
hearth. It is as if the fifties family were taffy. "Father Knows Best," "Captain
Kangaroo," "Wyatt Earp," "Gunsmoke," "Peter Pan" (TV's first spectacular

in 1955, starring Mary Martin), and Disney's "Davy Crockett" were all affirming family images inherited from the Victorians, setting up strong father figures, even while admitting between the blips that some children did not want to grow up or that they wanted their own worlds, as in both "Peter Pan" and the new "Mickey Mouse Club." In general, TV tried to solidify family images while films, fiction, poetry, and plays documented the family's beleaguerment and disintegration. This was the tension that James Dean and Marlon Brando rode to prominence, that Sylvia Plath would record in such poems as "Tulips" (which describe husband and children as "little smiling hooks"), and made James Agee's *A Death in the Family* so poignant. It was clear that there were many positions to stake out on the baby boom. It was clear, moreover, that the baby boom had grown into a lucrative target market and that business had anticipated that market.

The onset of consumer electronics vastly altered competing media such as print and the older electric forms of radio and cinema. Despite the famous McLuhanesque predictions, however, people have not stopped reading, nor listening to radio, nor viewing films. To the contrary, sturdy statistics indicate a higher proportion of readers, listeners, and viewers now than ever before, but by mid-decade they were attending to different art and attending to it differently (Dempsey 23). Literacy did not suffer. Rather, new sorts of verbal entertainments opened up new markets challenging the high literacy of elite readers whom the publishing industry had pampered — and who had controlled the calm flow of canonical culture as it entered the decade, before the flood of popular culture. Such elite readers confused the passing of their privilege with the passing of literacy itself.

Verbal complexity is what literacy protects and projects, encodes and enshrines. By that definition, literacy spread and increased during the fifties. New levels of verbal energy — much of its complexity still unplumbed thirty years later — emerged on record and in film, as the instances of Little Richard and other performers in the blues tradition show. Television and hi-fi spread the cultural franchise much more widely through the population. At the same time and as a partial consequence, new money, new classes, and insurgent ethnics injected their needs into the programming mix. Always looking for new markets, the disseminators of culture from record companies to TV studios to paperback publishers could and did supply these differently refined tastes all across the Southern Rim, and elsewhere. These new groups demanded, and received, their artful justification — from Eudora Welty and James Agee and James Baldwin, Elvis Presley and Cannonball Adderley and Ray Charles, as well as "Gunsmoke"

and "Davy Crockett"—just as all classes that ever before rose to prominence demanded and received from their arts similar assurances.

The combined forms of electronic home entertainment forced cinemas to close by the hundreds in the fifties and reduced the number of
feature films Hollywood distributed in 1962 to a mere 38 percent of the
number distributed in 1949. Delmore Schwartz pointed out early what is
now the cliché: "the owner of a TV set has the greatest of all cathedrals of
the motion picture right in his own living room." That is why Hollywood
and TV were then, he said in 1955, in "a state which can only be called *acutely*
transitional. This is also true of TV as a whole and of the entire entertainment industry since the new medium may dominate or devour all the older
forms" (21). Dominate, TV has done, devour, it has not. But Schwartz's
writer's anxiety stamped itself on the succeeding era anyway.

In his book, *Television,* Raymond Williams has coined a more accurate,
if more awkward, term for this cultural difference TV made. Williams calls
it the increasing "mobile privatization" of the West. As the media became
more and more massively centralized, some consumers diluted that condition, or countered its feel, by receiving it not in mass arenas such as the
previous era's film palaces, but in the privacy of their homes or cars. Indeed,
one of the more interesting forms fifties culture patronized—especially
because it melded together both mass and private experience—was the
drive-in movie: all through the decade the great bulk of newly built
cinemas were drive-ins. People were part of a mass culture at the drive-in.
But they had a metal cocoon protecting their vulnerable individuality; and
they had mobile potential, too. The driver of the car could always cut out of
the mass. Ultimately, cutting out has been more important than driving in:
the drive-ins are all gone now, but for a few fossils, and the cocoon is
everywhere more mobile in the omnipresent Walkman and its many progeny, such as the wrist TV and the ever-thinner portable compact disc player.

When this urge to privatization began, the bourgeoisie of the fifties
emulated the princes and princesses of yore much more than they imitated
the middle class between the wars. The modern middle class liked to
promenade in public and attended the theater to see and display. The
Sunbelt middle class, beginning in the fifties, used the new media as
switched-on, robotized court jesters, which they enjoyed in the privacy of
their own formica mead halls, now called rumpus rooms, with their feet up
and shirts open, banquets laid before them in individual aluminum trays,
brew and snacks as handy as at King Arthur's round table. With the lights
low and the blue glow up, even a tract home may seem a castle.

This quirk of history had gone so far by the mid-fifties that the studio system in Hollywood had developed Cinerama, Superscope ("the new anamorphic process of the giant wide screen"), CinemaScope, Todd-ao, Aromarama, Smell-O-Vision, 3-D, and other spectacular scams — among them Marilyn Monroe, Jayne Mansfield, and all their clones — to lure viewers back from the private, small, blue screen to the public, even wider, silver screen. At the same time, however, Hollywood also experimented briefly with the opposite tack. Such films as Stanley Kubrick's much-underrated *The Killer's Kiss* (1955), Richard Brooks's *Blackboard Jungle* (1955), Nicholas Ray's *Rebel without a Cause* (1955), as well as Elia Kazan's various films with Marlon Brando and James Dean from 1950 to 1955 demonstrated a refreshing independence. Each was willing if not eager to forego the mass audience for smaller, more fragmented, embattled, and alienated audiences than the prewar and pre-TV Hollywood had habitually courted.

Until TV atomized the film's appeal, there had been no financial need — or chance — to make such films. Likewise, in subsequent decades it was interestingly true that the citizenry pursued with almost equal frenzy both the mass society and its shards. Along with the growth of arena rock, for instance, came the simultaneous proliferation of bands clearly aimed at a minority taste, and independent labels to promulgate them. For example, one listened to the group Stiff Little Fingers on the Rigid Digit label.

Finding strategies to cope with consumer electronics united all the branches of culture in the fifties. As Hollywood explored new structural responses to the wired home, so radio, literature, foreign films, painting, and jazz all experimented creatively with style. After TV pinched radio's narrative content — stole the quiz shows, sitcoms, soap operas, horse operas, grand operas, grand ole opry, even the news — radio was briefly a void, but only briefly. In desperation, it turned to the previously denigrated content of black music, in the form of rhythm 'n' blues and the very new rock 'n' roll, and to the jive patter of blacktalk which young, white deejays absorbed imitating older, black voice artists. One favorite among the older originals was Baltimore's Fat Daddy, whose midnight sign-off had become legendary by the beginning of the sixties, and went something like this: "Great kooka looga mooga (BONG!), this is yo' Fat, Fat Daddy (BONG!) walkin' the backstreets of B-town (BONG!) like a fat, fat sparrow (BONG!) alone with the bells (BONG!) of Bald-mer, sayin' a fat, fat (BONG!) good night to *you*."

Radio's changes illustrate the bends taken in all the media and arts. Each followed a progression understandable as the principle of passé pursuit: each medium and each art most fulfills its potential the moment *after* it loses its mass audience and faces its apparent obsolescence.

Just as wholly new styles and directions in poetry and fiction, painting and jazz arose in the fifties in competition with the newly rewired home, so did wholly new radio chains spring up based on rock, ding-a-ling news flashes, the Top 40 format, and the slipping-sliding patter of the Fat Daddies, Rockin' Robins, Jumpin' Georges, Moondog Alans, and Wolfman Jacks spread across the land like so much peanut butter. This change at first was the intuitive response of local programmers struggling to fill the void caused when TV wrecked radio's network programming. If new formulae swept into the gap almost immediately — as with the Top 40 programming that Todd Storz's New Orleans-based chain first established in 1955 — at least this new pattern began as a real response to audience behavior (Gellatt 306). Originally, the impulse for the formula was bottom-up, not top-down. Having noticed that youths gathering around jukeboxes played their favorite songs over and over, rather than stressing variety, Storz had his stations mimic teen behavior. The Storz chain began playing popular songs as often as forty times a day. But this imitation soon became dictation of audience taste. Moreover, the repetition speeded up exhaustion of a song's popularity, providing the station with the powerful burden of supplying new alternatives faster and faster.

Because radio responded creatively to its threatened obsolescence, more radios were operating in 1955 than ever before — 111 million. Sales of the appliances were up 40 percent over the year before, and the total number of stations had doubled since 1947. Forced to reinvent its content after pessimists tolled its death knell, radio flourished as never before, fulfilling a potential it never suspected. Unlike old soldiers, old media do not fade away. Rather, they grow more vital in passé pursuit. They stop seeking the majority audience, formulate instead a minority aesthetic, and please fewer people more thoroughly.

During a period of passé pursuit, each medium pares down to what its controllers consider its unique strength. Hollywood film typically chose spectacles, as it is still doing today, stressing its gigantism and its capacity to bring off special effects. Radio emphasized its fleeting instability and, with its black and youth idioms, its very minority status. Painters redoubled efforts during this period to approach pure process: the action of painter confronting and covering virgin canvas. That's why Harold Rosenberg's term "action painting" came to apply generically to all the various competing painting cults in the postwar period, from abstract expressionism through combine paintings to subway-car graffiti. During passé pursuit, a medium streamlines itself, ups the beat and pace. Hence, bop double-timed swing, rock double-timed rhythm 'n' blues, and punk double-timed rock.

Jack Kerouac, Norman Mailer, and Allen Ginsberg double-timed Gertrude Stein, John Dos Passos, and William Carlos Williams. The principle of passé pursuit boils down to common sense: when threatened, people fight back with what they think they do best.

Passé pursuit in the fifties also illustrates recognition of new paradigms to pursue. The speed and staccato format in each of the consumer electronic media was a new model of energy's regulation and play. Beat poetry and the prose of Kerouac, Mailer, and Pynchon all emulated the new form of the era—momentous spasms of energy frequently linked together amorphously. Electronics had programmed the audience to attend in concentrated spans with heavy doses of information sandwiched between relaxed lapses. If contemporary artists were to claim attention from the audience they shared willy-nilly with the electronic media, artists would have to participate in the electronic parameters. They did: Joseph Heller's chapters grew as brief as the gap between television commercials; Robert Rauschenberg recycled newsprint images and automobile detritus into his assemblages; Robert Frank snatched photos of mostly Southern Rim subjects from his moving car window. That's one way art has always rejuvenated itself—by discovering new potential in new material relations.

The largest difference that the new material conditions made in contemporary culture, thus also in contemporary life, was the speeding up of cultural cycles. The new technology made information available so much faster that audiences could develop and exhaust forms as they had always done, but at an unprecedented speed. This speed meant that the old process of European validation of American popular art could occur more quickly. Kerouac's image of the road returned to these shores in Peter Handke's Austrian novel, *Short Letter, Long Farewell* and in the German Wim Wender's film, *King of the Road*. Nabokov excited loving attention to American motels and gas stations. French critics celebrated "hot jazz" and *film noir*. English youths permitted polite Americans to reattend to rhythm 'n' blues after the music of the Beatles and the Rolling Stones redeployed its vitality. All this happened quickly beginning in the fifties and is still continuing. The development cycles of fiction, jazz, film, and rock 'n' roll all stepped up.

Accompanying this redeployment came an emphasis on repetition, probably because electronics and plastics encouraged it even more than mechanical, industrial methods had in the century's first half. Everywhere one looks at mid-century, there was the same emphasis on replication, on control or manipulation or processing of surfaces (as in smooth, bright, and shiny plastic or chrome or Naugahyde). People wanted and designers stressed inheritance of familiar forms from popular culture (targets, flags, tires, detective formulae, blues lyrics, sexual clichés, and folklore). And people used those givens to serve certain common themes and forms. The aerodynamic *swoop* showed up everywhere, from auto fins and chrome, to coffee tables and couches, from ashtrays to jewelry to Steuben glass sculpture, and then became the registered trademark of a running shoe. It celebrated speed, it signified motion and the pleasure of plastic freedom.

The repetition of shapes and insignia and disparate themes in the decade had many implications. Initially it solicited the new syntheses necessary as the decade deepened because it allowed people to identify with and declare positions previously unavailable to them. Teenagers wearing coonskin caps in Syracuse, and craving Tex-Mex Fritos packaged in Dallas, might accompany their mother or older sibling to the supermarket, riding in Detroit's tail-finned Impala and listening to Macon's Little Richard sing a song with a New Orleans arrangement on Los Angeles's Specialty Records label. Such multiple juxtapositions, commonplace today, were still surprising then. They quickly stitched the crazy quilt of signs now charismatic in contemporary American life. The ease and frequent emptiness of the combinations contributed to their rapid consumption, so that Americans gobbled styles and information, form and knowledge, like they burned petrol, pushed back the night with neon and searchlights, smoked cigarettes, and swilled cola: ever more, ever faster.

Whether in abusing material resources or instigating thoughtful plans for urban redevelopment, social integration, and a steady-state economy, opportunities in the fifties ensured also the danger of new vulgarities. If an item could be replicated so easily, some said and continue to say, it must be cheap. If it becomes a best-seller, if it is popular, it must be worthless. So goes this plausible line. But does the democratization of culture and education really cheapen it? Or does it dilute its exclusivity, diminish its privilege?

The *life* of an idea or synthesized shape is much shorter now not only or simply because heavy-handed people have thumbed it but also because so many more hands—deft and sensitive ones, too—have kneaded and needed and used it up. Many more people attending to a form or an idea simply exploit all its possibilities, see through what it can do, much more rapidly than just a third of a century ago.

Compare the history of the novel to that of rock 'n' roll. Both started out a minority taste, became a mass taste, and then splintered into several subgenres. Both have been the typical cultural expressions of classes and epochs. Both started out aggressively fighting for their share of attention, novels attacking the drama, the tract, and the poem, rock attacking jazz and pop and rolling over classical music.

The novel in English was at first the scrappy street prose of the cony catcher and the parading of Aphra Behn fantasies. Then, with Henry Fielding and Samuel Richardson, through Charles Dickens and George Eliot, it became the proud voice of the middle class. When that class splintered, as reported in fictions by Henry James and Edith Wharton and Mark Twain, as confirmed in Joseph Conrad and Virginia Woolf, and as reinforced in Thomas Pynchon and Susan Sontag—and not incidentally when the media started to proliferate into film and radio and large circulation magazines—then the novel itself splintered. The novel fell back to servicing distinct minority tastes, from challenging consciousness extenders to formulaic revolving-rack anodynes. Now the novel is another of the varieties of *print*, small stuff compared to the clout of the electric media in all its immediate power. This rise and fall of the novel took just over three centuries.

The rise and fall of rock 'n' roll took just over three decades. From its minority start in the South in the early fifties, through its renaissance in the mouths of English imitators in the early sixties, through the second renaissance in California in 1967, through its mass acceptance and incorporation into college classes in the seventies, rock 'n' roll ran through its rapid ascendancy. Its severe splintering also began in the seventies, if not before, with punk and postpunk and new wave groups. This period of fall was really its period of passé pursuit, reflecting rock's reservicing of the minority tastes it had increasingly neglected while it was growing into a majority art form.

There can be no doubting the way the era's technological changes quickened the development of every one of its forms. Genres, forms, and idea-constellations in this time have taken on a deliberate speed, circling faster than anyone was accustomed to seeing them come and go. Rather than exhausting the stock of available ideas, however, the contemporary hands-on access to information has replenished and augmented it even while leveling the value of some privileged positions. When people could reproduce an idea or a form inexpensively, people did. More and more, they toyed with more readily available ideas, shapes, and bits of information

than they ever could before the material differences of the fifties yielded
such ready access. And they continue to jigsaw startling recombinations
that further contribute to the stock in a larger jigsaw possibility. As it
continues, this rate will seem more and more quaint like the rates of the
past, like the gait of a horse and buggy, like the pace of a Model T, like the
once blinding but now grinding 4.77 MHz clockspeed of the original
personal computers.

What is striking, and the subject of *Deliberate Speed,* is that every
cultural bailiwick in our time looks over its shoulder, alarmed in one way or
another, to its own crawling buggy past. In painting, sculpture, jazz, rock
'n' roll, drama, fiction, poetry, film, and architecture there was in the mid-
fifties a shift in both the velocity and vector of development, a kinking of
each form's cable. This bend in every art's history is interesting by itself,
providing many local examples, but the collective kinking of all the cultural forms together, more or less at once, has made the large difference that
preoccupies *Deliberate Speed.*

Far from there being no culture in the fifties, or its being the whining
sound of lower-class resentment, the truth is that conditions in the fifties
produced an aggressive and whole culture which was distinct from its
predecessor and is not yet replaced. All the elements of American contemporary culture were in place by the year 1955, when the civil rights movement began, when the TV takeover had reached the majority of the nation's
homes, when rock 'n' roll surfaced, when the consumer society and its
energy problems were as visible as the fallout and bomb shelters beginning
to obsess American citizens, and when the baby boom's outriders started
coming into their own. No wonder the sociologists David Riesman and
Nathan Glazer confirmed that year "a decisive shift in the American mind"
(48). It was neither good nor bad, this mind's gearshift into deliberate speed.
It was what beleaguered people could fashion to encompass their mate-
rially different experience.

To decide without much search that there was no important culture in
the fifties, or that the genuine voice to be heard then was Nixon's whine, is
to misunderstand the resilient nature of human culture in overcoming
adversity. Indeed, a considerable part of fifties culture takes that point as its
topic, emphasizing its resolute, dialectical relationship to the mainstream.
From Brando's omni-rebellion to Jasper Johns's ironic flattening and
palimpsesting of the flag, from Martin Luther King's bus boycott to Little
Richard's sexual rebellion in "Tutti Frutti," from Neal Cassady's stimulated
daze to Gary Snyder's Zen ways, fifties culture was an oppositional culture.
It was quite clearly and quite often about the need to have an effect, about

overcoming malaise, affectlessness, anomie, impotence — about overcoming the whole laundry list of accusations that the period's armchair commentators liked to toss its way. If there really was apathy in a significant part of the population after the war, the cultural record shows there were busy hives counteracting it well before the frenetic and supposedly uniquely active sixties.

The most important poems composed at mid-decade, for instance, doubtless include two by Allen Ginsberg, "Howl" and "America." He begins the first poem acknowledging his victimization. The best minds of his generation have been "destroyed by madness." They search "negro streets" for answers. He concludes the second poem overcoming this alienation. Converting his adversity into play, he promises his country in public to put his "queer shoulder to the wheel" (*Collected Poems* 148). Acknowledging and forefronting one's difference is the leitmotif of the art that came to counter the whine. The culture of deliberate speed, Ginsberg wrote in "Howl,"

> rose reincarnate in the ghostly clothes of jazz in the
> goldhorn shadow of the band and blew the suffering of
> America's naked mind for love into an eli eli lamma
> lamma sabacthani saxophone cry that shivered the
> cities down to the last radio. (line 77)

In using Christ's last words on the cross (translated at Matthew 27:46 as "My God, my God, why hast thou forsaken me?"), Ginsberg has slightly respelled and doubled the King James version's "lama."[7] Stuttering the question anthemically, Ginsberg blows it through a saxophone to shiver his existing cities as Joshua did Jericho. Importantly, however, this time around there will be amplification sufficient to shiver all the cities because poets will use the media. Ginsberg's appropriation of Matthew further indicates this extraordinary ambition of both the poet and the audience which accepted his lines as a creed. When Ginsberg located the famous Christian wail within the shadow of jazz storming social walls he made an imaginative gesture that would be iconic for deliberately speeding culture. His twisting, eclectic confidence documented, too, that culture's contemporary synthesis. He radically yoked aggressive Judeo-Christian myth with Afro-American expression.

Rather than ignoring or renouncing tradition, as many critics originally claimed, this deliberately speeding culture recharged tradition for its own uses. Ginsberg reimagined the wail of abandoned Christianity and resuscitated it into a battle cry against victimization. When he yoked this rebirth with the consumer electronics revolution (radio) and black culture (jazz), he put explicit alliances—indeed, the principle of alliance—at the heart of the aesthetic he delivered. Like the deliberately speeding culture which it helped inaugurate and for which it can stand, "Howl" filled any purported fifties hole in history.

DELIBERATE SPEED

Charlie Parker, the great saxophone player and bop jazz improviser, died laughing on 12 March 1955. Ill, propped on pillows in the suite of Baroness Pannonica de Koenigswarter at the Hotel Stanhope in New York City, laughing at a vaudeville juggling act on the Dorsey Brothers' TV show, Parker choked, then succumbed to a seizure. Although he was only thirty-four years old that spring, his attending physician estimated the age as fifty-five, for Parker had paced his life at the tempo he spurted conceptual innovation through his alto. Within days, all over New York but especially in its subways and alleys, the legend appeared spontaneously: "Bird Lives!" Charlie "Yardbird" Parker had joined the rare line of black cultural charismatics who were adopted by segments of both black and white culture.[1] Parker's music epitomized the newly emerging culture of deliberate speed.

All his discipline was devoted to intensity. One first heard his speed and nimble chaos, the sound of someone extraordinarily attentive to the present moment. Then the structure supporting the music's surface discombobulations gradually appeared. Finally one realized the moving—even mortal—risks Parker took circumventing limits others accepted. This progressive understanding of Parker's dimensions shows well in a comparison of two successive responses by two admiring writers. In 1952, Jack Kerouac defined bop as that music which surrounds its subject "indirectly and too late but completely from every angle except the angle we all don't know" (*Visions of Cody* 296). Twenty-one years later, Thomas Pynchon would remember hearing just that mortal angle nobody can verify in Parker's music: "down inside his most affirmative solos honks already the

idle, amused dum-de-dumming of old Mister fucking Death he self"
(*Gravity's Rainbow* 63). Parker's influence, like bop, like black culture, deepened its impression over time.

Within the month of Parker's lethal hilarity, the first international
meeting of unaligned nations, now known as the Third World, met in
Bandung, Indonesia. Mostly Asian and African states, twenty-nine in all,
sent delegates. Adam Clayton Powell attended from the United States as an
observer, but reported more hindrance than help from his government.
Nevertheless, he and Richard Wright, who analyzed the conference in *The
Color Curtain,* confirmed the gathering's inspiration. It had wide ramifications, ranging from tiny to large. From the beginning of the conference,
Wright claimed, its cohesion "smacked of something new, something
beyond Left and Right." Instead, races and religions were the "vague but
potent" new forces operating there. Quite consciously, the "despised, the
insulted, the hurt, the dispossessed — in short, the underdogs of the human
race" (12, 13) — were banding together not on ideological but on more
instinctive grounds.

Bandung generated Herbie Nichols's little-known piano composition,
"The Third World" (recorded 6 May 1955). On a grander, if less specific
level, it confirmed the self-consciousness necessary for the unaligned gov-
ernments to cohere as a policy-enacting group. Thus the Bandung allies
supported the Soviet threat to employ nuclear force against the British and
French invasion of Egypt in 1956 to regain control over the then-recently
nationalized Suez Canal. The Bandung Conference signalled that European control of the developing continents had ended, and thus marked an
international equivalent to the emergence of black culture at the national
level within the United States.

As their culture rose to prominence, blacks were continually in the
news during the last half of 1955. Walter White was surely the last important
Negro leader to have light hair and blue eyes. As Executive Secretary of the
NAACP, White had pushed the *Brown v. Board of Education of Topeka, Kansas*
case to the Supreme Court, and he had heard Justice Earl Warren's "Black
Monday" decision (17 May 1954) promising to integrate the public schools.
The Court did not then implement its decision; and Walter White died the
same month as Charlie Parker, so he never heard the famous ruling Warren
wrote and delivered to a packed courtroom the last day of May 1955. In his
last paragraph, Justice Warren ordered "the District Court to take such
proceedings and enter such orders and decrees consistent with this opinion
as are necessary and proper to admit to public schools on a racially
nondiscriminatory basis with all deliberate speed the parties to these

cases." The heaped syllables and perverse word order in Warren's sentence perhaps lack eloquence, but the terse phrase "deliberate speed" stuck in the mind like a dart in the bullseye.

Where did Earl Warren derive his most famous term, one "so untypical of the normal Warren mode of expression" (Bernard Schwartz 121)? The phrase came directly from Felix Frankfurter, who first passed it to Warren in a memo he circulated among his colleagues on 15 January 1954 (G. E. White 167). Beyond that, the remarkably resonant phrase "deliberate speed" echoes and evokes all of America's attempts to transform itself from an industrial to a postindustrial society. The real importance of the phrase is how it caught and crested a welling American mood. Warren would not have followed Frankfurter's suggestion, nor would the phrase have become centered in American consciousness, had it not risen from a larger momentum running deep in the national life at mid-century. In many ways the state was catching up with and codifying the already deliberately speeding society — which in its turn was cuing off black culture.

Making integration stick at the practical level proved even more difficult, however, than achieving the abstract transformation in the courts. Smooth on the surface, the summer of 1955 was hot and dry, and race talk crackled under northern neon and southern Jack pines. Justice Warren's decisions had stirred people on both sides of the issue, doubtless contributing to the Emmett Till case, which a few years before might have remained a routine horror, but in the summer of 1955 became instead a rallying point. The details remain lurid.

Emmett "Bobo" Till, a black and barely fourteen-year-old lad from Chicago, was spending the summer out of trouble and off the streets with his sharecropping uncle in the deep Delta hamlet of Money, Mississippi. Carolyn Bryant, a young white mother of two small boys, sold Till two cents worth of gum over her husband's grocery counter one Wednesday evening late in August. She accused Till of asking her for a date, whistling at her, and bragging of his success with white women. There are reports that polio caused Till to whistle when he tried to enunciate clearly (Raines 133). But Huie has written that Till was intentionally bragging and clowning in order to win favor with his country cousins. In any case, early that Sunday morning, Carolyn Bryant's husband and his half-brother, Ray Bryant and J. W. Milam, kidnapped Till at gunpoint and admitted later that they had done so. These men were the last to see young Till before the sheriff dragged him up from the bottom of the Tallahatchie River with the back of his head shot away.[2]

In Chicago, ten thousand mourners viewed his coffin. But the case was processed in Tallahatchie County, Mississippi, where there were then 19,000 blacks, 11,000 whites, and no blacks registered to vote. The all-male, white grand jury closeted itself for an hour and then acquitted everyone, claiming insufficient evidence. Nevertheless, William Bradford Huie's lucid articles in *Look* and *Reader's Digest* soon appeared with incriminating details and confessional quotes from the killers. Still, no one has ever served time for Emmett Till's murder.

The week of the verdict in the Till case was also the week that President Eisenhower had his heart attack in office, reason enough for some conservative commentary to ignore what passed for justice in Mississippi. But others worried more about America's than Eisenhower's heart. I. F. Stone wrote in his *Weekly*, 3 October 1955: "To the outside world it must look as if the conscience of white America has been silenced." Then he went on with uncommon foresight, because he could not yet have known of Martin Luther King, Jr., who was already waiting in the wings of Montgomery, Alabama: "The American Negro needs a Gandhi to lead *him*," I. F. Stone wrote, "and we need the American Negro to lead *us*." December fulfilled everyone's needs.

At rush hour on Thursday evening, 1 December 1955, Mrs. Rosa Parks, a forty-two-year-old seamstress at the downtown Montgomery Fair department store, sat down in the first Negro seat of a Cleveland Avenue bus in Montgomery, Alabama. Whether she was annoyed at the insistent Christmas decorations already up, thinking about larger indignities such as Emmett Till's murder, or simply angry at the repeated and stepped-up harassment of blacks on Montgomery's buses, she never said. When the white driver turned around and called out for the occupied black seats in the discretionary zone, however, neither Mrs. Parks nor three black men moved.[3] Driver J. P. Blake came back, explaining to his recalcitrant passengers that he would arrest them if they did not yield their seats. The three men moved, but Parks told him to do what he had to. She stayed seated until Blake fetched the Montgomery police, who booked her at the station.

There were many successful improvisations that percolated through black (and white) culture in the fifties, from Mrs. Parks's emphatic sitting to Little Richard's ecstatic keening to what Ralph Ellison has called the "wild star-burst of metamorphosis" in his novel *Invisible Man* (xxi). In each case, however, it is important to stress that there was much more work below than above the surface. Mrs. Parks was tired that evening from her job, surely, but her exhaustion was balanced by years of organizational homework. Just that summer of 1955, she had been studying political alternatives and interracial living at the Highlander Folk School in Monteagle, Tennessee; as a long-standing member of the Dexter Avenue Baptist Church political discussion groups, her temperament, inherited she has said from her father, was activist; and she had been both a youth adviser and secretary for the Montgomery NAACP, whose leader, E. D. Nixon, had recently been trying to challenge the city's rigorously segregated bus service.

Thus the conventional picture of a civil rights movement igniting spontaneously around the tinder of her passivity is inaccurate. Oppression caused lifetimes of scheming. A hardly incidental example is the time a Montgomery bus driver humiliated Jo Ann Robinson, a teacher at Alabama State College who had absent-mindedly sat near the front of a Montgomery bus, in 1949 (Robinson 16). In tears when she quit the bus, Mrs. Robinson took over the Women's Political Council of Montgomery and "prepared to stage a bus boycott when the time was ripe and the people were ready" (17). She and the three hundred other women in her organization were waiting. She has since estimated that before the boycott "twenty to twenty-five thousand black people in Montgomery rode city buses, and . . . about three out of five had suffered some unhappy experience on the public transit lines" (43). These were the people who were waiting for the civil rights movement, like people all across the South and in the North, too. It was no single event but the longtime push and pull of institutional racism against a complex response within black culture that initiated the movement. Until 1955, however, the scheming lives among blacks had been largely isolated, impotent, and invisible. At year's end they came together, gathered power, and marched in public.

E. D. Nixon's scheming brought most of the principals together. He was particularly skillful in uniting the local black clergy with Mrs. Robinson and her Women's Political Council, who worked militantly behind the male oratory. As early as August of 1955, Nixon had been impressed by a speech King gave, and had told a friend "I don't know how I'm going to do it yet, but someday I'm gon' hang [King] to the stars" (Raines 48). But more than E. D. Nixon's planning was involved in black Montgomery's response to the city's statutes and region's customs. There was also the readiness of the citizenry for change.

Nixon has recalled what he saw when he came out of court with Mrs. Parks the first day of the boycott: "I'd been in court off and on for twenty years, hearing different peoples, and very seldom, if ever, there was another black man unless he was being tried. But that particular morning, the morning of December the fifth, 1955, the black man was reborn again . . . . I couldn't *believe* it. When we got outside, police were standing outside with sawed-off shotguns, and the people all up and down the streets was from

sidewalk to sidewalk out there. I looked around there, and I bet you there
was over a thousand black people—black men—on the streets out there"
(Raines 46–47).

But it was Mrs. Jo Ann Robinson's political group, founded in 1946 by
teachers at Alabama State College "for the purpose of inspiring Negroes to
live beyond mediocrity" (Robinson 23), that started the idea of boycotting
the city's buses. Between midnight the Thursday night of Mrs. Parks's
arrest and 7 a.m. the next Friday morning, Jo Ann Robinson had written
and secretly run off tens of thousands of leaflets on the college mimeograph
machine. She and two students had distributed them all across town so that
the people would pass them around all weekend. The leaflet told of Mrs.
Parks, made its brief case, then ended with its plea: "Don't ride the buses to
work, to town, to school, or anywhere on Monday. . . . Please stay off of
all buses Monday" (Robinson 46). They planned to stay off the buses only
for one day. When they succeeded the first day in rolling the buses empty,
the encouraged community agreed to push principles originally so moderate that they did not even include integrated seating.

Because he was as yet politically unaligned, articulate, and Mrs. Parks's
pastor, the boycott's Coordinating Committee elected Reverend King to be
its president. In his first, improvised, speech at their first rally that Monday
night, 5 December 1955, King spoke most presciently. King had less than an
hour to consider his words, but his phrases were moving and mature
(Garrow 23). "If you will protest courageously, and yet with dignity and
Christian love," he intoned, "when the history books are written in future
generations, the historians will have to pause and say, 'There lived a great
people—a black people—who injected new meaning and dignity into the
veins of civilization'" (King 63). This early, then, King was consciously
cuing his country and beyond.

East versus West, love versus analytical struggle: that was the dialectic
in King's personality and advocacy. The synthesis he effected and represented first to the rally crowds, then to the nation at large, was in his
particular voice. Recordings still confirm its coal-tar opalescence and its
lingering latinate vocabulary, its cadence and balance, its entire amalgamation of South and North, heart and head. Like so many other crucial
personalities of 1955—Allen Ginsberg, Elvis Presley, Ray Charles, Little
Richard, Marlon Brando, Marilyn Monroe, and Richard Nixon—the voice
audibly bears and conveys the pressures of the moment. Of all the remarkable, physical voices of the time, however, King's resolved and bore the
most, carried furthest.

Surprisingly enough, the voice of the twenty-six-year-old man in 1955 spoke virtually the same phrases it spoke the night before he died, age thirty-nine, when he said, "It is no longer a question of violence or nonviolence: it is a question of nonviolence or nonexistence." He'd been to the mountaintop, was not afraid to die, when racists bombed his home in 1957. He had been to the mountaintop, was not afraid to die, the night before James Earl Ray killed him in 1968. Racism could do to him nothing it had not already done to his people and to his youth. The way he acknowledged his victimization but refused to play his conventional role touched men and women of all ages and hues. He changed the process of victimization that all of America felt in the fifties into a growing process of passive aggression. To his principled phrases about dignity and love injecting meaning into civilized veins, King remained true the dozen years left him.

Surely King had an individual genius, but part of it was to phrase the rhythms and moods reverberant across the country. His maturity and fullness as a person is thus both remarkable and commonplace. There were many other youths becoming adult, victims refusing victimization, bit players methodically grabbing lead roles, and schemers becoming movers in the fifties. The time was peopled with emerging new forces, both black and those learning heart from blacks. King's martyrdom has inevitably heightened his significance. Except for his martyr's end, however, King's career is also a fifties type, anticipated in song and novel, varied in politics and film. Blacks and youths and women and Southerners, individuals *en masse,* were leaping limits and coming out of holes. King's deliberate speed was theirs.

The civil rights *movement* began that early December in 1955 when Mrs. Parks stayed sitting, Mrs. Robinson wrote and distributed her leaflets, E. D. Nixon brought them together with the ministers, and King's voice reached out to consolidate the isolated angers in his audience, helping them into the mainstream. The Montgomery bus boycott spawned first the series of bus boycotts that spread across other Southern cities and towns during the late fifties, then directly inspired the Greensboro sit-in of 1960, which again in its turn stenciled the South. The antiwar movement, the women's movement, indeed, all the movements for social justice which people commonly associate with the sixties have their debts to pay to the overcome obstacles of the fifties. That was when the civil rights movement experimented with and created organizational strategies that have since served every other insurgent group both within and beyond electoral politics.

□   □   □   □   □

Shine swum on . . .
Shine was on the corner . . .
— "The Titanic"

The emergence of black culture into American prominence greatly altered the course of American art, balancing and lending it a completeness it had lacked. In addition to the civil rights movement, the other great force black culture unleashed on the land in 1955 was black music, most saliently and salably in the form of rock 'n' roll. "Tutti Frutti," "Maybellene," "I've Got a Woman," "The Great Pretender": all these were 1955 releases and represent the real beginnings of rock as a popular form.

Before rock 'n' roll came rhythm 'n' blues. Before rhythm 'n' blues came the blues. The progression had several causes, but the effect was to remake a minority, folk, form into a popular, pop, form. The real and rooted excitement of rhythm 'n' blues music thus prepared some musicians and some audiences (Chicago blacks, initially) for rock during the late forties and early fifties. Rhythm 'n' blues was the hybrid product of Southern, rural, "downhome," blues and the electric amplifier into which bluesmen plugged when they moved north to Memphis, St. Louis, and Chicago. Muddy Waters, B. B. King, and Jimmy Reed at first needed electricity simply to make themselves heard in the noisier night of the urban club. Then they learned to like — or at least to use — the whine and fuzz, feedback and sustain that an amplifier could create. They began making not only louder but also metropolitan music. Rock occurred as whites and blacks started spreading black music beyond its southside clubs across the whole metropolis and out to the suburbs, too.

Black music moved forward also in jazz. Jazz became freed for esoteric development when rhythm 'n' blues and rock began servicing those parts of the audience that prized primitive basics during the forties, beginning with the likes of Louis Jordan and Jackie McVea. These two were significant, and very entertaining, bridges between the swing jazz style and the sparer combos of rhythm 'n' blues.

The remaining audience cheered the jazz tendency to be continually avant-garde, deliberately speeding, constantly changing. Miles Davis broke his heroin addiction, attracted John Coltrane to his group, synthesized bop and cool jazz into smart soul, and urged Coltrane's famous "sheets of sound" (which convention incorrectly associates with the next decade).[4] Art Blakey formed with Horace Silver the most significant of his many Jazz Messengers groups, recorded Silver's "The Preacher," and so initiated the funk or hardbop movement; *The Preacher* was the first out-and-out jazz record to be released as a single and sell over 100,000 copies" (Sidran 131). Sonny Rollins took a sabbatical, he said, to cure himself of heroin addiction in 1955, worked sporadically in Chicago and then joined the important Max Roach–Clifford Brown Quintet four weeks before the Montgomery bus boycott. And not least important in this list is that by 1955 the jazz entrepreneur Norman Granz became the first jazz millionaire — via his Jazz at the Philharmonic concerts across the land (Wilson 143). Jazz was both moving out into the mainstream and moving on into untracked territory.

Why did black people have to wait so long? Why was the mid-fifties the precise moment when black culture should have become an apt symbol for the way millions of nonblacks wanted to be in the world? Within the United States, black culture had long determined much of Southern Culture, from cuisine to consciousness, gumbo to guilt, but it went national at mid-decade, crossed the Mason-Dixon line, jammed airwaves and stores and headlines, heavily influenced American literary form and styles, commanded the attention of the Supreme Court, and involved itself with aspects of every extant form of art. But why did people start acknowledging their vernacular cultural resources at this moment? Maybe when Holocausts and Hiroshimas, genocide and fallout, new technologies and demographic shifts all threatened the population, then even mainstream people began more frequently than usual to see themselves as dupes of their inherited ways of being in the world.

Then they wanted to change those duping patterns. Seeing themselves as victims, they turned to that black part of the nation and thus of themselves which had longest borne and coped with victimization. In fact, mostly unaware but all across America, whites had absorbed Negro culture long before the fifties. Music and sculpture and dance, speech and writing and lore, religion and food and costume — black life had touched every corner of American life, had long been a part of white life. The paradox that had propped up the shabby house of American racism, however, was the pre-fifties tenet that such ethnic cultures were somehow separable. This fiction was one of the most victimizing beliefs for Americans of all races. Belief in separability kept the largest two American racial cultures touching while allowing whites their fantasy of distance. It inhibited the powerful even from contemplating any aspect of the black ethic, because by definition they were not allowed to recognize it.

Mainstream citizens only started acknowledging their latent black values once they began sharing the doubts and began feeling the lack of control blacks had long known. Then many parts of the mainstream sped toward black culture deliberately. The alembic of black folklife showed how there was pride to win for those who survived displacement and dispossession. Had not Brer Rabbit and that famous trickster slave, John, and countless other wily figures on the periphery of American consciousness proved so? Yes, came back the answer. Yes, slaves and their descendants had proved expert in kneading feelings of displacement and dispossession into leavened accounts, songs, and tall tales of victory down all their American generations. Brer Rabbit could laugh all the way to his hole that he was back in the briar patch. John could outwit the strawboss, marry the Devil's daughter, and spin her father so fast he fell on his head and died. According to his wife talking to his child, John could outrun Ole Massa masquerading as the Lord himself: "You know de Lawd can't outrun yo' pappy—specially when he's barefooted at dat."[5] When all the white world goes down to its doom, the black trickster survives. Shine, black engine-tender on the *Titanic,* escapes the racist captain, the captain's seductive daughter, whales and sharks:

> And Shine swum on,
> Now when the news got to the port, the great *Titanic* had
>   sunk,
> You won't believe this, but old Shine was on the corner,
>   damn near drunk.[6]

This rich manipulation paraded in the complexity, the constant doubleness, the making much with little in black art forms. It strutted nowhere more clearly than in black music and speech.

The important aspects of black lore and music in American life corresponded exactly with the significance of Martin Luther King, Jr.'s improvising voice. Lore, music, and voice signified to American culture the capacity to turn adversity into play through orality. Just as rhythm 'n' blues grew from learning to incorporate the accidents and feedback trash which blues guitars generated when players plugged into cheap Chicago amplifiers, so turning adversity into play is what each of the secular black musics from jazz to reggae has always been about.

Behind all the Afro-American musics there is doubtless an Ur-music, some still-unmapped musical code about the merging of the African inheritance with European scales and instrumentation within the American experience. There is an adaptive genius there. Jazz, ragtime, blues, and rhythm 'n' blues all draw on that elusive source, but the stable form and commonly shared lyrics of blues provide the clearest and most convenient clues to it. Indeed, the persistent influence of the blues on American culture during and since the fifties necessitates analysis of the blues aesthetic and ethic.

The structure and content of the blues, reflecting that original music, indicate the ideals of black culture to which whites were particularly susceptible in the early-fifties slipstream of angst and possibility. Largely through its blues ethic, black culture taught a new generation to document its victimization so dramatically that the act itself became a way of coping, a way of playing within a repeatedly oppressive world.

Scholarship in the late seventies has debunked the old saw about blues being the taproot from which ragtime, jazz, rhythm 'n' blues, then rock all flowered in succession. A stable blues probably did not appear until the first decade of this century. W. C. Handy reported in his *Father of the Blues* that he first heard it in 1903, in the northwest or Delta region of Mississippi. The earliest evidence of the blues thus dates from some ten or fifteen years after the earliest evidence of jazz, and five years after our knowledge of ragtime. But these dates may well be misleading because while jazz appeared in urban New Orleans, and was accessible therefore to the people who write history down, blues players developed their art in the boondocks, in shacks known as juke joints far away from written history. In fact, one reason blues developed was to fill the story vacuum; blues became a loose oral history of the downhome folk's recurrently suffered moods, which singers might release and recount on Saturday night. Blacks' physical distance from the white world at the time was central to the music, partly accounting for its strangeness and subsequent mystique to people in Euroculture, and perhaps as well for its tardy appearance in written accounts.

Neither jazz nor blues developed until the end of the last century. The music came then, and not before, because the failure of Reconstruction in 1877 forced more segregation on blacks and their culture than they had known even under slavery—when, for instance, blacks had learned and sung European songs and hymns for mutually festive moments. For that while after Reconstruction during which jazz and blues developed, however, there were no racially mutual festive celebrations. Urban blacks developed jazz as their own music in a vacuum. Rural blacks developed blues in the even more feudally sealed vacuum of tenant farming.

Originally the stable blues form was popular only very locally. That is, the birth and earliest development of the blues was within the bounds of a few Mississippi and Arkansas Delta counties, and a few more in East Texas. Growth followed the chance movements of professional singers between jobs and mates, Saturday afternoon streetcorners to Saturday night juke-dances across the South—until 1920. Then Mamie Smith recorded "That Thing Called Love" backed with "You Can't Keep A Good Man Down" (OKeh 4113), which was the first blues record (Titon 204). But even in 1920 the recording location was Chicago; Mamie Smith was neither from the Delta nor in its jukedance performance style (she did not even snap her fingers); and her recording orchestra was white, a dilution that OKeh rectified on her subsequent records. Mamie Smith ushered in the trend of vaudeville entertainers performing the blues. The most famous and tal-ented vaudeville blues singers were Ma Rainey and her protege, Bessie Smith, both of whom made landmark recordings in the form before its inventors did.

From its very beginnings, therefore, blues history illustrates the speedy development of art forms in this century. Just seventeen years after it certainly existed, the first blues that anyone in the world outside a few cotton-picking counties along the Mississippi and Tallahatchie rivers could have heard was already a second-generation phenomenon. These classic, or jazz, or vaudeville blues recordings by female artists accompanying jazz orchestras (black or white) are distinct from the original, downhome blues. Vaudeville blues lyrics are usually highly organized, with development from stanza to stanza that is thematic and progressive, even narrative—like a poem, or a novel. That is, they have been influenced by literary aesthetic standards. Someone other than the usually female singer frequently com-posed (rather than improvised) classic blues songs. And the bands accom-panying these women were sophisticated if not urbane. This form's enor-mous popularity among the black audience, in backwoods and on back streets alike, skewed the development of the original downhome form, moving it away from its original looseness toward the tightness im-presarios thought necessary for the recording studio. Whether it belongs with blues or jazz, however, the musical accompaniment to the classic blues is frequently highly accomplished, yielding some of the most interesting examples of early combo work in black idioms.

Despite the jump ahead that classic blues took, the original form eventually did achieve documentation. Sylvester Weaver's instrumental guitar blues in 1923 inaugurated authentic downhome records by blacks for blacks, but had no voice track. A few obscure recordings exist between 1923 and January 1926, when Paramount finally produced sessions of Blind Lemon Jefferson's East Texas blues that cemented the trend to what even his own company called "weird, sad music" (Titon 113). Thus began the wide-spread distribution of downhome blues records in urban and rural black communities coast to coast. These sales represented a burgeoning recognition of and attraction to the ideals of the black experience in America. Although this music did not precede jazz, its audience has treated it as the root aesthetic, as the expression of the place from which they all came, the place which made them. Hence the name, downhome blues. However, not until June and November of 1926 did anyone record a blues by a singer from the Mississippi Delta, where field workers believe the style began. And not until 1928 and 1929 did Tommy Johnson and Charley Patton record their definitive, kernel blues style.

Given the nature of American society and white control of the recording companies, why, suddenly, the appearance of a black music whose lyrics, ambition, and basic strategies were beyond white ken or condonation? The answers lie within a new black market. Their ongoing migration north was conveniently clustering southern blacks in Chicago and to a lesser extent in New York, Detroit, Philadelphia, and Pittsburgh. Therefore, target markets were ready. Moreover, the post-World War I capacity for mail-order sales extended this market. Mail-order reached past cities and towns to the crossroads and remote plantation jukeboxes in Coahoma and Leflore counties, Mississippi, where record salespeople visited only reluctantly.

Most important, however, was a significant material difference in post-World War I technology. As Jeff Todd Titon reports in *Early Downhome Blues,* the radio's becoming available in 1920 provided listeners with fidelity superior to any on their extant records and players (204). Radio also supplied constantly changing live programming of white performers. At this point there were very few black artists on records and none on the radio. Because whites started listening to the radio rather than to records, and because there were no black performers on records for blacks to buy, record sales dropped precipitously. For instance, Columbia's pre-tax net in 1919 was $7 million; in 1921—after the onset of radio—it lost $4.3 million, causing its stock to drop from 65 to one and five-eighths. And the largest record company of the time, Victor, lost more than half its sales between 1921 and 1925, from $51 to $25 million. In their distress, the record companies were forced to turn to the black market. By recording black blues artists and by assiduously cultivating new black target audiences, America's record companies saved themselves. And the black audience gratefully, greedily, responded by buying some ten million records a year in the late twenties, according to plausible estimates (Titon 205).

Such turnings of record companies to black culture to save themselves, or, examples of black culture supplying the excitement to save a medium recently made passé, has therefore occurred twice in this century. It operated first in the twenties, when radio stole the audience from phonograph records, then second in the fifties, when TV stole radio's content. The incident in the twenties is an early confirmation of the law of passé pursuit: record companies added to the racial (thus stylistic) dimensionality of their product only after radio surpassed the fidelity of records and stole their market. Records did not regain their relatively superior fidelity until the thirties. When that happened, the white audience returned, white interests becoming again the primary content, the white market regaining dominance. But the black content and market also remained. That they stayed confirmed the principle of species proliferation rather than Marcuse's notion of species obliteration.

When TV created the fifties vacuum in radio's content, perhaps radio turned to black music so quickly because it had learned the trick watching the record companies respond to its own challenge some thirty years before. Both cases, in the twenties and fifties, indicate how racism provided American business a fallback, safety-valve market for its passed media and their entrepreneurial capital. Just so, the West would try with mixed success to use the Bandung Conference countries as an even larger market abroad.

The ace-in-the-hole subculture may be hidden one moment and appear bewilderingly everywhere the next. For instance, downhome blues existed twenty-five years on record before southern blacks and whites — Fats Domino and Little Richard in New Orleans, Elvis Presley in Memphis, Chuck Berry in East St. Louis — discovered how to jump it up a notch, turning the blues' regional appeal into national, even international, anthems.

Before blues and rhythm 'n' blues merged with white forms and voices and themes to become rock, popular culture had offered little more than silliness — "Oh, say, how much is that doggie in the window?" — to organize the values of the mainstream youth culture. Until the penetration of black music into the white mainstream, with recognizably black lyrics and vocal styles, there had been no capacity to create anthems alternative to the pop songs of Frank Sinatra, Rosemary Clooney, and Snooky Lanson. Their "Hit Parade" ethic was the only ethic *broadcast*. This emphasis on the mode of dissemination is important because there were so many material differences between the way black culture emerged in the fifties and the way it had moved before — as when jazz moved across the racial divide in the twenties. In the fifties, black culture had much greater possibility of becoming mass culture, and in fact it did spread much more widely the second time around. Thus black music's new content, style, form, and rhythm—call it the blues ethic—inserted fresh iconographic elements for black and white performers into the middle decade of the century.

☐ ☐ ☐ ☐ ☐

his song had been there all the time . . .
—Ellison, *Invisible Man*

A hard question in the aftermath of World War II concerned how American culture might resume. In his *Cat on a Hot Tin Roof* (1955), Tennessee Williams's Maggie posed this question when she reminded her husband, Brick, "life has got to be allowed to continue even after the *dream* of life is — all—over" (44). Along with the nightmare fruits of the analytical tradition, like Nagasaki and Belsen, there was the less radioactive but still pragmatic problem that the metastasis of cities and their communications media were closing off folk resources, one main lode for art and its dreams.

When the smoke cleared after the war, cities and their technology, autos and their asphalt, central casting and its celluloid, advertising and its billboard hype covered the landscape, dampening whatever impulses any remaining folk might have been murmuring. This bottom-up folk murmur had long served as constant choric commentary on the machinations of the state. In its place now was coming the glut of topdown popular culture, produced not by but for the people. Artists trying as they always had to hear the country's heartbeat by listening to its folklore were now like doctors placing stethoscopes against chests baffled by pillows. If folk hearts were beating at mid-century, artists couldn't hear them. Artists heard instead the external noise of the people's barkers and saw their bright electric signs. As early as 1953, in the first of his *Maximus* poems, written while he was in Mexico studying Mayan culture's ancient antidote to the recent American bafflement, Charles Olson asked:

> o my people . . . where shall you listen
> when all is become billboards, when, all, even silence, is
>   spray-gunned?
> . . . when sound itself is neoned in? (2)

Faster than anyone else, it also seemed, the folk were undoing themselves, like Lolita in her novel, by entering into willing partnership with developers who would dissolve their separate identities. By mid-century, few people in the United States would admit to being folk or lower class. With the entire population of the country joining the great middle in fact or consciousness, America seemed to be losing her folk resources for art and thus her agency of political change, as well. C. Wright Mills, as a left-liberal, lamented this loss of an alternative agency in *The Power Elite* (1956). Daniel Bell, as a right-liberal, claimed it meant *The End of Ideology* (1960). And so it might have been, had the lore of the folk truly disappeared. But it did not, not entirely, in two ways.

First, the position of black culture in the fifties helped demonstrate how contemporary culture might find ways to reclaim the lores that cities and media hid. Second, anticipating an even more blanketed urban future, Americans learned how to transmute the very obstacles to lore — electronic media and city life — into topics for a new lore, not folk this time, but pop: poplore. That second transformation is a topic in two later chapters, "Congeniality" and "They All Juggled Milk Bottles." The topic here is how the once essentially rural blues ethic became a significant model for the resumption of the increasingly urban and suburban American culture.

Ralph Ellison makes the issue of starting over a central theme and formal property of his novel *Invisible Man* (1952). The young man who tells the story (but never his name) continually plays parts providing only discontinuous identities. Every time he is reborn, every new father figure, or mentor, betrays him. He finally sees that the roles he has played have been external, thus have nothing to do with his intangible and invisible, internal and indivisible self beneath. That he has such a self and that it stems from black culture are the primary discoveries differentiating his latest societal engagement from his fumbling first. By novel's end, his roots no longer embarrass him, nor does he flee them. Rather, he understands his life as a continuing affirmation of the lores at his source, a testing of both the lore and the proper way to say yes to it, but no to the hostile, dominant world.

From the clear-cut racism of the downhome South to the displaced complexities of the urban North, the invisible youth's story recapitulates his people's emergence during this century, tracing its geographic course, as well as its psychological history. Winning a scholarship to a Southern black college, the invisible youth hopes he may excel and rise to assist his college president. Instead, the president expels him. Though daunted, the youth continues to New York where he hopes to rise in business. But his letters of recommendation in fact direct their recipients to "keep this nigger boy running." Now desperate, he takes a job in a factory which actually explodes in his face. Recovering from the explosion and the sinister hospital in which he awoke, he wanders onto the eviction of an old couple, rousingly speaks against their dispossession, is noticed by a communist leader, and trained to be their Harlem spokesperson. Adapting once again, he now hopes to rise as a prominent organizer. In the by now familiar pattern, however, his new "Brotherhood" mentor betrays him as all the others have before. The invisible youth watches his disillusioned followers drop out of the movement and a white policeman kill his best friend.

The invisible youth's final oration is a stirring eulogy for this friend. It is inspired by the music of the crowd as they march to the service — a spontaneous duet between a euphonium and a baritone voice rising from an anonymous man's knife-scarred neck. This will be a life-transforming moment for the invisible youth, not least because the song evokes in him latent, folk knowledge. The singer's "song had been there all the time" the youth confesses, "and he knew it and aroused it; and I knew that I had known it too." But he himself "had failed to release it out of a vague, nameless shame or fear" of such primitive ways. He thought he had been running toward goals, but was all the while running from the lore of his folk. Listening to the song, however, he says, "I was listening to something within myself, and for a second I heard the shattering stroke of my heart" (342). It took the whole novel long for the youth to lift the baffling pillows of miseducation, cultural interference, political dogma, and his own "shame and fear," so that he could hear the end which was there all along in his beginning.

In this key second the youth hears that his self connects to others who have no designs on him but do have designs — their own rich lore epitomized in their song — and that the connection is carried in black music. The music in this case, the funeral for the invisible youth's friend, is the spiritual "There's Many a Thousand Gone" (also known as "No More Auction Block"). In this eulogy, the youth tells the crowd to go home, which is code for returning to their roots, going downhome. But he also tells them to climb out of the boxes that keep them disengaged. Thus his speech captures the stirring contradictions of the blues ethic. So effective is this speech that it sets off a surreal riot in Harlem that engulfs even its instigator, leading to his final revelation.

White thugs wielding baseball bats chase him through the anarchic riot until he suffers a fortunate fall into an open manhole at the border area between Harlem and white New York. Closing himself up in a basement of a building abandoned significantly since Reconstruction, he mulls over his experience, repeating it imaginatively, then yet again as he reforms it into the narrative he calls *Invisible Man*. The youth holed off from the world — like black people during the nadir that spawned jazz and blues — grows up to create his blues novel as his folk created the form: "Ontology recapitu-

lates philology."[7] He narrates a story of black experience as well as his own.
It recounts coming to self-knowledge, learning by degrees to recognize,
remember, and trust the folk vernacular. It is also a parable of reengagement, showing everyone how to resume. It shows how to go on by going
home. As such, it moved to solve the crisis modern literature had reached in
the years before Ellison's novel appeared.

J. Alfred Prufrock thought at the end of World War I — and the end of
his "Love Song," by T. S. Eliot — that the asking of large questions would set
him ineluctably apart from his era. Prufrock wondered in his paralysis how
he should presume to "Disturb the universe." Neither daring nor disturbing, he drowned in his own sensuous ineffectuality. The invisible man at the
end of the next World War does disturb his universe because he realizes that
beginning is no longer presumption but necessity, no longer alienating but
integrating. Thus the novel's last line is also its largest question, "Who
knows but that, on the lower frequencies, I speak for you?" With that, he
leaves his hibernation hole, resumes social life, and poses his large questions
to everyone he meets — including us, via the novel. Like the Brers and bears
of folklore, like the blues singers of Saturday night juke joints, he keeps on
keeping on, reclaiming his past to make it over as art.

The story is thus peculiarly double. It speaks for the black individual
and also the largely white reading audience of the early fifties. It speaks to
their experience and of it. Telling how the invisible youth kept rushing
eagerly into yet another surely painful, explosive, and shocking trap, this
story strikes many readers as excruciatingly innocent. But it is wisely
controlled, too, with its obvious patternings, webbed symbols, and allusions to literary and extraliterary sources. Readers are soon aware that they
are reading a double consciousness dealing in doubletalk, delighting precisely in its capacity to improvise elaborately at length. These are of course
leading characteristics of blues performers at the Saturday night rite. Both
this novel and those blues performances stress the latent doubleness in
reality: something good may come from something bad; something bad
from something good. Complexity lurks in simplicity.

The doubleness also reflects the two sorts of attitudes the youth has
toward society as he gathers experience. First, he wants to rise within it.
Second, he gradually becomes aware, like so many other fictional characters who follow his wanderings across the postwar American landscape,
that he needs to break away from society's clutches.[8] Ellison is performing a
delicate integration here. He is signifying on the "twoness" that W. E. B. Du
Bois described in *The Souls of Black Folk* (1903) as essential in the experience
of black Americans (who feel always that they are both black and Ameri-

can). And he is making that twoness stand for the new culture of the fifties that is also both conventionally American and deliberately speeding.

Like the blues performances behind and in it, the novel must integrate those central conflicts in its own urges and those of its main character. Indeed, *Invisible Man* is at least as much about this intellectual and emotional integration as about its social counterpart. But since all these resolutions are difficult to achieve or even imagine, the youth spends most of his time either championing or avoiding his society's dominant creeds. Instead of integrating the central conflicts of his time, as a youth he listens to Louis Armstrong records, smokes reefer, has clairvoyant hallucinations, wires his walls with 1,369 light bulbs, and avoids the grid of conventional expectations that had so driven him before his fall. Will he come out of his hole?

He will as a man, no longer as a youth. His coming out to resolution, to a full manhood, will be the achievement pointed to in the title. He will come out because his novel is a blues book. It is structured like a blues song, based on the blues ethic and trying desperately to live up to the blues, reclaiming its endangered lore for literature. The invisible man might have rested on the telling of his story, might have remained an underground hermit, might have broken away to private places, real or fantasied, as Joseph Heller's Yossarian would do nine years later. He might have run like John Updike's Rabbit did in 1960. He might have gone trout fishing in America, à la Brautigan in 1967. Embittered, he might have preached apocalyptic fire or pushed political revolution, as so many in the meantime wished Ellison had made him do. He might have made a separate peace. He might have remained incomplete, a youth, but he did not.

Instead, he returns with his story to society. Early in the book he emphasizes in the language of lore and rite that "a bear retires to his hole for the winter and lives until spring; then he comes strolling out like the Easter chick breaking from its shell" (5). This is but the first of innumerable tropes about hibernation, birth, and rebirth in *Invisible Man*. From its beginning the novel addresses the American need to begin again, responsibly borne by tradition.

Just as the novel itself starts with the invisible man asking himself, "What did *I* do to be so blue?" so it is important to ask how blue is it really? Very. Often called an episodic novel because of its pulses and apparent disconnectedness, or a *Bildungsroman* because it recounts the invisible man's formation, both these terms coordinate the novel on the same European grid it takes pains to elude and which frequently though not alone oppresses its main character.

Recent critics have also recognized the novel's connection to folklore, in general, and to the blues, in particular.[9] Stanley Edgar Hyman and Albert Murray, two of Ellison's closest intellectual friends, have both written at some length about *Invisible Man* as a "blues novel" (Hyman, "American Negro Literature") and "a literary extension of the blues . . . scored for full orchestra" (Murray, *Omni* 167). Ellison himself confirmed this attention when he remarked in his introduction to the novel's Thirtieth Anniversary Edition that he began the book when its "ironic, down-home voice . . . as irreverent as a honky-tonk trumpet" and "persuasive with echoes of blues-toned laughter" disrupted another fiction he was composing (xv). He started *Invisible Man* knowing he "would have to improvise upon [his] materials in the manner of a jazz musician putting a musical theme through a wild star-burst of metamorphosis" (xxi).

That metamorphosis is significant because the novel not only simulates and orchestrates blues tones but takes its transformational shape from the ethic behind the tones. The blues ethic is its grammar. The episodes of *Invisible Man* are as disconnected, repetitious, and similar as the stanzas of a blues song, its themes as reiterative as the lines of a blues song. For all his eagerness to discover his authentic self, for all the existential overtones in this search, for all the rhetoric of individuality in the fifties, the formation in *Invisible Man* is not of a unique person but a socialized self. The youth hears his own heart when he acknowledges the specific shape of experience that his people developed living in America. The invisible youth's growth into the invisible man is his recognition of his blues self. What is truly unique about both the narrator and his author is the way both of them learn to manipulate and profit from their positions as members of a community.

The knowledge that *Invisible Man* teaches is the education of a blues song. Both proceed incrementally toward neither didacticism nor overwhelming revelation but toward understanding and engagement. Like the blues, *Invisible Man* offers its audience not the chance to transcend their condition but the capacity to cope with life's unconditional onslaught. Just as a blues song's opening stanza compactly conveys the singer's story and strategy, the first episode of *Invisible Man,* its often anthologized battle royal scene, projects the novel's themes and shape. Subsequent episodes elaborate that message, entertaining us more, emphatically repeating the world's evil. They indicate the same epistemology blues songs always express—the gradual dawning of a sufficient strategy for coping with, rather than evading or overcoming, the world.

By repetition of events in patterns as formulaic as those in blues songs, Ellison shows the invisible youth learning to see both the duplicity and the doubleness in things. Pieces of paper that purport to promote in fact deracinate him. The virgin statue at college is as covered as unveiled. Buttered yams are hot roots as well as Proustian madeleines. And men like Bledsoe, Trueblood, Rinehart, and Brother Jack are all many-faced. The youth comes to see these other aspects of his experience as he rethinks and reimagines it. He deconstructs what he originally experienced as the repetitions make him reexperience what he had naively felt.

But Ellison does not leave it there. Rather, he shows the youth reconstructing a new sense of the world and a new sense of identity. Like a singer gradually regaining control of embarrassing experience stanza by stanza while singing the blues, Ellison has the invisible youth regather and restate his story in the hole, putting it back before us as he felt it, by degrees. *Invisible Man* is a blues novel in structure, therefore, as well as theme. Those are important facts about the novel for itself, for its location in the history of black culture, and for its location in American culture, at the conception of the deliberately speeding epoch. *Invisible Man* is the novel that enacted the process of rebirth after the war, that showed people how to admit their differences from the shibboleths of high modernism. Ellison's blues novel enacted the process of rediscovering vernacular shape. It showed its characters and its readers how to resume responsible action.

☐ ☐ ☐ ☐ ☐

This familiar music demanded action.
— Ellison, *Invisible Man*

The story has its remarkable beginning at a southern "smoker" to which he, as the valedictorian from the town's black high school, has been invited to address leading white men. Before the speech, his audience forces him to watch a blonde stripper who has fear in her eyes and a smile on her face, just like a "circus kewpie doll" (16). Then he and nine other blacks, blindfolded and all together, must box among themselves until only one of them remains standing before their white elders. This is the battle royal. Still reeling from the punches they have dealt and felt at white behest, the youths then rim a rug on which town leaders have tossed coins and bills. Calling the invisible youth "Sambo," they direct him and his peers toward the money, mouthing the commercial creed, "You get all you grab" (21). Leaping for the coins and bills while still dripping-wet from the fight, the fellows are truly shocked to discover that the elders have electrified the mat. If they try to escape the charge, their audience throws them back, laughing at their contortions on the electric grid. That's where the invisible youth has the first of his characteristic cognitions — not yet recognitions — which will pulse as regularly as the summary lines of blues stanzas. He has perceptions about his self and situation that for all their truth he cannot yet absorb because he has not — or has not acknowledged — the conceptual framework to illuminate them. Only when he recalls them at the end, telling the tale, will he recognize their meaning and pattern. Only then will he have learned to illuminate his perceptions by sluicing off power from the monopolated power company (read: from tradition, from the establishment).

Back on the rigged rug, he does notice that he "could contain the electricity" (22) and even achieve the requisite detachment to observe as well as feel. He sees a boy heaved onto the mat to dance upon his back while his elbows tattooed the floor. He describes how he himself tried to tumble one of the whites onto the mat, was detected in the subversion and kicked viciously back onto the electric current, to fall as in a dream, fall seemingly for a century, fall out of one time sense into another more surreal. He notices these events but does not acknowledge their meaning. Acknowledgment comes only at his consummate fall into the Harlem manhole. Then he will understand that his particular sort of attention to these events is what makes him so positively blue and his story a novel, if universal, blues. Then he will illuminate his existence with electricity rather than dance victim to its charge, as he had on the battle royal rug. Understanding this positive and patterned side to his position, understanding his possibilities, will make the invisible youth at long last the invisible *man*.

Still very much a youth at the battle royal, however, he has no frame by which to understand. Such is the consequence, Ellison is clear, of the youth's flight from the lore and knowledge of his culture to the pitiable phrases of his schooling — which the authorities finally permit him to deliver in his speech, the novel's first of many. Its valedictorian mode earnestly reworks Booker T. Washington's epochal remarks at the Atlanta Exposition of 1895 ("separate like the fingers of the hand"), particularly stressing Washington's biblical figure "Cast down your bucket where you are" (Washington reprinted the speech in the fourteenth chapter of *Up from Slavery*, 1901). Ellison will play changes on this idea during the novel so that, by the end, exploiting one's apparently barren place has real menace beyond its evident meekness — as when, telling the funeral crowd to go "home," he starts the Harlem riot. But at this early point the idea is entirely traditional. Therefore, not until the youth chokes on his own blood still flowing from the battle royal and urges "social equality" when he means to advise "social responsibility" does anyone heed his words and reprimand him to know his place at all times. The elders award the youth a briefcase and a scholarship to the state college for Negroes. Excitedly thanking them, the youth drools bloody saliva on the leather, "forming a shape like an undiscovered continent." Characteristically still embarrassed by the unacknowledged mess of his experience, he "wiped it quickly away" (26). Although never named, the college he will attend is Tuskegee Institute. Ellison himself studied musical composition and trumpet there from 1933 to 1936, and Booker T. Washington founded it. The youth cannot yet go off to this school, however, because he must first dream the meaning of his experience and summarize his pain, as the blues form dictates.

As in so many other deliberately speeding books that would follow, *Invisible Man* rejects immediate authority figures, fathers and spurious mentors, for grandfathers — for the traditional lore which prestigious modernism baffles. He dreams his grandfather took him to the circus — but refused to laugh at the clowns — then made his grandson open the new briefcase to read a state document inside. The youth unfolds a series of envelopes, each inside another; "Them's years," according to his grandfather. The final envelope contained not the scholarship but these formulated phrases which fix his image throughout the novel: "To Whom It May Concern, Keep This Nigger-boy Running." The youth awakens with his grandfather's laughter ringing in his ears and "no insight into its meaning" (26). Later, when he is grown and able to recreate these scenes in the novel, able as a thinker to tinker with his experience, he will realize that he himself was the real clown all along.

His grandfather knew the significant guerrilla potential in clowning. That's why he refused to laugh *at* the circus clowns in the dream. He was temperamentally *with* them, for they were serious agents of the almost inevitably comic conversion into one's real self. Here, then, is the novel's first and most powerfully intimate representation of the "blues-toned laughter" which Ellison later fingered as the fundamental impulse of the narrative (xv).

In episode after episode of *Invisible Man,* the elements of this battle royal chapter will repeat themselves. At college, in New York's factory right and political left, even in Harlem, the youth will adopt and be adopted by such surrogate parents as the town fathers at the battle royal. They will make him dance the clown at their whim. They will make him entertain their purposes, not his, nor will he yet suspect his purposes might differ from theirs. Sometimes with their eloquence, sometimes with their intensity, sometimes just with their jargon they will hide from him his actual struggle and turn him against his peers. They will shock him sometimes figuratively but also really — as when corporate doctors try to erase his

memory in an electroshock coffin while he "fairly danced between the
nodes." (Noticing the rhythm of his spasms, the doctors urge him to "Get
hot, boy! Get hot!" [181].) His frequent speeches, until his final one, will
always be someone else's truths rather than his own. The real, if undiscovered, countries of his life will sometimes drool unwittingly out of his
mouth. Wherever he goes, mentors and their papers — such as the battle
royal scholarship — will define him in ways which inhibit his slowly
emerging real self. He will stash all these documents in his briefcase,
culminating in the paper Sambo doll that his friend, Tod Clifton, was
peddling when the police killed him. This doll showed people as puppets to
unseen hands, shuckin' and jivin' on invisible strings. Thus it capsuled
much of the symbolism of the story. But neither the invisible youth nor the
street audience then understood so much.

Bringing the youth and all his audiences to another understanding is
what the novel and its blues structure are about. The novel illustrates at this
juncture a facet of the black ethic that is a common denominator of all its
local instances, be they blues songs or fictions, dances or jokes. By being
stored in community memory and replayed, gestures of all sorts — lines and
tales, names and notes, dance steps and punch lines — become double. They
become charged nodes. They become representations of meaning beyond
the obvious — the way a fish, in the contexts of adolescents discovering sex
or early Christians hiding and displaying their faith, can be much more
than mackerel. As such these remembered gestures are particularly useful
tools for people under surveillance — adolescents, for instance, or early
Christians, or slaves' descendants, or performers of every stripe. Using
these tokens, performers make themselves seen and invisible, too. Using
these tokens, a tale teller or novelist converts the banal into mean-
ingfulness, even while hiding, as necessary, in the banality. These are the
tokens that make apparently accidental reality ritualistic and deliver its
inhabitants to their traditional selves.

In their instant of watching Clifton promote Sambo's features, the
crowd simply sees the doll's smiling surface — "little Sambo, the joy
spreader" (327) — and is thus irate when the youth spits on it. The youth,
however, is operating reflexively from an understanding opposite to the
crowd's. He sees the doll's demeaning spinelessness. Unlike his Grandfather, he still does not yet see how the art in clowning hides subversion
behind apparent harmlessness. If he sees its function at all, he understands it
as supporting not undercutting established prejudice. However, the police
do understand the threat, if only intuitively, when they hustle off and
summarily assassinate Clifton — Sambo's spieler — for "resisting reality"

(345). Likewise, the Sambo peddling infuriates the Brotherhood theoreticians employing the invisible youth. They call it obscene because its ritual way of working undercuts their declarative methods and united-front pretenses as thoroughly as it mocks the practices of the power elite.

Which is the Sambo peddling scene to be — the peddling of obscenities or a catalyst forcing the invisible youth to know himself in all his particularities? It is both but cannot catalyze without first banalizing. It must insinuate its commonness, must marinate in the audience's consciousness, before changing it. To set its hooks, a rite must not reveal its barbs, must not indicate that its function is to change people, or even to reorganize their thoughts. Partly, this necessary indirection is a case of not being able to have one's cake and eat it too. To have the experience, the audience cannot be reflecting on it at the same time. The reflection and its attendant clarification must follow if they are not to dilute the emotional experience of the ritual action. This necessity for unconscious ritual is particularly pronounced on American shores because of the national hostility to overt ceremony as that which clogged the arteries of antiquated cultures. Whereas older, for instance African or European, cultures "glamorize themselves through rituals," Ellison has written, "Americans tend to require supplementary rites that are more modest, more down-to-earth, and often it is these which serve to give dramatic form to our warmest emotions." What matters is that these rites not be noticed as rites: "it is precisely in their being regarded as unimportant that they take on importance" (*Territory* 50).

What importance? They have several, of which two are relevant here. First, rites cluster actions that reveal important truths about what their participants value, that speak especially acutely about the deepest needs — the "warmest emotions" — of the people who practice, so reinforce, the rite. Second, rites enact transfers of power. They cluster around moments of change when control or power transfers from one person or group to another. Thus, most of the community-disciplined performances of black culture, from blues songs to jazz dance, from the dirty dozens to rapping, from telling tales to writing certain sorts of novels based on oral culture and blues ethics — all these are rites, secular rites. They show the culture's gradations of power. And one way or another their performers know it. Ellison is particularly conscious: "rites are *actions*," he has written, "the goal of which is the manipulation of power; in primitive religions, magical power; in the South (and in the North), political power" (*Territory* 98).

By this principle, the birth of the blues was likewise the birth of a ruse. The blues, like other rites, comes on as entertainment — in a club or

backstreet alley — but ends fostering action, understanding, and reengagement. This "familiar music," Ellison's narrator wrote in his prologue,
"demanded action" (10). But this is a puzzling imperative. How can familiar
blues demand action? The answer lies in the connections between performers in apparently different roles. Essentially the blues performer is a Sambo,
a Sambo is a blues performer, and both are licensed fools who tell the truth
to audiences of every color and class.

□   □   □   □   □

This is a practice
As full of favor as a wise man's art.
— Viola in *Twelfth Night*

In the fifties, the nation was riddled with Sambo rites whose associations,
conventions, and license had been ripening since minstrel shows fixed the
role in the first third of the nineteenth century. What Sambo represents is
doubtless older than the recorded history of Euro-American race relations.
But by the middle of the eighteenth century, certainly, English speakers had
adapted "Sambo" from the Spanish for *mulatto,* thereby referring to the
mixed-race figure at the bottom of the pecking order of color. The significant doubleness of the Sambo figure thus inheres in the roots of the name.
Sambo is etymologically neither black nor white, by definition neither this
nor that. Rather, he or she is a figure occupying a middle ground between
races. Helped by such etymological solicitations, the Sambo figure developed into the masked figure who shuffled onto the minstrel stage enacting
formulaic, protective behavior: *yasSUH.* Ellison has picked a figure and
trope that is particularly suited to raising issues of how black foolery may
speak for the whole culture. Ellison's Sambo, however, is only one of the
Sambo figures that multiplied during the fifties. This spate of Sambo
spasms probably mushroomed from the time's increasing attention to race
issues, which always highlighted the role's usefulness. Equally important
for this proliferation of low-dignity figures was the concurrent hope on
actors' parts of transcending their role's demeaning features. To emphasize
it might mean to turn it inside out and move beyond it even while accepting
its protection.

The historical pattern in black performance is broad, having many
types and tributaries, but the doubleness of Sambo figures is one common
trait. A second is the standoff embrace audiences give their infra dig
performers. These two traits are related. Mocking or distancing oneself

from Sambo and from blues performers, downhome or classic, are variant responses to the same figure. Both sequences derived historically from the same source. Jazz players' light mockings of blues singers — which is evident in Bessie Smith's records — developed in vaudeville minstrel shows — at the fixing point, that is, of Sambo strategies. For it was in the minstrel show, the most popular form of entertainment in America in the nineteenth century, that the complex Sambo strategy developed.[10]

There, the natty Interlocutor grilled the raggedy endmen — Tambo and Bones, Sambo's cousins — during the formulaic show's first part. Cuing from the Interlocutor, vaudeville musicians likewise expressed their distance from the demeaning clowning by their ironic commentary on the staged activities. This glossing of the passing scene by vaudeville and classic jazz musicians was known as "signifying," a commentary which every successive jazz generation has carried on, and which black lore also voices in sophisticated verbal patterns.[11]

A good example of the way the minstrel tradition taught audiences to respond to blues performers and to the Sambo role in general is audible on Bessie Smith's "In the House Blues."[12] Her accompanying musicians are self-conscious about the singer's simple sentiments and display a flash attitude toward rubes and rural rudiments — perhaps particularly evident during the singer's moaning last stanza, where Louis Bacon's trumpet and Charlie Green's trombone go past complementing Smith's voice to cartooning it. As urbane jazz musicians, they absorb their primitive sources complexly but simultaneously insist that audiences notice their spit-shined shoes. Historically, supporting players have attached this affectionate putdown to clowns and other low-dignity performers at center stage. One present remnant of the gesture is the whack to the high hat with which drummers in the pit still mark corny jokes from talkshow comics. Such clues importantly indicate the constant labeling of blues performers, both by themselves and by others, internally and externally. They are infra dig either in projected demeanor or manner of audience acceptance, indignity being the price of their license. Similar indignity permitted the Elizabethan fool and other parasites to speak and sing their truths, too.

Given this wealth of associations attending on infra dig performance patterns in black cultural history, it is appropriate that the Sambo scene catalyzes the whole closing of Ellison's novel. That is, the invisible youth goes below ground after Clifton's peddling and murder, meets zootsuiters, thus questions the Brotherhood and its whole scientific theory of history, thus confronts Brother Jack's blindness and rouses the Harlem riot at Clifton's funeral. Consequently dropping out himself from Brotherhood politics, the invisible youth becomes a lone actor and spieler of his own private subversions, which he finally knows enough to improvise into his own literary blues. The novel is itself a sort of Sambo rite, but writ large, a long write and long rite of transformation. During the novel, power moves from others defining a youth to the youth becoming a man and defining himself—not lastingly, not permanently, but tentatively and still open to constantly continuing change.

The Sambo scene does all this in a small version of the larger novel's process. Like a stanza within the novel's song, Ellison set it up as early as the battle royal, the novel's first stanza. There the white observers called the youth "Sambo," made him dance for coins on their rug, paraded the woman before him on whom he merely wished to spit whereas he later does spit on Sambo, her paper surrogate. In both the battle royal and Clifton's Sambo-peddling scenes the audience ignores the power relationships so lucidly and obscenely on display—but for opposite reasons: the battle royal audience is too powerful and the street crowd too powerless to admit the social implications. And in both the rural and urban cases the transaction is all the more resonant because of the connotative baggage that clowning and laughing at clowns may trigger in communities that are repressing their unequal power distributions. In such situations clowning is: a way to make money, fawning to surveillance, a double masking and signaling of one's vulnerable fragility, a way to make others happy, and, through it all, a mockery of the controlling group's power.

All blues-derived performances share in this swampy ambiguity, perhaps most notably in the sexual clowning and fooling of blues lyrics and in the extreme characterizations performers project along with their stylized sound and words. Chippie Hill, Jelly Roll Morton, Louis "Satchmo" Armstrong, Charlie "Yardbird" Parker, Bo Diddley, Little Richard, even Elvis Presley and Jerry Lee "The Killer" Lewis (who performed memorably during the fifties in a leopard-skin bathrobe): all these performers extended their significance beyond what their often amazing voices and repertoire could achieve by fooling in a Shakespearean shadow area between propriety and promiscuity. Ellison recognized this aspect of black performance, too, with every outrageous performer in his novel's gallery, from the street-corner Clifton/Sambo to downhome Trueblood, from protean Rinehart and angry Rastafarian Ras to jive-talking Peter Wheatstraw. All are expert at multivalent black performance, but none more so than their author, Ralph Ellison himself.

Ellison based his character Wheatstraw on the real blues singer, William Bunch, from East St. Louis, who recorded and sang under the name "Peetie Wheatstraw, the Devil's Son-in-Law, the High Sheriff from Hell" (Palmer 115). At the beginning of Chapter Nine, Ellison has him sing a Count Basie/Jimmy Rushing song variously known as "Boogie Woogie" and "Boogie Woogie Blues." The song has lots of animal imagery, as Ellison cites it (*"She's got feet like a monkey / Legs like a frog"* 131), but its recorded versions and the variant Wheatstraw chants in the novel remain relatively polite. The actual Wheatstraw was considerably racier: "Well, the first woman I had," he sang on one of his slow blues, "she made me get down on my knees / And had the nerve to ask me, ooh, well, well, if I like Limburger cheese" (Palmer 116). Ellison's allusion to Wheatstraw is therefore just the sort of ambiguous connection with the taboo to which all black infra dig modes tended. His allusion was as scrubbed or as suggestive as the audience might make it. *He* mentioned no cheese; he just counted on cheesiness spicing the reference. Some audiences would be in the know and some would not; but the allusion would reach out doubly to tie both together.

Wheatstraw, or Bunch, was one of those performers, like James Joyce or Hemingway in this regard, who tossed around clues on how to understand him. As Hemingway would describe a bullfighter's economy of motion and grace under pressure in ways that suggested his own aesthetic, so Wheatstraw sometimes sang lines that telegraphed his extra level of meaning. For instance, take these chilling lines recorded in September 1931: "I did more for you than you understand / You can tell by the bullet holes, Mama, / Now, here in my hand" (Palmer 116). Here was a performer ambitious for extra levels of meaning and willing to display his stigmata to any interpretive doubting Thomas. It would be silly to romanticize infra dig performers, but it would be equally mistaken to ignore their scapegoat function. They suffered for their audiences what they sang about, talked about, danced about.

Black performers perfected their vernacular doubletalk because once they sang beyond the single-race, single-class, sealed-off world of the juke joint they were playing to many audiences simultaneously. Fanning out toward the villages and towns of the South, singers encountered an increasingly volatile and conflicting sense of audience expectations. Then the blues joined all the other black performance forms since the nineteenth century in the American force fields of complex surveillance. There were real differences between the conditions of blues performance and jazz or vaudeville or black theater and dance. But that all these types frequently traveled together and marketed themselves under the rubric of minstrel or "minister" shows (David Evans, *Big Road Blues* 187) corroborates their shared features. And their most frequent denominator was the especially multifarious meaning each developed to soothe the complex tensions it engendered, addressed, and suffered.

Because of the radical uncertainty prevailing in post-Reconstruction southern life, blues performers played to an even more unstable and shifting set of powers than prevailed in other national minstrel traditions, as in mead halls or medieval court, where race was not a dominant issue (though Negroes were traditional sources for fools).[13] Nevertheless, to be a professional fool has always been difficult, primarily because of the performer's multiple patrons and the relativity of truth. The central comment on this difficulty is in *King Lear*, when the fool tells his choleric master, "Thy daughters . . . have me whipp'd for speaking true, thou'lt have me whipp'd for lying; and sometimes I am whipp'd for holding my peace. I had rather be any kind o' thing than a fool" (1.4.179–82). And equally telling is Viola's remark in *Twelfth Night* about Feste—especially coming as it does in the midst of badinage about whom he serves—that to be "wise enough to play the fool / . . . craves a kind of wit":

> He must observe their mood on whom he jests,
> The quality of persons, and the time,
> And like the haggard, check at every feather
> That comes before his eye. This is a practice
> As full of labour as a wise man's art. (3.1.61–67)

Such were the conditions that might obtain for the historical fool, who must behave like an untrained hawk (haggard), checking every moving feather. If to be a fool was to be proverbially haggard in Elizabethan England, far worse conditions prevailed in the American South following Reconstruction. Such conditions were common for performers but also potential for all blacks until well after the mid-fifties and the onset of the civil rights movement. When the tenant farmer Mrs. Fannie Lou Hamer was asked if whites in her neighborhood knew in the fifties that they were treating blacks wrongly, she answered: "Some of 'em really didn't, 'cause I don't think they really saw us as human beings. We would smile and that would just fool 'em, that would just trap 'em. Now we have been some of the greatest actors on earth, 'cause we could smile when we would see 'em coming and they'd get about ten feet and we would say—you know it wouldn't be right to put it in the book what we would say" (Raines 255).

This fooling and acting was what the blues and minstrel performers of the region reenacted as art for their audiences, whose members were themselves practiced performers in Hamer's sense. Such performance was not political in the sense of consciously hoping to change or directly oppose the era's and region's pecking orders. But it indirectly reflected those orders and it certainly kept them in consciousness. Its representations of the human order included the political order. And that the blues and the civil rights movement had their greatest successes in the same spots throughout the Delta is doubtless more than coincidence. The blues prepared for the overcoming of victimization, even providing a downhome, passive-aggressive model for the movement's early ethic of nonviolence.

Say what one will about Gandhi and his Salt March to the sea, blues performers and their audiences knew about the long passive march toward what they needed just by treading between all the watching eyes, some powerful, some powerless. To sing the blues was to negotiate among many publics. The blues performer sang for nickels on a Clarksdale, Mississippi, loading levee on Saturday afternoon, for clear whiskey and smoked ribs at a tenant-shack juke party deep in a plantation that night, sometimes preached or sang in Sunday's church or social, then slipped over to Lula or Friar's Point for the next week's action. The immediate audience was usually black, but there were variations between the needs of town and plantation audiences, as between street-corner and juke-joint performance styles. Moreover, whites controlled most scenes and hung at the edge of the town circles. They certainly monitored the goings-on at the plantations, which they owned and where they pulled the ultimate strings.

Charley Patton and others of the distinguished songsters early and late in this development also played directly to whites in the big houses or social clubs for special occasions — even giving command performances at wayside for casually passing landlords. Both Ellison's Trueblood scene (*Invisible Man,* Chapter 2) and James Agee's moving report early in *Let Us Now Praise Famous Men* (26–31) document this role-playing on demand in ways that indicate the substantiality of the rite. Agee's scene is particularly apposite because so painfully clear in it is how varied the surveillance can be, thus how multidimensional the white audience for black performances can be. And Ellison's Trueblood scene importantly indicates how internally contrasting the black audience is also. In any case, everyone in the rite realizes at some level usually not conscious how the roles simultaneously collect and cover the social structure of the performance. Collecting it, they bring it to the fore. Covering it, they gird its transactions from conscious scrutiny.

Clowning and masking, then, became a way of transforming the constant surveillance, shifting patronage, poverty, and mandatory mobility into an art that appeared harmless even while it cut into and commented on all its formative forces. The more harmless it appeared, the more it showed the pressure and superintendence it felt. The trick was to stay in control of one's creation and therefore reside in that excluded middle area which resists concrete interpretation.

As Tod Clifton found out selling Sambo dolls in *Invisible Man*, to slip out of the shadow area into an identifiable interpretation could be fatal. This was no passing point for Ellison, who stuck by it years later in commenting on the way civil rights activists might need to slip behind Sambo roles for protection: "the outcome of abandoning the role is frequently tragic, for it leads to terror, pitiful suffering, and death" (*Territory* 101). Likewise, in the youth's dream at the end of the battle royal scene, his grandfather had "refused to laugh at the clowns no matter what they did" (26), but began the chapter advising clownish behavior: "overcome 'em with yesses, undermine 'em with grins" (13). The old man's puzzling remarks put an American twist to Shakespeare's images, and demonstrate how a similar strategy can develop equally along, say, the Tallahatchie and Thames rivers. By the banks of both streams, performers "ministered," to use the Mississippi metaphor, in a similar maw between power and powerlessness. Their lot was to "Live," as the grandfather commanded his charges, and as later rights activists knew, "with your head in the lion's mouth" (13). While the lion thought minstrels were tickling his tonsils, they were stealing some of his power.

Well aware of the covert but significant power of rites in black life, Southern and Northern, Ellison treated it often and richly in *Invisible Man*. The selling of Sambo, as street theater with mortal significance and power to transform the youth's life, is only one of the novel's zooms to ritual at key moments. Rites of passage and eruption, rites of recognition and identity permeate the work, from the battle royal to the Golden Day and the final riot, with Trueblood, Peter Wheatstraw, and Rinehart only some of its Masters of the Dance. Ellison learned, he claims from T. S. Eliot and "The Waste Land" (*Shadow* 159), the significance of ritualistic doubleness for the purposes of a novel: barren actions encased in rites permit uncannily fruitful meanings.

Subsequent to *Invisible Man*, Ellison has spoken steadily of the blues as ritual. He went to lengths in his groundbreaking essays of the fifties, collected in *Shadow and Act* (1964), to show how blues performers are secular ministers, singling out Jimmy Rushing as a "master-of-the-dance . . . the leader of a public rite" (237). Calling attention to the "mysterious potentiality of meaning which haunts the blues," and "their ability to imply far more than they state outright" (238, 239), he explains why he wanted a blues structure to hold his novel's blues content. As when folk rituals base Greek tragedies, Shakespeare's holiday comedies, or Faulkner's puberty madness in *The Hamlet, Invisible Man* also uses the doubleness folk rites provide.

One truly experiences a rite innocently without contemplating its meaning. Should conscious meaning come later, then it is all the richer for the first, unconscious, experience. Cesar Barber, who has thought best about the way Shakespeare used folk rites in his festive comedies, noticed a rhythmic pattern both in their performance and the audience's perceptions. Both performers and perceivers proceeded "through release to clarification," he wrote, and the plays therefore served functions similar to those of the rites they supplanted historically and fulfilled aesthetically (Barber 4, ff.).

"Through release to clarification" is finely descriptive of the blues as a ceremonial form, enacted in Saturday night juke parties, and perfect for *Invisible Man,* a literary reinscription of the folk form. The natural holidays Shakespeare drew on, as his culture was becoming rapidly urban during Elizabeth's reign, had developed during Medieval centuries, so were enriched by time and varied by region. Much more quickly, but in just that way, tenant-farming blacks developed their own distinctive ceremonies during their isolation between Reconstruction and the civil rights movement. The nadir generated blues, jazz, and their attendant rites much in the same way that the material differences of the fifties generated a distinctive aesthetic, ethic, and attendant vernacular rites in the national culture. In both cases, there was a deliberate speed, a willed adaptation of the cultural climate to the altered material reality.

Chief among these African-American rites were the Sunday morning gospel service, with its distinctive preaching and singing, and the secular frolic on Saturday night, the weekend's central eve. They have a clear connection perhaps properly understood as one extended rite: the weekend safety valve. The Sunday experience fed on the Saturday excitement — closing it off, chastising and clarifying it. And *Invisible Man* comments on both, linking them in one spectrum. The novel shows orality as their common trait, and establishes its narrator as a budding speaker. It parodies black preachers in blind Barbee at the book's beginning and unprincipled Rinehart toward its end. In short, *Invisible Man* followed, glossed, and made compact the complex structure of feeling that a juke-party blues performance must have raised in its audience.

The novel also expresses the rhythmic pattern by which rites teach and change their participants. The lyrics of blues songs follow a rhythm of depression and control, disengagement and engagement, psychological pain and its adequate mastery. Critic Cesar Barber generalized these elements as release and clarification, and Albert Murray particularized them as the blues and their stomping. Ellison achieves this rhythm when he disrupts both his novel's and character's calm growth with violence. The battle royal, Trueblood's volcanic story, the Golden Day, the Liberty Paint Company explosion, the police murder of Clifton and the invisible youth's spearing of Ras during the Harlem riot—all these, and more, stutter the story. They are reminiscent of Richard Wright's active fictions, of the razors and floods and kicking mules in blues songs. They disrupt his plans and depress the youth. But they are only a fraction of his novel.

The important remainder is in the quiet links which hold such violences together. There in the modulation, engagement, and sufficient articulation of his pain, the youth balances his violent disruptions into a blues rhythm. If the explosively memorable pieces of the novel are gems, the rest of the narration links, sets, and frames their sparkle. In vivid scenes, events break out of the youth's control; these moments happen to him. In the links, he regains control of his story partially as protagonist and, more thoroughly, as narrator; he stomps the memorable moments into place; he happens to them. Thus, clarification occurs in his life as well as for readers attending to it.

This linking process is as much a part of the blues structure of the book as are its explosive moments, dialogues, and diatribes. Indeed, they may have been more important to Ellison (*Territory* 53) because they show the youth becoming articulate, gradually learning to think for himself, seeing through his victimization and doing something about it. Ellison used the basically conservative tendency of folklore here in a radical way. By having his invisible youth follow blues repetitions to their incremental recognitions, Ellison made him into a figure who overcame the despair riddling the works of such modern predecessors as Eliot, Faulkner, Fitzgerald, Hemingway, Dreiser, and Wright.

Ellison was consciously going against such modern models in the novel, he says in his introduction to *Invisible Man*. Unlike Jay Gatsby, Clyde Griffiths, Joe Christmas, Quentin Compson, Jake Barnes, or Bigger Thomas—all victims of the times and troubles in the century's first half—the invisible youth would sidestep social forces. Specifically, he runs from the white men and their clubs during the Harlem riot, then has a fortunate fall out of their clutches into the manhole he will inhabit, allowing him to think over his predicament. This accident well fits the author's intention to write a novel that would show a "subtle process of negating the world of things as given in favor of manmade positives" (xix). Ellison wanted his youth, "like Brer Rabbit and his more literary cousins, . . . to snatch the victory of conscious perception from the forces that overwhelmed them" (xx). And to the extent that he does so snatch, he helped create a distinctively different aesthetic for the American novel since the fifties.

The simplest way to put it is to say that the links between excitements are the novel's equivalent to summary lines in blues stanzas; in them, the youth becomes a man. His growth follows the dictates of the novel's blues structure. Until *Invisible Man*, black fictions had not yet delivered such a full vision of maturity, because they had neither studied nor followed ruthlessly enough their folk traditions. James Baldwin noticed part of this point just months before the publication of *Invisible Man*. Writing about Richard Wright's *Native Son*, Baldwin claimed that Bigger's estrangement from his family, friends, and community in Wright's novel creates a

> climate of anarchy and unmotivated and unapprehended disaster; and it is this climate, common to most Negro protest novels, which has led us all to believe

—Baldwin is writing this in December 1951—

> that in Negro life there exists no tradition, no field of manners, no possibility of ritual or intercourse. . . . But the fact is not that the Negro has no tradition but that there has as yet arrived no sensibility sufficiently profound and tough to make this tradition articulate. ("Many Thousands Gone" 28)

That the invisible youth's crucial "second," when he hears black tradition sung at Clifton's funeral and thus hears his own heartbeat, comes during the song "There's Many a Thousand Gone" (341) is surely important in this connection. Responding to the Jamesian echoes in Baldwin's remark ("no field of manners. . ."), Ellison proves like Constance Rourke before him that there has indeed been a usable past. It has been as available and relevant for black writers in the lore of their community as it has been generally true for every writer, every citizen. Everyone is from someplace, everyone has a tradition.

Ellison stated this principle directly in the early sixties, at a seminar on "culturally different youth":

> The children in question are not so much "culturally deprived" as products of a different cultural complex. . . . If you can abstract their manners, their codes, their customs and attitudes into forms of expression, if you can convert them into forms of art, if you can

stylize them and give them many and subtle ranges of reference, then you are dealing with a culture. People have learned this culture; it has been transferred to them from generation to generation, and in its forms they have projected their most transcendent images of themselves and of the world. (*Territory* 68)

Ellison, along with diverse others of varying profundity and toughness, in music and politics, from Bo Diddley to Martin Luther King, Jr., did articulate those rituals and intercourses, did stylize and abstract them, did convert them into forms of art, rhythms, tropes with subtle ranges of reference. They did, therefore, prove a black tradition in the mid-fifties.

In Baldwin's terms, these varied performers individually and together composed a "sensibility sufficiently profound and tough" to articulate their tradition and teach it to the world. It is as difficult, now, to suppose a time when customary perception hid that black tradition from everyone as to imagine when consensus claimed Americans had no usable tradition setting them off from the European inheritance. There is always a usable past, as there is always a usable present. The problems are knowing where to look and staying open to the news.

OUT OF THE HOLE

. . . wishing I were a Negro.
—Jack Kerouac to himself

The American mainstream still owes its unpaid debt to fifties black culture for showing paths through their mutual thicket of troubles. To those who would listen, the blues ethic discovered how to mine and kindle the deeply buried lodes of energy in its history. That Ellison wanted to lever this energy up for all is clear from his novel's last line: "Who knows but that, on the lower frequencies, I speak for you?" It was the postwar period and he would show everyone—blacks, novelists, Americans—how to come out of the hole.

For Ellison the idea was to return to the sustaining lore and traditions that preceded and—he demonstrated against the grain of his time—*were succeeding* modern despair. When he discovered literature at Tuskegee Institute in the middle of studying trumpet, Ellison later reported, "'The Waste Land' seized my mind" (*Shadow* 161). He found ritual the organizing basis for modernism. He also saw how the longing in modern writers for the putative completion they attributed to ancient culture led them awry of their own time. Nevertheless, Eliot's poem staggered Ellison, by his own account driving him back through American literature seeking answers to the poet's riddles and paralysis, searching for the sources of the poem's greatness, which he has always saluted in print. But Ellison is a particularly cagey man and *Invisible Man* is no simple extension of Eliot's poetry—as deliberately speeding culture does not simply extend modernism.

"I learned a few things from Eliot, Joyce and Hemingway," Ellison has told interviewers, "but not how to adapt them" (*Shadow* 174). He learned about lore's importance to art from these modern mentors, but he came to reject their despairing relationship to it. He pioneered instead the untold and living lore of his own lifetime and people: "When I started writing I knew that in both *The Waste Land* and *Ulysses* ancient myth and ritual were used to give significance to the material, but it took me a few years to realize that *the myths and rites which we find functioning in our everyday lives could be used in the same way*" (174–75, my emphasis).

This daily lore was not the stuff of debauched Sweeney, from Eliot's poems, nor Eliot's lament for an impotent Fisher King casting the polluted Thames for a catch that will never bite. Instead, Ellison gave vivid instances of this daily lore in Trueblood's blues (Chapter 2), Peter Wheatstraw's jive energy and the laughter of Robin's pluckers (Chapter 9), and the sneaky duplicity of Sambo's smile (Chapter 20). Those were instances of lore alive and present. They eventually taught the invisible youth he was whole, so could grow into manhood. They made him engage his world, put his lands in order, so to speak, by elaborating his story.

Ralph Ellison's complex relationship to the modern writers was like the poet Charles Olson's, himself an important shaper of contemporary attitudes in his own genre. Both admired the formal achievements of the previous generation's best writers. But both eschewed the content and tone of that achievement. Olson's early poem "The Kingfisher" (1949) rejects the modern axiom of one declining lineage from the classical past. "The Kingfisher" reflects Eliot's Fisher King becoming impotent. But Olson quite differently notices that, although the kingfisher (around which the ancient Fisher King myth developed) does indeed raise its young in a nest that grows "fetid" with repeated use, its fledglings actually fly away to build new nests and begin afresh. Olson identifies with the fledglings.

At poem's end, Olson adapts from Rimbaud his own new conditions for culture: "if I have any taste / it is only because I have interested myself / in what was slain in the sun." He addresses these lines indirectly to Ezra Pound, whose cantos' form he was emulating. But the lines reject Pound's modern content in favor of ideas which the moderns overlooked, even "killed," in pressing their imperial modes. Less discreetly than Ellison, Olson challenged his forebears with their own — specifically, Pound's own — words: "I pose you your question: / shall you uncover honey / where maggots are? / I hunt among stones." Olson's stones were the Mayan hieroglyphs that he traveled to Yucatan to study.

Olson was leaving the fetid nest of his modern mentors to prove the living existence of lores that he insisted had a present bearing on contemporary life. And twenty years later, continuing the contemporary epoch, Thomas Pynchon was to have one of his more sympathetic characters, a

black Southwest African living in Germany just after World War II, similarly insist, "Somewhere, among the wastes of the World, is the key that
will bring us back, restore us to our Earth and to our freedom" (*Gravity's
Rainbow* 525). Olson, Ellison, Pynchon, all these contemporary voices,
insisted that the resources that would carry culture forward reside outside
the narrow purviews of the late modern aegis. The point was to know how
to use tradition, how to choose pertinent strands, and then to recontinue
their weaving.

Ellison pursued the point most noticeably with his mentor, Richard
Wright. Ellison wanted to leap the black community's hedges which the
attention of Wright's stories had paradoxically made the more impassable
even while protesting them. Ellison's title and his novel's action emphasized
the capacity to grow into manhood, while the last word in Wright's titles
always reinforced stunted immaturity: *Uncle Tom's Children* (1938), *Native
Son* (1940), and *Black Boy* (1945). By 1956 and his account of the Bandung
Conference in *The Color Curtain,* Wright, too, was noticing and trying to
account for the emergent full personalities of people of color. The mid-
fifties was when that all came out of its hole, in fact and fiction.

Allen Ginsberg read Ellison's *Invisible Man* in July, 1954 (*Journals* 87),
fourteen months before he recited the first part of "Howl" in San Francisco,
7 October 1955. "Howl" gauged its era in many ways, and perhaps most
closely in showing how the "best minds" in Ginsberg's generation depended on black culture to fix their needs. The oscillations between withdrawal and engagement that mark most of Ginsberg's mid-fifties poems,
their struggle against the affectlessness and victimization common in the
previous generation, their allusions to jazz — all these were lessons garnered
from black culture. Just as Ellison's invisible man returns to society from his
hole on the novel's last page, so Ginsberg usually closed his poems reengag-
ing the wheel of his society. The blues ethic fomented and confirmed both
Ellison's and Ginsberg's already existing concerns.

Kerouac had written *On the Road,* in April 1951, partly about the need
to connect with a literally derelict American lore. He represented this
dereliction in crazed wanderers from the ghost of the Susquehanna, at the
end of Part I of *On the Road,* to "Old Dean Moriarty the father we never
found," in the novel's last sentence. A year later, April 1952, Allen Ginsberg
wrote a significant early poem, "Wild Orphan," about this same felt
lovelessness, similarly shown as separation from the mentor. The orphan
tries to construct a mythology too wild to inherit about forebears too
derelict to create it themselves. He is consciously investing a usable, romantic past. Meanwhile, across the country, the mentor grieves for the lost son,

unaware of the youths "bumming toward his door" (*Collected Poems* 78–79). In this poem orphans forgive fathers who in turn need and want the sons.

Clearly, Beats and blacks were both on the same track in the fifties, both reaching to connect with an only apparently lost culture. Thus when Beats could not connect with white fathers — symbolically, when orthodox mentors proved inadequate — they adopted black jazzlore. Kerouac wrote in *On the Road:*

> I looked everywhere for the sad and fabled tinsmith of my mind. Either you find someone who looks like your father in places like Montana or you look for a friend's father where he is no more. . . . I walked . . . wishing I were a Negro, feeling that the best the white world had offered was not enough ecstasy for me, not enough life, joy, kicks, darkness, music, not enough night. (148)[1]

His mind's tinsmith is a fantasy of derelict and black culture compacted into a blues ethic.

Kerouac learned from this ethic to send down his bucket where he was, much as Booker T. Washington had urged, and as Ellison's narrator had repeated. However, Kerouac was in the apparently barren desert of lower-middle class popular culture, a sepia world of baseball cards and the stations of the cross, Joan Crawford and the Three Stooges.[2] He transformed it into *Visions of Cody* and *Dr. Sax.*

The connection between the blues ethic and its sympathetic outsiders passes directly and consciously through Jack Kerouac. When interviewers in 1968 asked Ginsberg about William Shakespeare and Christopher Smart as sources for "Howl," he told them, "Lester Young, actually, is what I was thinking about," referring to the great jazz tenor saxophonist who came out of Kansas City with Count Basie and went on to name Billie Holiday "Lady Day," as she named him "The Pres." "'Howl' is all 'Lester Leaps In'" Ginsberg continued to claim. "And I got that," he said, "from Kerouac . . . he made me listen to it" (*Composed* 43). In fact, with the enthusiasm for black music in his novels, Kerouac made a lot of people listen to it. More significant than their enthusiasms, though, were Kerouac's and Ginsberg's reenactments of the blues ethic. Kerouac's improvisations, repetitions, stuttering starts and stops, insistence on coexisting with the world as it is, and love of late-night performance all came directly from the jazz worlds he entered on both coasts and both banks of the Mississippi River.

The first inkling of the blues ethic as it would crop up in *On the Road* and, much later, *Visions of Cody* appeared in 1955 under Kerouac's pseudonym "Jean-Louis," as "Jazz of the Beat Generation":

You can hear Lester blow and he is the greatness of America in a
single Negro musician—he is just like the river, the river starts in
near Butte, Montana, in frozen snow caps (Three Forks) and
meanders on down across states and entire territorial areas of dim
bleak land with hawthorn crackling in the sleet, picks up rivers in
Bismarck, Omaha, and St. Louis just north, another at Kay-ro,
another in Arkansas, Tennessee, comes deluging on New Orleans
with muddy news from the land and a roar of subterranean
excitement that is like the vibration of the entire land sucked of its
gut in mad midnight, fevered, hot, the big mudhole rank clawpole
old frogular pawed-soul titanic Mississippi from the North, full of
wires, cold wood and horn—Lester, so, holding his horn high in
Doctor Pepper chicken-shacks, backstreet, Basie Yaycee wearing
greasy smeared corduroy bigpants and in torn flap smoking jacket
without straw, scuffle-up shoes all slopey Mother Hubbard, soft,
pudding, and key ring, early handkerchiefs, hands up, arms up,
horn horizontal, shining dull, in wood-brown whiskey house with
ammoniac urine from broken gut bottles around fecal pukey bowl
and a gal sprawled in it legs spread in brown cotton stockings,
bleeding at belted mouth, moaning "yes" as Lester, horn placed, has
started blowing, "blow for me mother blow for me," 1938, later,
earlier, Miles is still on his daddy's checkered knee, Louis' only got
twenty years behind him, and Lester blows all Kansas City to
ecstasy and now Americans from coast to coast go mad, and fall by,
and everybody's picking up. ("Jazz" 14–15)

From such long sentences derived the long-lined ecstasies of "Howl," some
of the impetus for Thomas Pynchon's catalogues in *V.* and *Gravity's Rainbow,*
and verification for many readers that there remained untapped resources in
the energy of jazz. That is why he can end with "everybody's picking up."
Indeed, everyone was cuing on the "muddy news from the land" that was
the blues ethic.

   Kerouac's extended simile links jazz to the tumble of muddy news that
the Mississippi bears to New Orleans. His words imitated both that tumble
and the syncopated beat of a Lester Young solo. This passage is striking
first for its volubility gushing from Kerouac's typewriter as from the river's
springs at Three Forks and from Young's horizontal horn. But also important is its precision—he says "Kay-ro" as the natives do; he says it as Huck
and Jim did when they passed it in the night. Abetting this precise gush is
Kerouac's concision. Dropping articles and pronouns emphasizes his allit-

eration and speeds his logic. These conceits couple with the surprising rhythms to create a density that hinders the horizontal flow of the passage and also its linear time, until Kerouac even confounds 1938 in "later, earlier."

Although he sanitized it for *New World Writing* ("fecal" and "urine" were otherwise), the editorial alterations hardly disturbed its spirit. Kerouac improvised his news the way Young had his, out of innumerable previous rundowns of the same material. For example, he sliced the part quoted here not from the famous roll manuscript to be published two years later as *On The Road*. It came, rather, from the manuscript for *Visions of Cody* (392–93), which by 1952 was Kerouac's fifth obsessive attempt to account for his friend Neal Cassady, though it would not be published in its entirety until 1972 (Hunt, "Composition" 534). The spoors of Kerouac's improvisation are everywhere in the passage—in its offhand allusions (Miles, Louis, Basie) and unfollowed ideas, as in its ambition to exhaust its topic and self. The passage tries, for example, to amplify into audibility "the vibration of the entire land." This prose lives up to the blues ethic in its reflexive image of the performer returning to his audience their moans, the matter of their porcelain bowls. That's one way to understand such writing.

Another way to understand it is to notice Kerouac offloading so many of his own needs and fears onto jazz and its black soloists that he created what Flannery O'Connor termed, in the same year, an "artificial nigger." Like so many other writers-performers of the fifties, even those who were sympathetic, even those who were black, Kerouac used the Negro as a metaphor of his needs. Ellison's invisible youth, Kerouac's Lester Young, the Emmett Till that James Baldwin and *Newsweek* made,[3] Richard Penniman's and Bumps Blackwell's Little Richard, Chuck Berry's brown-eyed handsome man, and Norman Mailer's host of notions about black sexuality conveniently clustered in his famous essay *The White Negro*—all these shared, at least in some measure, with O'Connor's statue, with the minstrel Interlocutor and Tambo and Bones, the uses of artifice and the abuses of artificiality. They were all Sambos. Use and abuse was what each in its way was about. They were all figures accustomed to slipping successive yokes of perception and becoming whatever their viewers needed to see in them. Sambos survived their surveillance no other way. The Sambo strategy was particularly active in the fifties, and of course still operates.

□   □   □   □   □

They ain't got enough real ones here.
— Flannery O'Connor's Mr. Head to Nelson

Flannery O'Connor's "The Artificial Nigger" is the brilliant centerpiece of her first collection of stories, *A Good Man Is Hard to Find* (1955). Her volume's title refers to the 1927 same-name recording by Bessie Smith (Columbia 14250-D), which was a staple in the singer's repertoire (though hardly a blues, for all its inflections). Important to "The Artificial Nigger" is one of those cast plaster statues of a miniaturized black man that sometimes light suburban driveways. In this story the statue perches on a yellow brick fence around an Atlanta lawn to eat a piece of brown watermelon: "He was meant to look happy because his mouth was stretched up at the corners but the chipped eye and the angle he was cocked at gave him a wild look of misery instead" (*Complete* 268). Nothing, she wrote to one correspondent, "screams out the tragedy of the South like what my uncle calls 'nigger statuary'" (*Habit* 101). But another more common vernacular euphemism for such a statue was "Sambo."

A frequent strategy of O'Connor's stories was to move tractable characters on pilgrimages through alien country where a shock propels them out of their complacency, through an epiphany, into a different consciousness. Her best stories often derive their deepest irony from the way a trig grandmother, hefty matron, or huffy philosophy student ricochets from a first to a second false consciousness without being able to sustain the painful clarity passed en route. Some inadequacy in the redneck way of knowledge is less to blame here than the general insufficiency that makes most people prefer comfortable conclusions to difficult truths. In "The Artificial Nigger," the Sambo statue incites both the characters' skid and their readers' realizations about the paths of human understanding.

The story of their skid begins when Mr. Head and his grandson, Nelson, leave their rural shack, where the moon "cast a dignifying light on everything," to visit Atlanta, where everything "looked like exactly what it was." Mr. Head has wanted to inoculate Nelson against the evils of the city. To that end, he has Nelson peer into a sewer entrance. The mentor describes the system so that the boy "connected the sewer passages with the entrance to hell and understood for the first time how the world was put together in its lower parts" (*Complete* 259). But Mr. Head's *pièce de résistance,* he is sure, will be the city's Negroes, whom the grandson has never seen.

The two pilgrims encounter several. On the train to the city, Nelson had noticed a man, coffee-colored, well-dressed, and majestically stomached, but missed the only characteristic Mr. Head disgustedly insisted on: "That was a nigger." After they walk in the city, pass the sewer, and admit they are lost in a Negro section, Mr. Head is too chagrined, horrified, and scared to ask for help. So Nelson approaches a lolling black woman, asks directions, and senses in her power exactly the charisma white youths were beginning to feel all across America at just this fifties moment in the history of race relations:

> He suddenly wanted her to reach down and pick him up and draw him against her and then he wanted to feel her breath on his face. He wanted to look down and into her eyes while she held him tighter and tighter. He had never had such a feeling before. He felt as if he were reeling down through a pitchblack tunnel. (262)

The grandfather pulled him away. And they walked ever deeper into what Mr. Head was by now calling "nigger heaven" (261).

Under the pressure to convey to his kin their race's regional wisdom, Mr. Head further compounds his mistakes. He leaves their lunch on the train, loses their bearing down urban streets, allows blacks to fascinate the boy, and, crowningly, when angry women threaten to call police against Nelson, even denies he knows him. Thus, instead of cementing the boy's commitment to the mores of his own kind, as he had anticipated, Mr. Head discovers blacks separating his kin from him. He is living out the fifties nightmare of the racists who called the Monday of Earl Warren's desegregation ruling "Black Monday." He is encountering the altered conditions that necessitated the era's deliberate speed. Like so many others, of every political and aesthetic tendency, Mr. Head is discovering that the old ways of coping do not suffice.

O'Connor musters her considerable religious rhetoric to manifest the unglued empire these two novitiates now inhabit, at least for the nonce. She shows them so lost that home, even, is nothing to them. They have grown so bereft of bonds in the world that they grasp what "man would be like without salvation" (*Complete* 268). Just then they arrive before the plaster statue. It seems to them "some great mystery, some monument to another's victory that brought them together in their common defeat." Mr. Head sums up the meaning of this black minstrel image in precisely the wrong way that will make everything right for the two of them as whites. "They ain't got enough real ones here," he tells the boy, "They got to have an artificial one" (269).

Such grandfatherly misinterpretation is neither more true nor more convenient, however, than the lie about its topic that the Sambo statue itself indicates for its owners. One of O'Connor's most interesting implications concerns the inevitable uses of totems and art. Mr. Head's interpretation of the statue is a lie about the lie that the statue represents. The demeaning statue presides over that lawn because of its owners' anxieties about the many threatening Negroes looming large in Atlantan, American, life in the fifties. The owners' inoculation of their greenswards against black menace differs mainly from Mr. Head's dose of the city to Nelson in that the Atlantans consider their dose successful. Unlike Mr. Head, who began his enterprise knowing what he was about, their effect depends on repressing their intents especially from themselves. The artifice of the statue carves Negroes down to manageable miniature, proposes their happy smile, and insists that watermelon sugar will appease them. Mr. Head imagines just the opposite. The interpretation he makes — his impromptu artifice in rejoinder — is that white Atlantans so belove the black populace that they multiply them in statuary.

Their interpretation serves O'Connor's pilgrims because it brings them together and allows their return to their moonlighted garden in the woods, where Nelson announces "I'm glad I've went once, but I'll never go back again!"(270). Blacks and their urban home have shocked the boy out of further experience, which is what the old man had wanted, but clearly not what O'Connor advises, and perhaps not what Mr. Head would now wish, for the Sambo figure has also affected him. But in what way, and how lastingly, is not certain. He now recognizes the size of his sin, but that he judges himself "with the thoroughness of God" is surely a tell-tale pretense. He also feels God's mercy so completely that he suddenly "felt ready at that instant to enter Paradise" (279). Some readers consider O'Connor earnest with her ending, arguing that Mr. Head has had full and satisfying conversion in this one event. Others suspect his second static understanding is as fatuous as his first, so merely the haunting beginning of many such moments in a late life of agony. That the story arouses such arguments indicates why Flannery O'Connor judged it the best she ever wrote, having more in it than she knew (*Habit* xvi).

Beyond its private associations and its early contemporary instance of embedded deconstructions, what's important in "The Artificial Nigger" is its intuitive scrutiny of that Sambo figure, smiling miserably, in the center of mid-fifties life. Well beyond O'Connor's story, the Sambo figure is the agent of change making for deliberate speed in both black and white communities. He is part of the black wedge into the white community which initially divides but ultimately connects the cultures, however fragilely. Cast plaster or paper ruffle, encoding ancient lore in apparent non-sense syllables as Little Richard did or prompting painful self-examination as Emmett Till did, he is a good man. But he's double, as Bessie Smith knew: "nowadays," she sang, in "A Good Man Is Hard to Find," "you always get another kind." In his resistance to scrutiny, his slippery double significations and ability to absorb all audience needs, he remains hard to find. If he was hard to pin down, still he was everpresent in the era, especially on the airwaves.

☐   ☐   ☐   ☐   ☐

> *They were outside in the dark with Sambo . . .*
> *running and dodging the forces of history.*
> —Ralph Ellison's invisible man to us

The Sambo figure was the conceit enabling the popularity of rock 'n' roll. After the mid-fifties, the separate white and black markets for records came closer together because in 1955, for the first time, black groups and indi-viduals began achieving large hits on the white charts. These crossover songs nearly always leapt across smilingly, enacting the I'm-whatever-you-need tomfoolery. Buck Ram's memorable hit "The Great Pretender," which he wrote and elaborately produced for the Platters in October 1955, was the first crossover song to snatch number one on the black rhythm 'n' blues charts and also top the then-white pop charts. Not even Elvis Presley had yet achieved peak popularity in both markets with one piece of product.

Behind lead singer Tony Williams's operatic enunciation of the lyrics, themselves significantly attractive, Ram's echoic production distinguished the song and surely influenced the wall of sound Phil Spector took credit for creating in the sixties. Ram used fifteen-year-old Zola Taylor's wail as a foil to Williams's tenor. She and the Platters repeated each phrase in-creasingly as the song progressed, punctuating their three lamenting verses with a total of thirteen affirmative yesses. *Too reeeeal* was Tony Williams's feeling of make believe. (Yes, sang Zola Taylor and the rest of the Platters.) Ohh-OHHH YES! answered Williams, pretending to be the Great Pre-tender. (Yes, called the Platters.) He seems (he seems) to be (to be — with some more yessing) what he's not (he's not) you see (you see).

The stage images of make-believe and clowning, the reiterated *you see,* the very present Platters watching Williams and echoing his every move all reinforced the Sambo doubleness which Williams confessed in the lyrics.

He was a clown under double surveillance, from his group and his audience, this great pretender, who would make himself whatever "you" in his audiences saw him to be. His American audiences made him number one, twice over. The great pretender lived up to his boast.

The limits of that boast, however, tied the Platters to their moment. Ellison and O'Connor could stick their Sambo figures into contexts that peeled away their minstrel masks, uncovering the strings behind the smiles. But the three-minute limit of the pop single held the Platters to elaborating the commonplace, indicating its tensions and complexities. They could not subvert the Sambo figure's racist associations so simply, in the fifties, because the inherited cultural images were too common. As you listened to Tony Williams sing how his smiling was make-believe, for instance, you might have been browsing in a *Newsweek* from that spring, and noticed the full-page advertisement for Chicago's Ambassador Hotel Pump Room. It pictured a black man, well into his thirties, wearing a brocade coat, white gloves, a turban, and a plume. With him ran the hotel's caption: "In Chicago He Pours Your Coffee . . . Say 'Pump Room' to anyone who knows Chicago's top restaurants and this turbanned coffee boy comes instantly to mind" (7 March 1955, 93). Such conventional cultural associations were the context that limited early rock uses of the Sambo convention.

As it turned out, the trick was less to transcend the common ground of American racism than to speed the Sambo figure across it, showing him in alternative contexts, indicating to each audience how the others viewed him. By putting the figure in the many lights of many audiences, his many facets would become apparent. This was essentially the strategy toward which Martin Luther King, Jr.'s tactics gravitated. King learned to make vivid dramas in public that projected passive victims bearing their condition through hostile crowds toward banal goals—a front seat on a bus, a registrar at a county courthouse, a bungalow in a white neighborhood, use of "white only" lavatories. He directed and starred in these dramas before curious national audiences in the print and visual media, before local audiences passionately for and against his principles, before the close scrutiny of the press, police, and FBI. These dramas shared much with the minstrel show, the passive figures with the Sambo figure, and King's nonviolent protest with the Sambo strategy. They shared the passive aggression, the doubleness, the covert mockery of the dominant position. They shared the largest audiences of their respective eras. They shared, too, the prime attribute of the Sambo figure—both protesters and performers carried the mask into new contexts, revealing its surprising dimensions. Thus the Sambo figure could participate in the same dignity that the protesters kept, for it was neither the performer nor the protester that was obscene, but the operating conditions. Their contexts lacked dignity: that was the clarification both rites proclaimed.

Taking the Sambo figure through multiple contexts, then, expanded its message. Whether or not performers, entertainers, and activists consciously learned the principle is difficult to say, but many of them came to apply it. Songs like "Speedo," toward the end of the year, caught some of the regular guy's engulfment in speeding past barriers — "They often call me Speedo," sang the Cadillacs' Earl Carroll, "but my real name is Mr. Earl." It was Chuck Berry's "Maybellene," however, during the Summer of 1955, that really illustrated the principle.

"Maybellene" begins as a song about class in a race: about a poor man's V-8 Ford dueling a rich man's Cadillac for a black woman.[4] But it ends being a song about race in a race. Berry's apparent desire was to ignore race somehow and grab the same American promise of Fords and proms, jukeboxes and guitars offered every adolescent. But his quiet conviction, ever deepening from "Maybellene" on, was that the ways of his people claimed him. And he claimed them, in song after song increasingly more complexly. His career in that way recapitulated the pattern Ellison's invisible man fixed just three years earlier.

Berry's singer is nevertheless very different from Ellison's invisible youth. His reservoir of street smarts and a mind portrayed as uncluttered by nagging introspection place him more happily behind a wheel than podium or desk. "Maybellene" concerns a black trickster's tactics of speed within a life understood as competition, all dodging through the hillbilly patina that attracted producer Leonard Chess in the first place. So it was an interesting match when Chuck Berry, at age 21, contested America's sense of itself with his pomaded hair, white bucks, seemingly cute lyrics, and stage moves that would soon become his phallic duck walk — itself a passive-aggressive contradiction in terms worthy of the minstrel tradition. He was armed with a potently sneaky mix of folk conceits and contemporary insouciance. Surrounding him that summer of Emmett Till's lynching was the general aura represented in the Pump Room's advertisement for its turbanned coffee server. He was arriving for the contest just after Earl Warren's enforcement decree, and a few months before the Montgomery bus boycott.

Victim of a woman who has started in doing the things she used to do, just "motorvating" around in his jalopy, Berry glimpses Maybellene in a Coupe de Ville. Whose Cadillac she rides Berry never tells, but he also never admits the fancy car's superiority to his Ford. Rather, Berry committed himself to the proposition that he was its equal. Their cars may go bumper to bumper and side to side, may jump the speed past ninety-five to 104 and even 110; the Ford may slip behind in its uphill battle, but Berry has reserves of energy and determination. When his Ford loses ground to the Cadillac's power, he relies on trickster wiles to pull him out: When it started to rain he tooted for the passing lane; all that water under his hood surely did his motor good. Berry inserts a bridge with the old blues chestnut of the guitar imitating a train whistle, but updates the motif, whistle becoming Ford horn, toot, and wail. He is Mobileman.

Mobileman masters his own technology, but remains in league with sun, cloud, and rain. With the elements on his side, he is soon speeding so fast you might swear he sings he spies Maybellene half a mile ahead *settin' like a toe on a leg* but, no, she's merely sitting like a ton of lead. Whichever, there's no stopping him now and Mobileman catches Maybellene on the crest of the hill. The open-ended capture of Maybellene is what still holds audiences decades later.

A man who has overcome his victimization by chasing down the fanciest Cadillac on a rainy road, intuitively drawn on the language and riffs of his folk ways, intertwined them with the twang and rhythm of his neighbors' counter tradition, and snuck his resulting anthem of pride past all the natural and cultural roadblocks — what might such a sly agent do with straying Maybellene at their peak moment? Nobody knows, least of all the singer. Berry exhibited the excitement of competition as well as anyone on the pop scene. At his career's outset, however, he could not imagine the result as success, which remained for him as undefined as death.

Berry would have to accrue confidence before he could propose victory in his songs, as in the last stanza to "Brown-Eyed Handsome Man." What was constant and thinkable in 1955 was the sport, the longing to score, the competitions, the reeling and rocking, the women doing all the things they used to do in fancier cars than he had, the fiancées like Nadine who, every time he sees them, "got something else to do." Berry fused his blues vision with a veneer of pop and "almost grown" optimism. But the blues vision was what was left at the end. Maybellene is caught for now, but he and she being what they are, and their world the same, their proclivities will prevail. There is a maw at the end of "Maybellene," as at the end of nearly all his other major songs, a maw which the title of a 1964 song minimized as "No Particular Place to Go."

Berry's earnest investment in the present and uncertainty about ends was inevitable for fifties performers in his position trying to bridge cultures. They are pronounced in Berry's classic songs for at least two reasons. First, because of the country spin to some of his early songs, their lyrics were unusually narrational; their inconclusiveness was therefore the more pronounced. Second, his blues tradition consoled Berry more and he relied on it more deeply as his career progressed, as he continued to commit "naughty-naughties . . . [e]very fifteen years" (xv–xvi) for which he spent prison time, and as the doubleness of blues and minstrel imagery came, therefore, to make more conscious sense to use.

As the very first song he recorded, "Maybellene" showed fifties consumer fetishism vying with blues determinism. Mobileman has faith that cars and the energy he shares with them can overtake Maybellene's waywardness. He catches her at the peak. But reality returns and the song simply fades when all the singer's V-8 momentum must still cope not with a wet Cadillac but with a woman outrun. How does it turn out? Berry's Ford chugs on into the night. That steady running, with neither defeat nor transcendence, is the return of the blues when adolescent, consumer, fifties hope fails. Berry was shrewd enough to know his optimism connected him to the larger audiences, canny enough to know his blues told him truths that sustained him between reaches. Certainly both ethics dueled in his songs, the first propelling their speed, the second providing their deliberation.

This doubleness personified the Sambo figure from the beginning, but it grew more complex as Berry proceeded, as he became more complex and defensive and distrusting. Over the next few years, Berry developed more levels to the figure than first appeared, showing that the symptoms of "Maybellene" were not aberrant but diagnostic. He sugar-coated cultural threat in "Roll Over Beethoven," perhaps his most famous song, the next spring. And he returned in the fall with "Brown-Eyed Handsome Man," an anthem of black power as devious as "Maybellene," and even more ambiguous because Berry crafted it to create an unreadable opposition at the end.

The brown-eyed handsome man is a trickster in the layabout present. In the song's wonderful opening line, he is in court, in the witness chair, being grilled because the authorities arrested him for "unemployment." The sprightly economy of the stanza proceeds to dramatize his powerful hidden allies, fantasying a whole vernacular sociology: the judge's wife called the D.A., told him to free the brown-eyed handsome man if he wanted to keep his job. Stanzas four and six, after the bridge, further this placement of him as a wily fellow shifting charismatically in the American fifties, attracting the lovers of lawyers and doctors, hitting clutch pitches into the stands. But the song has its wider context, too, for the brown-eyed man is also a Bandung man: the second stanza glimpses a woman walking across the desert to Bombay to find a brown-eyed handsome man. This brown-eyed Bandung man is also historical: he goes back to when the world began. And he's mythical: Venus lost both her arms fighting to win him in the penultimate stanza. So by the time the last stanza finds him in the baseball game, that most American pastime, Berry's brown-eyed trickster is a deepened figure. Berry has pulled tighter the initial tension of a watched witness judging the D.A., of a lover whose jobless freedom will ensure his prosecutor's further imprisonment in a job. By the end, Berry's song has yanked him across epochs and continents, dislocating him even beyond the usual trickster detachment. That is why the last stanza is so supremely empty and loaded at the same time, itself a Sambo fragment. At two strikes and three balls, the brown-eyed man hits a home run and rounds the bases, the crowd cheering as he takes third and goes home. But for what home is he heading?

Is he a conventional American sport doffing cap to fans while heading for home plate in a hot dogs and mustard baseball game? Or is he a sly fellow heading home to his briar patch, to the traditional blues code for the sanctuary of one's culture, as when the invisible youth urged his Harlem crowd to "go home"? He wouldn't be the brown-eyed handsome man in the mid-fifties were he not running toward both destinations simultaneously. The difference between "Maybellene" and "Brown-eyed Handsome Man" is that the singer's vagueness in his first song's ending has become controlled ambiguity in the second. "Brown-eyed Handsome Man" throws doubt about the nature of the game at the audience. He announces that was the game in the last line, as if the song had made game and outcome all clear. But just the opposite — the song has called into question just what sort of game brown-eyed tricksters play.

While he was riding high, Berry hid behind a smile, relying on his distinctive backbeat to propel the songs' seemingly teenaged sentiments. Nevertheless, the deliberative side lurked below for those who watched for it, as some did. For instance, Berry's best song from the sixties is "Promised Land," recorded in February 1964, and released that autumn. It is significant that he wrote the song in prison.

"Promised Land" is ostensibly about journeying across the land from Norfolk, Virginia, to Los Angeles, totemically naming many of the home-towns along the way. The travel is quick, but the speed itself starts to become suspect early on. The high energy of the song, its mandolin-style guitar riffs, and its road motif lend it a happy sound, but that is its minstrel mask. The catalogued places soon indicate another America not often the topic of *Billboard* "Hot 100" songs. That is, the early lines of "Promised Land" signify about the South of the Freedom Rides as the poor boy traced their tracks across the country in a Greyhound bus in 1964, that year of Mississippi Freedom Summer, when activists Michael Schwerner, James Chaney, and Andrew Goodman were all killed for registering black voters. They topped off the "sixty-three [black] people killed around the question of the vote before '64" (Raines 288). Berry rode his Greyhound into Raleigh, across Carolina, stopping in Charlotte to bypass Rock Hill.

Rock Hill? The town famous to locals for its mills where the Klan bought its sheets? Why mention such a small place? Here is James Farmer, national director of the Congress on Racial Equality (CORE) in 1961, when the Freedom Rides went through Rock Hill, reporting on events at that town's bus station:

> John Lewis [veteran civil rights activist, later U.S. Congressman from Georgia] started into a white waiting room in [Rock Hill] in South Carolina . . . and there were several young white hoodlums, leather jackets, ducktail haircuts, standing there smoking, and they blocked the door and said "Nigger, you can't come in here." He said, "I have every right to enter this waiting room according to the Supreme Court of the United States in the Boynton case."
>
> They said, "Shit on that." He tried to walk past, and they clubbed him, beat him and knocked him down. One of the white Freedom Riders . . . Albert Bigelow . . . stepped right between the hoodlums and John Lewis. . . . They then clubbed Bigelow and finally knocked him down, and that took some knocking because he was a pretty strapping fellow, and he didn't hit back at all.
> (Raines 111)

No wonder Chuck Berry wanted to bypass Rock Hill on his way to the promised land. And, since he knew that about Rock Hill, it is no wonder he was scared crossing Alabama, where the Freedom Riders encountered mobs who shot into and burned their bus, beating them even more. And it is no wonder he fled when the bus developed motor trouble in Birmingham that "turned into a struggle." This was, after all, the Birmingham of Reverend King's "Letter from Birmingham Jail," of Police Chief "Bull" Connor with his dogs and cattle prods; this was the Birmingham of the church bombings.

Like "Brown-eyed Handsome Man" and "Maybellene" — only more so — "Promised Land" smuggled black reality and black anxieties into the smiling heart of America, grafting them there so artfully that most listeners never dreamed Berry's incubus had visited them. In these early lines of "Promised Land," the singer is playing Mobileman again, but with the deepened awareness ripened during the civil rights movement, his prison term, and a decade of dealing with people on both sides of the microphone.

Mobileman is now running the gauntlet of recent American history even while plying his evident optimism about ends. This is quintessential Sambo strategy. Ralph Ellison pegged it correctly in *Invisible Man* when the youth discovered zoot-suiters in the subway after his friend's killing, and intuited their way of coping: "they were outside, in the dark with Sambo... taking it on the lambo with my fallen brother... running and dodging the forces of history instead of making a dominating stand" (333). In "Promised Land," Mobileman is dodging from and through America, a zoot-suiter's spokesman, while running toward his goals. The Freedom Riders made their stand and absorbed their abuse; Berry's way is complementary and only evidently more normal.

There really is nothing normal in "Promised Land." Even its goals turn inside out and deepen after its initial hearing. They are in fact as apocalyptic as that clock, set at X minutes before midnight, on the cover of *The Bulletin of Atomic Scientists:* at song's end the pilot told Mobileman in thirteen minutes he would set them at the terminal gate. "Swing low, chariot," he responds, "come down easy, taxi to the terminal dome." The multiple conjunction of ends with gospel imagery validates the sense of surviving doom, of speeding deliberately through a national madhouse, that permeates "Promised Land."

The song ends with the old blues conceit of calling home that Berry had used successfully in so many of his tunes, and which stems back to the original downhome artists, as in Charley Patton's "Pony Blues":

> Hello central   'sa matter with your line
> Hel- lo central   matter now with your line
> Come a storm last night   tore the wires down. (Yazoo L-
>   1020; syncopated transcription by Titon 67–68)

Patton's traditional stanza is about the failure of communication. But Berry's variant surmounts that difficulty. Mobileman believes in technology, can use the tools of his time, has no doubt that he can connect. But his connection is the eerier for all that. He achieves the promised land only after a hell of a trip; everyone the poor boy cares about is still in hell; and now he is "on the line." The line may be innocent; but if so it would be the only innocent line in the song. Maybe the poor boy is simply happy to be calling home. Maybe also the poor boy is strung out on drugs, "on the line." And most surely the closing has enacted a nightmare journey, through the forces of history, to relief, miraculously to paradise. Whether that is a real or a phantasmagorical, drugged, promised land is another one of Berry's open questions.

Whatever the ending means, it refers to a breakthrough that is double, a connection that throws in doubt the whole enterprise and concept of a realizable promised land. Indeed the phrase *promised land* has multiple connotations for blacks then as now.[5] Its use is ironic because no such place can exist in a racist society. No such place has yet materialized for blacks in white America, not even in California. The term signifies a place necessary but impossible to believe in on earth. Hence the plane has become the chariot swinging low as it lands, the airport has become the terminal gate, both as real and unreal as the signifying term can pump up.

Throwing the apparent event under additional doubt and scrutiny is what all the watched witnesses, all the Sambo performers of the minstrel tradition have always done. Berry is another in their line playing for the same sort of stakes and with the same sort of intensity that made the minstrel shows before and after the Civil War such risky business. Berry deliberated his speed because he recognized the apocalyptic nature of both his text and context.

Beneath his smiling patina, Berry's song is as apocalyptic as Martin Luther King, Jr.'s last speech improvised in Memphis at the Mason Temple, rain beating the windows and pelting the roof, on 3 April 1968, the night before he was killed. King spoke of death and fear, the movement's peaks and depths, and his own. But none of that mattered to a man like himself, he said, who had "been to the mountain . . . looked over, and . . . seen the promised land. . . . I want you to know tonight, that we, as a people will get to the promised land" (Garrow 621).

Reverend King and Chuck Berry shared images and concepts that stem from a root source. Both the strategies and their spoken signs refer to American hope and belief in revival, beginning again common to gospel and blues musics, broadcast on the airwaves and preached from pulpits. But so much incantation of the phrases betrays doubt about their claims. King, Berry, and their followers both believed and disbelieved in America as a promised land, were sure that democracy was real and sure that it was a carrot cruelly eluding its most dogged pursuers.

This pursuing of dreams, sexual and political, was what Berry's songs were about. From speeding Ford in "Maybellene" to careening jet in "Promised Land," Berry was a master of pulling his Sambo personae — watched witnesses, all of them — through the fields of American surveillance that were harmless only within the construct of the song. Each song additionally displayed the complexity beneath its witness's smile, as well as the fractures among his observers. Like the invisible youth's grandfather, Berry yessed 'em to death, sang about being *so* glad to be back in the U.S.A. But he also called attention simultaneously to those who saw him flash through his differing modes that it was hardly a straightforward "Promised Land." No matter how expeditiously he came to perform in his mature career, his was no simply speedy trip, this land not always promising to every poor boy. His presence was intense enough to make audiences ignore the mask he was wearing, but it reappeared in the afterglow. The ends of his speeding journeys were always suspect. They were always more deliberate than his first audiences suspected, less stable than his mass public believed.

Chuck Berry made a particularly accessible brand of pop music out of blues, out of the spots and strategies in black culture that he imagined might excite young Americans, white and black. He was cunning from the start, trying to make something new in a new form, rock 'n' roll. There was about his role always the salesman's, even the conman's, pitch. He was making something artificial for the public to buy. He was putting over a line. The line seemed distinctively new, but it drew for protection on cultural strategies and performance roles deeply rooted in black tradition, specifically in minstrel shows. Thus, blacks and whites both knew how to respond to it. Beneath its new patina was a known quantity. Moreover, his musical instincts further rooted him in a substantial culture, aided him to a signature guitar line that remains as distinctive today as when "Maybellene" appeared, and ballasted his essentially pop optimism. Without that blues genius he might have spieled Magipeelers in five-and-dime kitchenware departments or sold burial plots, or continued to create the hairstyles in East St. Louis that were supporting his young family while he wrote those early songs. Yet the blues genius was always there, in "Maybellene" to sustain his Ford at the end, in the later songs to ripen his latent understandings.

Berry, then, created an early variety of rock 'n' roll by stamping the emerging world of pop culture with Sambo strategies sinister enough to satisfy those seeking menace, smiling enough to please audiences hoping to escape. He was an artist profoundly ambivalent about his cultural roots, always shucking them off to imagine himself in the new vehicles, the new clothing, the new suburban high schools of the glossy magazines and TV culture of his time—but returning to the roots increasingly as bouts with the record industry and the Internal Revenue Service dampened his enthusiasm for American hope.

Berry represented a man from nowhere entering history. He thought of his roots as nowhere, suburbia as somewhere, and his leap between the two as historic. He tried at first to leap beyond black culture, but in pulling himself into the consciousness of Americans he pulled black culture in, too, like a black Trojan horse—which is a Sambo figure seen from another angle. He is important because his songs reached so many people and because they so publicly live out their relationship to the blues ethic. By example, Berry proved its value. Another sort of relationship to that blues culture is evident in the case of Little Richard Penniman.

□   □   □   □   □

You're doin' something no one can.
— Little Richard to Miss Ann

One of the most obscuring claims critics make about the origins of rock music is that individual genius conceived it. Talent was significant, surely, but such theses serve stars rather than understanding. They also deter acknowledgment of how significantly rock 'n' roll is a development of American folklore. For instance, *The Rolling Stone Illustrated History of Rock 'n' Roll* passes on as authoritative Little Richard's account of how, since his family disapproved of rhythm 'n' blues, "Bing Crosby, 'Pennies from Heaven,' and Ella Fitzgerald were all I heard. And I knew there was something that could be louder than that, but I didn't know where to find it. And I found it was me" (Winner 52).

What he does not say, of course, is that before it was in him, the music was in the milieu of after-hours bars, minstrel shows, gay clubs, carny midways, folk patois, blues lyrics, road bonding, and the postwar leisure of Northern soldiers bored in Southern towns. Little Richard found rock in its social roots, which he cultivated. Rock was not his invention anymore than it was Chuck Berry's or Elvis Presley's. It was a hybridization of pop and folk seeds, for which Richard Penniman was a medium favoring the folk as much as Berry favored the pop germs.

One of the most compelling cases for situating the origins of rock 'n' roll in folk culture rather than in personal genius took place in New Orleans shortly after noon on 13 September 1955, when legend asserts just the opposite, that rock rained out of a blue sky. That day Little Richard went to lunch after a disappointing morning's recording session, and wowed the lounging musicians at the Dew Drop Inn with an obscene ditty he had polished in gay clubs across the South. It was a protoversion of "Tutti Frutti" and it truly sounded like nothing else either on the radio airwaves or in the studio that morning. Its surprising sound was disconnected from the current pop modes. Where then did it come from?

It was deeply entwined with surviving minstrel modes and homosexual closet humor. The sound, the style, the delivery are all audible in the music Esquerita, one of his cronies from that time, was making. Esquerita[6] (puns on "esquire-ita" and "esquire-eater" and "excreter") is Eskew Reeder, Jr., from Greenville, South Carolina. He has vouched that every part of Little Richard's act from pompadour to countertenor final syllables, manic piano triplets to Pancake 31 make-up, was all conventional in the gay clubs of Southeastern cities between 1947 and 1955 (Billy Miller 5). Little Richard confirms that Esquerita taught him piano, especially his characteristic treble phrasing (Charles White 30).

At first hearing, Esquerita's wild album, *Esquerita,* sounds more like Little Richard than Little Richard does. But then the extremity of his performance emerges as something that was probably there before he met Little Richard (as both have said) rather than parody of the latter's success. Esquerita's "oooohs" sound like sheets of stainless steel tearing in the wind. His bawdy lines remain bawdy ("Hey, Miss Lucy, you're too fat and juicy for me"), unleavened by Little Richard's punning wit. Audiences first hear how important the connections were between Little Richard and his roots. Then they notice how significant were the singer's changes in his sources. The two perceptions are complementary and equally valid.

Another direct source of folklore and repertoire for Little Richard was Louis Jordan. His "Keep A Knockin" is the model for Little Richard's song of the same title, especially confirmed since Charles White's account of Little Richard's recording sessions notes that Jordan's line, "I'm drinkin' gin and you can't come in," was deleted from Little Richard's final release (229). That line was the single major difference in lyrics between Little Richard's and Jordan's version of this old blues standard associated with Storyville, the New Orleans brothel district. Indeed, David Evans has pointed out that "Keep A Knockin" was a folk song from a prostitute's point of view; she is with a john in her stall, so cannot let in the knocker, but urges him to try again tomorrow night (Letter 1).

Here then is another pertinent example of the multiple signification in black performance tradition. These songs repeatedly offer opportunity for performers to bootleg taboos into clean, well-lighted places. Delight in such scatting, in such soiling, was older than the minstrel shows which had conveyed it in America, but in making it new, in perfecting its libidinal excess, Little Richard built out of it both a meteoric career and the supercharged form of rock 'n' roll associated with him and with New Orleans.

The considerably tamer version of "Keep A Knockin" by Louis Jordan (Charly Records CRB 1048) inadvertently demonstrates yet another feature of the changes such speeding fifties forms made in their folk lodes. Cliff White's liner notes to this album claim that there was an earlier recording of the song by James Wiggins in the late 1920s, and David Evans reports that Clarence Williams first copyrighted it, preceding many subsequent recordings of the song across the whole spectrum of taste from jazz through country music (Letter 1). Yet this late reprinting of the Louis Jordan version, originally recorded 29 March 1939—when Little Richard Penniman was still only five years old—credits "Mays / Penniman / Williams" for its composition. Here then is an example of a song slowly rising through the oral tradition but suddenly acquiring a rendition so definitively popular that it monopolizes attention and thus so powerful that it reverses chronology. The power of the electronic media, which Little Richard exploited at their fifties inception, arrogate proprietary rights to anonymous lore. Thus individual performers stamp their private names onto traditional anonymity. But what was lore remains lore, beneath the bogus credits.

What then was Penniman's own contribution, or, what was it that he and his producer Bumps Blackwell exploited to make him perhaps the greatest rock 'n' roll stylist? His talent was promiscuous. Personally unmoored, he easily slurred beats, quavered all around notes, and, most significantly, jumbled extant styles. That was how he appealed so widely across American racial and sexual barriers simultaneously. The ability to jumble multiple worlds seamlessly—white and black, straight and gay, gospel and blues and pop—enriched his music even if only subliminally. And it later dictated his remorse about his career.

His legendary claims about himself include being born in Macon, Georgia, on Christmas 1935, taking his diminutive name eight years later while singing in hometown schools and churches, and being disowned at thirteen. In fact, however, he was born well before Christmas, on 5 December, and well before 1935, in 1933. His was not a second coming, nor was he any longer a teenager in 1955 when he broke into the public eye. Moreover, schools and churches were only two of his less important venues. More telling in his music were the minstrel shows and bawdy revues he played for the ten years preceding "Tutti Frutti."

If Richard left home at thirteen to live with the white club owners Ann and Johnny Johnson, as Langdon Winner reports, Charles White's biography confirms neither the move nor even their existence.[7] In any case, at age fourteen or fifteen Penniman left home, whether his mother's or Miss Ann Johnson's, and began a career of one-night stands with a series of hucksters, carny circuses, and minstrel shows.

The titles of these shows are themselves an evocative folk exhibit. Following a Doctor Nobilio's advice, the youth joined Dr. Hudson's Medicine Show (which sold snake oil for $2 a bottle). Then he quit selling dubious cures to sing blues in B. Brown's Orchestra[8] which followed migrant laborers across South Florida's muck farms around Lake Okeechobee. Then came a stint as a transvestite, billed as Princess Lavonne, "the freak of the year," he said, in a show called Sugarfoot Sam from Alabam. Little Richard described this act as a "minstrel show—the old vaudeville type of show. . . . That was the first time I performed in a dress" (Charles White 24). This was clearly a significant period in the development of Little Richard's repertoire, a time when he would go to any length to win an audience. While he was with Sugarfoot Sam he met Esquerita, who taught him some of his piano style and, significantly, a mutual trademark which Esquerita calls their "obligato holler." (Little Richard later taught Paul McCartney this falsetto OOOOOHH! when the Beatles warmed up audiences in Hamburg for him during the early sixties.) "When I met him," Esquerita has said about Little Richard, "he was dancin' with a table and chair in his mouth. . . . He used to stand up and dance and balance a chair in his mouth then put the table on top" (Billy Miller 5).

The King Brothers Circus, the Tidy Jolly Steppers, the L. C. Heath Show, and the Broadway Follies were four subsequent traveling shows in which Penniman developed his transvestite act across the South. Nor was he alone. Even before Esquerita taught him piano, Little Richard has said there were mentors in Madames Kilroy and Merle as well as fully pancaked—and very popular—rhythm 'n' blues performers like the influential Billy Wright.[9] This minstrel lore ballasts the gospel fervor and blues inflections in his style. Most importantly, the enforced double-talking patois of the underground taught Little Richard to signify different meaning to different audiences at once.

He learned to be a many-faceted fetish, to play the minstrel Sambo, and to project the artificial figure who survives by being exactly what perceivers want him to be.[10] To this end, Little Richard has stressed his crippled status to many interviewers (Charles White 6, 7). He thus reinforces the connection between his act and its indirect origin in the dance of Jim Crow, the black and crippled hostler said to have inspired T. D. Rice's impersonation at the beginning of American blackface minstrelsy (Rourke

80). But we do not look to Little Richard for exegesis of his performance. Rather we turn northeast about fifteen miles from Macon to Milledgeville to reread Flannery O'Connor's "The Artificial Nigger," which she published the same year her neighbor released "Tutti Frutti."

When her rustics granted the statue "all the mystery of existence," they interpreted that mystery in ways that ratified their preconceptions, without any reference to the reality behind or inhering in the image. O'Connor showed therefore something that Little Richard and Bumps Blackwell instinctively used and confirmed. The backgrounds, educations, interests, and proclivities of Blackwell, Penniman, and O'Connor could hardly be more radically different. Their mutual use of the artificial figure's radically disconnected status therefore demonstrates the ultimate condition of the black *image* at the end of the American minstrel tradition. It was free-floating and ripe for use.

Like so many other performers of these years, from writers to Supreme Court justices, O'Connor shows how the image of the Negro in postminstrel America had become so detached from specific anchors that it was a Rorschach blot, on which people flung their fantasies. At some level, Little Richard recognized this seeming vacuum. What's disturbing in his work is that, like nearly all the black minstrel performers before him, he was not so passive as the watermelon-eating statue in O'Connor's fiction, but active. He crafted his own image to emphasize his own indignity. He chose to project a self that allowed, even provoked, the audience's private interpretations.

The singer's volatile relations with several folk domains all over his region from 1947 to 1955 taught him that the Sambo role could hide and express meaning simultaneously. From housebroken happiness to libidinal eruption, the meanings audiences caught in it were what they needed to catch. Of great interest, however, is that none of his Sambo complexity is recorded prior to "Tutti Frutti" in late 1955. On not one of the four previous recording sessions Little Richard did with RCA and Peacock did he make compact the many parts he was working. He must have thought the Sambo foolery was too rude, dangerous, or threatening to display in the mainstream, despite his nightly strutting of it in minority culture venues from Macon to Miami.

What he was recording, rather than performing, before 1955 was above all safe. For the large public, he contained his burgeoning counterlore behind conventional surfaces. Indeed, despite the hints of an eccentrically plastic voice, his early sessions produced merely the era's usual jump blues. Little Richard's performance in this vein is distinguished primarily by his sententious and sometimes mother-ridden lyrics. I love my mother, he confessed in "Thinkin' 'bout My Mother," January 1952, like nobody else — "She formed me as she fed me, when I couldn't even feed myself" (*Every Hour with Little Richard* [Camden LP 420]).

He recorded those feelings, and his vacillating career later confirmed that he truly meant them, but they were not the whole story and certainly not the moods by which he chiefly lived. The problem was that he did not yet trust the underground emotion and counterlore that were creating his persona and which, in turn, he would shortly redirect. Either he did not trust them, or he feared them. In any case, he rightly suspected the treachery at the center of the minstrel–Sambo joking. It would gain him access to the mainstream because it seemed harmless, but it was not. In fact, no other American folkway had a more complex history or bore more evocative energy. That a gamut of performers from Amos and Andy through Elvis Presley and Flannery O'Connor to Little Richard all squeeze under the umbrella of the postminstrel Sambo indicates the sheer span of the term's meaning for America in the fifties. In short, no other native lore had more meaning, certainly not in the year of Earl Warren's integration enforcement decree.

Therefore, by September 1955, just a few months after the Chief Justice had ordered blacks and whites together with all deliberate speed, Little Richard had gathered up all the lore, stigmata, and accoutrements of the old Tambo and Bones walkarounds. He had supplemented that with elements from the blues and sideshows and medicine spiels, had compressed them into one persona, and had paraded that act — testing it — around all the home regions of the old minstrel troupes. But he had not brought it out of the hole to the mainstream surface, yet.

He surfaced with it only when he met Bumps Blackwell, the conservatory-trained producer whom Specialty Records sent to New Orleans to record him. All the evidence indicates it was Blackwell who had the initial confidence in Little Richard's relationship to the lore. Moreover, that Blackwell had the shaping instinct is clear because Little Richard never made a successfully complex record without Blackwell's collaboration. Conversely, Little Richard's experience was absolutely necessary. The songs written by others which Blackwell brought him successfully confirm his catchy style, are energetic indeed, but remain lorelorn. Having later also worked with Sam Cooke at the crucial moment he moved into the pop world from gospel, Blackwell is often said to have helped assimilationists bleach their blackness. The charge is too simple. He helped them deliver product. Some of it was empty; but he also found ways to push profound aspects of black lore into the white mainstream.

What Blackwell heard Little Richard sing at the Dew Drop Inn during that legendary 13 September lunch, knew enough to process, and tried to reproject was:

> Tutti Frutti, good booty
> If it don't fit, don't force it
> You can grease it, make it easy. . . . (Charles White 55)

Blackwell claims he immediately knew that Little Richard's song had the energy Specialty Records wanted. So he gave the task of sublimating the words to Dorothy La Bostrie, who wrote new lyrics suggestively heterosexual. Nevertheless, they retained the fay hint in the title, and particularly in "Sue" (who knew just what to do) and "Daisy" (who almost drove him crazy), for *Sue* and *Daisy* were gay argot for transvestites.

What Blackwell heard was similar to what Chuck Berry's producer, Leonard Chess in Chicago, heard in the protoversion of "Maybellene," and what Sam Phillips, Presley's producer in Memphis, heard lurking behind the blues tradition—but unrecorded even there. They believed, too, that it would stun, express, and enrich the consonant empathy of the emerging baby boomers. Little Richard, then, was part of a common, national movement. But if there is more uncommon vitality in his "Tutti-Frutti" and in the rest of his best songs than in Presley's or Berry's or even Bo Diddley's, it is because Little Richard tapped further into more underground lores than the others did.

The difference all the producers could sense and were hoping to document was the difference between the conventional jump blues Little Richard recorded for RCA in the beginning of the fifties, released on LP as *Every Hour with Little Richard,* and the rock sound of "Tutti-Frutti," at the midpoint of the decade. Beyond the significant reinforcement that Chess, Phillips, and Blackwell gave their singers to be true to their formative lore, the difference was essentially dimensional. The RCA jump blues songs like "Every Hour" and "Thinkin' 'bout My Mother" were treacle with the thinnest sort of commercial relation to the audience. But "Tutti-Frutti" and most of Little Richard's hits tapped into several vital folk groups at once. For instance, the puns on "Sue" and "Daisy" titillated uninitiated audiences simply as references to good opposite-sex partners. At another level in those days of desegregation, Daisy and Sue were racially moot names— unlike "Maybellene," who sounded specifically black in Chuck Berry's scenario. Was Little Richard probing the delights of miscegenated sex? At a third level, and to other audiences, Daisy and Sue were knowing referents to drag queens in the clubs where Little Richard had presented himself as Princess Lavonne.

In seeming to sanitize "Tutti-Frutti," so it might penetrate suburban bedrooms, Blackwell, La Bostrie, and Penniman had instead sublimated it with small nodes of latent excitement. Most audiences probably did not suspect any of this — "You don't know what she do to me," Little Richard admitted as he sang — but the singer knew, Blackwell knew, and so did the musicians in Cosimo Matassa's J & M Studio, where they were recording. Their performance took on a licentious exuberance commensurate to their release from restraint. Having found a strategy for eluding the censors, public and private, their speed and joy in the song memorialize both their freedom and the trick the song pulls off: ramming its underground reality to the mainstream airwaves. This is the quintessence of the sort of complex Samboing Little Richard enacted.

Although "Tutti-Frutti" is the most famous of Little Richard's songs because its mania far surpassed anything white listeners and most black audiences had heard, it actually did not yet beam all the fervid sureness of his next year's hits — "Rip It Up," "Slippin' and Slidin'," and especially "Long Tall Sally." This first time out, Penniman was still one quarter expecting lightning to strike from on high at any minute. Blackwell reports, for instance, that Little Richard was so embarrassed the first time he sang the original "grease it" lyrics to Dorothy La Bostrie that they could only induce him to perform facing away from her toward the wall. He did not yet have confidence in the sufficiency of his songs. Out of the closet into the corner: such are the unsuspected stages of a man's growth — and a music's. Little Richard did not know that the rocking moment he was winching up from the underground would have an intensity immunizing it against authority — so long as the song lasted, so long as it built its own armature.

What audiences hear in Little Richard's definitive versions of rock songs is just this capsulated moment between duties and responsibilities. His songs enact a joy of love that is but a moment long:

> Good golly, Miss Molly, you sure like to ball.
> And when you rock 'n' roll, *I can't hear no mama call.*
> ("Good Golly, Miss Molly," emphasis added)[11]

Little Richard actually stretched his moment out less than two years, until late 1957 when he did hear something like his Mama call. Then he renounced rock for Bible study and preaching. This stage in turn lasted a full seven years—with lapses in Europe to train the Beatles—until his rock comeback in 1964, when he trained Jimi Hendrix. The orthodoxy of the mother church and the joyful release of his rock songs are the opposite poles between which his career always oscillated. He never synthesized nor repressed either side. These poles in Little Richard's music drove him back and forth, each whipping the other into more extreme expression.

His heyday songs between 1955 and 1957 explore the terrain of liberty enjoyed only in such foreshortened freedoms as shore leave, sexual ecstasy, and carnival revelry. The best of these singles was his second hit with "Long Tall Sally" and "Slippin' and Slidin'" on opposite sides, released March 1956. "Long Tall Sally" is an incredibly energetic tableau with a curious origin in three lines scrawled on a doily by Enortis Johnson, a scrubbed and plaited innocent of sixteen or seventeen. She had walked to New Orleans from Opaloosa, Mississippi, in order to raise money for her aunt. Her lines were as follows:

> Saw Uncle John with Long Tall Sally
> They saw Aunt Mary comin'
> So they ducked back in the alley.

"Aunt Mary is sick," she said, "and I'm going to tell her about Uncle John" (Charles White 61). From this unpromisingly poor and vengeful beginning, Bumps Blackwell and Little Richard Penniman fashioned one of rock's most richly tolerant songs, with understanding for all parties. This fashioning occurred in the studio, with Blackwell pressing for speedy delivery of the line he liked, "they ducked back in the alley," trying to make it so fast that Pat Boone would never be able to "get his mouth together" to cover it. One can hear this speeding up on the alternate early versions. The first was recorded 29 November 1955 (available on a bootleg, Redita LP-101). It is roughly half the tempo of the great Specialty release recorded 10 February 1956.

If Blackwell was trying to outspeed the competitors—a standard strategy in musical revolution as prominent in bebop's development as in rock 'n' roll—Little Richard was pursuing additional dimensions in the material. He was pumping minstrel and gay lores into it. "Long Tall Sally" is an acting script, a quick treatment of visual actions, lightly directed by the scenic directions for players' movement and behavior on the flipside. They slip and slide in both songs. They peep and hide. They hope not to be life's fools anymore. Alternatively, one can understand this record as Crescent City cubism with accounts of adultery seen simultaneously from multiple perspectives. Taken together, the songs on both sides sympathize with the cheaters, the cheated, and the hardly passive or innocent onlookers—the omnipresent surveillance. Moreover, several layers of identity mask the characters in "Long Tall Sally," as befits a tale that all the musicians collaboratively assembled. As Blackwell reports, "we pulled stuff from everybody" (Charles White 62).

Traditional black folk figures scamper through this song in scandalous antics. Uncle John is a stock figure in black lore from the "John cycle" of tales about a slave who outwits the authorities. On this level, the song's Aunt Mary is a good wife, not unlike the Mary Rambo who counsels and shelters Ralph Ellison's invisible youth in Harlem, inspiring him with her kitchen rendition of "Back Water Blues." But "Aunt Mary" is also gay argot for a possessive queen. So she operates on at least two levels, apparent nurturer and drag possessor. In any case, Uncle John in this song is ducking out on Aunt Mary's authority, whatever she represents. It's Long Tall Sally, "built for speed," who "got everything that Uncle John need." But where did Sally come from? Nightmare to every Aunt Mary, Sally is the newly noticed, old, subtraditional freak. Not only long, tall, and speedy, she's "bald-headed." As such, she's figuratively phallic, flashing in and out of alleys in the hand of Uncle John, that trickster. That is attractive enough in the male-bonding context of the studio where all this cropped up mutually among these men, but there is more. In the transvestite shows of Little Richard's apprenticeship, baldheadedness was preparation for one's wigs. Clearly Sally is a freak, the same term the singer had applied to his own incarnation as Princess Lavonne. Long Tall Sally, in addition to her other meanings, is therefore a transvestite fantasy figure slipping and sliding through life's niches. She delights the nephews and seduces the uncles. A transsexual variant of Sambo, and just like this new rock form which her surfacing embodied at this mid-fifties moment of family breakdown, she represents whatever anyone wishes her to represent. She bears variant and deviant fantasies. She is as new as rock 'n' roll. She is as old as the oral tradition, old enough to be a stock runaway tease, as in Blind Lemon Jefferson's "Pneumonia Blues" from the 1920s, which someone in the recording studio had surely heard:

> I went slipping 'round corners, running up alleys too
> Watching my woman, trying to see what she goin' do.
> (Sackheim 72)

As an observant nephew and our stand-in, Little Richard plays this scandal every way against the middle. He is far removed from the innocence of Enortis Johnson and her simple, single original attitude, which he has dusted over the song's surface, like sugar on a doughnut. On the one hand, he identifies strongly with John's escape; if Penniman tells us of John's fun once, he relates his own fun half a dozen times. On the other hand, hanging over the joy is the song's first line like a guillotine primed to fall, thus increasing the excitement: "Gonna tell Aunt Mary about Uncle John." Thus he enacted the censor, the tattletale, as well as the cheater and releaser.

"Long Tall Sally" knotted up in four verses all the contrary tensions of Little Richard's career. In his life, he tried to relax his contrary impulses by switching from one to the other, from censor to solid sender, mama's boy to phallic performer. But in "Long Tall Sally," as in his other strongest rock songs, his success depended on the way Blackwell helped him compound that tension into his rich Sambo persona.

At the climax of this capsulated period, when the rock charts were filled with his hits about the joyous moment, Little Richard delivered "Miss Ann," in June 1957. This song shows perhaps best of all how deeply he mined lore's lodes. The first line of its first couplet is a seemingly suggestive tickler in which Richard gasps to Miss Ann, "you're doin' somethin' no one can." And audiences are free to impose a sexual interpretation on the line, as the performer's Sambo strategy prompts. However, the song illustrates the use of that strategy to express and repress meaning simultaneously. The minstrel tradition had presented an artificial image of Negroes that seemed detached from significance even while the image smilingly conveyed modes of black culture into nooks of consciousness blacks were segregated from entering straightforwardly. Just so, Little Richard's Sambo strategy made him seem the very figure of nonsense — to this day critics usually discuss his lyrics as babytalk meaninglessness, wop bop a loo bop — when in fact he was projecting folk substance. That is, Miss Ann's doing what no one can was not only exact, in fact it was hoary. It seemed empty, it seemed nonsense, but it was not.

The encyclopedists of children's lore, Iona and Peter Opie, writing only a few years before Penniman sang his song, reported the use of the same rhyme in a riddle verse from the English "storehouse of popular memory":

> Little Bird of Paradise
> She works her work both neat and nice;
> She pleases God, she pleases man,
> She does the work that no man can. (82–83)

The Opies find its earliest printed instance appearing as a devotional riddle in a 1511 manuscript, and show it published at regular intervals thereafter, right up to the 1939 version they cite.

Both the English riddle and Richard's sly variant on it imply that the song's subject is performing promiscuously. But both riddle and song surprise us. The answer to the riddle is that only a bee can busily please the Maker while providing man with both wax and honey. And the Miss Ann of the song is no counterpart to the pleasing, spinning, balling women and/ or freaks who populate Little Richard's other rock songs. Here the singer probably refers to the white woman, Ann Johnson, who mothered him as a young teenager (Winner 52). She was serving both God and man by nurturing him when he was young and homeless. A further dimension stems from the common use of "Miss Ann" to refer to a maid's white female employer, and by extension to all white women.[12] And the song came as close as he dared to talk about God in a rock song, for when he was with Miss Ann, he sang, he was "living in paradise." Little Richard was once again bootlegging interracial love into the radios and pop charts of the fifties. All this he chocked into the confines of the blues form.

Of Little Richard's hits, "Miss Ann" most patently follows the AAB stanza pattern of the downhome blues and its middle two stanzas are straight from the stanza storehouse. Stanza two of "Miss Ann" is for instance Blind Lemon Jefferson's fifth stanza in his first blues, "Got the Blues," recorded probably in March 1926.[13] Both singers like to hear their lovers — "good gal" (Jefferson) and "Miss Ann" (Little Richard) — call their name, as they say in the A lines. Their B lines are virtually identical. First Jefferson sang "She don't call so loud, but she call so nice and plain." Then Little Richard substituted "can't" for Jefferson's "don't" and "sweet" for Jefferson's "nice." Whether or not Little Richard had heard Jefferson's recorded variant, he certainly was drawing on blues tradition, just as he pulled the riddle in stanza one from an ancient English oral tradition.

The poles of his career remain those of black folklore. Little Richard Penniman is a perfect example of folklorist Roger Abrahams's figure, "the man of words." As preacher and singer, Little Richard has used language to mediate visions unavailable in the sanctuary of orthodox reality or even the opportunistic media, except at ripe moments such as the mid-fifties. His songs were literally good booty. They were the repressed stuff of underground lore, which he made charismatic for public consumption. In Little Richard those lores found a vehicle prepared to bear their chocked energy. He transferred that energy from its underground holes, putting it in capsulated form on vinyl, where it now resides as a public storehouse, which the whole culture continues to use and occasionally pauses to decipher.

Congeniality

Little Richard and his motley retinue of rock 'n' roll performers were significant in themselves, in their relationship to electronic media, and as the biceps in the cultural arm of the civil rights movement. But they also indicate another feature of the fifties. Like Robert Frank's photography, like Allen Ginsberg's poetry and Jack Kerouac's sketches and Miles Davis's improvisations, like the so-called folk revival that the Weavers and *Sing Out!* crew pumped through the fifties and that graded into Bob Dylan in the early sixties—like all these, Little Richard's chocked songs show a shift in the nature and use of contemporary lore.

This new material behaved like folklore and sometimes had folk traditions. But identifiable individuals were making this lore in the city now, assembling it with cameras and electric instruments, propagating it on TV and radios and records, multiplying it in books. So it did not fit the current definition of *folk*-lore, which specified anonymous creation by rural illiterates. Nevertheless, contemporary lore was serious. It widely organized and artfully expressed people's lives. It was poplore.[1]

Poplore was threatening some of the elite or minority arts, rousing others. Whatever its effect, poplore surprised them all because the immediately preceding modern generations had argued that vernacular resources were no longer available and no longer possible. If someone were to say, "Wait, listen to this song about all the wires down," or "Did you hear that rhyming ditty about the monkey and the lion?" or, "What's going on with all these signs of flags and targets, arrows and body parts?" Then the conventional response from the late thirties until the mid-fifties was,

"That's not lore, that's kitsch. That's beneath contemplation, or worse." Nevertheless, the songs, ditties, signs, stories, and customs persisted, as did the outsiders enjoying and employing them. The persistence of this poplore and its ramifications on the cultural scene in the United States, then abroad, are two of the best reasons to suppose that epochal change had come to the period of arts known as modernism.

Naming that change "postindustrial modernism" or "late-late-modernism" or "postmodernism" is less important than recognizing how the mid-fifties represents a distinct phase in the maturation of the lore cycle. It constitutes a phase similar to the fin de siècle years when high modernism gestated in Paris, London, and isolated outposts along the Atlantic coast of North America. People in those capitals were then exchanging their Victorian values for modern counterparts so undefined but real as to be nameable only chronologically. In the mid-fifties of this century, first this time all across North America (in the South as well as western and northern cities), then in European capitals, citizens were once again exchanging their aesthetics, and their concomitant sets of values, for others that more closely matched their expectations and perceptions.

In the mid-fifties in America the clogged arteries of official modern culture finally popped open. This release occurred when it became obvious how the prestigious wing of every art had cut itself off from its potential public to follow its own heedless autonomy. Massive examples were the skyscrapers on Sixth Avenue in New York City, with their rectilinear gleam and hermetic one-way windows. The internal dynamics between architects and their tiny clutch of corporate clients shouldered aside the real needs of the large public for fresh air, for vagrant space with personality, for the human touch, for interaction with evident purpose. Likewise, the museum orientation of advanced painting had come to crisis in the late forties in this country, a crisis captured in the title to Calvin Tomkins's account of the fifties generation, *Off the Wall*, which suggests the upstart strategy of breaking out of appointed and anointed spaces, out of the sealed museum, toward a more interactive and less established relationship between object and observer, painter and public.

A similar crisis had surfaced also in symphony halls. There the dilemma was the relegation of classical music to excruciating formality — black-tie music in chandeliered chambers. By then Euromusic had lost its autonomy, for its primary important pieces were, until John Cage and Philip Glass, pieces of a curated repertory. Furthermore, poetry had become an almost entirely academic scene in the early fifties. It had not always been so. As recently as the thirties, queues formed at Scribner's in

New York and Hatchard's in London on the days Eliot and Auden published volumes. By the fifties, however, a poetry reading was rare in itself and took place in a library or university lecture hall. By then, modern poetry was primarily a property of *readers;* it mediated between two persons operating as individuals and meeting in hushed spaces—a library reading room, a home study. The late modern poetry of the early fifties was a transaction occurring in two-dimensional space between hard covers. By the mid-fifties, queues formed for Elvis Presley and Fats Domino. They reformed for literary figures like Jack Kerouac and Allen Ginsberg only when writers learned to use poplore. On a fortieth birthday tour of California colleges that happened to follow Ginsberg's working of the same audiences, Robert Lowell discovered that he could raise a lively response if he made up and slipped in a personal line. Consequently, the anthologies gave *him* credit for inventing confessional poetry.

In fiction, too, there was emerging by the early fifties a deep dissatisfaction with the hermetic spaces modernism had constructed for itself. The novel during its American modern period was the realm of the cut-off individual, the man or woman unable to reach beyond what Sylvia Plath called her "bell jar." In this claustrophobic hothouse wandered Henry James's Christopher Newman in *The American,* severed from the vital washboard culture that had formed him at home but "stopped short before [the] blank wall" (358) of European high culture. In such vacuums wander the idiot, intellectual, and racist white protagonists of Faulkner's *The Sound and the Fury.* Each Compson brother is in his different way oblivious to the reliable wisdom of Dilsey, their black retainer. And each is differently estranged from other infra dig resources present but unavailable to them because of the retarded brother's mind, the intellectual brother's narrow obsessions, and the boorish brother's xenophobia. Read this way, *The Sound and the Fury* is a parable for the perplexing condition of vital lore during the modern first half of the twentieth century. The white Compson lore is an exhausted impediment to their lives. Meanwhile all round them, teasing and mocking, teems the rich vernacular lore of the black servant class, Northeastern ethnics (when Quentin goes to Harvard), and white itinerant circuses. Whether Dilsey's faith might have saved her employers, whether vernacular ways in general were appropriate for them or entirely other, is part of the issue. Another part is whether any group may learn from the vitality of another. Faulkner certainly shows that the ineffectually specialized Compsons do not avail themselves of the wholeness Dilsey and her relations evidence. The Compsons vanish in suicide and rage, castration and abnegation—while Dilsey's people "endure." Such romantic statement is easily overdone, but if it turns out to be true, it will have been hard-scrabble persistence of vernacular ways that underwrote the prophecy. Just so, the shotgun house and the market square, the row house and the pub may well endure after the high and narrow World Trade Center has gone the way of the Crystal Palace.

At issue is congeniality. As a cultural strain matures, it may go awry. Rather than heeding wide social needs, a cultural strain may develop autonomous values that lock into its own traditions, as did modern painting. Rather than heeding the human needs of its current context, it may follow the seductive money of its caretakers, as did modern architecture. Rather than using the medium's force to clarify the condition of its audience, a few pied pipers whose charisma at first seems liberating may eventually march the medium over a far cliff, as happened in modern poetry and music. When as in these cases the art does not return sustenance to the culture that originally set it up, then the larger audience, too, withdraws its attention and pockets its support. It is no wonder the maturing, straying art then grows defensive and makes a fetish of its independence from mass tastes. But wilfully autonomous forms end up curated in collections. Sooner than later, new arts connecting congenially with a public will replace them.

The cycle is natural. An art may be promising at its outset, develop richly even toward its end, and still flounder. To speak of its cycle is not to judge its quality, but to account for its internal changes by noticing how it negotiates congeniality with its public. These are the issues that this chapter addresses and illustrates with examples from American culture in the fifties. A late-fifties composition by jazz composer Ornette Coleman, itself titled "Congeniality," provides the rallying point.

Like Little Richard's rock 'n' roll, Ornette Coleman's free jazz seemed to come to New York out of nowhere. Nevertheless, Coleman, like Richard Penniman, had been around. He had even been around in some of the same ways Little Richard had, in rhythm 'n' blues bands and that incubator of so much American music, the minstrel shows. Therein lies a story.

When he was a boy, Coleman had taught himself first the alto then the tenor sax. He could afford neither lessons nor a horn of his own, so would pick up and fool around with a saxophone that belonged to his cousin. Before he had his own horn at about age fourteen, Coleman had taught himself to play by ear all the rhythm 'n' blues tunes he heard coming over the radio. His fingering was more inventive than orthodox and his tone sounded self-taught, different, more like someone playing with a human cry in mind than written notes. Hence, his stuttering and sliding, plaintive and untempered sound. Although he was playing in rhythm 'n' blues bands and earning $100 a week during high school (when his teachers were earning less), he read music poorly, never learned to write musical notation well, and continues today to sound odd to those who have schooled themselves conventionally. Gary Giddins has described this oddness exactly; he calls Coleman "a musician who effortlessly pitches his notes in the cracks, as it were, of the tempered scale with unerring intervallic consistency" (242–43).

Coleman's "total immunity to the notational aspect" helped ensure what Gunther Schuller has called his "unique contribution to contemporary music" (*Collection* 2). But it also stopped traveling bands from offering him a job when he wanted to leave Fort Worth. That's why he finally had to accept a tenor seat in the lowest prestige visiting band—Silas Green from New Orleans, a minstrel show, which took him all over the South. They ultimately dumped him in Natchez, Mississippi, he has recalled, because he was teaching the other tenor player bebop tunes and the Silas Green organization feared the style would infect the show's music.[2] There followed a stint of one-nighters with Clarence Samuels's rhythm 'n' blues band that ended violently in 1949 in Baton Rouge when roadhouse customers pummeled him and destroyed his tenor horn. Without instrument or money, he found his way to New Orleans, called his friend Melvin Lastie, who invited him over to recuperate a while—and, in doing so, brought nearer the point of this story.

The Lasties were then, and still are, one of those New Orleans clans that have made the Crescent City sufficient unto itself and a hybridizing source of black American music since Reconstruction. Often those families stay at home to make the musics which become famous elsewhere, from Chicago to New York, Los Angeles to Jamaica. The Lasties go way back and they come way forward.[3] Melvin Lastie was a trumpet player. One of his brothers had just quit playing the alto—so, once again, there was Coleman without a horn living in a house with a saxophone lying around inviting someone to invent ways to play it by ear. "That's how I started back playing alto," Coleman said at the end of the fifties. "It was while I was staying at Melvin's that I started playing like I'm trying to play now. The things that me and Cherry were doing, Melvin and I could do that then, and that was 1949" (Spellman 102). By 1949, then, Ornette Coleman had soaked up the gut bucket style of rhythm 'n' blues in Fort Worth roadhouses, amalgamated it with knowledge of the minstrel songster book, and stewed in the New Orleans jazz of one of that city's oldest musical families. All this happened before Ornette Coleman had turned twenty.

He was making his music an entire decade before the Lenox (Massachusetts) School of Jazz in the summer of 1959 when his intentionally untempered, out of key, and out of time playing there so angered at least one faculty member enough that he quit in protest. But Coleman so impressed some others that they transcribed his solos for publication (see Schuller) and booked him, an unknown in the City, into the avant-garde New York venue, the Five Spot, that November. It was Ornette Coleman's first extended gig in his life. That is where his song, "Congeniality" became known.

In his liner notes to Coleman's *The Shape of Jazz to Come* (Atlantic SD 1317), which included "Congeniality," Martin Williams reports the song "was originally named for a wandering preacher but, Coleman says, 'I'm not a preacher, I'm a musician, so I named it for what I think a *musician* feels toward an audience.'" These innocent, ideal words came at a time when modern art had moved far from mutual generation, which is the etymological referent of the word, *congeniality*. Coleman's aesthetic was unusual even within ambitious jazz itself ever since bebop had (for whatever reasons, however justifiable at the time) turned its back on some of its audiences in the forties, as had all the modern arts in one way or another. Coleman was proposing, however, that he and a public play out a rapprochement together. This traditional spirit of kindred empathy as his ideal for art remains an important aspect to remember about Coleman's "radicalism." His was the aesthetic of someone early in a lore cycle.

Coleman would come to his kindred improvisation and composition by paying more attention to impulses that united him with his public — "how a musician feels toward an audience" — than to the body of conventions that had grown up over the years. These keys, harmonic progressions, specific bar structures and tempos that had arisen originally to protect and connect the delicacies of musical intuition seemed to some players by the mid-fifties and to some in their audience to be hindering improvisational impulse in the music. For these reasons, Ornette Coleman paid more attention to the melodic idea and its "inner musical necessity" (Williams's liner notes to SD 1317) than to the forms that he thought many people were mistaking for the music. His concept of melody was primary in his music (and this, too, is a surprisingly conservative point). Incorporating rude and dissonant sounds, Coleman's idea of melody was broad in what it took to be melodious. It was also capacious, Coleman quoting classical as well as popular fragments, for instance, in his "Congeniality" solo — "The Peanut Vendor" cohabiting with Rimsky-Korsakov's "The Flight of the Bumblebee."

The phrase in poetry equivalent to "inner musical necessity" was Ginsberg's "rhythm of thought" near the end of the first part of "Howl" (l. 75). Ginsberg there is paraphrasing Wordsworthian sentiments — really recurring Romantic sentiments — in his desire to make the pulse of common talk ("poor human prose") express the teeming rhythms in his "naked and endless" mind. All of which shows that Coleman's stubbornness paralleled a similar reshuffling of priorities taking place at the same time among poets on both coasts identifying with "naked poetry." This movement included the Beats, the Black Mountain poets in North Carolina, and many in New York as well as on the West Coast. The Naked Poets called for a stripping away of conventional meter, rhyme, and stanzaic shape in order to release and follow an essential feeling or cry. For jazz or poetry really to follow that cry meant in theory to ignore whatever bar pattern or rhyme scheme, key or tempo that convention may have proposed. The composer must let the snatch of melody or rhythm of thought dance itself out, much as players follow a planchette across a Ouija board.

The earliest and most influential formulation of this idea among these artists probably was Robert Creeley's "FORM IS NEVER MORE THAN AN EXTENSION OF CONTENT," which Charles Olson centered in his 1950 essay "Projective Verse" (148). If it works, as it frequently did with Ornette Coleman (and the members of his group, Ed Blackwell, Don Cherry, and Charlie Haden); with Allen Ginsberg and Jack Kerouac; with Robert Rauschenberg and Jackson Pollock; and with Marlon Brando — then the practice justifies itself. Then there is a congeniality with feelings that are in the audience as well as in the performer; then the artwork expresses its persistently underlying vernacular. For all the advanced and radical aura surrounding Coleman's achievement, he like many other avant-garde performers simply returned to colloquial priorities — in Coleman's case to the perception that because melody was primary, it determined harmony and structure. These were old and resilient notions that refused to go away.

Vernacular culture never disappears. Like the people it serves, it is always with us, sometimes driven beneath scrutiny, sometimes outlawed, patronized, deprecated, repressed, always infra dig. But it continues parallel and self-sustaining: a patient resource. When elite culture weakens from stewing in its own entropy, then vernacular culture surfaces. It judges the collapse of insubstantial elite culture and it fuels the forging of new cultural forms. On the last page of *Rabelais and His World,* his climactic study of folk humor's relationship to literature, Mikhail Bakhtin cited a passage from Pushkin's *Boris Godunov* that clarifies this position: "In all periods of the past there was the marketplace with its laughing people, that very marketplace that in Pushkin's drama appeared in the pretender's nightmare:"

> The people swarmed on the public square
> And pointed laughingly at me,
> And I was filled with shame and fear.

"We repeat," Bakhtin concludes, "every act of world history was accompanied by a laughing chorus" (474). Bakhtin omits saying that the chorus is often not heard. He implies that the laughing chorus is sometimes ineffective, in fact rarely has a leader so effective as Rabelais, the French Renaissance writer, to voice its values. But the brilliance of the chorus's leader even when he is noticed probably does not change conditions for an era. Epoch-altering conditions depend on more widespread conditions, on the exhaustion of the old forms and on a widely felt sense of extra-official vitality that demands and demonstrates new arrangement. In other words, epoch-altering conditions depend less on individual genius than on lore cycles.

Lore cycles have a natural history very like the surge, peak, and decline of the scientific paradigms Thomas Kuhn proposed in *The Structure of Scientific Revolution* (1962), a book he conceived and researched during the fifties (ix). By accounting for critically important data and shaping important ideas, scientific paradigms and cultural forms rise to prestige. They remain influential by continuing to explain matters and by rejecting insubordinate data, interpretations, or organizations. That is, their influence depends not only upon apparently adequate explanation of important puzzles but also on efficient gatekeeping, or sorting out of the unacceptable — defining it as insignificant. Over time, however, the rejectamenta inevitably loom larger than the acceptably explained heap. The insignificant or taboo trash becomes a compost heap for the future. It collects and compacts energy more multifarious, more vigorous than the overexplained, overused ideas in the paradigmatic pile — especially in these days of fast information and increased access to ideas. In cultural terms relevant to American modern literature, for instance, the lore cycle inevitably delivers moments that show life beyond Eliot's waste land, outside Fitzgerald's valley of ashes, independent of Faulkner's dramatized hypochondria, idiocy, and suicide. At such breakthrough moments as the fifties, not all

behavior will button into Hemingway's toreador costume, nor relax in the
rentier's longeur Henry James idealized. In times like the fifties, a new
paradigm or cultural form may rise to organize and make sense of the
wasted data, the outlawed experience, the preterite form.

The mid-fifties was a time when many people felt more exciting
connections were possible in vernacular than in polite culture. Like poetic
and musical convention, polite culture was in the way. Similarly, when the
maverick mathematician and journeyman scientist par excellence Benoit
Mandelbrot began in the 1960s to notice repetitions of shapes large and
small, from vascular branching to the branching of broccoli and ferns,
which he would call "fractal scaling," he knew that he would not find it
described in then-paradigmatic botany or biology. "I started looking," he
said, "in the trash cans of science for such phenomena. . . . My gamble paid
off" (Gleick 110). From such trash cans researchers draw data to construct
new paradigms.

Poplore broke through as a laughing chorus. Because it was coincidental with the electronic changes of the fifties, it had decibels and force
enough to be heard. Because it was coincidental with the postwar baby
boom, it had a ready-made public. Because it had the example and mentors
of black culture, it had a reinforcing tradition and store of strategies. These
multiple conjunctions created the conditions for a new paradigm. That's
why poplore raised resistant hackles among the gatekeepers of prestigious
minority culture—just the same way early modernism had gotten in the
nose of nineteenth-century expectations, and so on back *ad infinitum.*

This is to say, first, that the significance of pop performers' presence
was not at first a given, and, second, that the hostile division between the
two cultures, this "great divide,"[4] had gone back a long way. How long? At
least as far back as the origins of early modern European culture. Until
then, the cloistered and courtly few controlled access to written information; after that, upstarts could command literate skills and their culture
could be considered an alternative to the elite version—no matter whether
the upstarts thought of it that way. With his "small Latin and less Greek,"
Shakespeare struck his colleague Ben Jonson as a pop artist in late six-
teenth-century London, albeit in the same pop ranks as "Aeschylus, Eu-
ripedes, and Sophocles." With his swinging shepherdesses and swollen
goats, Antoine Watteau, painting in early eighteenth-century Paris, also
seemed a popular artist to his audience.[5]

Intellectual nostalgia to the contrary, as far back as records go, history
reports no unified culture—no nirvana where noble and peasant slipped
equally easily into the same cultural slipper. That a cinder-sweeping peas-

ant girl might fit into a noble slipper, glass or otherwise, has always been one of the great cross-cultural dreams, treasured everywhere because it was so fantastic. Great house and thatched hovel always had different cultures. Even when the great house *was* but a thatched hovel made huge; even when it had a great hall with a rude floor, a fire in the middle, and a hole in the thatch to act as a chimney; even when the master's family and servants together shared the diurnal tasks — even then lord and lady retired to a raised bedroom where a peep hole allowed spying on the servants bedded down around the hearth, to ensure those jaspers stole no silver.[6]

Behind the nostalgia for an invented unity in culture is the present, conscious, and very long-lasting recognition of the real split between elite and popular cultures. Indeed, although the phrase "the two cultures," coined by C. P. Snow in 1959, referred originally to an incommunicability between physical scientists and literary intellectuals, it might better, then as now, have referred instead to the bitterness between high and low, top and pop, formal and informal, ambitious and inadvertent, minority and majority, hieratic and demotic, elite and vernacular cultures. As far back as urban history goes, as far back as there is concomitant evidence for the cultures of leisured people *and* the culture of working people, there was between them neither a spatial nor cultural fit. From the onset of early modern Europe around the beginning of the sixteenth century, the butcher and the baker and the candlestick maker had different fantasies and jokes, distinct dialects, fears that varied and hopes that deviated from the rich families that bought their meat, ate their bread, and burned their tapers.

This division between the cultures is important enough to linger over longer, establishing assumptions. Modern life began when the middle class commanded enough power to force its vernacular languages into official status, prying official discourse away from its exclusive circle of Latin-reading clerics and nobility. In a series of breakthrough moments in all the nations of western Europe, the language, faces, dress, festivity, anxieties — the lore — of common people with money enough to play patron became memorialized in painting, drama, and literature. Bakhtin has identified this renaissance moment as one in which "folk culture . . . with its popular (vulgar) language [played] an essential role in the creation of such masterpieces of world literature as Boccaccio's *Decameron,* the novels of Rabelais and Cervantes, Shakespeare's dramas and comedies, and others. The walls between official and nonofficial literature were inevitably to crumble, especially because in the most important ideological sectors these walls also separated languages — Latin from the vernacular. The adoption of the vernacular by literature and by certain ideological spheres was to sweep away or at least weaken these boundaries" (72). Modern life began therefore when vernacular people *(slaves born in their master's house)*[7] asserted the principle of public self-definition, and made space for themselves and their idiom in prestigious discourse—including canonical archives. With the vitality of its living language, rich lore, and material plenty, the middle class appropriated culture unto itself, dividing the ancient from the modern world.

Among their many other significances, this rising class fulfilled a necessary phase in the lore cycle. This phase of epochal style formation occurs whenever a class or a public scrambles onto the historical stage, looks into the existing mirrors of art and sees not themselves reflected there, but the previous producers', directors', managers' visages, dress, festivities, and intentions. The new group scurries to mirror *itself*. Provided that it is sufficiently new, thoroughly ingenious, and has innovative lore crafted out of the distinctive experience supporting it, then a new style may take hold and, beyond that, a new form may result.

The succession through history of epic poetry, lyric poetry, drama, opera, fiction, film, soap opera, and rock music has consistently followed successively emerging populaces who needed their own art forms to blazon more permanently the values, ethics, and aesthetics embedded fluidly in their lore. Which is to say, each emerging populace has developed the art forms latent in the lore which encouraged its surge to power.

Each public therefore earns the forms that have in that sense already created it. The operative rule of thumb is that each emerging class or public has particular tensions and anxieties; each generates a particular form to soothe those anxieties, express its particular form of heroism, champion its values, and ban its bugaboos.

One might well ask what these factions required before they scrambled onstage. Did they not need reflections of themselves when they were powerless, perhaps even more so then? Of course they needed them, and had them, in the uncollected and unmemorialized phase of art called lore. Lore: the stories, customs, patterns of belief and behavior and gesture which inculcate and maintain the structure of belief by which a community knows itself, expresses its common features, and explains to itself its dilemmas. People perform lore outside of official institutions. Schools do not teach it; few books value it; churches disparage it; city halls ridicule it. Like the relatively powerless people it bespeaks, lore is part of any era's rejectamenta.

"That's just folklore," people say when they want to negate an idea. So when a new social class climbs on power's stage it memorializes its lore.

Then outsiders will not label the new group's belief structure "just folklore" anymore; it will become truth; in such ways, ideas in the trash heap contribute to a new paradigm.

Powerless people refresh their lore in constant retelling and rough reproduction in fragile form (on newsprint and other cheap records, in unrecorded pageants and fairs and daytime TV). Empowered people inscribe truths on tablets, protecting it in libraries and vaults; powerless people write lore on sand, preserving, maintaining, and augmenting it in incremental repetition. When they achieve power, they accord what had been slapdash lore the full treatment of hard covers, of canonized and curatorial attention (museums and concert halls and cinemas). This full protection severely slows lore's changes and feeds its audience's illusion that their lore is sempiternal. The new public has the power to place its lore on a pedestal in the costume of art. Academics write books about it. Institutions collect it. Its darkness becomes visible, its seeming chaos takes shape. What had been gossip, proverb, and nostrum winnows down to news, wisdom, and therapy.

Tablet inscribing has never proved easy or instant. Not even at Bakhtin's Renaissance instance of vernacular breakthrough did folklore leap immediately into art. Then, as in every subsequent cycle, there was an intermediate stage of popular culture, of poplore. The phase of poplore takes place when an emerging *public* [8] unselfconsciously entertains itself in its inevitably urban environment, so replicates its lore with mechanical (then, later, electronic) means. Peter Burke calls the early instances of this stage "chap-book culture," saying it was "the culture of the semi-literate, who had gone to school but not for long. . . . This chap-book culture might be regarded," he continues, "as an early form of what Dwight Macdonald calls 'midcult,' situated between the great and little traditions and drawing on both" (63). The chapbook culture shading into poplore is also exactly what Clement Greenberg has derogated as kitsch. Chapbooks and histories recorded the oral tales. Woodcuts and printed sketches replicated architectural design and dress. In later periods the Three Stooges of Saturday-afternoon B-movies, then Porky Pig cartoons in comic books and on Saturday-morning TV, represented values and inculcated legends in the uninscribed places of minds looking for their own values. Everyone, in every age, needs a narrative fix. [9]

Shakespeare's and Ben Jonson's play texts were early examples of poplore, as were the broadside ballads that appeared as penny sheets until well into the Victorian period. No one took them as art at the time, though the few surviving examples now reside in air-conditioned library and

museum vaults, with guards to ensure that currently reverent thumbs do
not flake them away. In their day, however, they were common tools,
wielded and thrown about like hammers or fertilizer with no fine finagling.
That's the way Shakespeare used Holinshed's *Chronicles;* that's the way
Rabelais used the chapbook *Grandes et Inestimables Chroniques de l'Enorme
Geant Gargantua* (Burke 62). Likewise, Jack Kerouac put the Three Stooges
to work in *Visions of Cody,* and Thomas Pynchon absorbed Porky Pig into
Gravity's Rainbow. A second reason poplore is so valuable to artists bearing
standards is that it sets their art off from previous generations. Poplore is
not only their lore, but it is also *not* the lore of previous art. Nor will it be the
lore of later generations, for they will have their own.

The poplore phase is relatively unselfconscious, but it does have its
own aesthetic. It is closely related to folklore values but enjoys the possibility for control that mechanical and electronic reproduction provide.
Like folklore, poplore is nearly always involved with narrative development, with violence, sentimentality, and the excesses of pornography.[10]
Unlike folklore, poplore is able to use technical means to ensure slickness,
spectacle, and ready accessibility. These attributes are particularly important to groups that are defensive about any country stain remaining in their
lives. Urban soul music exaggerates its slickness and synthesizer capacities,
its plasticity and jetset speed, for instance, as a way of distancing its
audience from the tinge of barefoot backgrounds, of times when there was
no plastic and only two important paces: the all-too-real mule cart and the
dreamed-of Terraplane that Robert Johnson sang about. James Brown
plays it both ways when he engineers his sound in dustproof studios and
disciplines his band to lockstep precision but stutters his music with the
earthy grunts of a fieldhand; Brown celebrates himself as "the Godfather of
Soul" and also "the hardest working man in show business." From Stevie
Wonder to Whitney Houston, younger soul singers are more determined to
hide any earthiness under synthesized surfaces.

When marginal poplore publics achieve truly secure positions in
society, they discard qualms about stains from their past. Their next typical
phase, in fact, is to memorialize their roots. But by then the recently
absorbed public has begun also to pick up other values, cue on other signs
that disrupt those original intentions into skepticism. Consequently, when
poplore pushes its way into the studios of the minority arts — or is raided as
a resource for them — the resulting mix is usually a disruption of narrative, a
reprojection of violence and sentimentality and pornography in ironic and
abstracted ways — as Roth did in *Portnoy's Complaint.* Jazz is another complex example of this point, it being an art that has welcomed into all its

styles the splinters and clods of blues, but skeptically, as when urban combos answered downhome remorse with exaggerated horn boohoos. This standoff embrace of blues' otherness has provided jazz an assimilated aesthetic and legerdemain frequently quite beyond the ken even of well-trained classical musicians.

In every case of a public's real assimilation both performers and audiences grow fond of roughness as a mark of authenticity. That's the way, in photography, Robert Frank's hasty composition works, for example, or, in poetry, Allen Ginsberg's creed — "First thought, best thought" — which devalues revision and seamlessness. This rough-hewnness is paradoxical because such works as Frank's *The Americans* and Ginsberg's "America" make their way on the initial assessment that their roughness is unworthy of art, when in fact their disturbing rudeness is one sign among many that they are keepers.

This vital stage in the lore cycle is an interval of risky boldness when artist and early public strut together in big boots, pushing rather than protecting their achievements, including rather than excluding influences. In later stages, the economic success of the patrons encourages the mutually reassuring genius of the performers; in this early moment, however, neither performer nor public may have large money; indeed, they may act as if it were unimportant. Conspiring to ignore or attack wealth (itself a sign of those they aim to supplant), they stride forward together into history and the canon. Pynchon chalks the stages in music's progress according to this logic when he has one character in *Gravity's Rainbow* argue that Western music has been "the incorporation of more and more notes into the scale, culminating with dodecaphonic democracy, where all notes get an equal hearing." And Anton Webern stood "at the far end of what'd been going on since Bach, an expansion of music's polymorphous perversity till all notes were truly equal at last" (440). There is a democratic reach to works of this stage, a formal elasticity, and a revelatory unguardedness through which hemorrhage both prejudice and faith without reservation. Earlier examples in the history of literature in English would include Shakespeare's *The Merchant of Venice* and Cooper's *Leather-Stocking Tales,* Fielding's *Tom Jones* and Twain's *The Innocents Abroad.*

The period after the Second World War is just such a moment in the American lore cycle. Jackson Pollock's paintings from 1946 to 1950 fit this concept, as does the postbop jazz of Miles Davis and John Coltrane, Thelonious Monk and Ornette Coleman. Other exemplars are Kerouac's sketched novels, Nabokov's *Lolita,* Frank's photographs, Jasper Johns's fifties paintings, Robert Rauschenberg's assemblages, much of Lee

Strasberg's work at the Actors Studio, Nicholas Ray's films, and Marlon Brando's acting. All appearing within a few years, even months, of each other, all reworking popular lore (from the flags of Frank and Johns to the cars and American West of Nabokov and Ray to the only apparently anarchic gestures of Pollock and Coltrane), all spewing sociological clues and prejudices like sparklers on the Fourth of July, all trying anything that comes to hand (house paint, old quilts, plastic saxophones, motel names) while they improvise the forms at their disposal—these are behavioral examples of artists at the beginning of an artistic epoch and at the moment that a new public clambers onto its stage of history.[11] The artist and the public confirm and embolden each other. In confidence they build their culture together, justifying and confirming one another.

The cost of confidence, however, is overconfidence. If the partners progress, they are more and more likely to mistake their proverbial ways, their lore, and their achievements for values that are singularly correct and universally applicable. Their political power and their cultural aesthetics consolidate to impede the development of opposing politics and new cultural aesthetics. Having climbed on stage, occupied the set, and played out their performance for a while, that is, each public and its cultural gatekeepers—sometimes artists, but more usually its professors and critics, its persons of letters—turn around to block the paths through which they entered.

Surely the fifties generation will also submit to this tendency when it has completed making monumental the lore of its public and closed in on itself. The style wars in the youth fashion industry, the skirmishes between successive styles of avant-garde painting, the anger between moldy old figs and beboppers in jazz (then between bebop and free jazz aficionados), for instance, show small instances of the impending larger process. That larger stage of closure is most recently full-blown in the instance of the high modern period, particularly because its confidence until the fifties was so high and its achievements so momentous, culminating in the works of what appeared to be "the American century."[12] Then modernism choked.

An overt instance of the high-modern choke is in the stunning impact of Clement Greenberg's early work. His book *Art and Culture* (1961) has been called "the most influential book about art of the past twenty-five years" (Sanford Schwartz 535) and his second and third published essays, "Avant Garde and Kitsch" (1939) and "Towards a Newer Laocoon" (1940), clarified and fixed the grounds of the late modern attitude toward popular culture.[13] These essays underwrote the then–increasing disengagement of modernism.

Greenberg's maneuver was to locate the vague hand–washing disdain for vulgarity within a spurious, but specific, logic of art's necessary refinement. Greenberg claimed in "Avant-Garde and Kitsch" that, following the example of music and in order to avoid being "stooges of literature," (*Essays* 1:25), modern painting boarded a train of increasing abstraction, studying "the various means of its own composition and performance" (9n). "The history of avant-garde painting," he continued the next year, "is that of a *progressive surrender to the resistance of its medium;* which resistance consists chiefly in the flat picture plane's denial of efforts to 'hole through' it for realistic perspectival space" (34, my emphasis). Greenberg trusted modernism had competent engineers who, braking and accelerating, might moderate their "progressive surrender." Competent or not, their surrender switched their train down a runaway track whose political or even socially savvy progressiveness was moot. Certainly the end of the progression removed the art from its instigating public, so that it had no longer a congenial connection with the people that set it going. But what did set it going? And how had Greenberg clambered from the caboose to the controls?

His strong pieces appeared at the embattled moment the Second World War began, a nexus of confident feeling that modernism had thoroughly won the day, combined with anxious worry that outside forces endangered its achievements. The growth in the universities of the New Criticism, itself consolidating in the time of Greenberg's essay, had promoted this attitude, and helped focus prestige on modernism's then-dominant Eliot-Joyce-Pound wing. That is, Cleanth Brooks and Robert Penn Warren published their textbook *Understanding Poetry* in 1938 and Brooks followed with his influential *Modern Poetry and the Tradition* in the year of Greenberg's "Avant-Garde and Kitsch."

Far from being a New Critic, Greenberg nevertheless shared many assumptions with these literary cohorts. They shared a formal emphasis, an indulgence in close readings of technique, a preference for artifacts isolated from their social dimensions, and a willingness to insist on something that Greenberg would call "taste" as ultimate arbiter. *Taste* is a euphemism for the inherited repertoire of shibboleths by which the empowered recognize one another. When people blame their likes or dislikes on taste, they need not examine the roots of their judgments. There is nothing sinister about this process — taste is simply the re-loring of examined principles that happens once those principles have occupied the stage of history for a while and become thoroughly assimilated. Expressing this principle as he nega- ted it, Robert Frank scrawled on one of his late photo-montages of the avant-garde: MORE SPIRIT LESS TASTE (*Nova Scotia* 52–53).

The tone in Greenberg's "Avant-Garde and Kitsch" and "Towards a Newer Laocoon" is aggressively defensive, overstating the achievement of the moderns he valued, and therefore condemning indiscriminately the varied constituents in the threatening context. "Since the avant-garde forms the only living culture we now have," continued Greenberg aware of neither his myopia nor his elitism, "the survival in the near future of culture in general is thus threatened" (*Essays* 1:11). Greenberg's aggression here is based on two implications of modern industrial society. First, the major achievements of modern art, science, and organization seemed to dwarf the achievements of less-industrialized cultures, including earlier stages of Euroculture itself. Second, moderns feared that urban living had killed off the peasantry that had generated past folk cultures. The urbanization, factory conditions, and standardized machinery of the industrial revolution eroded peasants' agricultural and oral-aural life—long the sine qua non of folk existence. Lacking this unlettered and rural peasantry, the theory went, there could be neither folk nor folklore.

Greenberg used precisely this crisis to propel his attack on poplore, the urban replacement for folklore, which he denigrated as "kitsch":

> The peasants who settled in the cities as proletariat and petty bourgeois learned to read and write for the sake of efficiency, but they did not win the leisure and comfort necessary for the enjoyment of the city's traditional culture. Losing, nevertheless, their taste for the folk culture whose background was the country- side, and discovering a new capacity for boredom at the same time, the new urban masses set up a pressure on society to provide them with a kind of culture fit for their own consumption. To fill the demand of the new market, a new commodity was devised: ersatz culture, kitsch, destined for those who, insensible to the values of genuine culture, are hungry nevertheless for the diversion that only culture of some sort can provide. (*Essays* 1:12)

In this crucial last sentence Greenberg employs his characteristic passive voice with anonymous agent—"a new commodity *was devised*"—implying a conspiracy by cagey capitalists to exploit the innocent, but leaving open also the possibility that the people brought this "culture fit for their own consumption" down on themselves.

In fact, there was no more intentional devising than at any other time in this or any other lore cycle. It all happened involuntarily, inadvertently, as always, everywhere. City people needed to screen their fantasies and fears, needed totems around which they could cohere into publics; people created, therefore, poplore which reflected their urban-literate condition.[14] It was no more ersatz culture than they were ersatz people.

Peasants-come-to-the-city were people living real lives, however different from the lives admissible to modernist gatekeepers. Moreover, their culture was authentically different either from its rural predecessors or from that of urban elites. To the outsider, unfamiliar with its associations and history, its codes and connections, it was as meaningless and silly as a Jackson Pollock painting soon would be to your harried New York cabbie. This is not to argue that the cabbie's Betty Grable poster or Frank Sinatra lyric was a masterpiece, equivalent to *Cathedral* (1947) or *Autumn Rhythm* (1950). It is simply to point out that the totems on either side were incomprehensible to the other side. Greenberg would never understand the sinews securing the working-man's affection for Sinatra's doing it his way against the scorn of the polite papers, nor the gratitude in the street when Grable raised her bare arms to her hair, smiling vaguely. On his side, the cabbie would never understand why eggheads desired art he believed four-year-olds were finger-painting in the nursery schools of every borough.

The popular culture that Greenberg derogated as ersatz and kitsch was simply what people were improvising out of their jetsam, some of which was elite culture's rejectamenta. But Greenberg's problem ran deeper than a blindness to the promising flux of his general culture. A passage a few pages later in "Avant-Garde and Kitsch" betrays his doubt in the value of *any* culture assembled inadvertently by nonprofessionals:

> There has always been on one side the minority of the powerful — and therefore the cultivated — and on the other the great mass of the exploited and poor — and therefore the ignorant. Formal culture has always belonged to the first, while the last have had to content themselves with folk or rudimentary culture, or kitsch. (*Essays* 1:17)

To isolate statements such as this and to contemplate their implications in or out of context is to feel empathy for Rumpelstiltskin's foot-stamping rage. What is "rudimentary" about the protective skein of feelings and gestures, signs and patterns — the culture — that has shellacked the lives of working people against the weather of history and the wind of the elite? In remarks like this Greenberg demonstrated that it was not merely modern kitsch he disdained, but all people's cultures, all "folk or rudimentary culture, or kitsch." That he assumed deficiency in all vernacular culture undercut Greenberg's purported crisis with the kitsch of his own time.

His real interest was to trace to the inception of modern art the seeds of anomalous, runaway momentum that in his time was "detaching" the avant-garde "from society . . . [and r]etiring [it] from public altogether" (7, 8). By this view, modern art had never really been about its "subject matter of common experience" by which it merely seduced patronage, but rather about "the very processes or disciplines by which art and literature . . . imitated the former" (9). This then was his justification for the modern withdrawal, against which Ellison and the Beats, indeed many of the painters that Greenberg has most famously defended, including Jackson Pollock, were in the fifties so desperately struggling. By Greenberg's argument, dropping the subject matter of common experience was the logical result of modern art's progressive surrender to the resistance of the medium. It was the victory of the medium against its clients.

In this dissociation of the public from the roots of art Greenberg managed his most important and most telling pass. At the same time, he coined a wonderfully true phrase about the relations of artists to audiences. The avant-garde may have withdrawn from society, he wrote, may have negated the values of its day, but it had never been without a "social basis . . . a source of stable income . . . provided by an elite among the ruling class of that society from which it assumed itself to be cut off, but to which it has always remained attached by an *umbilical cord of gold*" (10–11, emphasis added). With all its associations of symbiosis, bloody parturition, the initial parental spank, as well as its reminders of the material reality, Greenberg's umbilical cord of gold was just the phrase to substitute for the traditional congeniality between artists and their social roots. His point was that the conditions were no longer salubrious: "the avant-garde is becoming unsure of the audience it depends on — the rich and the cultivated" (11). There was nothing for it but that the modern avant-garde must forget that it developed out of artisans grabbing power and instituting their culture. Now that the originally artisan public had become "an elite among the ruling class," their artists must find a way to continue art's own autonomous momentum, and leave the rich to discern how it memorializes them.

This aspect of "Avant-Garde and Kitsch" is not so much true as it is a true sign of its times, like a crooked ring in a tree stump indicating a forgotten tornado that determined the tree's warp. Greenberg feared fascist manipulation of kitsch. Dictators could (and in 1939 did) use it both to foment cheap racial fictions and to bludgeon high culture's achievements: "In the name of godliness or the blood's health," Greenberg wrote in one of his many memorable sentences, "in the name of simple ways and solid virtues, the statue-smashing commences" (19). The fascist danger was genuine and poplore was surely manipulable. Still, manipulation was not exclusive to poplore. Certainly avant-gardists were also highly manipulable — as in the famous instances of (monarchist/Royalist) T. S. Eliot and (Fascist) Ezra Pound and (accommodationist) Gertrude Stein and (collaborationist) Le Corbusier.[15] But beyond the dangers of poplore's illegitimate use, to define it as the "rear-guard" and the real danger to living culture was surely to throw out the mule with the manure.

Greenberg's definition of the relationship between advanced and vernacular cultures so expressed the powerful version of the modern aesthetic — while it ran so extremely against other, healthier variants — that its function deserves straightforward assessment. Greenberg's attack on poplore extended the maturing logic within modernism's prestigious wing, the very logic that had most enabled its dominance. Simultaneously, however, this reasoning was suicidal. As the ultimate installment of a costly bargain, Greenberg's denigration of poplore completed the sealing off of modern values into an entropic hothouse of technique and medium which he argued had begun at its medieval beginnings, when "the medium became, privately, professionally the content of. . . art" (18).

Yeats, Eliot, and Pound had all pursued this point extensively in remarks that schooled Greenberg. They had been, in their turn, echoing Verlaine's remark, "Take eloquence and wring its neck." Yeats described poets in his time saying to one another over their black coffee, "We must purify poetry of all that is not poetry."[16] And T. S. Eliot was trying to avoid "the pathology of rhetoric" even before Pound more extremely pruned for him his draft of "The Waste Land." What was happening was a general but not universal turning away from the contamination of social engagement among some modern performers of every art.

This characteristic modern turn is even in the documentary photographs of Walker Evans, whose creed was "absolute fidelity to the medium" (Appel 150) and Berenice Abbott: "Photography can never grow up if it imitates some other medium. It has to walk alone; it has to be itself" (6). All these modernists, of every medium, were negating the conditions of their time, and returning they hoped to something pure and separate from social soiling. Their urge to purification pushed toward the feverish consumption of Yeats's verse, toward the arcane difficulty of Eliot's *The Four Quartets* and high-cholesterol punnery of Joyce's *Finnegans Wake,* toward the rectilinear severity of Bauhaus architecture. They likewise battened the hatches against social resources, vernacular transfusions. In other words, it is not so much peasant culture that was disappearing as that elite culture abandoned and derogated it.

Very much the same retreat into the rigor of compartmental discipline was contracting hard science and mathematics at the same time. Focusing on what was special to one's own tradition lighted up the ever harder and finer advances available within modern paradigms for particle physics, molecular biology, astronomy, and pure mathematics. "Few laymen realized how tightly compartmentalized the scientific community had become," wrote James Gleick in *Chaos,* an account of the "revolution" in contemporary physics and mathematics; science was "a battleship with bulkheads sealed against leaks" (31). Modern mathematicians and physicists had purified themselves into separate, pristine entities—in the U.S. as in France, for instance, modern "mathematicians were pulling away from the demands of the physical sciences as firmly as artists and writers were pulling away from the demands of popular taste. A hermetic sensibility prevailed. Mathematicians' subjects became self-contained; their method became formally axiomatic. A mathematician could take pride in saying that his work explained nothing in the world or in science" (89).

When the change developed into a new integrative mathematics that could begin to solve the problems differential equations had to ignore, that could address the messiness of population ecology and turbulent flow and weather, then the new science made its advances in exactly the same way as did the art culture—it dropped its insularity, it became eclectic again. As a matter of fact, it stopped trying to differentiate itself from folklore and folk wisdom, but began again to confirm intuitive shape and scale. Gleick: "Often the scientists drawn to [Stephen Smale's dynamical systems and Benoit Mandelbrot's chaotic] fractal geometry felt emotional parallels between their new mathematical aesthetic and changes in the arts in the second half of the century. They felt that they were drawing some inner enthusiasm from the culture at large" (116).[17]

Modernism's position in the lore cycle has proved to be a specially paradoxical case because it has been at once so brief and so protracted. By 1953, Roland Barthes was already calling it a "miraculous stasis" (39). But in comparison, say, to the languorous development of the epic it is brief. Its apparent protraction stems from its early self-consciousness. With so much historical information at their disposal, modern artists were perforce self-aware. And self-consciousness has, of course, been a major theme of modern poetry and fiction, film and painting. What needs insisting, however, is that this theme derived at least largely from social necessity. Modernism's originating public was changing so quickly that no artist could continually champion its values. Having drifted so far from the values of its originating public, modernism had to be self-conscious, if only because it had little else to consider. If modernism's originating public had in any way remained constant, perhaps its art might have stayed more socially committed. But the patron public was busily blobbing and reblobbing, faster than mercury spilled on a mirror, almost faster than Dizzy Gillespie could say bop or rebop, faster than Pynchon's McClintic Sphere could say Set or Reset.

The patrons of early modern art began as carriage-conveyed and barge-borne merchants at the rise of Renaissance cities. They then metamorphosed through various stages including the locomotive and subway periods of the Victorian and Jazz ages, when high modernism commenced, to the helicopter-commuting merger-managers descending on helipads in the American, European, and Asian megalopoli four hundred years later. Trying to remain constant to its own values while serving such vastly altered, and differently sped, publics—all the while grafting onto their vastly different umbilical cords—made modern art the most-stressed art period in history. Almost since its inception, therefore, modernism has practiced defending against its demise. Its practice adopted two conflicting tendencies.

One characteristic high modern wing proceeded by renewing itself regularly in vernacular relationships—in painting, the artists following the different models of Manet, then Duchamp and the Futurists; in literature, those following William James, William Carlos Williams, even Wallace Stevens; in architecture, those like Robert Venturi who picked up the severely deliquesced vernacular strands of Frank Lloyd Wright and early Le Corbusier and followed them to the shock of Las Vegas neon. This is the modern wing that a few recent critics of literature and painting have tried to reclaim and reassess, as for instance Richard Poirier, Marjorie Perloff, and Calvin Tomkins. A second wing, which prevailed between the two world wars, pulled the wagons round itself, withdrew into the purity of its traditions, and tried to generate its future from the nothingness of spirit, of mind, of pure intelligence operating on the monuments of the past.

For these high modernists, everything became rejectamenta except, to paraphrase Yeats's "Sailing to Byzantium," the monuments of each art's magnificence, its artifice of eternity. Eliot had begun closing the doors on the outside world when, in his magisterial essay "Tradition and the Individual Talent" (1919), he declared that no poem had meaning unless it was set "among the dead," in "relation to the dead poets and artists" (*Essays* 4). This tradition comprised the complete world of meaning for the new artist:

"The existing monuments form an ideal order among themselves. . . [that is] complete before the new work arrives" (5). In *The Tower* (1928), the volume which began with "Sailing to Byzantium," Yeats published a short poem called "Fragments." It quickly demonstrates the realm to which this strain of avant-garde modernism was tending. After a perplexing, nightmarish four lines telescoping Locke, Eden, God, and Eve as a spinning-jenny, the poet asks himself where he got his "truth." It came, he tells himself, from the mouth of a medium: "Out of nothing it came" (*Collected Poems* 211).

Yeats's claim is reminiscent of the confrontation in *King Lear* between Cordelia and her father, which Yeats turns inside out. Lear's "nothing will come of nothing" response to his daughter's skeptical muteness at his ritual may be literature's most famous clash between a dispensing patron and umbilically connected offspring. Cordelia is the first modernist negating a patron's principles because his values violate her own, which she holds superior. Would that her successors had been so involved in the processes of the state and so caring about the conditions of the patron. Her successors adopted her withdrawal but not her ministering follow-up. Withdrawing to their media while claiming they owed their patrons nothing, modernists negated the foolish, old, soiled world dispensing its riches awry.

Yeats and Eliot, and to a less-enunciated degree painters since Fauvism and Cubism, stayed in that closed tradition to which they retreated. It became the world for them. Unlike Cordelia, who returned to redeem her patron, these high modernists tried to generate the semblance of life completely within the tradition, within putatively abstract "standards." As in Yeats's case they got their truths out of "a medium's mouth," "out of nothing."

□   □   □   □   □

This closure into phantom forms of the mind, or what the retaliating contemporary poet Charles Olson called the "fetid nest . . . where maggots are," is what the bulk of the postwar generation avoided. They did so by negating the negations of the most prestigious modernism. They affirmed what was affirmable around them — daily life and poplore and the stained working world. What they affirmed was in the waste heaps thrown out during the previous generation.

They were in good company, some of it modern — for the practice of Eliot and company, however predominant, was by no means the whole of what was modern. In the plastic arts, Marcel Duchamp had constantly eschewed technique for ideas and real objects in his art, even at the time the Picasso wing of painting was pointing at technique and breaking objects down. In writing, one now sees that the examples of Robert Frost, Wallace Stevens, and William Carlos Williams, and the James brothers (yes, including even the modern master himself, Henry) had all been at ease with common things. They thought everything depended upon a red wheel barrow glazed with rain water (Williams) or Strether's tomato omelet next to a bottle of straw-colored Chablis on white table linen (James, *Ambassadors* 176).

It is important that Henry James, that paragon of modern refinement, could celebrate Barnum's Great American Museum as the place in his New York youth of which he was fondest, then continue for pages in reminiscence about its value for his life. One of his most vivid "Barnumite scenic memories," for instance, was how *Uncle Tom's Cabin,* a prototypical instance of poplore, triumphantly broke all classification, "gathering in alike the small and the simple and the big and wise, and had above all the extraordinary fortune of finding itself, for an immense number of people, much less a book than a state of vision, of feeling and of consciousness" (*Autobiography* 92).

James approves of *Uncle Tom's Cabin* in prose too tightly interested and involved to paraphrase. It is an amazing torrent, his enthusiasm for kitsch — as surprising in its commitment as in its acknowledgment of depth. And both features contradict Greenberg's derogation. Can James's enthusiasm for Topsy and company possibly be as real at the end of his life as when, a child, he sat in those vaudeville American "lecture-halls"? Yes. He insists on it too earnestly often to doubt even his most elaborate praise of this formative culture. "The social scheme, as we knew it, was, in its careless charity, worthy of the golden age," he wrote, "though I can't sufficiently repeat that we knew it both at its easiest and its safest: the fruits dropped right upon the board to which we flocked together, the least of us and the greatest, with differences of appetite and of reach, doubtless, but not with differences of place and of proportionate share" (93). Here James the famous elite aesthete is the most robust aesthetic democrat.

James of course knew all the arguments against popular culture. It is possible to infer them from quick readings of his novels and criticism, as for instance in certain notorious passages in *Hawthorne* (1879). But in his consummate work written during the years that Yeats was imbibing Verlaine, James carefully counters the antivernacular charges one by one. Here then is a modernist whose elite credentials are without parallel, a writer devoted just as much as Clement Greenberg to "the best standards of the past." But modernist Henry James is entirely at ease with popular culture.

Do not imagine that James found this ease only through the rosy filter of memory. Popular culture fits just as easily into the center of his most advanced late phase, as in *The Ambassadors* (1903), when Jim Pocock frequents the Follies in Paris rather than that city's cathedrals or museums. Jim Pocock's program is to have a good time, nothing more nor less. James's view emerges when his rapidly learning central character comments that Pocock will "sniff up what he supposes to be Paris from morning till night, and he'll be . . . well, *just what he is*" (233, emphasis added). And this is the point — Pocock and po' cock culture remain for James *just what they are,* fairly percipient facts of life, with which sensitive observers coexist, extracting from them what they offer, expecting not what they have not, and certainly not blaming the Pococks nor their poplore for the deficiencies of avant-garde culture.

Something happened to part of modernism and part of the avant-garde in the years following James. It took a wrong turn away from social engagement of any sort into believing that somehow the nothing of the mind might generate sufficient matter to support great art. Then, when the way grew faint and the resulting poems and painting wound themselves into tighter thickets than their publics would penetrate, gatekeepers like Greenberg came along to pout and point at the innocent insouciance of poplore. "Is it the nature itself of avant-garde culture that is alone responsible for the danger it finds itself in?" he asked in "Avant-Garde and Kitsch"; are there not "other, and perhaps more important, factors involved?" (*Essays* 1:11). That is when he introduced kitsch as the central danger for formal art. Through the power of his essay, reinforcing and channeling ideas already operating in the major avant-garde arts, poplore became the enemy, the "rear-guard" of modern culture.

The gains in Greenberg's 1939 and 1940 tactics were that he provided a rationale for the first-generation Action painters. He bought them time and bolstered their market. By proposing an aesthetic, Greenberg reassured those who worried whether the New York avant-garde had a professional ethic squarely within a modernist tradition. But the costs were greater than the benefits because valorizing modern withdrawal further caulked off from congeniality an understanding of the art Greenberg favored. Postwar New York painting in fact still awaits its adequate social account.

Beginning in the mid-fifties, in painting and fiction, jazz and rock 'n' roll, drama and film, poetry and photography, too, the move was to extend formal sophistication achieved under modernism, but also to regain social connection. Conscious of their sophisticated inheritance, fifties artists nevertheless wanted to return, like Cordelia, like many of their less prestigious modern mentors, to social connection. That's why in every important case contemporary artists remained difficult but accessible, avantgarde but replete with a recognizable repertoire of signs for the newly emerging public. Thomas Pynchon's vision "receding in an asymmetric V to the east where it's dark and there are no more bars" (*V.* 10) could, for instance, exceed the perversely Adamic pessimism Eliot demonstrated in naming the modern world a waste land. But Pynchon dealt also in a panoply of characters ranging from recognizable dropouts and sailors, absurd sound-effects engineers and moody jazz musicians, all across the spectrum to comic-book fantasies of talking automatons, technicolor monkeys beneath the polar ice, and characters with servoswitches implanted in their arms, clocks in their eye sockets. This circus of serious types (holdouts from high-modern and Victorian fiction) mingling with Yahoos dredged from four-color pulps and Saturday matinee movies absorbs modern despair into a rainbow rhetoric. Pynchon's is a nay- and yea-saying that can grade from the utterly dark to a light whimsy, even ecstasy.

Awareness of the bomb and recognition of nuclear fallout danger during the fifties were at least as intense as anything the interwar moderns had to acknowledge. But there were features of fifties life to balance those anxieties. Chief among the balancing features was the recovery of connection to a common public that looked the better for not being tainted by the mistakes the elite public had made. The lore recovered in this readmission of the vulgate came to balance and replace the loss of age-old belief Eliot dramatized, the unsponsored consciousness Henry James thought he showed his major characters achieving, and even the "Ambiguous undulations . . . / Downward to darkness, on extended wings" Wallace Stevens described beautifully in the last stanza of "Sunday Morning" (1923). By 1973, a work like Pynchon's *Gravity's Rainbow* could insist, in such robust set pieces as its scratch choir compline service (127–36), that the grave downward cycle was part of a larger circle, whose bottom was a composting for an advent, the rainbow reach beyond the grounds of our normal being: "our scruffy obligatory little cry, our maximum reach outward—*praise be to God!*"

In the significant art of the deliberately speeding years, from *Rebel without a Cause* to *Gravity's Rainbow,* Ralph Ellison's *Invisible Man* to V. S. Naipaul's *The Enigma of Arrival* (1987), reanimation of ritual that works poises against ritual inherited in fossil form from the past. In all of them is a recognition that ritual starts off helpful and optimistic, maturing through phases that end as a dampening, even a deadening, burden on the legatees of its originators. But this catastrophe is less a conclusion than a way-station, something to be overcome.

The rebirth cycle is one of the oldest American tropes, of course, with perhaps its most notable previous expression being Thoreau's hatching bug. The bug was deposited long past as an egg "under many concentric layers of woodenness." On the last page of *Walden,* Thoreau reports hearing of it "unexpectedly come forth from amidst society's most trivial and handselled furniture, to enjoy its perfect summer life at last!" (587). In the mutuality of this handselled rebirth imagery, as in so many other ways, then, the deliberately speeding generation is in fact restoring as much as disturbing cultural direction. Its return to jokes and coke bottles, the insistent recognition of goats and tires, chickie-runs and rhythm 'n' blues riffs is in no way homelier than Thoreau's culminating reliance on an old New England story of a strong and beautiful bug.

Contemporary artists entering the now-electric arena not only felt the pressure but knew from the modern example where it was going, so could also intuit its non-conclusion. They were living, after all, in the aftermath of Nagasaki and Belsen as well as the protracted waste land. They were surviving doom. By the sixties, demotic poets like Bob Dylan were broad-casting these ideas, as in the lyrics he wrote to "This Wheel's on Fire" — recorded simply with The Band in 1967, bootlegged widely, and finally officially released on *The Basement Tapes* (1975). He was on fire as he rolled down the road, he sang, and he expected it would explode. It did, he did, and yet he went on several times in his career, just as he was doing when he composed the song in convalescence from a motorcycle crash and from imagery too surreal jamming his songs. Life goes on past apocalypse. Or, apocalypse is as much a beginning as an end. Cultural apocalypse is the moment in the cycle where the disruption occurs that powers the cycle, kicking it along, setting its spin, employing new bards and artists who can accommodate themselves to the constancy of change.

Dylan's lyrics quickly demonstrate his working awareness of the patterns of development modernism bequeathed culture. But the words of song, poetry, fiction, and film are not necessary to show the patterns, which are manifest also in painting and photography. Robert Frank's still photographs from the mid-fifties, particularly in the way they addressed sequencing and narrative, concentrate this modern legacy as one of their topics. Of these photographs, one stands out as an instructive totem of ideas about catastrophe, the force of narrative, and the relations between ambitious and inadvertent arts: "Hoover Dam, Between Nevada and Arizona" (1955).

This complex photograph is a picture of other photographs, and of their standing. "National Color Card[s] from Koda[color]," says a label on the back of one of them. They are all on a revolving rack raised slightly on a plywood stage and displayed for sale between the fragmented words advertising them and an auto (not Frank's) pulled up perhaps to buy them, its Cyclopsian headlight scrutinizing their rear as Frank's lens does their front. "Hoover Dam, Between Nevada and Arizona" pictures poplore in the fifties, its content, conditions, and context. And it pictures its power: Frank's photo shows that by 1955 poplore had digested into totemic signs items as grand as the canyon and as apocalyptic as the bomb.

The crude rack holds nine stacks of prints, three stacks to each vertical side in its triangular arrangement. Moreover, the box of replacement alternatives behind the rack reinforces an impression that any sequential pattern is accidental in this jumble. However, Frank *has* caught a sequence in this photo that is chilling—and all the more headlong for its being unacknowledged, innocent, apparently random. The top picture on the rack is of Arizona's Grand Canyon in precivilized splendor—the fragmented word next to it is "UR," in the largest letters of the picture, labeling the canyon as the original, the ur-state of life. The rack's next photo shows that monument of modern American can-do knowhow, the Hoover Dam, flag waving gaily above it. (Throughout *The Americans,* for which "Hoover Dam Between Nevada and Arizona" was intended but not included, the flag veils from citizens the reality of their lives. Flags are the bunting by which they proceed toward their headlong catastrophes.) The last photo on the rack is of an atomic cloud mushrooming over the Nevada test grounds after a nuclear explosion. As these three elliptical frames tell it, Frank's implied story speeds from origin to catastrophe, modern civilization being the merest membrane between the two. After the world's pristine origins, modern (American, flagged) culture is the dam which holds back and also opens gates to the ultimate flood. But the extreme ellipsis of the telling, the headlight scrutiny, and the roadside condition of the story also give this ultimate flood a comic aura. Frank, like Nabokov and Dylan and Pynchon, is standing outside the modern apocalyptic narrative to take his picture of it. There is another, external perspective, after all. There is life after apocalypse.

The whole question of story or ordered narrative is a real issue in this photo, as it is in *The Americans,* as it is in the era's art and science, as it is in the apparent chaos of the cities and towns Frank visited. Are there stories? If so, what are their conditions? The stacks of Color Cards in "Hoover Dam, Between Nevada and Arizona" imply that the narrative might be shuffled; the rack suggests that turns to different sequences and stories are easy. The top words on the wall behind the rack disclose alternatives: "2 maps," they say. However, there are no people in "Hoover Dam, Between Nevada and Arizona," just their aftereffects — the photos, the car, their broken words, the stage for their artifacts. Agency being absent, the likelihood of someone shuffling the Color Cards is moot, as is the very sense of a narrative. The rack was designed not to display narrative, but to offer stills in random order, like the apparently turbulent presentation of *The Americans*. That there is a narrative order Frank only suggests minimally in the title of the photograph, and then only if viewers accept that his "Between" signifies temporal sequence as well as geographical location. Moreover, since the customary ways of sorting the progression would be top to bottom on the rack (Arizona over Nevada) or the direction of Frank's trip (east to west that fall of 1955, Arizona before Nevada) the title's reversal of expectations by putting Nevada before Arizona may suggest a turning inside out of catastrophe, a hope of return to ur-peace in the canyon after the explosion. In other words, Frank's catastrophe may be a beginning as much as an end. His picture shows eddying — which is to say neither linear development nor clean cyclical periodicity.

The point of the photograph, even with its apparently linear implications, is entirely open-ended. It catches a story, but does not dictate, impose, or read it tightly. It recomposes the work of commercial photographers into a new clutch of meaning that is not condescending, condemnatory, nor parodic. Neither is it celebratory. Frank accepts the dam, the Grand Canyon, the rack, the headlight, the words, the stage, and their messy conglomeration as components of the terrain. They are not so much equal as equally likely candidates for significant inclusion in the narrative which Frank's choices enable. But it is significant that he does enable narrative, for that is the dimension of his work distinguishing and charming it still.

This distinction shows clearly when one compares Frank's ordering to the sort of sequencing in Walker Evans's modern masterpiece, *American Photographs* (1938), or the photos Evans collected as Book One of *Let Us Now Praise Famous Men* (Agee and Evans, 1941). Order is important in Evans's texts to orchestrate their subjects' authenticity and the photographer's sincerity, to emphasize grand decay, to pick out dogged persistence. Everything takes place against a background of long time; everything is at the end of a tradition, yet suspended as if in a museum case. Walker Evans values stamped tole (*American Photographs* II-1, II-37) because its timeless design is terminally discarded here, and because it is the essence on a more pitifully devolutionary scale of the stamped descent of everything else: that's why these tinny images are the alpha and omega of Part Two.

Order reinforces the wit and essence Evans discovers in these simple objects and portraits, in themselves and as separately lasting valuables. Evans insists on the superiority of his art over the inadvertent picturing of the "License Photo Studio, New York, 1934" that is his book's first photo; and his first direct shot of people is of the two handsome boys pricked out from their anonymous background in "Faces, Pennsylvania Town, 1936." This order says that in mass culture there is anonymity and lack of differentiation, while in such high art as his own, the singularity of things becomes known. His photography points out a callousness in the mass world that does not recognize the poignance of handmade objects passing away. But Evans is conscious of objects and people, individuals all, passing grandly and with little relation toward amber solidity, toward a museum of infinite capacity that recognizes the democratic worth of each body and every thing. Evans's sequencing is thus something which calls attention to the art of photography as the medium best able to frame discreteness with discretion. While Evans clearly "loves" and is "entertained" by billboards and other signs of inadvertent culture — and has said so (Newhall 317) — he continually strives in his work to isolate and hold it still. He loves inadvertence the way Humbert Humbert loves Lolita, who tries to hold her in one stage of her development. Both try to stop the growth process of their love objects.

Robert Frank's ordering in the mid-fifties and after is quite different because he relates people and objects to each other. He never removes the inadvertent sign from its process. Frank's content moils in a conglomeration whose essence is motion, change, and odd shape. Eternity is not part of Frank's picture, although sometimes his characters seem to ponder it from a distance (*Americans* 17, 29, 67, 79). Frank's eternity is impermanence. His ordering is rich and calculated not to call attention to his art and his choices, not to point out the rightness of photography for this content, but to respect the intricate flux of the world he is snapping. When a student at Yale in 1971 asked Frank what sort of still photography he then would make, Frank replied, "I certainly would double print or do all kinds of things so that I wouldn't be stuck with that one image" (Frank and Evans, *Still/3* 6). In its jostling and speeding compositions, its tumescent relationships across pages, and its latent narratives, *The Americans* already displayed that dissatisfaction with the static image that his whole career would play out.

Frank's genius emerges from the way he played the cards on this issue of relationships. He was an innovative photographer with a style that changed the vector of American photography, but the impact of *The Americans* then as now hangs on its approach/avoidance conflict with narrative. He was always telling and denying a story, always catching and freeing a connection, encouraging and discouraging an interpretation. In the shooting of his photos, Frank found hope and narrative flow lurking. In the sequencing of his photos, Frank both enhanced and hid that connectivity. The experience of going through *The Americans,* looking at the lowering skies and the claustrophobic interiors, searching for meaning in the chain of pages, is so baffling at first, and grows so concentrated as viewers learn to gather clues, that narrative and its resolution or abandonment takes on special intensity.

Viewers attach themselves to any throb of connection between images that might multiply into a rhythm, might become a snatch of story. And when those snatches snag, when some competing cluster bumps them out of the way, when these light growths of meaning deliquesce or simply disappear—then it is not too strong to describe the effect as *catastrophe.* That's the way it feels when a reader of his sequences has built up a chain of associations and meanings, only to find them deserted or destroyed by the rush of new images and associations that the book propels. Frank suggested and contradicted catastrophe, just as he pointed toward pessimism and also seemed optimistic.

The Americans flows like a rapids, with eddies that turn back against its current and whorls within larger whorls that gesture like earlier sequences and will be echoed later. Its achievement is to be as turbulent as the real world with as much order cohabiting with its disorder. Frank's *The Americans,* then, is one of many important signs of its times that propose—like the new physics still latent then in the late fifties—an interest in the glancing, unpredictable, seemingly spontaneous ordering that occurs simultaneously with the flowing disorder of crowds jumbling individual consciousnesses into complex whole scenes.

The spontaneous complexity that Frank photographed in 1955–56 would receive defense twenty years later from the architect Robert Venturi. "Relations and combinations in city streets between signs and buildings, architecture and symbolism, civic pride and honky-tonk," wrote Venturi in the catalogue to his "Signs of Life: Symbols in the American City" exhibition at the Smithsonian, 1976, "express a messy vitality and produce an unexpected unity. It is not an obvious or easy unity but one derived from the complexity of city life 'which maintains, but only just maintains, a control over the clashing elements which compose it. Chaos is very near; its nearness, but its avoidance, gives. . . force.'" To that description add people and subtract half the anxiety about chaos, and you have Frank's insight. From Frank through Venturi, American artists have been finding force and taking hope in the vital combinations in city streets. They have been congenial with the vernacular vitality they find around them.

Frank's sequencing in *The Americans* is as associative as the sequencing of stanzas in a downhome blues song. As a Swiss immigrant, Frank had the early-fifties European's curiosity about vernacular American music across its whole spectrum. Anne Tucker reports that the first record he bought on these shores was by Johnny Cash on the Sun Records label, and that he followed jazz innovations at the Five Spot in New York (95). (In 1963 he hired Ornette Coleman to do the soundtrack for his short film, *O.K. End Here.*) Like transitions in the early Delta blues songs, Frank's connections in *The Americans* are hardly lockstep or strictly story-line. He repeats elements in photo sequences the way essayists abut paragraphs or poets yoke dissimilar entities with rhyme.

One example among hundreds is his pairing of the charity ball matron, with her jewels, coiffure, and hard-sequined composure ("Charity Ball — New York City," 143), with the working man vulnerably forking his chop on a cluttered formica table ("Cafeteria — San Francisco," 145). The way both the woman and man occupy the corner of their tables, the surprised angles of their necks, their like emergence from dark backgrounds and messy foregrounds, the verticals of her liquor bottle and arm, his coke bottles and coat, her candle and his salt shakers, the circles her necklace and his collar make, the pursings of their lips — all these rhyme the two pictures visually while maintaining the separation of their subjects.

As viewers move out from those two photos, forward and backward in their surrounding sequences, they see similarly evocative connections in the crook of necks, arrested perceptions, pursed mouths, and vertical lines that relate these photos with others across the text and the country, San Francisco to Detroit, New York to Indianapolis. The society woman and the eating worker also focus Frank's interest in askance glances that have been accumulating throughout the book, but come to the fore in this last section, beginning with the grotesque, cyclopean tuba-as-face in the Adlai Stevenson "Political Rally — Chicago" (125), succeeding to the disembodied Eisenhower and televised talking head in the next two photos, then the headless man heeding the neon arrow in "Los Angeles" (131), skipping a few photos, then coming on again in "Rodeo — New York City" (139) where the background New Yorker confronts the camera over the self-absorbed cowboy's right shoulder while to his left the wonderfully ironic tailgate commands: DODGE.

Flipping the pages, then, viewers build a memorable repository of glances some directly confronting the camera and viewer, some turning away or into themselves. Robert Frank turns and returns to this issue at a fairly apparent level with his repeated structuring or interval-establishing photos of flags and jukeboxes, cars and crosses, courting and death. But he pursues it most interestingly with his even more pervasive imagery of windows.

Windows as apertures of illumination and vision, windows as membranes between experience and comprehension, windows as shapers of points of view, windows as location of judgment and scrutiny — these are the dominating images in *The Americans*. Frank chose "Trolley — New Orleans" (45), his most arresting shot of windows, for the slipcover illustration of the first and every subsequent American edition (Brookman 1). The book begins and ends with windows, and windows permeate its content in countless ways. Many of the frequently noticed signatures of the book — its jukeboxes and cars, its vistas from and of buildings, its flags, its televisions — are about windows or lenses, which screen, project, absorb, frame, obscure, and mask visions of reality. Flags become metaphorical windows, for instance, when they obscure and frame the images of Hoboken (11) and Jay (43). Televisions and movie screens are lenses for a shaped reality, as are the large glasses on the front of the vintage jukeboxes Frank favored, as are the windscreens on the front of fifties autos (especially "Motorama — Los Angeles" [31] and "U.S. 91, leaving Blackfoot, Idaho" [72], the series from 163 to 169, and the book's last photograph). And as in the cleverly important photo "Barber shop through screen door — McClellanville, South Carolina" (85), Frank has a knack for piling up dimensions in window images that others had not noticed.

"Barber shop through screen door" shows how a neutrally viewed plane such as a screened glass door can contain and reproject at least three dimensions — the interior of the shop behind the screen, the house and trees far in front of it, and the shadow image of Frank himself, close in, at the instant he snaps the other two dimensions. In fact, the physics of the reflection on the screen door would inhibit the image of the barber chair were it not for Frank's shadow negating the glare. The effect is that the barber chair is a dream contained in Frank's head — yet it is the real interior of the shop that he has never seen before. The photo is an image of how

photographers—even while imposing their fantasies or ideas on a scene—
are also within and part of it. In that way the photo is a picture of Frank's
own self-consciousness: he has *his* hand to *his* face here, the way many of his
subjects do at moments of discovery, but in Frank's hand is a camera.

The other windows looking in on the empty barber chair imply
alternative views; and the one in the rear of the shop occupies—within the
superimposed shadow of the photographer's head—precisely the locus of
Frank's Leica's viewfinder and his eyes. This window at the rear of the shop
does at least two things, then. It emphasizes the photographer as viewer,
peeper, scrutinizer in an abstract way (just as it abstracts Frank's face). And
it helps Frank catch the chair in a viewer's crossfire. It emphasizes the
potential scrutiny under which even this placid barber chair might come—
just as Arkansas troopers arrested Frank himself while he was taking these
pictures because his accent was suspicious, because he had a New York
license plate, because "he was shabbily dressed, needed a shave and a
haircut, also a bath" (*Nova Scotia* 24). The several windows opening to the
calm of the barber shop imply that it can bear, even elicit, a mishmash of
cross purposes. But "Barber shop through screen door" is not only a
paradigm for Frank's window shots running through *The Americans.*

It is also a photograph of the concept of congeniality. The photographer is an audience member viewing the content. The photograph is a
picture of the process that goes on when publics view content. It pictures
an artist as an involved member of the public who is a co-performer with
the subject. In a photograph like this, the subject multiplies. The subject
remains the chair, but it also becomes the gesture of the photographer
composing the chair's context to include his scrutiny. Because it is a picture
of its own genesis, this photograph reveals as well as any of the others in
The Americans Frank's close kinship with the Action Painters in the New
York fifties. Moreover, it is a picture in a middle present between a particular past and future. As Tod Papageorge has clearly shown (42–43), its
content is based on the sixth photograph in Walker Evans's *American
Photographs.* Frank photographed a comparatively less-cluttered barber
shop than Evans, but his concept is much more involved than his mentor's.
When he took the photograph, Frank of course did not know where it
would lead—that it, too, would engender imitation. But it did call up its
homage, as in Lee Friedlander's *Self Portrait,* a 1970 volume of photos that
show Friedlander laying his shadow on, and being framed in, forty-three
roadside and storefront subjects à la Frank. Therefore, Frank's photo of
depth in an apparently serene plane has also inspired its own temporal
sandwiching and fulfillment in the stream of art photography's history.

While many of his pictures develop that simultaneous complexity, with or without windows, he also used window imagery to suggest sequential intricacy, of which the masterpiece in *The Americans* is "Trolley — New Orleans" (45). Much of Frank's later work in still photography, with his then-characteristic multiple images, reinaugurated in the seventies, is an extension of elements in "Trolley." So also are the "bus photos" which he took in 1959 after publishing *The Americans*—photographs taken through the windows of a public bus as Frank rode at random (see *Nova Scotia* 43). Each window in "Trolley — New Orleans" is a separate framing, on a string like a movie strip. The boy in the center, however, has broken the separation by wrapping his right hand through the solitary woman's space in front of him and dangled his left hand out his window, into the viewers' space, as has the black man behind him.

The tiers in the photo also grade into each other in ways that are meaningful for Frank (as in "Hoover Dam," with which "Trolley" is formally allied). The richly shaded black band with its many tones along the bottom yields via the white boy's and the black man's hands to the middle tier's expressive busts, all signifying realistic lives and clear meanings but separated each from each by their white vertical bars. This middle tier yields via the shared patterns in the closed window at the front to the tier of abstraction above it. Along this top row, the five abstracted windows show unrecognizably distorted images, scenes of motion as tantalizingly impossible to read as clouds scudding a sky. One puzzles in vain to find correspondences among these three tiers. The realistic window tier is thus squeezed between layers of uncertain meaning. Like Hoover Dam, it shows a brief moment between different states, implying process.

Most of the commentary on this photograph has centered on the despairing face of the black man in the fourth window, with good enough reason, for this is perhaps the most famous art photo of blacks occupying the rear seats of American public transportation. What still requires emphasis along these lines, nevertheless, is how the Jim Crow practice on the trolley jails all the characters, young and old of each race. The passengers handle this trolley's window frames just the way prisoners handle the bars and rails of their conventional cells. Moreover, what Frank has centered in the picture is the background nurse or mother, of indeterminate race, with her flowered cap, who is presenting the children in the third window. (The beautifully printed 1986 edition particularly highlights her presence.) If she were black in 1955, when Frank took the picture the year of the Montgomery bus boycott, she would have had to sit behind the children in the very place she is, behind her charges and with her people.

The conventional reading of "Trolley" is that it is a political photograph of the despair in the black man's face and the stolidity of the woman behind him. Yes, the photo does show that, and is important for it. But Frank's story has as much to do with the fate of these white children between the stony white woman before them, in the second window, and the appeal of the black man behind them, in the fourth. The children will mature in some version or combination of these directions. But which? Frank's photo does not insist or predict. He just snaps one space in their development.

Frank's work is very often about these interfaces between states. His photos imply, then, a before and after that are open to conjecture but which are estimable on the basis of the lore embedded in the delta-t he has snapped. For example, the filmstrip middle tier of the Trolley photo puts the central children into an elliptical narrative that constitutes an important class in Frank's work. Other major examples would be the second "Movie Premiere — Hollywood" (140) and "Hoover Dam." There is nothing in Walker Evans's work to prepare for the reversible logic or narrative of these photographs. But it is not any narrative; the photograph is not free abstraction. In its middle, representational tier, the photograph is not the Rorschach blot that the top and bottom tiers are.

It is a strip that tells of Southern American mores, coming to an official end in the year of the photograph. It therefore pins these two children within a social structure that could encourage their sympathy toward the contextual frames before as well as behind them — in the sort of perverse English that spun Southerners like James Agee and Elvis Presley into fondness for black culture. It confines interpretation of the photo to the lore that Southern mores embed in the picture. Viewers might legitimately project about those two children that in the next decade, for instance, they would be old enough to participate in the later stages of the civil rights movement; or, contrarily, to stone the Freedom Riders as they bused through Louisiana. But it would be unwarranted to project about them, on the basis of the picture's signs, that they grew up to become real estate agents specializing in beach property.

Frequently, Frank's subjects are between windows which convey forces jousting for control. The baby between the towering jukebox and the window glare of "Cafe — Beaufort, South Carolina" (53) is caught in the new sort of fifties tension Frank is noticing between electronic and natural authority. Likewise, but farther along in this struggle, is the man turning his back on the streaming natural light of the bar windows as he studies the jukebox playlist in "Bar — Las Vegas, Nevada" (57). A televised Oral

Roberts turns to another window blaring light in "Restaurant—U.S. 1 leaving Columbia, South Carolina" (99); this eerie photo is of a competition between televised light and the sun's natural version, and this time the sun seems to be winning, but no one except Frank is there to notice. The next picture is the famous one of a "Drive-in movie—Detroit" (101) with all its cars facing into a large screen obscuring a sunset; here poplore is vanquishing the traditional world and the audience is vast. The two lumberjack-shirted men pictured on the screen are lookalikes of Neal Cassady and Jack Kerouac, which is to say of the Beat characters Dean Moriarty and Sal Paradise whom Kerouac would celebrate in the late fifties (though he had written his manuscript by the time Frank took this picture). Frank is capturing the authority of iconic images that cut across film, photography, and literature—and whose light competes powerfully with previously traditional lights.

Frank took photos, then, not from outside the vernacular reality staring in—as had been the tradition of American documentary photography—but from inside. Many of his photographs were of his cohorts. But quite frequently his most striking pictures came when he peeped out like a vulnerable pest at the immense host. "Drive-in Movie—Detroit" is a good example, shot as it is from the viewpoint of the buglike autos at the looming humans on the media screen. Other good examples are his political photos (13, 15, 25, 111) in which the politicos are burly bullies with broad chests and elephantine backs, huddling in crowds. He pictures insiders the way marginal people see them, as hulking, formidable, threatening presences. And he relates to those host presences the way pests do, by scurrying to take sharp, small bites.

In that way, Frank can be both the outsider he is usually described as being, *and* the photographer who has most tellingly entered and photographed from within the vernacular vision. Frank himself thought photography the ideal medium for an outsider like himself, because he did not have to talk to or know people to take their pictures. In his photos he could regularly achieve the "cold sincerity" with which he sometimes closed letters (*Nova Scotia* 64).

This sincerity is an apparent link with Walker Evans, but the more one compares Evans's photos to Frank's, the greater grows the difference in their aesthetics, indeed their whole personal outlook.[18] Evans's sincere composure is very different from Frank's jump to catch his moving targets, his "lonely solitary chance conscious seeing," as Ginsberg called it, his "accident truth" (*Nova Scotia* 74). Frank's cold sincerity kept him moving back and forth over the interface of inside and outside. He was part of a time when the windows on the reality before him, as well as the technology to capture it, multiplied immensely. And that's what gives the complexity and power to *The Americans*. There are as many ways of seeing as windows and they all have their validity. They open up mini-sequences, tiny narratives, within larger ones. These sequences are linear, as strings within a book must be, but because they develop within larger patterns, they nip at and pester their hosts. They break down obvious development, setting it awhirl and creating turbulence. But they are orderly still, in a finely fragmented and humane way.

Reviewers trained to honor the sentiments of American documentary and art photography as distinct entities took time to appreciate how sturdily Frank had webbed the strands of his sequences. Unlike the modern variant of American documentarists, Frank featured no stalwart yeomen eking satisfaction out of a desperate scene. Instead, Frank noticed a proto-intellectual process among common people. He noticed individuals discovering their difference from the community values around them (especially see the photos following "Fourth of July—Jay, New York," his second flag [43–47, 51, 65–67, 75]). Unlike American art photography, Frank did not favor unanchored abstraction for its own sake. He printed no pictures of wave or leaf patterns (like Ansel Adams), no flowery or riparian convolutions in light and shade (like Evans, Steichen, or Stieglitz), no abstractions of human sensuality. It is important in Frank's work, as in that of the Beats and Jackson Pollock and much of fifties jazz, that his abstractions were anchored congenially in a specific time and place.

The deliberately speeding aesthetic of the fifties was to incorporate more of the nonlinear complexity of the nature of reality. It was to try to understand, in the arts as in science, the messy whole with its shifting moiré of structure and meanings. It was to recognize that there can be no certainty about ends in a matrix shifting so speedily and continually. Robert Frank's photographs illustrate all this through their incorporation of what earlier photographers rejected or scrubbed or displayed taxonomically, and through his sequential displays that mirrored the flow of the reality obsessing him. Like his comparable forebears, Frank also represents the vernacular South, the effects of social change, and class interaction, but he shows these very differently because his intent is different. He no longer resists or retards the processes of social change and the lore cycle. He is congenial to the outsiders, to their lore, to their self-recognitions, to their stop-and-start stories. In his pictures, Frank shows reality's deliberate speed.

5

THEY ALL JUGGLED MILK BOTTLES

I want to bite the hand that feeds me.
—Elvis Costello to himself

Robert Frank coursed his photo sequences to his era's stuttering rhythms, and Charlie Parker had a fatal weakness for TV jugglers, but less-secure talents were not amused. However lamentable kitsch had been in 1939, it blanketed all the scenes after the war. With new technology spinning the lore cycle and new publics snatching chances to clamber on stage, jugglers shouldered aside artistes like so many dominoes all the way to the deepest heartland. In Tonganoxa, Kansas, the mock-savage site of William Inge's play *Bus Stop* (1955), one young chanteuse named Cherie killed time during a blizzard by recalling her initiation into show business:

> I won a amateur contest. Down in Joplin, Missouri. I won the second prize there . . . a coupla boys won *first* prize . . . they juggled milk bottles . . . I don't think that's fair, do you? To make an artistic performer compete with jugglers and knife-throwers and people like that? (Inge 166)

Cherie illustrates Greenberg's concept of "folk or rudimentary culture, or kitsch" (*Essays* 1:17) as the rear guard danger to art. She mouths it now in the homeliest reaches, using it even there as an excuse for failure and translating it into a chorus girl's whining terms. Cherie will end her play and resolve her competition with "jugglers and knife-throwers and people like that" by retiring from the stage to marry a cowboy in Timber Hill, Montana. But the question is whether poplore threatens authentic art and artists as much as it does the pretensions of warbling artistes. The answer is no. Artists will not solve their competition with poplore as simply as

Cherie did. The range of their solutions will prove, however, that poplore is hardly the danger to art, but rather its bracing natural resource.

So thoroughly was poplore blanketing the fifties that artists had to own up to the challenge. They had to admit and incorporate some of poplore's risk, edge, and spontaneity into their own work. Some ventured so aggressively to the desolation rows and waterfronts and rebel youth gangs to seek geeks and grab their imagery that it characterized their work. The most notorious case was Bob Dylan in "Ballad of a Thin Man," who kept shoving Cherie's rivals into his audiences' faces to shock those who didn't know what was going on. Dylan's sword-swallowing protagonist dismembered and borrowed body parts from his public—"here is your throat back"—sneering thanks for the loan (*Lyrics* 198). The several peers for whom Dylan's instance stands cherished rather than regretted both the new material and the opportunity to exploit it.

Lesser artists would find other aspects of popular culture to imitate— its sentimentality, for instance, and sometime naiveté. This exploitation is what Greenberg had most feared back in 1939. Sentimentality and naive family loyalty in the face of deliberately speeding times were the values the United States Information Agency promoted when it sent overseas *The Family of Man*, the powerful photography exhibition Edward Steichen had collected and curated at the Museum of Modern Art in 1955. Steichen designed it for direct competition with the jugglers, sword swallowers, and animal acts of poplore on an international scale. One USIA memo described the reception Djakarta gave *The Family of Man* in 1962: "The exhibition proved to have wide appeal [although its] period coincided with a circus sponsored by the Soviet Union, complete with a performing bear" (Sekula 142).

More challenging annexations of poplore's welling emotions appeared in a long list of cultural achievement from the late forties through the fifties into the sixties: Miles Davis's ballads and characteristic trumpet tone; Kerouac's imitation of blues performers and competition with tape-recorded conversations; James Agee's tender-tough remembrance of his father's death in a Southern family; Jackson Pollock's absorption of prewar jazz, postwar advertising, and nuclear anxieties; Nicholas Ray and Elia Kazan's cinematic collaborations with James Dean and Natalie Wood *(Rebel without a Cause)*, James Dean and Julie Harris *(East of Eden)*, Marlon Brando and Eva Marie Saint *(On the Waterfront)* to show adolescent anxiety about failed fathers; and even poet James Merrill's extended elaborations on his Ouija board.[1]

The leisure and artisan cultures diverging ever since the industrial revolution (and scaring Greenberg just at the Second World War's outset) achieved a diagnostic and sustainable split after the war. The split occurred because of modernism's exclusivity, because of mass culture's dominance, but most directly because a rising culture built up separate steam. The popular media developed enough power that bards could create national and international audiences the way their coeval advertising mates created consumers.[2] The tape recorder and 35-mm camera, the paperback and television were able to record and disseminate such a wide array of cultural activity that the traditional competition between jesters and poets, bear-baiting and drama, extant since the beginnings of court and urban culture, went into an even more rigorously competitive gear.

This competition did not weaken the traditionally advanced arts. It sped their development. It enriched cultural material all along the cycle by rudely composing, thus making more manifest, free-floating lore. It was not Charlie Parker the jugglers threatened, not Jackson Pollock, not Jasper Johns, neither Jack Kerouac nor Miles Davis. The milk bottle jugglers drove out of business William Inge's snowbound artiste, Cherie, who was in any case pleasantly talentless.

This Darwinian aspect of the deliberately speeding fifties was one severe consequence of the relationship poplore had achieved with the rest of culture. Another consequence was that the host and pest categories in culture had reversed. The concept of the folk is partly truth and partly fiction. But since time immemorial it had occupied a privileged position as culture's very host, in the sense of gracious source. Until late into the industrial revolution elite cultures remained pests on the folk culture's host. *Culturally* the elite poet and painter drew inspiration, plot, melody, motif, structure, and insight from the folk artist's storehouse — until the interwar period of modernism. It is true that in days of yore the court jester and the traveling troupe were social and financial *parasites*. They literally *sat next to* the host — entertaining him in order to eat, trading stories and song for cakes and ale, bartering humor and a narrative fix for bread and bedding. Each supplied the other. The Manor house provided food and protection. The jester provided legends and values. In that way, folk culture was host to the rich pest that refreshed itself in folk art. There were two currencies: the umbilical cord of gold trickled one way while the umbilical cord of lore trickled the other.

That mutually refreshing relationship obtained for centuries, even and especially after role professionalization — when dramatists, composers, and poets skillfully raided the host folk culture time and again. Some classic examples are that Mozart often derived his operatic melodies, Shakespeare his tragic plots, and Yeats his conceits from host folk resources. During the first half of this century, however, before the ascendancy of the deliberately speeding lore cycle, middle-class culture became the host because it absorbed the folk.

By drawing in and suffocating any folk culture surviving outside its value systems, middle-class culture had *in theory* resolved all tensions. This was the nightmare of left and liberal intellectuals in the fifties and early sixties — from Daniel Bell to David Riesman, C. Wright Mills to Herbert Marcuse. These writers described the various processes by which they said the middle class expanded with its repressive tolerance (Marcuse) inhibiting any agency of change (Mills), creating henceforth a crowd that was lonely (Riesman) but sufficiently satisfied (Packard) or desublimated (Marcuse) that it would not, could not, think to challenge the dominant ideology (Bell).[3] All these writers considered the large center of society in one way or another insufficient, deeply uninviting, and largely unchangeable. And they called it Mass Culture.

This intellectual anxiety is germane to a defense of serious fifties culture because its theorists insisted nothing oppositional could breathe under the middle-class blanket. An ironic and instructive contradiction of this position occurred in the publication of Marcuse's famous *One-Dimensional Man* the very year, 1964, of the powerful Mississippi Freedom Summer, the movement to register black voters in the South. Whatever else it managed, the black and student (and, later, the women's and gay) movements riddled Marcuse's thesis that late capitalist society had "invaded and whittled down" the contemporary individual's "private space" (10) and created a one-dimensional "Society Without Opposition" (ix). Despite its radical reputation, *One-Dimensional Man* is in many ways a culmination of the modernist logic. It speaks of a single Key or theory (Freudian-Marxian, in Marcuse's case) that controls the populace. It assumes the populace is generalizable, that it will follow laws predictably. Its premise is that the psychosocial process is rational from the individual to the social level. It supposes and prefers an earlier epoch — the end of the nineteenth century, the beginning of modernism — when healthy alienation produced an ongoing critique of the status quo. Finally, it posits the late modern present as a serious decline, and the indicated future as a probably disastrous nadir . . . . Yet, if the world would only listen to his modern logic, then all might reach a new, corrected nirvana.

Hermetic theories like these encounter similar problems. Their authors cannot explain the provenance of their own insights, which cannot be conceived if the society is sealed and homogenized. If they can conceive their criticisms, the society is perforce multidimensional. Even as a tendency rather than an achievement, a truly one-dimensional society is impossible; the very moment Marcuse claimed it, the most popular and multifaceted oppositional spirit in the hundred years since the Civil War erupted all across America.[4] How could this oppositional culture have emerged from the purported one-dimensional crowd?

The absorption of oppositional agency within the middle class had generated its own resistance. Everything within the culture became charged with potential subversion, became a potential flea ready to bite the hand that fed it. The totemic features of middle-class culture that seemed most tawdry and used-up to its critics—flags and George Washington crossing the Delaware, radios and disk jockeys, frontiersmen and fatherhood, hula hoops and the highway—were likely to undergo retitillation into perverse new fetishes.

The "Society Without Opposition"—this "end of ideology" which Marcuse, Bell, and other late-modern intellectuals imagined and described—spun out subcultures which resisted it and contradicted its putative name. These internal lore groups organized around insights such theorists could not foresee; and once the insights or totems became apparent, theorists could or would not validate them. That is what happened to latenight radio patter of the Wolfman Jacks and Fat Daddies, to new jazz and rock 'n' roll, to Brando and Dean's Method acting, to action painting, to Beat poetry and spontaneous prose. Resistant subcultures specialized in finding images and melodies and concepts within the mainstream to redefine, recharge, and refetishize; they validated themselves by celebrating their talismans and (if they worried about it at all) waited for criticism to grow up.

Living like everyone else in the mainstream's midst, Pynchon derived his jumpcut structures from Porky Pig cartoons, Nicholas Ray his *Rebel without a Cause* from Robert Lindner's pop psycho-social theory of the same name, and Miles Davis his songs from Arthur Schwartz and Cole Porter. In fact, nearly all jazz has made its standards from alterations of popular formulae. The way jazz siphoned off vitality from its ambient mass culture is in fact the prototypical principle for the invisible youth at the end of Ellison's novel, growing whole in his hole, stealing power from the Monopolated Power Company. Unlike the victimized characters in the preceding generation, Ellison's invisible man does break through to self- and social knowledge. Fitzgerald's Jay Gatsby, Faulkner's Quentin Compson, Dreiser's Clyde Griffiths, even Wright's Bigger Thomas all die in their novels never knowing what really happened to them. But Ellison's character not only survives, he also swipes from the mass cultural monopoly adequate consciousness of the forces arrayed against him. He remains prototypical for his generation because he discovered an alternative, pest consciousness despite concerted efforts by management of both races and two contending ideologies to eradicate and replace it with a generic servitude. The pesty youth wins, the monopolated host fails.

Pest groups regularly and significantly discover the shape of their existence by resisting incorporation into mainstream consciousness. This discovery has caused a change in folklore theory and in the social theories dependent on it, has changed ideas about the provenance of culture and its transmission. Until the 1950s, a folk was a group that lived outside and independent of the elite culture. A folk generated independent cultural items which organized its world in its own way for itself. And a folk shared this homegrown lore with the elite parasites who sought contact with it.

This traditional folk became an endangered species when the industrial revolution began creating a new, mass cultural host in urban areas. The mass culture had been absorbing folk culture gradually since before the Victorian William Thoms, anxious even then that the folk were disappearing, coined the term "folklore" in 1846.[5] A century later, by the mid-fifties, everyone shared this theory about folklore's deliquescence. Academic folklorists, mass culture's liberal theorists, and the anonymous Disney drones reworking Crockett and Fink for Tinker Bell's TV presentations — all agreed that what had been exterior and independent was by then interior and domesticated. Mass culture had acted like a large amoeba digesting its ambient host. Twenty years later its happiest self-representation would be Pac Man electronically eating his assailants.

Nevertheless, something that acted like a folk was still there — as the examples of jazz, independent fictional characters, disk jockey patter and rock 'n' roll freaks, Method actors and Beats, student activists and civil rights workers, an avant-garde, and all the rest of the resistant subcultures indicate. Maybe they were literate and urban, maybe they gathered and hunted sweaters and geegaws in malls rather than mushrooms and berries along hedgerows, but there were still groups generating their own meanings and forms different from the host's.

These folklike groups were feeding off the mainstream culture, but creating alternate meanings for the signs and ideas they recombined, as did the invisible man in his hole. This process became clearer during the fifties as events and groups confirmed its existence. Therefore, even as the dominant modern theory of despair over the loss of folk culture ripened during the decade, so too did the grounds to dismiss its despair. The despair and its dismissal were both real in a culture as riddled with information as then obtained. Neither was powerful enough to erase the other.

The industrial host did absorb the old folk host, turning it into an internal pest. But it could not eradicate independent interpretation and use of information. When mass culture ingested what had been exterior to it, ideological dispute did not end, but came from inside now, like a war with one's conscience that never reaches equilibrium. Over time the host culture accepted impulses from its new pests, resynthesizing them into the host culture, often defusing their oppositions and turning their bite to anodyne. But the oppositional process continued because the pest groups continued to create differentiating lore. Once one granted that there were independent lore groups within the mass society as there had been externally independent peasants, then the process was not astonishing. It followed the pattern established when the Lord of the Manor adopted and defanged the lore of the jester sitting beside him at his long table in days of yore. Only now, with the material differences that consolidated the fifties, the cycle turns faster.

The aggression of the pest group angers, therefore speeds and intensifies, the blanketing response of the mass host. Within a few years after the Beatles had returned Berry's songs to the suburban purview, Muzak had relaxed their tensions in synthesized strings. What had begun as aggression ended as aural environment for elevators and sprightly stimulation for shoppers. To that extent, then, Marcuse was correct. But he did not foresee how this functional pacification would instead wind up a further response — sending successive lore groups in search of further material to recharge. Instead of the flattened and domesticated society that the theorists of mass society envisioned, a deliberately speeding society has as one of its governing principles this *autohype,* in which the contending parts of the culture stimulate each other more and more intensely, to subdue and subvert, exhaust and retitillate.

Elvis Costello's 1977 song, "Radio, Radio," is about this important contemporary pattern. The singer begins by describing living within the "shine of the latenight dial / Doing anything [his] radio advised." From a Marcusean perspective at the song's opening, Costello is a robotized individual, with no private space. To achieve such perspective, however, one must derogate the pop glow illuminating Costello. In the modern view, which Marcuse sums up extremely, poplore does not exist in any significant sense beyond its homogenizing danger. It has no quality, no usable history, conveys no critical content, and deletes dimensionality from the lives it illuminates. But audiences can maintain that perspective only by not listening.

Time and again, writers and singers have celebrated the weird, wired world of radio late at night, especially, when the AM band bounces off the night sky, seems to cross synapses and hallucinate all on its own, bringing home to its auditors distant aural delights nowhere available within their locally predictable regions. Many a postwar American youth retired to expanded consciousness in a darkened bedroom or auto speeding across the flatlands of the West, tuning in the latenight radio. Kerouac and Ginsberg describe it in the East (Lowell, Paterson) and in the West (San Francisco, Wichita). The remarkable taped section of *Visions of Cody,* for instance, ends transcribing a mad call-and-response at a black revival meeting late at night, its voices making only approximate sense, challenging the ambition of any experimental writer. It is more incomprehensible in its ecstatic fervors than even the marijuana-goosed screeds of Cody and Jack. The American night is always farther gone than the furthest personal realities. It makes the loneliest listener feel normal and collected. Top this, it seems to demand:

PREACHER. I HEEEARD – I HEEEEEEEEEERD – I HEERD A
          MAN MAY DO WORKS
PEOPLE. MOTHER!
          MOTHER!
          PREACHER. I GOT MY SURANCE!
          BUT THEY CAN'T DO IT! –
          I HEEEEEEEEEEEEEEEEEERD!
          (247)

And Kerouac, in his next section, "Imitation of the Tape," will in fact compete with the vernacular anarchy caught on the tape. He will try to "do works" no one had ever written before.

In the same spirit, though perhaps clearer in its intent, is Ginsberg's "Wichita Vortex Sutra" (*Collected Poems* 394–411). Certainly the radio bolstered Jonathan Richman in Gloucester, Massachusetts, as he rode highway 128 in the dark. "Roadrunner," his 1976 paean to the airwave bond, kept him "from being alone late at night." From the forties through the fifties and into the seventies, when it began to revert, the latenight radio was the great glue of countercultures. It recruited members, changing the directions of their lives, as it turned John Lewis – who later played with Miles Davis and led the Modern Jazz Quartet – from the Anthropology and Baroque music he had been studying in Albuquerque toward bop jazz piano. At least that is how he has described the effect of first hearing Charlie Parker on the radio broadcast from New York's Savoy ballroom in Jay McShann's band.[6] And once those members were initiates, latenight radio reassured them that they were not alone, that they could overcome their feelings of being lonely in a vast crowd.

Costello begins "Radio, Radio" tuning his dial in *that* perspective. He recalls for himself and evokes for his public an entirely real history of poplore, however invisible or mute it might have remained to outsiders whose theories forbade its existence, or their noticing it. But Costello soon realizes that radio in the seventies is not what it had been twenty and thirty years before. By the mid-seventies, authorities were reining in even radio, which had been relatively free compared to the processing of books, TV, and film. To Costello, the radio world was starting to seem like the modern one that the social theorists feared, the one without niches of private space, where fools "anesthetize" audience feelings.

Because he knows radio's tradition Costello sees its doubleness, knows that the control is a recent affront rather than something permanently wired in. Costello reckons he can fight back, nipping the host that is his matrix. That is his difference, the pest's difference, from modern mass-culture theory. Both for his lore group and for the "fools" who would try to control it, "Radio is the sound salvation. / Radio is cleaning up the nation." That is, salvation and nation-cleaning may wipe both ways — maybe against Costello's lore group, maybe against the lot of fools. If the radio can wipe against the authorities, can tell people the truth that is in the world, then Costello would be agreeing with no less an historical authority than Huddie Ledbetter, who as Leadbelly sang "Turn Yo Radio On" in the thirties (EKL-301/2). In any case, "Radio, Radio" shows an internal lore group well along toward self-conscious defense of its territory.

"Radio, Radio" is a creed for a self-aware pest that has learned how to thrive within the media of would-be mass culture. Thus its memorable three lines after the first chorus:

> I want to bite the hand that feeds me
> I want to bite that hand so badly
> I want to make them wish they'd never seen me.

"Radio, Radio" is hardly an ideological statement and would not be useful as a rock poem if it were. But it points to the conditions which ensure that ideology never ends, especially in a mass culture. The more robotic the conditions of a society, the more its establishment reproduces cultural totems as placebos and tries to turn its public communicative channels into anesthetic drip tubes, then the more anger it arouses in the recipients and the more the whole design turns inside out. Resistance happens.[7]

The doubleness that "Radio, Radio" represents, showing the way a too-compacted mass society can turn inside out, is parallel to the doubleness of black culture. Both blacks and youths (although resistant subcultures are hardly defined by ethnicity or age) seize evidently innocuous terms or totems'—Buckeye the Rabbit, blue suede shoes, ducktails—and give them significant new associations which maintain group identity against attempts to erase it. The poplore implicit in "Radio, Radio" is, like folklore of yore, an aggregate of associations with a history that matters. Like all lore, it has a usable past which not only enriches but also determines its effect. When Costello realizes how the lot of fools is warping his latenight radio illumination, it angers him unto resistance. Not only his anger and resistance are important. Also significant is the history of latenight radio lore that leads to and allows his responses. Together they mean that enriching, determining lore—not impoverishing, random kitsch—is activating Costello.

☐　☐　☐　☐　☐

. . . lackadaddy, I was on the road again.
—Sal Paradise in *On the Road*

The chain of poplore's history and its kinking in the postwar years are readily apparent in film, too, where the specificity of the references is sometimes particularly convincing. One chain of such references is the Pop-in-the-apron scenes in Nicholas Ray's *Rebel without a Cause* (1955), François Truffaut's *The 400 Blows* (1959), and Robert Benton's *Kramer vs. Kramer* (1979).

The image of the father-in-the-apron as a model for his son is an extraordinarily resonant one from the moment Ray levered it up out of diffuse jokes to center it in *Rebel without a Cause*.[8] There it was the prima facie indictment of emasculated malehood—Jim sees his father wearing an apron at the top of the stairs, mistakes him for "Mom," and watches with mute disgust as this man in an apron mops up a mess. Jim later drives off with tires squealing when his still-aproned father cannot answer his son's question, "What can you do when you have to be a man?"

This disgust and condemnation persisted when Truffaut coddled the same image four years later in *The 400 Blows*. It was the director's first feature and a movie heavily indebted to *Rebel without a Cause* for its analysis as well as iconography, but without Ray's self-pity. (*Blows* is as good an example as any in film of the international exportation of the culture of deliberate speed.) In Truffaut's film, twelve-year-old Antoine (played by Jean-Pierre Léaud) and his father (played by Albert Rémy) make eggs for dinner, father in apron à la *Rebel*. Whereas American Jim had run disgustedly away from his too-womanly father, French Antoine breaks into damning laughter at the whole idea of such a father making dinner while their mother and wife cheats on them. Truffaut, one might say, reveres and fulfills Ray's talismanic image by adding the realism and turning the screw. The boy's laugh is his one moment of mirth in an otherwise somber performance.

Two decades down the deliberate speedway, Pop-in-the-apron scenes come at both beginning and end of *Kramer vs. Kramer,* framing the movie. In an indebted reversal, the final incident of the father and son cooking together indicates male strength. Its first occurrence proves the Dad, whom Dustin Hoffman plays, incapable of performing simple household tasks or of caring for his boy. But at the end of the film when Hoffman breaks eggs to make French toast (nice nailing down of the allusion to Truffaut, that) he shows how entirely coordinated are his patter, performance, and camaraderie with his boy. He shows their growth together, the rightness of his fatherhood, and the wholeness of his manhood.

What a different world the late 1970s are from the fifties, yet still taut with the same underlying sinews. The material was lore enough in 1955 to make the scene a revelatory icon, then it gradually deepened and gathered inference as it crossed and recrossed the Atlantic, still legendary after all these years. Hoffman and son can accept the apron, so are not so easily male chauvinist. They have grown, yes, but they have grown into mastery of the male fantasy of control and destiny. Now father and son can bond together self-sufficiently, can bust, scramble, and devour those female eggs faster than you can say James Dean. "In James Dean," declared François Truffaut somewhere, referring to the end of the fifties, "today's youth discovers itself."

One repeated issue not only in this chain of allusions but coursing throughout the deliberate speed period is the failure of father figures. The father in the apron; the man who could not take charge, or who dominated too totally; authority unable to convey itself to the next generation; authority which had stood by during the breakdown of modern culture and managed the Holocaust — here was the cause of rebellion that Hollywood could enact but would not name. While stroking its chin and claiming its rebels were inexplicably without a cause, the mainstream culture was enacting a search for adequate mentors. Meanwhile, the fragmented forms of the vanguard arts displayed their sense that the tradition was in shambles.

A major problem after the war was what to do when the father, God, authority in the abstract died not only as an intellectual concept (The Death of God), or as a political problem (the governance of conquered zones), but as a diffuse enigma running through all the experiences of culture expressed top to bottom. In films, records, plays, and novels — all the narrative arts — this basic problem appears: the father is gone, is illegitimate, is corrupt, cannot stand up to women or his children, is effete, is mortally ill. He left, was killed, committed suicide, miraculously died. His messages to his dependents are faint, quaint, or nonexistent. In his absence, peer pressure, or brotherly love, or mob rule, or participatory structures emerge.

The missing, dead, or derelict father in contemporary texts shows people feeling an inadequate authority. As this theme plays across the spectrum of cultural expression, it develops more and more dimensions, becoming increasingly self-conscious as it serves different publics. The constant anxiety about it at every level shows people wondering how to live in a world without some one, tradition, or form inculcating wisdom sufficient unto the day.

The most popular media generally tried to prop up the father figure, thus denying any problem while telegraphing an obsession with it. Examples are such long-running television series originating in the mid-fifties as "Father Knows Best," "Ozzie and Harriet," "Leave It to Beaver," "Bonanza," and "Gunsmoke." More interesting was Edward Steichen's concomitant visual presentation, *The Family of Man,* which the Museum of Modern Art published as a book in June 1955. It was doubtless the most popular photography show of all time.[9]

The Family of Man is an internationalist soap opera that had the feel of a promotional trade fair in its museum version and retains the layout of a high school yearbook in its published variant, sentiments by Carl Sandburg. Belonging to a family is its highest value. All life's functions are family functions. Babies are members of a family, of course, and nations are large families, themselves kin in the world family. Everything is from a family point of view. Backyards, for instance, open to continental vistas. "With all beings and all things," claims one of the captions, a Sioux proverb, "we shall be as relatives." The exhibit pretended no politics clouded its vision, but its sequencing showed that the move from underdeveloped to developed countries was as indisputable as growth within the family: the women marching through the desert with baskets on their heads would mature into the row of women in New York City (in a photo by Robert Frank) a few pages later, smoking, smiling, drinking coffee in a burger parlor. The captions progress from Genesis to St.-John Perse. Steichen filled the exhibit with fundamental narratives of the family story. He showed individuals are: unhappy, scared, hungry, broke, begging, "alone with the beating of [their] heart," asleep, dreamy, thirsty, sometimes working, sometimes dead. Family groups are: fulfilled, strong, laughing, dancing, loving, playing, preying, praying, enchanted, rapt, proud. Families are repositories of individual memories. They carry forward and make individuals eternal. *The Family of Man* is a too-obvious example of how photography's selection can seem to be documentation while presenting a particular point of view. The Museum of Modern Art, like television and pulp comics, tried to prop up fatherhood, family togetherness, and universality at the moment all three were failing.[10]

Moving away from such a massively popular easy target toward what originally had a subcult public, one finds an *auteur* film like *Rebel without a Cause* caught between Warner Brothers' ambition for popularity and the film crew's snatches of germane sociology. *Rebel without a Cause* oscillated between propping up and knocking down the father figure. With an apron, director Ray dressed down the ironically named Mr. Stark, but stood him up with his son at the end against his wife and mother, showing how his son has taught him manly, husbandly, behavior. In *East of Eden* (1955) a heart-attacked father and his rebellious good/bad son (again James Dean) come together among violins at the end, united by the loving woman who has understood and loved them all. Big Daddy in *Cat on a Hot Tin Roof* (play 1955; film 1958) has cancer, a thoroughly intimidated household, and a son who deals in mendacity, bourbon, and dubious heterosexuality. When the family is finally more or less frank with each other, their honesty enables the son to climb crutchless back in bed with his back-scratching cat of a wife. He becomes a "Little Father" if not a Big Daddy.

A complete list of damned, effete, sick, or corrupt mentors as icons in the mid-fifties would be long. It would certainly include chief characters in *On the Waterfront* (1954) and *Blackboard Jungle* (1955), whose union boss, priest, and classroom teachers stand in for the head of the family in domestic dramas. All these films interestingly present the authority figure as bad indeed, but nevertheless conquerable, teachable, or redeemable. On the one side these films contrast with the cuddly TV father or sheriff who can do no wrong. On the other side, they contrast with the father in serious books and poetry, who is dead or derelict.

The range in ambitious literature of the deliberate speed period runs from the "Meinkampf" father cursed as a fascist in Sylvia Plath's "Daddy" to James Agee's deeply loved but weak and drinking father, seen from the perspective of his six-year-old son in *A Death in the Family* (1957). No matter how bad or good they may be, they are gone—dead in these cases, but frequently simply missing. This lack of an adequate father lurks behind *Invisible Man.* It runs through Flannery O'Connor's stories. The abstract issue dominates Pynchon's *Gravity's Rainbow,* in which Broderick Slothrop sells his son, Tyrone, to a Harvard stimulus-response laboratory, causing the grown boy's wartime traumas, including V-2 bombs dropping wherever Tyrone has enjoyed an erection. And in Kerouac's work the lacking father is quite literally the determinant bringing *Visions of Cody* and *On the Road* into being: *"lackadaddy,"* lamented Sal Paradise as he tamped his problem into one word, "I was on the road again" (85).

Throughout *On the Road,* Sal and Dean seek his father, Old Dean Moriarty, though one of the points of the book is that he is not to be found. His son, young Dean Moriarty of *On the Road,* will become Cody Pomeray in *Visions of Cody.* Kerouac built both Dean and Cody closely on the real Neal Cassady, the same man who came to drive Ken Kesey's famous Merry Pranksters bus in reality and in Tom Wolfe's *The Electric Kool-Aid Acid Test* (1968). His father, Neal Cassady, Sr., was a derelict "in the depths of alcohol," said Neal (*Visions of Cody* 178), who grew up with him in flophouses and freight cars. Largely because they derive no help from such a father figure, Moriarty/Cody and Sal/Jack must turn to each other—to brotherly bonding. They deliver the "fervid comradeship" Walt Whitman had awaited in his preface to *Democratic Vistas* (1871), claiming that without it democracy would remain "incomplete, in vain, and incapable of perpetuating itself."[11]

Recognizing, moreover, that they cannot find their desired authority embodied in a physical mentor, Jack will discover Cody's essentials spread across poplore incarnations of legendary material—will compare Old Cody to W. C. Fields (181) and, in one of his most masterful fantasies, liken young Cody to the Three Stooges (300–306). At one point in the taped third section of the novel, Cody and Jack receive a letter from Old Cody. The father's misspellings embarrass his son but excite Jack, who incorporates them into his romance of the man. Jack and Cody's eager decoding of Old

Cody's insufficient letter represents the orphaned origins of their congeniality.

The occasion of the letter leads into Kerouac's declaration of his novel's central strategy. His ballooning style (178) will transform an American derelict into a "King." As they decipher the old man's scrawl, Jack tells of a story he has written that includes a "Rex," so named because "he was no king, he was a guy who never wanted to grow up" (178). At this virtual midpoint in *Visions of Cody,* calling a wino sidekick of Old Cody "Rex" at least amuses Cody. But Kerouac and his narrator "Jack" are serious when the novel's last word crowns Cody "King."

This conclusion of *Visions of Cody* differs sharply from the ending of *On the Road.* Sal ruefully deserted his reduced and pitiful friend in the earlier novel, choosing stability and a settled life over the cross-country caravansaries and crazy consciousness that Dean embodied. As a novelist, too, Kerouac clearly likewise withdrew in the last pages of *On the Road* from his own tentative early commitment to the vernacular instability he had shown Moriarty living. At the earlier novel's end, Dean comes across the country three thousand miles to see Sal, five days and nights on his railroad worker's pass. But Sal turns away from him to attend a Duke Ellington concert at the Metropolitan Opera with his wife and other friends.

Dean Moriarty is a failure; Cody Pomeray is King. The difference between the two is that in the second book Kerouac has made it impossible to retract recognition either from Cody or from the techniques that encompass him. *On the Road* withdraws from its insights as from its hero and is leery of its own implications; *Visions of Cody* is uncompromising about these points from beginning to end. It presents truths about Cassady's restlessness even while insisting, too, on his protean sufficiency in each instant.

Visions of Cody brings out, opposes dialectically, and accepts without synthetic resolution *both* Cody's *and* Jack's creeds. Jack's driving force is to "get it down," to record and interpret life for eternity. Cody's is to live in each moment, which is "kicks enough in itself. . . that's my interpretation," he says succinctly (134). Expunged from this ending is any derogation from Jack's previous friends. Cody is King, Jack his interpreter, and they have shouldered out of the picture any other conventions—just like the two flannel-shirted variants on Cody and Jack who have taken occupation of the crepuscular screen in Robert Frank's "Drive-in movie—Detroit" (*Americans* 101). Now everybody is watching *them.* It is not so much that they have stopped wanting the father's authority as that they have discovered their own adequacy and strategies to sustain it. It is their moment of hearing the tick of their own heart (as in *Invisible Man*), their trusting in the gonadal glow climbing the jukeboxes *(Lolita),* their putting their hands to their faces (as Frank's people do in *The Americans*).

□   □   □   □   □

All interspersed with white bottles of rich mad
milk— Then the bread bun mountain— Then the
serious business.
                                                          —Jack Kerouac, *Visions of Cody*

To point out the way *On the Road* ultimately betrays its ambitions and gestating principles is less to gainsay its considerable achievements than to notice their fulfillment in *Visions of Cody. On the Road* stood way out from the modern surface temper. It was an extreme extension of the American orality and volubility that the art critic Bernard Berenson in 1955 called "glossolalic triumphs," referring to Gertrude Stein (128). Berenson might as well have been referring to the odd, dense and tense, allover form of Jackson Pollock, Ornette Coleman, John Coltrane, or Jack Kerouac. These artists would all surface toward the end of the fifties, but their voluble techniques developed under the rose early in the decade. They derived in part from latent clues in, say, Cezanne and the Surrealists, Stein and James, Armstrong and Ellington. And they derived also from their common urge to incorporate popular lore into the forms the artists all inherited from the history of their media. Specifically, it was the persistence of poplore, its ability to start over after dead ends — as in the blues, as in Maggie of *Cat on a Hot Tin Roof,* as in Bakhtin's laughing chorus, and as in Neal Cassady — that was so valuable to the avant-garde, which needed most of all that very capacity to bend to it again, to crop up against all odds. So this volubility had its genealogy high and low, in minority and majority culture, in Gertrude Stein as well as Little Richard. To miss one or the other antecedent is a mistake.

Their American volubility is in marked contrast to the postwar European effacement, which characteristically tried to blot personality in its "literature of silence," as Roland Barthes termed it. Robbe-Grillet, Barthes, Sartre, even Camus aimed for rigorous control of emotion and withdrawal from affect in what Barthes famously called "writing degree zero." Anonymity was the continental way of accommodating the psychic damage of the Second World War, the Holocaust, and the bomb.

But Kerouac is in a tradition that unifies even Walt Whitman and his apparent opposite Henry James. These three rely mutually on the play of the voice to represent the process of discovery and the idea of American humor. Walking back and forth between the window sofa and the writing desk in his garden study at Rye, his booming voice audible out on the road's cobbles, James too "composed on the tongue" — in Ginsberg's memorable phrase[12] — dictating his three last, long masterpieces to a secretary, who typed out the sustained sentences in the rhythm of James's abstracted meander. Certainly this American tradition in its triumphant glossolalia uniting writers as deeply different as James and Twain, Stein and Faulkner, Kerouac and Heller is distinct from the calculated conceptions of "writing degree zero" eking out of Western Europe in the postwar period.

While Kerouac and others in all the contemporary media are voluble, however, they are also distinct from their modern predecessors in this line. The modern American writers from Walt Whitman to Henry James, Gertrude Stein to Ezra Pound, and on through William Faulkner, all teemed their profuse sentences in arcing manifestation of what they took to be both the mind's and mother earth's infinite carrying capacity. There are many meanings and intentions in the structures that the contemporary avant-garde created, but one of the ideas that Ornette Coleman, John Coltrane, Robert Frank, Jackson Pollock, Bob Dylan, and Jack Kerouac most clearly enacted was consciousness exceeding its carrying capacity just at the moment the earth was exceeding its own. Here was matter and music, here were people and pictures more complex and chaotic than the mind could model through its act of will. This was the main principle that Neal Cassady embodied. *On the Road* delivered some of the implications in Cassady's chaos, but contradicted them with its pat form culminating in an exclusive conclusion.

The paradox is that Kerouac and company had struggled to explore the limits of catholic expressiveness. Kerouac pioneered in catching and elaborating experience that poplore was already composing in ritual form. A prime example among many others would be Kerouac's rendering of jazz performance and audience interaction. Outside the club, an establishment tradition and mentors had dissolved or disappeared, but, inside, the jazz club continually recreated a secular, vernacular rite that substituted for religious sacrament. Kerouac was colporteur for that underground faith, his fiction (like many a central artifact of the fifties) so much vernacular sacrament.

Frequently the jazz club or scene is a surrogate mass in Kerouac's work. The blowing soloist stands in for the priest, his horn for the censer, his stimulants for the chalice. His playing enacts the richest sort of tradition—so alive that it feels invisible, weightless, immanent, supportive rather than confining. The San Francisco club scene of *On the Road* is the clearest instance (162–64). Elsewhere, Kerouac clinches the connection when he has Dean Moriarty describe George Shearing's vacant piano stool as "God's empty chair" (106).

Although jazz history hardly confirms Moriarty's reverence for Shearing, the spirit of such moments is nevertheless important in Kerouac's prose. They insistently demonstrate a knowledge in his characters beyond the ken of standard discourse. Kerouac piles prose catalogues in these passages as Gatsby in an earlier day heaped shirts. He coins onomatopoetic sounds to emulate squeals and squawks in frenetic saxophone lines that themselves strain to represent ecstasy. Throughout *On the Road,* until its end, Kerouac's general move is to push against the limits of form and memory, discourse and the sentence—to move *out of the place,* which is to move ecstatically. These jazz passages are his most driven exemplars of that romantic urge. Kerouac's enactments of jazz rites are to his intent as Hemingway's description of a bullfight is to his meaning, descriptions of flooded rivers and corralled Texas ponies are to Faulkner's, sailors kneading whale sperm are to Melville's. They are atomic representations of larger schemes.

Here, in *On the Road,* is Dean explaining to Sal Paradise the significance of a saxophone solo they had egged on in a Little Harlem club south of the Southern Pacific station the previous night in San Francisco:

> "Now, man, that alto man [in fact, Kerouac had described him playing *tenor* sax (162 and 163)] last night had IT—he held it once he found it; I've never seen a guy who could hold it so long." I wanted to know what "IT" meant. "Ah well"—Dean laughed—"now you're asking me impon-de-rables—ahem! Here's a guy and everybody's there, right? Up to him to put down what's on everybody's mind. He starts the first chorus, then lines up his ideas, people, yeah, yeah, but get it, and then he rises to his fate and has to blow equal to it. All of a sudden some where in the middle of the chorus he *gets it*—everybody looks up and knows; they listen; he picks it up and carries. Time stops. He's filling empty space with the substance of our lives, confessions of his bellybottom strain, remembrance of ideas, rehashes of old blowing. He has to blow across bridges and come back and do it with such infinite feeling soul-exploratory for the tune of moment that everybody knows it's not the tune that

counts but IT"—Dean could go no further; he was sweating telling about it. (170)

This passage is a romantic fantasy of filling moments with "infinite feeling" of inexpressible truth. But perhaps more importantly marking Dean's own epoch is his warm evocation of the mutuality audiences feel with performances that convey their "bellybottom strain."

The saxophone player blazoning their substance jolts a corresponding effort from them—which process the novel is in its turn also recapitulating. "Then I began talking," reports Sal, "I never talked so much in all my life" (170). He tells Dean his childhood fantasies of riding in cars scything trees, posts, and hills that zoomed past the window. And Dean excitedly remembers his own Western scything fantasies. They trade choruses in this fashion, competing in their East and West Coast styles, until the driver complains that they are "rocking the boat" (172). And off they go again, talking to beat the band.

Beating the band, competing with the excitements popular culture rouses, is the common need across all the art media of the deliberately speeding generation. Ornette Coleman tries to make his horn sing like a human voice; John Coltrane talks in religious tongues; Jasper Johns paints his sculptured ale cans and sculpts his painted flags; concrete poets sculpt their pages; Joseph Heller models the snippet chapters of *Catch-18* (not yet *Catch-22*) on the concentrated attention-span television programming fostered; Frank O'Hara competes with lunchtime gossip and tabloid headlines in his "I do this, I do that" poems. All around, the avant-garde absorbs the challenges of multiform popular culture.

In contradistinction to the prestigious high modernist generation that preceded them, these artists of the deliberately speeding years did not turn tightly within the demands of their specific media (forms or traditions), but often looked outside them for inspiration, for subject matter, and for technique. Meeting at places like the Cedar Street Bar in Manhattan or the City Lights Bookstore in San Francisco, they looked to each other across forms, and together they looked specifically to the excluded world of poplore. They looked affectionately in most cases, realistically in the rest. There was no hiding anymore from the need to draw on poplore's capacities. The choice was to use it one way or another, or else to relinquish connection with the lore that was organizing the potential audience.

It would be wrong to insist that this use of poplore form and impulse in itself distinguished the era of deliberate speed from high modernism. In fact, many moderns had themselves contradicted the Yeats-Eliot-Pound-

Greenberg dicta of withdrawal into the purity of the tradition and recoil from rhetoric. Fitzgerald's, Dreiser's, Faulkner's, and West's use of the Horatio Alger poplore legend, for example, shows that many modern writers heavily mined popular material, the very process T. J. Clark has insisted characterized modern painting. But they used it with disdain, as a way of signaling how their era necessitated a coarsening of theme. In short, they showed much the same aspersion that led Eliot to hold his nose when describing the "young man carbuncular" assaulting the typist at the center of "The Waste Land" (ll. 222–48).

Therefore, the diagnostic distinction comes not in the fifties generation's use of lore, but in their no longer disdaining it, rather finding in it affirmable rituals and ideas. This finding is what drove Kerouac immediately on, after *On the Road,* to the extremity of *Visions of Cody.* He must have recognized the disjunction between his positive feelings about Cassady and his culture and how the formal expectations of the novel pushed him into disdaining his friend at the end of his book. He must have known there was more to the lore than he had achieved in *On the Road.*

But knowing it was there and knowing how to use it were different. That is what the conjunction of *On the Road* and *Visions of Cody* clearly shows. When Kerouac and company involved themselves deeply in lore's openings, they found them leading centrifugally into a milky way of form, spread nebulously. What started as promising exploration in Jack Kerouac's and Ornette Coleman's cases (and John Coltrane's and Miles Davis's, and many more) turned into a danger zone whose unforeseen traps they each had to try to map and pass among. Because it turned out unmappably complex, they did not all make it through. And none passed easily.

Sal Paradise's recoil from Dean Moriarty's life at the end of *On the Road* shows the typical impulse. Jackson Pollock did not commit happily and quickly to his allover paintings in 1946–47, when he was beginning them. Ornette Coleman did not intuit his long-line melodies and group improvisations, and he explored them only after internal as well as more famous external resistance of audience goons beating him and smashing his horn. Jasper Johns at first thought his dream of painting the American flag was "crazy," said so at the time (the mid-fifties), and has told every interviewer since. Still, all these and others, too, persisted in their use of poplore, and their exploration of its apparent chaos.

Persisting, they learned to resist the obloquy with which the media doused them. For such sons of the blue-collar provincial poor as Coleman, Pollock, and Kerouac, ridicule in *Life* and *Time* must have been deeply frustrating. But as they kept on, more important than their embarrassment and anger were the ways they found to use poplore increasingly richly to overcome their own doubts, pullbacks, and self-censoring. Cherie, in *Bus Stop*, competed once with bottle jugglers, came in second, and soon quit to marry a cowboy. The modernist critics from Marcuse to Greenberg defined poplore as the flattening enemy and variously prescribed frontal attacks or retreat. The artist pretenders (Cherie and her ilk) as well as the theorists would therefore deal with the problem by keeping their distance. It was only the artists themselves who were solving the problem at last by pushing through poplore, absorbing it and its strategies into their work. When artists did so, their positive commentators ignored the content and the means of its incorporation to hail it as *formal* advance — overcoming Picassoid space (Pollock), scotching standard chord progressions (Coleman), or breaking with linear narration (Kerouac).

The deliberately speeding artists surely did achieve formal successes, and in the way their interpreters claimed. But these ways were ancillary to their root question of how to pump poplore into the artifact and, once it was there, how best to use it. In other words, persisting with poplore caused artists to face consequences with which they could not quickly cope. Ginsberg read Kerouac's roll manuscript to *On the Road* and wrote to Neal Cassady on 7 May 1951 (about a week after Kerouac finished it) that "Jack needs . . . an ending. Write him . . . so he can have courage to finish his paean in a proper apotheosis" (*As Ever* 107). The problem of the proper apotheosis was not confined to Kerouac.

Poplore is hot lore and hard to handle. A character like Neal Cassady can overwhelm both his chronicler and his novel. Robert Frank had to sequence carefully the images he found on his road for *The Americans* — and what controls that book is still up for grabs. Pollock's sense of the world's teeming, rhythmical infrastructure overwhelmed first his canvases, then him, then the world of New York art. Ornette Coleman's fidelity to the melodies dancing in his head drove him away from the conventional forms that had framed improvisation and glued jazz together; instead he groped toward alternative resin for group play that would permit the odd lengths and harmonies of his tunes.

Like these other artists, Kerouac's way of coping with the impact of poplore after *On the Road* was to use more of it. Rather than turning away to propriety and literary acceptance, and despite the deal Ace Books offered him to publish *On the Road,* Kerouac plunged into "sketches" that became the opening of *Visions of Cody.*[13] Then, like Ornette Coleman finding resin for his melodic bits, Kerouac built up a structure to show off the sketches.

He sketched an old diner grill "like the ones Cody and his father ate in long ago" (novel's first line). He sketched scenes that reminded him of flophouses like "the Skylark in Denver where Cody and his father stayed" (6), where men "leaned elbows over their humble meals of grime—I saw the flash of their mouths, like the mouths of minstrels, as they ate" (7). He also sketched himself in these descriptions, his prejudices and enthusiasm leaking out between the sentences. His romantic racism shows in the way he buys the Sambo image whole, sketching "a Negro cat . . . with the strangely humble clownish position of the American Negro and which he himself needs and wants because of a primarily meek Myshkin-like saintliness mixed with the primitive anger in their blood" (18–19). On a single page he spills these phrases: "big cowlick Irishman," "Sharp little rich Jewish lady . . . with a hairy husband Aaron who deals in high finance with the gravity and hirsute slowness of an ape" (21). He sketches his own misogyny: "My vision of men enslaved to cunts, to women who at or near thirty become lost in a dream of maternity as men die in the night with slavering thirst for the eternal food, the inexpressible security of a conscious caress (or dreamy unconscious)—poor Mac, Cody, broken by their cunts—but not me" (116).

Regrettable as these passages are, they warrant the unguarded thoughts of a son of immigrant Lowell, a mill town that conspicuously did not melt its citizens into one happy consciousness, but in fact reinforced their separation. These confessional sketches mark Jack's class and background in *Visions of Cody*. They are not attitudes which the school of hard knocks will convince him are wrong, that a superior education will convince him to repress, or that writing his novel will erase. He will not vanquish them. But he will fight their constant presence throughout the text the way other explorers swat mosquitoes or cut through underbrush. They are limiting climatic effects, but their gravity also enables some significant insights.

Jack Duluoz's prejudices establish his simultaneous attraction to and alienation from the "ancient redbrick—1880 redbrick" (6) that makes up the modern infrastructure of America from Lowell to Denver. His Lowell anxieties of class, gender, and ethnicity make Kerouac see the brick stolidity of modernism's economic base. More than any comparable American writer of his time Kerouac shows that the seductive neon playing across the modern surface promises more than it delivers to the youths and bums of the land. Those who do not understand this principle stay derelict. Those who learn how to live with its meaning can poach lordship over their uninherited demesne.

Jack recognizes how the Cassadys, father and son, fetishized the class

barriers of America as their "prime focal goal." His sympathetic differentiation of their approach to this redbrick barrier established his brotherhood
with them:

> Cody's life in Denver entered a second phase and this one had for
> its background, its prime focal goal, the place to which he was
> forever rushing, the place his father had only known as a bum in
> meek stumbling uplooking approach. . . nothing less and nothing
> more than the redbrick wall behind the red neons: it was
> everywhere in Denver where he went and everywhere in America
> all his life where he was. (78–79)

The novel will turn and return to the attitudes that separate its characters,
including its narrator, from each other and from the implied host culture.
The phrase "redbrick neon" is a plangent reminder of the inhospitable host
throughout the novel. It is what Cody and Jack have in common; it sets
them going; and it is what they are trying to understand and address better
than old Cody's "meek stumbling uplooking approach" to it. Their mutually ripening understanding of the flashing signs' relationship to the industrial structure will allow them their genuine bonding. These sketches were
shafts Kerouac sank into "the bottom of the world, where little raggedy
Codys dream" (5). Kerouac boasts that their effect is "deep form." They
record the mire of the world.

Rather than letting the narrative skate across time in linear, chronological narration, the sketches also catch on the vertical associations en-
crusting any moment or image. The sketches therefore created temporal
snags and dislocation important to subsequent writers as different as Susan
Sontag (*I, Etcetera*, 1975), Thomas Pynchon (particularly *V.*, 1963, and
Gravity's Rainbow, 1973), Norman Mailer (*An American Dream*, 1965, and *Why
Are We in Vietnam?*, 1967), and Tim O'Brien (*Going after Cacciato*, 1978). Still,
this formal innovation was an adjustment Kerouac made in order to pack
his fiction with the poplore necessary to turn Cassady from the frozen-out
derelict he remained at the end of *On the Road* into the King Kerouac felt
him to be and wanted to show him being at the end of *Visions of Cody*.

These shafts of poplore counterbalanced the middle-class judging of
Cassady that had inevitably occurred so long as Kerouac employed the
chronological, conventional narrative of *On the Road* to explain his pest
hero's life within the mass-cultural host. The sketches of *Visions of Cody*
dredged pest silt up to surround Cody, restoring to him his cultural armor
against the hostile scrutiny of the host world. The attractions of middle-
class family life were absorbing him and he was choosing, too, to encounter

it. But in real life Cassady carried his poplore, pest, culture with him to gird against surrender to middle-class ways. In fiction about a pest hero, the writer had to restore that poplore context, provide that nacreous shell, or watch helplessly as the host conventions ground up his pearl.

To describe Kerouac's intent this way is to show another significant difference between *On the Road* and *Visions of Cody*. The first novel has an author who is a voyeur in the pest world of the road, the derelict, the cotton-picker, and the Mexican peasant. Acting as a conventional narrator, Sal observes but takes no responsibility for the connections he makes; he loves and leaves subject after subject. *Visions of Cody,* the mature novel, shows Jack as a narrator responsible to the subject he has introduced into the vicissitudes of the host purview. In *Visions of Cody,* Jack's sketching restores enough of Cody's poplore ambience so that he protects his friend.

Kerouac performs this protection richly, achieving much else at the same time so that his concern for Cody's tenderness is never demeaning or mothering, so that he also is doing interesting takes on the form of presentation. An example is the sketch of "Hector's, the glorious cafeteria of Cody's first New York vision" (10). It includes a page of food celebration as tacky and excited, hallucinated and real, as a Busby Berkeley musical:

> . . . general effect is of *shiny food* on counter — walls are therefore not too noticeable — sections of ceiling-length mirrors, and mirror pillars, give spacious strange feeling. . . . But ah the counter! as brilliant as B-way outside! Great rows of it — one vast L-shaped counter! — great rows of diced mint jellos in glasses; diced straw-berry jellos gleaming red, jellos mixed with peaches and cherries, cherry jellos top't with cream; great strawberry shortcakes already sliced in twelve sections. . . vast sections reserved for the splendors of coffee cakes and Danish crullers — All interspersed with white bottles of rich mad milk — Then the bread bun mountain — Then the serious business, the wild steaming fragrant hot-plate counter — Roast lamb, roast loin of pork, roast sirloin of beef, baked breast of lamb, stuff'd pepper, boiled chicken, stuff'd spring chicken, things to make the poor penniless mouth water — big sections of meat fresh from ovens, and a great knife sitting alongside and the server who daintily lays out portions as thin as paper. The coffee counter, the urns the cream jet, the steam — But most of all it's that shining glazed sweet counter — showering like heaven — an all-out promise of joy in the great city of kicks. . . .
> (Poor Cody, in front of this in his scuffled-up beat Denver

shoes, his literary "imitation" suit he had wanted to wear to be
acceptable in New York cafeterias which he thought would be
brown and plain like Denver cafeterias, with ordinary food) —
(10–11)

This Whitmanesque catalogue links back to the most basic story-telling
traditions, to the food fantasies of folktales, to famine ordeals, yoked with
budding megapolitan disorientation ("mirror pillars, give spacious strange
feeling") and excitement about the plasticity of food "showering like
heaven."

Many passages in Kerouac's work display his hunger, from the matter-
of-fact ten salami sandwiches prepared for a cross-country bus ride (*Road*
86) to the "foody esculence" in his hallucinatory "ah-dream of San Francisco" (*Road* 144). They function like the wish-fulfillment fantasies Robert
Darnton has analyzed in Old Regime French folktales, bespeaking folk
desire: "Wishing usually takes the form of food in peasant tales, and it is
never ridiculous" (33). *Visions of Cody* begins in a diner and constantly
discusses food and eating, partly because cafeterias and truck stops are
warm havens with tables for writing in a dufflebag life, more intuitively
because the poplore mode that Kerouac is working out entails a nakedness
to need. Dropping the residual ambition for success that had partially
veiled Kerouac's misogyny, racism, and desire, in *Visions of Cody* Jack
Duluoz lets it all flow — for worse and better.

The openness of the narrator's prejudices seeping from his every
paragraph recalls folk-telling. Folk bards serve just one group's awareness,
so their telling is unchecked by the palimpsested consciousness, the self-
censoring civility to all groups, necessary in modern and mass culture. One
looks long and far to find this openness today in literature because it is
vestigial. It is the first truffle authors and editors root out of manuscripts.
One finds the rooting process wherever literature has absorbed and published folk tales, as when the Grimms and Perrault scrubbed peasant
fetishes and fears for middle-class readers. In America, however, the openness rare in literature was rampant in the early nineteenth-century almanac
tales of peddlers and frontiersmen, in the minstrel skits, and on the vaudeville stage. Just to skim Richard Dorson's anthology of the Davy Crockett
figure, a man the almanacs made legendary much the way Kerouac was
working on Cassady, for instance, is to be thankful that Kerouac's racial
warpings were celebratory and romantic, that his misogyny was related to
mother love, and that he was pacific. Crockett was the most famous of the
Coonskin figures that occupied the American tall-tale tradition in the early

years of the Republic. Kerouac was trying to make Cassady the tallest poplore King in the early years of deliberate speed.

For the same reasons that Sal Paradise turned away from Dean at the end of his novel, and as civility always tries to souse raw spontaneity, most of the best accounts of these poplore resources housebreak them even in discussing their crude vigor.[14] But it is this sub rosa vernacular culture that Kerouac is deliberately reaching for in his sketches. He wanted to realize it, pull it up onto his page, and make it crust Cody the character the way it projected and guarded Cassady the man. That way it would counterbalance the censoring judgment inevitable when the pest culture comes under host scrutiny. These are the reasons Kerouac juggles the rich, mad milk bottles of poplore all throughout *Visions of Cody*.

□   □   □   □   □

. . . moments of self-possessed thought.
—Jack Kerouac, *Visions of Cody*

The sketching was, however, only the beginning of this juggling, kicking off the novel, delivering Jack to Cody and San Francisco, pushing readers toward the transcribed tape section at the novel's center. The taped section seems to have been a main impediment to the publication of *Visions of Cody*, of which New Directions published extracts not until 1960 and which McGraw-Hill posthumously released entirely only in 1972. Yet Kerouac insisted on the tape as the centerpiece in his novel because it hoists poplore right onto the novel's pages. The two men refer to the recorder, perform for and so enter into it, and comment on its representations of them. As early as the middle of July in 1951, Kerouac knew he wanted to use the tape to experiment with narration (Hunt, *Crooked Road* 119). From the beginning of its use, he and Cassady used the device in the way that would become standard in poplore—to provide the feeling of "live" performance, as in the titles "Saturday Night Live," "Live at Budokan," and others running across TV, jazz, and film. But of course Kerouac edited the transcriptions. He may not have altered or revised them, but he broke them where he wanted and dropped material, for example, to emphasize their opening ("I'm an artist") and conclusion ("I HEEEEEEEEEEEEEEEEEERD").

There seems to be an annoying amount of dead matter in this long, problematic section but it is essential to the novel, which takes off from it, imitating and competing with it. What is he competing with? With the latest in popular gadgetry, the tape recorder having been released first for sale just five years before, about the same time Kerouac met Cassady. He is competing also with the fitful rhythms of artificially stimulated conversation (both men were drinking wine and smoking marijuana continually through the taped sessions). Also with combined layers of conversational commentary on performance in other media — Billie Holiday and Lester Young on records, and radio preachers, for example — and with minor subcompetitions in which Cody and Jack would try to imitate the sounds they heard each other make or that they were tuning in on the radio. Also with Cody, Jack, and Evelyn commenting on Jack's transcriptions of their previous night's conversations. So that even with this sometimes elementary and obscene conversation, there are always eddies, undertows, and freshets to their improvised flow that inevitably challenge the simplicities of composed, edited, written prose.

The whole tape section of *Visions of Cody* is Kerouac/Duluoz's attempt to trepan Cody/Cassady into rehashing events to which Jack had not been privy — the same way Lee Strasberg was pulling actors through his Method training. For instance, Jack spends much effort searching through the records on the floor for a specific Billie Holiday recording of "Body and Soul" because that is what Cody/Cassady had once listened to at Bull Lee's (William Burroughs's) house in Texas years before (122, 134). Finding the record, putting it on, and talking through it are all part of Kerouac's Method: "trying desperately to be a great rememberer redeeming life from darkness" (103). Jack Duluoz echoes this, telling Cody he is trying "to evoke the musical sound . . . of the *Texas* that we were talking about last night" (135). This procedure parallels Strasberg's affective memory. All of Jack's questions in the subsequent interchange are pointed to physical objects — where were the washtubs? Where was Lee sitting? Were they inside or outside the window? By such tactics, American actors from Marlon Brando to Eli Wallach were intensifying their responses to one another. By recalling an emotion's physical scene and imaginatively reoccupying it, they would represent the original emotion that much more vividly. This methodical intensity, shared beyond the drama and film, is part of the emphasis on deliberate speed among intellectuals of the era. Kerouac developed his variant on the underlying need in uncanny parallel to Lee Strasberg and Elia Kazan. It was part of his creed of getting it all down.

In accord with *his* creed, however, Cody resists this dredging. He wants to listen for the central voices of black culture — or whatever else he is attending to — for their own sake: "listen to the man play the horn, that's all" (142). It is an important argument to Kerouac, one that he respects but cannot follow because it would inhibit his writing. During the taped section, Cody often talks about a related issue in terms of "rehashing." He says going over an idea or event too many times means "there's no more spontaneous, there's no more . . . first happenings any more . . . no more opening" (145). When you reiterate an event, it ends up disconnected from its context, "just a dry, drab nothing . . . without all the things that are between that build it up into a solid building, like you can't make it out of just bricks" (216). By this insight, Cody connects the Method to that image of the modern infrastructure as "1880 redbrick" (6). Cody is counseling his friend to favor the active spirit of his characters over their physical ambience. Let the mortar of their actions build their form, he implies, rather than reconstruct for them the mercantile and modern redbrick infrastructure that kept them derelict. Don't brick them in, emphasize their "opening."

What then is Kerouac to do? Is his methodical memory a tic making more modern walls of abstracted dry, drab nothing? Yes, unless it is also a new opening, an action that is for itself rather than trying to represent or rehash something or someone else. It must be as much for itself as for Cody. It must be its own action if it is to have the necessary spiritual mortar to make a structure.

Visions of Cody, not "Revisions of Cody," is what he must conjure — if he wants them congenial to Cody's creed. Following the taped section, this is the aesthetic which Kerouac tries to follow, and it is the underlying justification for the sketches of Section One. Therefore, Kerouac did not reach his experimental formal properties by competing with Faulkner, or trying to extend the tricks of Djuna Barnes. Although literary referents stimulate the novel, Kerouac's experiments do not derive from any canon-centered anxiety of influence. Rather, his experimental intensity stems from the sense Cody reinforced of time flying and the need to "report- . . . well and truly" (295) the visions the man aroused in him. Kerouac's work gives good instance of avant-garde techniques primarily progressing from an urge to match poplore practice rather than to pursue evermore esoteric tendencies in late modern tradition.

Kerouac's visions run a gauntlet of types. Cody "Out-Marxes Marx" (390). He is "Robert Burns, a Carlyle a Hero of Hero Worships" (296), and he is also "an empty minded, vacant, bourgeois Irish proletarian would-be-Proust tire recapper — a nothing" (318-19). Jack compares Cody to the Greek and Roman heroes Oedipus (83), Odysseus (257), and Caesar (320), on the one hand, in a casual extension of the modern "mythical method."[15] On the other hand, Kerouac compares him to American legends Franklin Delano Roosevelt (298), W. C. Fields (299), and "maniacal Ahab" (371). In the nexus of these visionary references, Kerouac both digests and extends the modern tools at his disposal.

Take, for instance, Jack's crowing that he and Cody are sons of "great Homeric warriors. . .just like that, Cody and Me, *only American*" (303; emphasis added). The point is not, as one often feels it is in Joyce and Eliot, that contemporary characters are worthy of literature because they unconsciously embody universal patterns still percolating through them despite their own banality. Cody is no cipher that external patterns ennoble willynilly and despite his ignorance of them. Rather, he is valuable because the vital persistence and ambition, which exemplify his tire-recapper hustler roots, liken him quite within his ken to traditional heroes.

Kerouac uses the mythical method of his forebears as secondary reference, but he reverses their hierarchy of celebration. It is as if Homeric warriors are still pertinent because Kerouac discerns their relevance clinging to Cody's present. Cody has his own values, is trying to achieve them, and Jack — his bard — is inscribing them into public awareness.

Moreover, that he and Cody are like Homer's warriors, "only American," indicates a second important difference in Kerouac's achievement. The phrase marks literature's shifted anthropological underpinnings. Sir James Frazer's monumental study of worldwide vegetative ritual, *The Golden Bough* (12 volumes, 1890–1915), had codified the general modern urge to find a universal key to experience — though others, like Freud and Einstein, hoped for a more elegant formula. The great modern texts from *The Golden Bough* to Freud's *The Interpretation of Dreams* (1900), from *Ulysses* to "The Waste Land," all stressed that chaos was pressing and near but that unity was possible. This stress on unity was the great modern achievement, the momentary stay, in Frost's famous words, against confusion (vi). But unity's cost was a blindness to the social coloring of themes. Late modernism lost the intense experience of community that calls literature, as it does all lore and ritual, into being to serve that experience. And of course its best texts, like "The Waste Land" and "Sunday Morning" and *The Sound and the Fury,* are partly about that loss.

Kerouac's "only American" phrase demonstrates his intent to restore that local coloring. Jack is quite clear that he is writing about Cody to celebrate him, not using him to bemoan the feeble and ironic shadow of Odysseus or Caesar. Call it nationalism, if you will, but remember that English was Kerouac's second language, that the closest representation of his thought was French-Canadian patois (which he records and translates in the novel, 362–63). More important than the nationalism is the way Kerouac insisted, even against his friend's argument, on methodically recalling the details correctly — and then taking off on fantastic actions of his own.

These take-offs mark epochal shifts in assumption. Within the novel, though, they protect Cody from the sort of depreciation that occurred at the end of *On the Road*. They embed him in poplore mother-of-pearl. Probably the best example is Jack's vision of Cody, staggering like the Three Stooges, in the "Union [railroad] Station" in Los Angeles (303–6). The public building has "the carven arches of a great white temple of commercial travel in America." Its name, its creamy propriety, and its power signify to these two both the canonical assumptions and the power of America that exclude them. Cody's capers enact how he felt "about his employers and their temple and conventions" (304). Kerouac's own capers enact his feelings toward the literary conventions that he had not yet succeeded in escaping, not even in *On the Road*.

Kerouac asks, Supposing the Three Stooges were real? And then he provides the Stooges plus Cody silently by their side goosing, goofing, and grabassing down the street, offending the conventions of traveling executives at the station. This is Kerouac's rude variant on the journey to Emmaus that Eliot included in "The Waste Land" (ll. 360–66) — just like that, Kerouac might say, "only American" — Cody beside not the disciples but the Stooges, B-movies standing in for the gospel of Luke. This is "the baroque period of the Three Stooges" and Cody is one of them, one with them, his style is theirs:

> I knew that long ago when the mist was raw Cody saw the Three
> Stooges . . . suddenly realizing . . . all the goofs he felt in him were
> justified in the outside world and he had nothing to reproach
> himself for, bonk, boing, crash, skittely boom, pow, slam, bang,
> boom, wham, blam, crack, frap, kerplunk, clatter, clap, blap, fap,
> slapmap, splat, crunch, crowsh, bong, splat, splat, *BONG!* (305–6)

Here then is Cody absorbed into and reprojecting the energy of poplore: "providing scenes for wild vibrating hysterias as great as the hysterias of hipsters at Jazz at the Philharmonics" (305–6). He justifies them and they him. *Visions of Cody* justifies them both. Their lineage lives in Cody, lifting him as it heaves up *Visions of Cody,* which in turn now buttresses them — a congeniality of circumstantial evidence if there ever was one.

Once Kerouac has learned his lessons, as he thoroughly has in the last third of the novel, then the sun falling simply on a pile of Cody's clothes provides Jack with secular immanence: "still-life geometrical images of Cody's poor attempt to stay alive and strong beneath the skies of catastro-

phe" (327). More importantly, such uncharged objects are physical stimulants for their transformation — for their recharging, not their rehashing.
They show how far Kerouac and Cody have come. They contrast with an
early memory of young Cody's. He and his father picked their teeth in the
mirror of a Ford fender, talking about the meaning of words that were
beginning their vogue on theater marquees. The boy asked the man the
meaning of "slay." The answer came back, "'it means you kill somebody
with a spear. . . . Er somethin,' he added a minute later" (327). Here is the
central theme of the novel gently capsulated: the failure of the mentor to
understand and explain the poplore signs, the marquees that matter, to
youths who recognize this loss affectionately but absolutely. To gloss their
lives, they turn to each other rather than to a derelict past. They empower it,
not it them.

All these speeding experiments and deep-form involvements, whatever their interest and value, nevertheless deliver the novel to its end as to
Cassady's ragged exhaustion, the same exhaustion which ended *On the
Road*. Duluoz in *Visions of Cody* analyzes Cody's collapse as his friend's
capitulation to marriage ("he went back to his wife and daughters"), just as
Duluoz busied himself in his own new marriage (395). But there is no direct
talk of his pitifulness, as there had been in *On the Road*. Instead, Kerouac
includes a much more significant comparison of Cody to Lester Young, the
poplore mentor whose rhythms and stance inspired all the Beats. When
Jack asks why their friendship has gone stale, Cody responds, "Makes no
difference, Jack" (388). He is paraphrasing the mood in "You Can Depend
on Me" as Jimmy Rushing sang it to Young's accompaniment with Basie's
band. Rushing's vocal led directly to a famous — and Jack and Cody's
mutually favorite — chorus by Lester Young. Young performs in it his
signature extension of syncopation; he "leaps in," as he plants the feet of his
chorus — a light *bap, bap* — one bar early, under the end of Rushing's last
notes. (That Cody is referring to Young's brilliant chorus is confirmed in
the successive references to the song and its sentiments over the next several
pages, most explicitly on 391 and 395.)[16]

Cody is as Lester Young — doomed like Young to be the one who
patched together the sense of what was modern in his time, and like Young
to be broken by it. This reference is where Kerouac and Duluoz let the
analysis end. It is an appropriate touch for the aims of the novel. Says Jack,
"Lester started it all, the gloomy saintly serious goof who is behind the
history of modern jazz and this generation like Louis [Armstrong] his, Bird
[Charlie Parker] *his* to come and be — his fame and his smoothness as lost as
Maurice Chevalier in a stagedoor poster . . . what doorstanding influence

has Cody gained from this cultural master of his generation?" (392). Among other things, Lester Young was famous for his stance that kept his soft shoes on the floor, his pork pie on pate, and his horn tilted to the horizontal before him. He was a soft man with a laconic legato horn, a sad singular man complexly related to the most sensuous jazz singer of their time, Billie Holiday, whom he accompanied and from whom he received his nickname, Prez (for President). Then she died of drug complications and a string of abusing relations. Young suffered severe racial trauma and a marijuana court martial in the wartime army. When he returned to peacetime playing, younger horn players were receiving the attention.

He fell apart and his horn fell by stages to the vertical. Cody "is connected with Lester, all our horns came down" (393), says Jack. And Cody agrees: "I, much like him, incline, and do fall, I've given up just about like Lester you'd say" (393). With Cody "blank at last" (397), unable even to talk any more, Jack might well have let him go forlorn, as he had in *On the Road.* But not this time. Jack resuscitates the man in the spirit of Lester Young's upbeat chorus, just as in the clichés which Jimmy Rushing sings but which Kerouac had the sense to elicit even while avoiding.

This time the whole structure of the novel was built around buttressing Cody, not betraying him. The protection of the poplore sketching permitted narrating his irresponsibilities frankly, to understand him as "a devil, an old witch, even an old bitch" (298) and like a "Zenzi witch King" (394), even to imagine killing him in hand-to-hand combat, and to describe scenes far too perverse for *On the Road,* such as the "slambanging big sodomies," Jack peeking from the toilet: "He'd treated the boy like a girl!" (358). But the function of these details beyond their eddying of the formal flow, breaking up its thematic focus, is to deepen Cody's complexity, rack up his protean extremes, and crown him finally in the novel's last words the perverse poplore American king:

> Goodbye Cody — your lips in your moments of self-possessed thought and new found responsible goodness are as silent, make as least a noise, and mystify with sense in nature, like the light of an automobile reflecting from the shiny silverpaint of a sidewalk tank this very instant, as silent and all this, as a bird crossing the dawn in search of the mountain cross and the sea beyond the city at the end of the land.
>
> Adios, you who watched the sun go down, at the rail, by my side, smiling —
> Adios, King.

This passage summarizes most of the themes and formal signals the novel has mastered, with tendrils webbing it to the culture of the fifties. The first point to notice is the mutual achievement of sufficiency these two men share. They have come through — not only relative to *On the Road,* but also to the either/or conventional senses of the fifties as despairing of bomb culture or displaying phony brush-a, brush-a Ipana optimism. Like Lolita, the invisible man, Little Richard, and Robert Frank's harried thinkers, these men have used the sustaining poplore of their times to find "moments of self-possessed thought" within the governing attitudes the host culture imposes. It shows in Cody's lips, the locus of his teeming talk. This is the same image Robert Frank used in *The Americans:* the pursed lips at the moment of self-discovery indicating a tough-enough sufficiency.

This quintessential fifties sufficiency is a beginning again, an over-coming of victimization, not the "passivity and fadedness" that Diana Trilling's mothering 1959 account of the Beats attached to them (222).[17] But it is a beginning that knows its pest status, silent and without claim on the host as a bird crossing the land and seeking release, like a narrator (and reader) surviving the book and seeking its surcease. Jack had referred to "flights of doublecrossing black birds" in the previous paragraph and probably had in mind the crossings he and Cody had made recreating themselves, on the move like the blues performers whose pesty presence they admired. Their silence is the survival strategy of a pest within a host — for those who have read this far know that Cody is anything but silent among friends. It is a reminder that the silent interstices of host life are as full of laughing choruses as of the random glints tossing automobile reflections off any sidewalk tank. The quietness is a reminder of the vulnerability of the pest culture, a signification that it must hide away. But the reminder is also that the pest culture quietly penetrates every niche and cranny with its reflective surprises.

Jack sends his friend not into the lonesome cold this time but to God, *a Dios.*[18] At the end of *Visions of Cody,* therefore, Cody is as successful as his narrator. Whatever failures they represent are cyclical. Kerouac's pun has it that these sons, like the sun they watch together at the rail, will rise. Therefore they are smiling. Because they are equally competent in fulfilling their creeds, and have reached real comradeship by acknowledging their differences, Jack can coronate his friend. It is an American, a poploric coronation in the tradition of bestowing titled names to figures who represent community values: Duke Ellington, Count Basie, King Oliver, Nat King Cole, King Curtis, Elvis is King (and Costello's later "King of

America"), Prince of Darkness (an early moniker for Miles Davis), Lady Day.

In the sketching, the tape transcribing, and increasingly in his competitions with the tape, therefore, Kerouac was constantly demonstrating the resource of poplore. For him it was a lode of precomposed experience ready to resuscitate the host fictional tradition. In showing Cody's complex enactments of its energy, and in his own, Kerouac was engaging in a mutual valorization between pest and avant-garde cultures. When he wrote with the conviction and force that concentrated his best passages, usually when he was competing with a B-movie ("Joan Rawshanks in the Fog," 275–90), with a jazz performance, with the immediacy of a tape recorder — then he quilted together an alternative tradition out of the preterite lore underlying modernism.

> *You know what a miracle is . . . another*
> *world's intrusion into this one.*
> —Jesús Arrabal talking to Oedipa Maas, in
> Thomas Pynchon's *The Crying of Lot 49*

In the fifties, juggling poplore's artifacts substituted for the absent, embarrassing, or insufficient mentor. Such juggling maneuvered to compensate for and overcome the lonely, empty life which failing fathers bequeathed. Participating in the juggling of poplore linked the sons and daughters in distinct sibling gestures. These incorporations of poplore came at the moment the electronic media were discovering their increased power to tie together even distant isolates and their need for new content to broadcast. These factors complemented each other to create a sense sufficient to set off deliberately speeding culture from the high modernism between the wars.

Epochs establish a new lingua franca the way Latin linked earlier regional, national, and class cultures with a common language and a set of rituals, the way "literariness" provided a common set of signs to set apart elite culture and bind its participants. So too did the milk bottle jugglers aggressively dominating the arts in the fifties set up their own standards, signs and rites, their own traditions and features that could link participants across cultures. Ellison's invisible man in his introverted hole, believing he was existentially alone even as he rediscovered his folk community, existed on one side of this new possibility. The extroverted Beat brotherhood, convening spur-of-the-moment parties from the left to the right coasts, confidently participated in a counter community of their own making. They walked just the other side of the possibility. The Beats were more aware of the networking capacity of radio, more attuned to the media and to continual coast-to-coast travel, able to find sustaining groups in San Francisco, New York, Denver, New Orleans, and Mexico.

Loneliness was one instigating common denominator. Finding a lore group to ease their loneliness was another. Ellison's youth acknowledged the continuation of his ethnic folklore in the city as he became a man. Kerouac turned thirty and reached his artistic maturity during the writing of *Visions of Cody*—recognizing, that is, the armoring use of poplore. Characteristically mocking his own serious attraction to this idea fifteen years later, Thomas Pynchon wrote many underground cults into *The Crying of Lot 49*. One of these cults called itself "a society of isolates" (85) — no meetings, nothing face to face, but signs in common, congeniality, and mutual aid: "You get a phone number, an answering service you can call. Nobody knows anybody else's name; just the number in case *it* gets so bad you can't handle *it* alone." In Pynchon's case, "it," just like pop songs warn, is unrequited love: "That's the worst addiction of all" (83). In the culture of deliberate speed, the media make impersonal connection especially possible. That way, people who loathe meetings can still be members of groups they never see.

The mass society Pynchon shows in his novels is so crazed with underground collectivities that there are not enough signs to go around, memberships tangle like spaghetti, and groups share the same tokens. Citizens so overcompensate for their loneliness that their multiple associations become more problematic than their instigating solitude. Far from there being no loric life in the mass society, according to Pynchon, lore so besieges folks in the trenches, who so oversubscribe to its competing messages, that the divisive loyalties tear them up like confetti. Disk jockeys come on like a "walking assembly of man" (104). Housewives who thought they could contain life in Tupperware taxonomy discover legacies and fermenting connections that continually lift their lids and spoil their seals. And psychiatrists who tried to believe in modern rationalizations of the happy mass future blow their tops most dramatically of all. "Freud's vision of the future" argues one as he fumes over the edge, "had no Buchenwalds in it. Buchenwald, according to Freud, once the light was let in, would become a soccer field, fat children would learn flower-arranging and solfeggio in the strangling rooms. At Auschwitz the ovens would be converted over to petits fours and wedding cakes, and the V-2 missiles to public housing for the elves. I tried to believe it all. I slept three hours a night trying not to dream, and spent the other 21 at the forcible acquisition of faith. And yet my penance hasn't been enough. They've come like angels of death to get me, despite all I tried to do" (102).

The point here, as in Kerouac and Ginsberg, as in Jackson Pollock and Miles Davis, as in Rauschenberg and Johns, as in Joseph Heller and Elvis Costello, is always the irrepressibility of the repressed. The theory of its disappearance was a modern dream. The fact of the repressed's persistence has therefore become a major theme for subsequent culture. It is a way for writers, muted trumpet players, and painters to represent their own status.

In *The Crying of Lot 49* the sign for the society of isolates is a muted post horn. For Pynchon the muted horn is a symbol of a culture struggling through opposition to announce itself, to surpass its suppression, just the way Jack in *Visions of Cody* thought "everything's waiting for me to understand it" (88), "it seems to want to tell something intelligible to me" (10). Can anyone say what the muted trumpet meant for Miles Davis, who played it persistently in the mid-fifties, even on up-tempo tunes when to stick with it surely was an impediment? Perhaps it stood for something abstract as it would later for Pynchon. Was it a way for Davis to implicate at once both the constraint and the openness he was yoking in the fifties wake of Charlie Parker?

Davis changed his life as well as his music in the mid-fifties. He began both again. Davis's addiction to heroin had reached infamous status by late 1953, when he was pimping, stealing friends' goods and money, nodding through solos, and collapsing curbside — a clichéd vegetable of dependency (Chambers 159–79). But during the winter of 1953–54 he regained control of his life by locking himself in the East St. Louis bedroom of his childhood, and sweating out his addiction. After a reentry recoupment in Detroit, Davis returned to New York able to sustain concentration on the changes to emerge in his music commencing that summer of 1954, and continuing for the next five years.

By the end of the decade, with *Kind of Blue* (1959), Davis in one blow consolidated avant-garde dissatisfaction with the elements of song form, which were still vestigial after bebop's assault on them, and he popularized alternative structures. Instead of prescribed chord changes at prescribed bar intervals, *Kind of Blue* used modal structures. Davis was also interested in free group improvising on this record, as Bill Evans's liner notes emphasize. Davis had been heading toward this freedom for five years. In the summer of 1954, recording "Oleo" (by Sonny Rollins), Davis began to try soloing without piano accompaniment.

Like Gerry Mulligan, who first organized his West Coast quartet without a piano in 1952, Davis wanted a wider panoply of choices than was available when a keyboard offered harmonies behind him. He would sometimes silence the piano during the next several years working with Horace Silver, then Thelonious Monk, Red Garland, and on to Herbie Hancock. That this was a stubborn intention comes clear in Davis's famous argument with Monk while recording the "Bag's Groove" takes on Christmas Eve, 1954. Davis insisted on going it alone; Monk bristled at depreciation of his role. This squabble over sound control continued between Davis and all his pianists, in whom he favored extreme reticence and tact (the virtues he heard in Ahmad Jamal and Bill Evans). Meanwhile, however, serious disagreement among these players has not surfaced about the provenance of their music. None of Davis's sidemen registered dissatisfaction with the leader's important return, like so many advanced fifties artists in every form, to the sustenance of poplore.

Davis was fully cognizant of working poplore into his art, rather than stealing from and denying popular culture, as the modern boppers had done. Let Parker stand in here as the quintessential jazz modernist, performing art for art's sake — a plausible enough hypothesis when he was with Savoy and Dial, 1944–47. As much as ever, Parker was then in control of his music. How did he control it? He cued his reflexive composition off pop tunes, using their chord changes but annihilating their surface sound. To his cult audience, the way Bird metamorphosed melodies and rendered standard structures unrecognizable was a brand of superiority that lifted bop above its smoky context of clubs and sweet tunes. In his original melodies, they say, Parker was responding to internal and autonomous cues in the music, not representing an exterior reality. They say his music was not subservient to an outside world it was trying to represent, but pursuing lines of pure musical development.

Actually, there is no such thing as pure art. Parker's abstract flights represented an attitude if not an object. But because many in his crowd appreciated him as a pure artist, and tried to understand him in that way, he stood during his moment in relative contrast to Davis's path. Thinking his music was autonomous, Parker had few titles for his compositions, which were numbers to him and to the Dial studio people: "Klactoveesedstene" was D-1112, for instance.

Thus, although cognoscenti were aware of the transformations on poplore material, their delusion was of a Yeatsian "out of nowhere" purity. "Usually, I dreamed up some kind of a title," reports Russell who was then his producer, "when it was time to release the record" (252). Bird's practice was much the same as Jackson Pollock's, who for an interval in 1948 resorted to exhibiting his paintings with numbers for titles, and who was too obsessed with painting and signing his works to name them at any time. That task fell to his wife Lee Krasner, or to friends, although Pollock himself later said that the color of an eggplant in his garden or his fascination with night sounds or creepycrawlies in the grass — or the energy in jazz itself — was what he was painting (Potter 141; du Plessix and Gray 51). No more than Parker was a pure musician was Pollock a pure painter. But Pollock's crowd also received him that way at the time — see any of Greenberg's reviews of his exhibits[19] — and relative to, say, Rauschenberg's goat constructs, Johns's ale cans, and Warhol's multiple paintings of his patroness, Pollock seemed purist.

Unlike Parker and Pollock in the late forties — who used but sublimated their relations with lore — the fifties generation artists visibly or audibly affirmed their connection to poplore. If Miles Davis changed titles, for instance, it was mainly those of his own compositions so that he could rerecord them separately, as with "Weirdo" (United Artists UAS 9952), "Walkin" (Prestige 7608), and "Sid's Ahead" (Columbia CL 1193). When he played George Gershwin *(Porgy and Bess),* Cole Porter ("All of You"), Irving Berlin ("How Deep Is the Ocean?"), or Jerome Kern ("Yesterdays"), he always said so, insisting on the connection even when he had changed the songs until they occupied none of their original form and only slipped in allusions to their original melodies.

Davis's music was coming together strongly in 1954, with "Four" and "Walkin'" both recorded in the spring and "Bag's Groove," "Bemsha Swing," and "The Man I Love" that winter. But it was in mid-1955 that he put together the basis of his first steady quartet, appeared at that summer's Newport Festival playing a moving solo on Monk's "'Round Midnight," and incited the critical buzz that has since waxed and waned, but never abated, except for his six years of retirement between 1975 and 1981. A month before Newport, Davis went into the studio for Prestige and cut four tunes with the men who would remain with him for years. To Philly Joe Jones, who had been barnstorming with Davis and anchoring his pickup groups, he added pianist Red Garland, a Southwesterner from Dallas (though a few years older than Ornette Coleman) with a tendency to chord sweetly with his left hand, and bassist Oscar Pettiford. These four became a quintet when he added John Coltrane and replaced Pettiford with twenty-year-old Paul Chambers before the next Prestige session.

The first session came out right after Newport, when critics were watching for Davis's new work. Its original title was *The Musings of Miles*

(Prestige P7007), later appropriately renamed *The Beginning*.[20] What's important about these records is that the spare, emotional music reconciled the avant-garde and funk developments that were ongoing and separate through the fifties. Davis's trumpet is lucid, piercing but generally soft. He phrases in mixtures of largely clipped, pure notes resting on a spicing of long notes that he suddenly kinks. Davis's sound is limpid. He runs the gamut on the blues "Green Haze"—from muted to crowing, sometimes breathy. Davis is seeking a voicing that will establish a place for his new fusion in the developing jazz scene, and for black music in the mainstream. He achieved it by choosing sidemen who would amplify the ambiguous aspects of his own personality—divisions in himself that matched those in jazz tradition. By emphasizing these parts and shoving them together in the same group, pieces, performances, and albums, Davis used each to call attention to and correct the other. It was an important strategy that tucked in popular romanticism with avant-garde astringency.

Davis started both sides of his next record with tunes Ahmad Jamal had recorded in 1952, "Will You Still Be Mine?" and "A Gal in Calico" (Epic LN 3631). Especially with this last song, although perhaps Davis neither knew nor cared, he was participating in one of the earliest strategies of avant-garde art. Remarking the posturing dress, style, and attention of nightclub-goers reaching for fulfillment beyond their capacities is exactly the same strategy that Edouard Manet painted in the bars and cafés of Paris at the onset of high modernism. The strategy was to engage and place the congenial audience whose lore occasioned the art—those who sold the cloth by day and touchingly dressed in it by night.

Here is T. J. Clark on café-concert habitués in late nineteenth-century Paris:

> The most effective code name for these unfortunates—it appears repeatedly from the 1860s on—was the simple metonymy *calicot.* They were what they sold, the metonymy said, for all their wish to be something better; the word came into widespread use around the time that shopworkers were forming a union and going on strike, and its nearest equivalents in English are "draper's assistant" or "counter-jumper"—the latter perhaps to be preferred for its period flavour and less than affectionate snobbery. ("I don't want to see my daughter spinning round a public assembly room in the arms of any counter-jumper," as the dictionary quotes Miss Braddon in 1880.) (214)

Beyond its connection to Hollywood's frontier West, where cowboys and cowgirls dressed in such cheap cotton, *calico* in American English had the same associations explicit in France and implicit in England. Webster's Second gives a jocose usage of the term to mean "a woman; a girl; womankind," a definition which Wentworth and Flexner's *Dictionary of American Slang* fulfills with the signification of "a flirtation; a love affair." Ab Snopes's daughters are dressed in calico in "Barn Burning" (1938), William Faulkner's study of class struggle in the rural South. James T. Farrell's collection of short stories *Calico Shoes* (1934) shows the term still in use among whites on the streets of American cities in this century. Duke Ellington demonstrates the idea in use among blacks, in July 1941, with his recording of "The Brown-Skin Gal (In the Calico Gown)" — interesting carnival lyrics by trumpeter Paul Webster (RCA 5659-2-RB). Therefore, the persistence of the *calicot* concept displays more than a remnant of the same social conditions from the last half of the nineteenth century still extant in the twentieth.

Within this persistence, the history of "A Gal in Calico" is a thicket in itself. Arthur Schwartz wrote it in 1934 (with different lyrics by Howard Dietz) for the radio series, *The Gibson Family*. He then copyrighted it (with even more banal lyrics by Leo Robin), May 1946, for a remake of the 1929 junk Hollywood musical *The Time, the Place, and the Girl*. The song proved sufficiently popular for both Bing Crosby and Tony Martin to cover even before Jamal and Davis did.

These instances of the *calicot* concept illustrate how subliminal congeniality persists in poplore. It perseveres in codes that are both harmless and implicitly charged. These codes are easy to ignore yet ready, too, for a new calico chorus to decipher and reinvest with meaning. Men like Manet, Ellington, and Davis use and reactivate this perseverance in their art. So do men like Schwartz and Robin, Crosby and Martin. They touch and retouch it differently, but however they use it, they keep it cycling. The best of them allow the miraculous intrusion of another, riper world into the harmless, recreational one.

In between the Ellingtons and Crosbys exist performers like Ahmad Jamal. Martin Williams has said that at times "Jamal's real instrument is not the piano at all, but his audience" (*Melody* 181). Jamal's consideration of audience emotion is manipulative, or congenial, as you wish, but it lingers nevertheless in the Davis quartet's rendering. The impressive part of Davis's recording of "A Gal in Calico" is the way he and Garland emphasize during Davis's solo the tension on which the young *calicot* thrives. Davis's trumpet and Garland's piano complement each other, broadening their response.

Garland's solemnity in this instance undercuts Davis's willfully buoyant surface insistence. (The two usually worked the other way, Davis tersely spanking Garland's romance.) These ambiguous poles represent sympathetically the eager and unacknowledged stress of any gal or guy in calico. Neither the song nor the sympathy would be complete without either the sentiment or the seriousness.

Accumulated enthusiasts in calico are the avant-garde's public. Hardly ideal, this is nevertheless the root condition. *Calicots* encourage the music (or the painting, the writing), while they pose and strive for completion at night that their day jobs do not supply. This dependency between unfulfilling life and cultural satisfaction has held since the dawn of religion and tales; it existed in the café-theaters of Paris in the 1880s; it crops up in the jazz clubs and cocktail lounges of fifties cities in America. Davis's sentimentality simply acknowledges these facts. His music responds to and documents the tenuous support for the uncurated arts. They depend on such shifting and green publics. Material differences in the society and the turning lore cycle generate and combine these enthusiasts into publics who cannot long live the life, cannot survive the tension and the indeterminacy. So they constantly give way to other short-term publics to whom artists must each in turn extend sympathy and whatever snippets of their tradition they can contribute before the public dissolves, their calico skirts, shirts, and shoes bequeathed like their energy and club-going idealism to the next lot. The problem is not an absence of rigor or an edifying past, but the speedy turnover of audiences who ride by the tableaus offered them so quickly that they too seldom have time to extend or elaborate their meanings.

Audiences in general care nothing for these historical conditions which obsess performers and their critics. Indeed, one of the most vexing issues in cultural study is wonder at what makes individuals leap across from relatively passive participation in a public to active involvement with the edifying tableaus of any art, any rich lore. What turns a member of a public into a fan, a fan into a performer or critic who transmits the lore? There is a quick illustration of this gap in *The Crying of Lot 49*. Stumbling into a bar filled with participants in the cult-jammed underground she has begun to suspect props up contemporary history, Oedipa Maas confesses her budding connections to a man wearing a lapel pin of the muted horn. He says: "'I never thought there was a history to it.' 'I think of nothing but,' said Oedipa" (82).

Oedipa has proceeded from passive innocent to involved participant asking the tough questions of performers in the world. She suspects something of the tradition and puts its performers on the spot. You would not call her a laughing chorus — she is too surprised and perplexed for that. But she queries their conditions. She is a solemn chorus. In her way, she too is acting on the lore that seems to her a miraculous intrusion. She, too, is recoding impulses and passing them on. Her drama is in finding meaning for the clusters of exhausted but still pregnable signs others bandy so carelessly.

For others the problem is not so much in finding these secret signs, kernels, and tokens as in delivering their structure. Like Jack Kerouac, Miles Davis used the history and attitude carried in the coruscating flashes of aggressionless assertion Lester Young practiced. Young's intelligence came down to Davis via Charlie Parker, who had himself digested Young's effect in Kansas City and reissued it in the pastiche flurries he sprayed where others played discrete notes.[21] Working this tradition, Davis infused his own playing with the logical connections that Young had compressed into Basie's choruses and that Parker had pulled out into his brilliant three-minute miniatures. On those sessions, Davis was a sideman. But when he became a leader, Davis drew out the structure further and further.

The kernels of Davis's late-fifties compositions are organically delicate, an idea of melody, a hint of a relationship coded, say, in the sound of his muted horn whispering a centimeter from the mike's ear. He always had this attention to sound, even when in Parker's shadow he was aiming less to compose or arrange, much less beat the living legend, but simply trying to hang tight after the master's solo. His development through the fifties shows him learning to protect this kernel of himself. It is much the same story Kerouac played out between *On the Road* and *Visions of Cody*. Just as Kerouac had to learn to embed Cody's vulnerability in poplore's armature, so too did Davis have to learn how to use and structure his sound in relation to the congenial resources of deliberately speeding culture.

At barely 21, Davis could not hope to equal Parker's dexterous flights but he could and did learn from Bird's adaptation of the blues-toned waver, adding tones that imply a higher note beyond the chord as the sound settles to its place, flourishing like a mockingbird alighting on a wire. It is all there on the minute and a quarter of solo that Davis pulls off after Parker's legendary two minutes on "Embraceable You."[22] It is there over and over in these early sessions, always most noticeable on the ballads, where Davis's protracted notes avoid vibrato but underscore that blues indeterminacy, thus compensating for and complementing in his own cunning way Parker's flurried demisemiquavers. Davis's notes project a man struggling to achieve his own sonority — his clatter and veering angst, his metallic hiss, brakes grabbing and rolling stock accelerating behind the repartee, all in a night's work, nothing to get hot about. Don't show or shout pain; admit it and clip it. Thus Davis threaded through the opening between his schematic intelligence and his developing fluency on the horn, standing nightly next to the fastest fingers and surest improviser in jazz. His was a kernel of precariousness out on its own.

As in "Weirdo" (recorded 6 March 1954, then repeated a month later as "Walkin'" and four years later as "Sid's Ahead"), the practice was to harry this precariousness until it took on viable life—then protect it. Think of Davis as scarifying the kernel of his sound to make it sprout, then improvising a precisely shaped cloche to house it. Here he is very like Kerouac, whose sketches were as tender as Davis's sonority. As the recording format opened up for Davis, and as Kerouac abandoned belief that his work would be published, so turned himself loose to write what he imagined, Davis's music and Kerouac's prose both became architectural from within. They held together by connecting internal tensions rather than fulfilling external expectations.

Here's Jack Duluoz, in *Visions of Cody,* admiring Davis's structuring:

> And meanwhile Miles Davis, like the sun; or the sun, like Miles
> Davis, blows on with his raw little horn; the prettiest trumpet tone
> since Hackett and McPartland and at the same time, to flash some
> of its fine raw sound, some wild abstract new ideas developed
> around a growing theme that started off like a tree and became a
> structure of iron on which tremendous phrases can be strung and
> hung and long pauses goofed, kicked along, whaled, touched with
> hidden and active meanings; to come in, then, like a sweet tenor
> and blow the superfinest, is mowd enow [*sic,* for "more den enuff"].
> I love Miles Davis because, send in your penny postcard [imitating
> Symphony Sid, the radio jazz deejay]. (323–24)

Duluoz summarizes significant aspects of Davis's style here, but more important is how the passage also webs Kerouac's own prose with the music. Acutely linking Davis's raw, pretty tone to Lester Young's "sweet tenor," Kerouac was also showing his own values. Like their music, his prose grew from riffs—penny postcard perceptions anyone might mail—into unusual iron structure, sufficiently strong to goof on, more than enough to protect the jelly of developing insights.

□ □ □ □ □

. . .get on with it, keep moving, keep in,
speed, the nerves, their speed, the perceptions,
theirs, the acts, the split second acts, the
whole business, keep it moving as fast as you
can, citizen. . .fast, there's the dogma.
— Charles Olson, "Projective Verse"

Where did goofing or improvisation come from? As the central feature of all the Afro-American musics, of course, it has been continually belittled. But improvisation was also active in many of the European avant-garde movements of the century — in the automatic writing that ran from Yeats through the Surrealists, in Constantin Stanislavski's System for the Moscow Art Theater (which became Strasberg's Method), in Marcel Duchamp's dada objects — his ready-made urinal fountain, the bicycle wheel sculpture, the mustachioed Mona Lisa — and in the principled incompleteness of such pieces as his large glass, "The Bride Stripped Bare by Her Bachelors, Even." Important as these early examples of spontaneous energy have proven to be in hindsight, no one would claim that improvisation was a central tenet of mainstream art in the first quarter of the century. Even as a cardinal feature of surrealism, improvisation seemed a sport confined to the hothouse of the avant-garde, to cotton-picking worksongs, and to barroom ribaldry. It did not occupy the middle, did not blanket all the scenes of art. By the mid-fifties, however, improvisation became a linchpin in North American art, and is still a major criterion in the contemporary aesthetic, high and low. Improvisation on the models of poplore is the link making possible one aesthetic for both minority and majority culture.

By the fifties, improvisatory principles were becoming codified. An example is Charles Olson's manifesto "Projective Verse" (1950), where the poet stressed listening to himself "where breath has its beginnings, where drama has to come from, where, the coincidence is, all act springs" (158). Poets attending to the spring of their own voices, Olson thought, would not heed the "verse that print bred." They would take up speed deliberately, remembering that "ONE PERCEPTION MUST IMMEDIATELY AND DIRECTLY LEAD TO A FURTHER PERCEPTION" — thus causing the form of the poem to come out of its own impetus, rather than using form as a Procrustean bed to hack and rack momentum. Olson's creed underwrote the era: "fast, there's the dogma" (149).

One critic who independently noticed this new dogma was Harold Rosenberg. In "The Parable of American Painting" (1955), Rosenberg attempted to decode and account for deliberate speed in the then-recent New York School of painting. He argued Americans have backed steadily away from style into something he called "Coonskinism"—"the search for the principle that applies, even if it applies only once. For it, each situation has its own exclusive key" (19). The great American Coonskinners are, he wrote, "Copley, Audubon, Eakins, Ryder, Homer, Marin, Stuart Davis, de Kooning" (20). And with de Kooning, during World War II, because Europe was sending over no new styles, "American artists became willing to take a chance on unStyle or antiStyle. Statements in interviews and catalogues emphasized the creative bearing of such elements of creation as the mistake, the accident, the spontaneous, the incomplete, the absent" (21). He was describing improvisation in rawhide terms, and Coonskinism conscious of itself is deliberate speed.

The problem with Coonskinism is hardly that Rosenberg made fun of improvised art, saying it "studied manoeuvers among squirrels and grizzly bears" (18). The problem is rather his calling it "unStyle or antiStyle" as if it merely or even significantly reacted against European style, or, worse, had no tradition, was noise. Neither is the case. The New York School, or Abstract Expressionism as it came to be called, was hardly against Europe. And because it has a distinct tradition, thus its own logic, it is not noise. It is homegrown and deeply within a tradition which the term Coonskinism aptly catches. As Rosenberg's list correctly shows, Coonskin style originated earlier than high modernism. It has its antecedents in the poplore of the land.

In that way, Coonskinism predates the remarks by Melville and Whitman that Rosenberg noted even while insisting Coonskinism has no tradition and is merely a series of one-off potshots. To the contrary, Coonskinism is profoundly part of America's lore going back to the minstrel shows and Yankee legends and Mike Fink tall tales of the early nineteenth century. In short, there *is* a usable past—"a style outside of art," in Rosenberg's excellent phrase—to which art may connect. It existed long before Van Wyck Brooks called for its invention in an article in *The Dial* (11 April 1918) and Constance Rourke wrote *American Humor* (1931) to prove it.

There is, moreover, a usable present composed of the anxieties and fears clustering around such promptings as the period's material differences occasioned. The bomb and atomic power, the violence surrounding the civil rights movement, the barrage of information that the consumer electronics revolution ushered in—all these created a distinctive present.

The fifties generated a usable and recognizable cluster of impulses calling up yet again the Coonskin creed of finding the one appropriate, perhaps homemade, surely improvised solution. The tradition of one-offs continued. Moreover, the wide references to Crockett and Coonskinism ten years after the war demonstrated that the subliminal processes of lore production had been busy all along. They had been turning anxieties into embryo practices that artists in each field could nurture into sturdy shapes able to stand recognizably on their own.

This is all particularly relevant to the case of Jackson Pollock, because the history of his reception tells a good deal about his achievement. Initially receiving him as "Jack the Dripper," the popular press has not much cared to alter its belittlement since the fifties. Dealing with that hostility, his advocates in the quarterlies and art press divided in their accounts of his radical effect. One camp that most notably included Harold Rosenberg argued in effect that he was an American existential hero, a man of action out of the West, quite in the mode of Kerouac's Cody Pomeray (whose first name is Pollock's birthplace in Wyoming). Another camp soon gained more favor because its adherents substantiated Pollock's intelligence and the logic of his painting. Clement Greenberg, then Michael Fried, William Rubin, and Elizabeth Frank have been adamant that Pollock counted because he solved formal problems rooted in the mainline European tradition. These problems included point of view, the crisis of the easel painting, three-dimensional representation inhabiting painting's two-dimensional plane, and the blurring between subject and ground. But this bright accounting for Pollock has begun to fade after some twenty years in the sun.

It fades because its formalist grammar is quick and fecund as a rabbit but hardly a longhaul carrier. Pollock's brilliance depended not alone on the fix he made in painting's problems but also on his involvement with the conundrums of his era. The formal explanation described his painting's surfaces but little of the social power Pollock's paintings revealed and aroused. Like the withdrawn aesthetics of the high modern forms which generated it, the formalist commentary on Pollock's work pointedly ignores the social conditions which Rosenberg's action theory originally stated too bluntly and humorously, too vaguely.

As Pollock's effect on the art world continually grows, its impact clearly extends well beyond the Eurocentered problems Greenberg and company admitted as solely significant. Those American problems and traditions which they belittled have held their ground not only in his work, but also in the events of the art world after him, in Jasper Johns and

Rauschenberg, in all the subsequent New York and Los Angeles generations.[23] Critics can discuss them in formal terms, and should, but their social dimensions also remain viable and connect more immediately to significance and meaning—aspects which formal discussion too often demotes.

One example of this formal exclusiveness appears in the highly touted introduction to Michael Fried's catalogue for *Three American Painters: Kenneth Noland, Jules Olitski, Frank Stella* (1965). After elaborating Greenberg's concept of the retreat from society in modern art (though neglecting to mention anything about the "umbilical chord of gold") Fried cartoons the assumptions justifying formal criticism of the New York School: "Only the most general statements . . . may be made about the relation between modernist painting and modern society. In a sense, modernist art in this century finished what society in the nineteenth century began: the alienation of the artist from the general preoccupations of the culture in which he is embedded, and the prizing loose of art itself from the concerns, aims and ideals of that culture" (7).

Fried's remarks are a capsule expression of the central modernist fallacy, which was helpful as a driving and motivating creed, but true mainly on superficial and misleading levels. The modern artist remains as tightly tied to the preoccupations of a congenial lore group as ever any shaman to tribe, artist to patrons. Both the artist and the lore group remain involved with the preoccupations of the larger culture embedding them, and of course there is plenty to discuss about that relationship. Because social connections are not necessarily obvious when artists feel general alienation, descriptions of a new art's formal properties or startling technique may be more readily apparent. It is understandable, therefore, that critics needed to describe Pollock's line and its configurative complexities, his experiments with ground and color. They needed to validate his dripping and pouring technique, his rebounding relationship to the canvas edge, and so on—especially in the teeth of the Yahoo derision coming Pollock's way in the late forties, early fifties. But it is diversionary at the very least to insist that such preliminary discussion either exhausted the topic or staunched the continuing duty to describe painting's complex fit to its era. Despite Fried's claim, Pollock's radical technique did not prize his art loose from the aims or ideals of contemporary culture. Inarticulate and painfully reserved as he was, Pollock knew differently, knew just the opposite, and said so in 1950:

> The modern painter cannot express this age, the airplane, the atom bomb, the radio, in the old forms of the Renaissance or of any other

past culture. Each age finds its own technique. (O'Connor and Thaw 249)

No more than Little Richard was Jackson Pollock distinct from his era. Nor did either ever claim he was. It was their followers who explained Penniman and Pollock as somehow distinct. To the contrary, Pollock's and Penniman's profound absorption of their time enabled their achievements. Of course they were alienated from the large turnpikes American macrosociety was bumbling down. But their work followed paths more meandering and exploratory, less governed by billboards, more in touch with local resources and private feelings subsisting amidst the gross facts.

Although Pollock had done an "allover" painting as early as 1937 in New York, it was not until he moved to Springs on Long Island for the winter of 1945 that he began to paint a meaningful *series* of paintings that encountered the allover idea in consequential ways. This series was the *Accabonac Creek* and *Sounds in the Grass* paintings that he displayed in early 1947. For all their flattening of the field, principled blurring of focus, and attack on easel painting, these paintings also embody a community's feelings about at least as many living issues. For example, as de Kooning's art also did, Pollock's painting distinctively changed color when he moved from Manhattan to the Island. Greenberg noted this in Pollock's work at the time and described it without attributing meaning. Pollock, he said, "has now largely abandoned his customary heavy black-and-whitish or gun-metal chiaroscuro for the higher scales, for alizarins, for cream-whites, cerulean blues, pinks, and sharp greens" (*Essays* 2:124). Had Greenberg wanted to admit any aformal impulse, he might have said that Pollock's newly rural paintings showed the drab-bright, shimmering colors of potato farming by the sea.

Pollock was painting a distinctive Long Island light which his new uses were taking over and refracting, breaking down. Pollock addressed postwar fragmentation of recognizable reality, as well as its opposite: persistence of fundamental principles (shapes, feelings, ideas) against the odds. The persistence shows not only in the stubborn shapes of his line but also in his fascination with the sounds and creepies to which Lee Krasner alluded when she titled the canvases. It is not so much that he was painting local life as a folk artist might have, as that the life of his locale and the stress of those years was a presence that vitalized, quirked, his new work.

It *is* possible to speak of representation in the case of such postwar performances even though they are inarticulate by prewar, modern, criteria. But one must broaden the means and vocabulary of representation.

One must adjust "representation" to mean not illustration but parallel exemplification. The hysteria in "Tutti Frutti," the mannered hiccupping in rockabilly songs, the allover rhythms of Pollock's paintings are not pictures of something but are themselves something lyrical. They exemplify reality made hysterical, driven to gasp and drip. They perform the energy underlying the billboards—the sounds in the grass by the roadside, say, that the official voices were ignoring as they went their public ways. Pollock said as much in his notebook when he reminded himself of what he was trying to put on his canvas: "Experience of our age in terms of painting—not an illustration of—(but *the equivalent*)" (O'Connor and Thaw 253). Pollock sought equivalent form.

He never proceeded easily through his search, nor did he finish it; *Search* is the title of the last painting he did, in 1955. His first significant stage was an involvement with totems and ritual (for example, *The Guardians of the Secret* and *The She-Wolf*, both 1943, the latter the first of his paintings acquired by the Museum of Modern Art). In these paintings, private references and noisy, apparently chaotic, gestures already besiege the looming charisma of the governing totems. Beset totems persist throughout his career. They loom less, even shrink to signature squiggles under the pressure after a while, but they hold on in his work, and he holds on to them. Although he is famous for his late-middle period of allover dripped or poured paintings, 1946–1950, in fact there are recognizable shapes or gestures—elbows, curves, circles, lines, signature "loops and snarls" (Fried 13)—even there. His career snags on the issue of motifs and figures, never passing by them entirely.

When at the end of this phase he seemed to have pushed entirely past figures separable from a ground, then he proceeded sometimes to overlay shapes onto the canvas (*White Cockatoo* and *Wooden Horse*, 1948), and to remove shapes from it (*Cut-Out* and *Out of the Web*, both 1949). The last painting in this period is the one Hans Namuth filmed him painting on glass—*Number 29, 1950*. It is dramatically suspended in the air, evidently groundless, rather more like Miles Davis's suspended solos, like Pynchon's favored "excluded middles" (*Crying* 136), than like the modern, static, and puzzling suspensions of Duchamp's "Large Glass" (1915–23). Pollock, Davis, and Pynchon give equivalences for a fluid place in which swim its elements (rather than Duchamp's still-coherent shapes).

Deliberately speeding art shows a difficult interface in which figures both fade and persist. Within individual artworks and careers, there is the fifties-typical problem of pattern within apparent chaos, the same problem that pushed photographer Robert Frank, novelist Jack Kerouac, mathematician Benoit Mandelbrot, and saxophonists from Ornette Coleman to John Coltrane. The appearance of this issue not only throughout Pollock's painting but also in photography, literature, music, and science indicates a root social dimension beneath formal tinkering. Pollock and company were enacting social anxieties of pest cultures vis-à-vis a besieging host, lonely individuals anxiously confronting crowds, scientists and others concerned to understand hardy anomaly, and the capacity to survive doom.

In describing the perception that became the science of Chaos, James Gleick said scientists noticed "mingled regions of periodicity and chaos" (230), periodicity being that which figured something, chaos that which did not. This mingled reality is Pollock's. It is what he noticed and, in enacting, made his paintings represent. When *Time* attacked his work as "chaos" (20 November 1950), Pollock dispatched an angry telegram that started with "NO CHAOS, DAMN IT." He meant any accident in his work was something that he absorbed and made part of the design, the way chess players replot their planned game as their opponents move unexpectedly. Pollock included detritus — glass shards, sand, cigarette butts and ash — in the texture of his painting precisely in service of this end. Incorporated trash in his work is an example of overcoming accident, accepting and coping with chaos, as well as recycling the wasted material from the previous order, as well as using local material that would imply the feel of its time and place, of the painting's making.

One of the best descriptions of Pollock's working process came in the first monograph on him, by Frank O'Hara, the poet and a curator at the Museum of Modern Art. O'Hara limits application of Rosenberg's "Action Painter" to those very few who have achieved "spiritual clarity": "This is not a mystical state," he argues, in the process defining improvisation in both Method acting and jazz, as well as Pollock's sort of action painting and O'Hara's own snapshot poems of emotion and popular flotsam:

> This is not a mystical state but the accumulation of decisions along the way and the eradication of conflicting beliefs toward the total engagement of the spirit in the expression of meaning. So difficult is the attainment that, when the state has finally been reached, it seems that the artist has reached a limitless space of air and light in which the spirit can act freely and with unpremeditated knowledge. His action is immediately art, not through will, not through esthetic posture, but through a singleness of purpose which is the result of all the rejected qualifications and found convictions forced upon him by his strange ascent. (21–22)

In jazz argot, Pollock could improvise because he had spent his time woodshedding.

One might wish to substitute something like *shrewd decisiveness* for O'Hara's "spiritual clarity," and perhaps point out that despite the dance of composition that Hans Namuth memorably photographed Pollock performing around his canvases and the one glass, their composition invariably took place over long periods of time — weeks, months — that included stretches of anguished, still, meditation. Their composition was a dialogue between speeding improvisation and deliberative planning. They clearly embody both these aspects the way Ellison's *Invisible Man* alternated between action and acknowledgment that necessitated further action. In fiction, those stages show linearly. But in the compressions of Pollock's painting they disappear among the palimpsested layers of his composition. One sees only the "strange ascent" of the built-up actions that make it all seem unpremeditated. That is why O'Hara's sort of description is particularly useful. It suggests the way Pollock could claim to subdue accident. It shows how his work connects deeply to the other improvised arts of the fifties. And in spite of its mystical terminology empathically reflecting the art community's initial awe, O'Hara's description preserves a climate receptive to judgment. It does not remove Pollock's painting to some performance preserve beyond painting (which Rosenberg seemed to beg, and Namuth's photographs seemed to enforce) but keeps it subject to the same standards of quality that prevail for any piece of art.

It is subject to the common standards because to a much greater extent than critics normally admit Pollock painted a reconstructable reality. Barbara Rose's and Rosalind Krauss's second-generation essays on Pollock help in this reconstruction, as do Serge Guilbaut's commentary and the useful oral biography by Jeffrey Potter.[24]

While some early critics felt his unfocused canvases reflected the uncentered Western vistas of his early boyhood, several of his neighbors thought his work pictured local conditions. Julian Levi, who helped the Pollocks when their house had a path, not a bath, and they had no car, has said, "Lee may have given him the title for the *Sounds in the Grass* series [of which *Shimmering Substance* is the most famous], but certainly the feeling in them is his. We don't think of Jackson as a poet, I suppose because of the hazard words were for him. These words of his stay with me, although he said them between pauses: 'You can hear the life in grass, hear it growing. Next thing, there's a dry spell — doesn't take much in Bonac [the local name for the backwoods Hamptons] sandy soil — and the life is gone. Put your ear to it then and all you hear is the wind'" (Potter 141). Pollock painted that instability. Hans Namuth concurs with a similar image: "One day as I was driving . . . to Pollock's house, I glanced up and watched the way in which the leaves of the elm and maple trees blurred as I was passing them. Squinting my eyes, pictures seemed to form above. It seemed to me that this was what Pollock was trying to do. His work was close to nature" (n.p., in "Photographing Pollock").

The paintings these friends have in mind are especially the transitional ones that came first at Springs — eight in the *Accabonac Creek* series and seven in the *Sounds in the Grass* series. In them he tried to work through his compulsion for ritual totems and move ever more wholly toward the allover structures that would dominate his work for the next several years. Pollock diffused the idea of the painting, totem-borne or not, all over the canvas. This diffusion is the way he beat the Cubist perspective game, sometimes known as "Picassoid space." Without a doubt, Pollock wrestled with these evolving problems of his discipline.

Doubtless also is that Pollock attended to stimuli to which his best contemporary critics were programmatically blind. In the same article that touted Pollock as "the most powerful painter in contemporary America and the only one who promises to be a major one" (*Essays* 2:166), Clement Greenberg severely propounded his own aesthetic of removal from "general middlebrow taste [which] constitutes in itself a danger" (162). The problem for the contemporary American artist, Greenberg claimed, was "to keep a step ahead of a pedagogic vulgarization that infects everything" (163) and yet still "find, in either décor or activity, impulses strong enough to send him further" (160). The surprise in hindsight is that Pollock's work did draw, in fact, on this very competition with the vulgar world that Greenberg warned against. Although Pollock's painting still seemed pure to Greenberg, it was not pure and could not be: the dangerous décor did infect it. Jackson Pollock lived in postwar America, lived anxious about the draft that he avoided, lived concerned about the environment, worried about atomic power. Jackson Pollock juggled milk bottles, too.

The 1946 painting *Shimmering Substance,* in his *Sounds in the Grass* series, illustrates Pollock's breadth. It is a hinge between the hands-on technique of easel painting and the composition by dripping, pouring, splashing, and flinging. *Shimmering Substance* is a painting of contemporary anxieties. Pollock paints in it the apprehensions of the postwar years in quite specific ways that are as important as its beautiful bright palette and formal composure. Indeed, Pollock's growing mastery of new representational equivalences was itself a formal achievement dependent upon his intense contemplation of the life of his time.

William Rubin has said *Shimmering Substance* is one of the paintings in which Pollock's evolving technique "acquired sufficient acceleration to literally 'take off' and leave the orbit of description, definition, and containment which had always been the traditional sphere of line" (part 1, 17–18). There *is* a jubilant speed to this painting, and it probably does have to do with the artist's frustration with the limitations in painting's rhetoric as it came down to him. As usual, however, the critic does not mention what the frustration means or to what his overcoming it, his Coonskin improvisation of a new rhetoric that works (if just this once), might refer outside the supposedly hermetic evolution of advanced painting.

Maybe the speeding lines represented what they seemed to represent: the ambiguous emergence or embedding of the shimmering totemic circle just beneath the washed bright surface skein of paint. What one needs with Pollock and his cohorts is a way of putting these formal considerations into their significant place. They are not the meaning but its means. They are metaphors that need further explanation. The formal structure of *Shimmering Substance* is the vehicle for Pollock's ambiguous excitement about moving to a sun-drenched locale, right after his marriage to a strong woman on whom he depended, during a growing anxiety about atomic power that affected every alert person in America. Every spot on *Shimmering Substance* is equally charged with energetic potential, yet there is a sober circle near its center.

Is the circle coming or going? For that matter, is the striking, uncharacteristic, bleached brightness (which embeds the yellow orb) the last glow of an apocalyptic moment or the dawning light of a happy Hamptons beach? It is both, and it would be as much a mistake to decide for one or the other as it is either to insist Pollock's painting was a flinging dance of rampant improvisation or, contrarily, a ruminative period of mulling and planning. Both his speed and his deliberation contributed to his composition. Ominous and optimistic moods complemented his paintings. *Shimmering Substance* is a deeply ambiguous gesture, an irresolvably deconstructive image. It is one of many works in different media with an aesthetic which muted what it proposed, talked in tongues that both declared and denied meaning, and seemed to veil what it unveiled.

The orb at the center of *Shimmering Substance* is the perfect image of this trope central to the art of deliberate speed. But there are many others: the statue on the campus of Tuskegee that Ellison discusses early in *Invisible Man* catches the college Founder with a veil lifted or lowered halfway over a kneeling slave's face. The invisible youth wonders whether he is "witnessing a revelation or a more efficient blinding" (28). Similarly, this practice of veiling or embedding signs and surface gestures presses on Pollock from the Cubist collage of Braque, Picasso, and Gris. And there were sources for *Shimmering Substance* in the New Orleans jazz which Lee Krasner has said her husband listened to for days on end until their "house would be rocking and rolling with it" (Rose, n.p.). The buzzing subliminality of words in early jazz, rhythm 'n' blues, and the era's rock 'n' roll is a sonic counterpart to Pollock's yellow orb and Ellison's (un)veiled slave. These black musics thrived on lyrics which the recording technology of the era as much as the singers' intentions frequently made indecipherable. The lyrics suggested more than they actually delivered, a promise that Bob Dylan made explicit in his late sixties underground throwaway "Nothing Was Delivered" (*Lyrics* 319; *Basement Tapes*). Rock 'n' roll lyrics of every style were uttered with absolute conviction even when, perhaps especially when, they made no sense or were buried in the noise of the city which their surface din enacted. From the Satchmo-ized lyrics of Louis Armstrong's wonderful "Big Butter and Egg Man" (1926) to the deliberate doubletalk of Little Richard and Chuck Berry in the mid-fifties, this undelivered, coming *and* going quality was diagnostic in American vernacular music. The new digital remasterings of this music help listeners decode it, but in making it clear they alter its effect as much as if *Shimmering Substance* were reproduced with the yellow orb clearly released from its surface embedding, prominently visible.

Therefore, the ambiguous *status* of the orb at the center of *Shimmering Substance* is not only important to the painting, as important as the speeding vector of its apparent surface, but also deeply part of American vernacular and postwar culture. The painting reenacts that important irresolvability of the culture. Its status is however only part of what it represents.

That orb had a particular meaning in 1946, when Pollock painted it: atomic power. Serge Guilbaut has noted that even such upscale popular magazines as *Fortune* and *Harper's Bazaar* educated their audiences about the force of atomic power. This "macabre warfare," *Fortune* called it in a 1946 caption to a photo of the famous atomic test explosion at Bikini Atoll, 1 July 1946, in the Pacific Marshall Islands (96). Furthermore, *Fortune* yoked this photo to an abstract painting by Ralston Crawford of the blast's force and the human "compulsion to disintegration" evident at what they called "the heart of chaos."[25] An abstract painter, Crawford had been Chief of the Visual Presentation Unit, Army Air Force, and observed the Bikini explosion. The photograph and his painting both show the moment in terms of the circles of its force.

These circles were becoming richly iconographic. *Fortune* employed them as sinister totems in their yoking; but elsewhere other people trying to put a happy face on nuclear power used such orbs optimistically. It is as if its anxiety were so mammoth that the public refused to hold its terror in mind, displacing it therefore into happy, or at least diversionary, images — like that of the "Bikini" swimsuit, whose name they coined and took to heart a year later (1947), surely as a result of this test.

Pollock was converting the barn in his new home that summer; the blast came in the middle of his enterprise. Thus, the Bikini news would have been on his mind for the first paintings he did within the barn studio, *Shimmering Substance* among them. He would have painted *Shimmering Substance* before the *Fortune* article in December, so it was not a specific determinant of his imagery — rather confirmation that the imagery was present that year, ready for Crawford, *Fortune,* Pollock, and others to employ. In fact, the orb images were soon ambiguous images everywhere in the era's poplore, circles of contention for those people competing to control the future of American attitudes on issues ranging from energy to the economy, appliances to art.

One of the corniest, time-bound examples of the nuclear orb used positively appears on the costume of Atom Man. A General Electric double-page-spread ad in *Newsweek,* 27 June 1955, showed Atom Man as a smiling giant hygienically costumed in a white jumpsuit with a matching white cowl. He is a priest for a new era, plugging in an atomic power cord for a petite housewife. She wears the generic fifties apron cut to the same pattern as the one Jim Backus wore playing Jim Stark's father in *Rebel without a Cause* that same year.

On Atom Man's chest is the large emblem of atomic power, its three upright circles within a horizontal one, like multiplied and dizzy circle pins with which fifties maidens blazoned their chastity on *their* breasts, like the plastic hula hoops budding adolescents swirled at their hips in rhythmic pelvic thrusts that made even the most innocent children blush to perform in public. As she stands next to Atom Man, on the housewife's apron are random cherries in the happy, hectic domestic style of the period. This ad is playing all the stereotypes straight on: she wears the apron, he wears the jumpsuit; he dictates, she smiles. She holds firmly, if a bit uneasily in her capable hands, the long hose and chromed pipe of a GE vacuum cleaner motor at her feet, its domed shape echoing the domed "symbolic view of an atomic reactor housed in [its] protective steel sphere" pictured on the facing page of this advertisement. At the center of the reactor again appears the symbolic totem of nuclear power, its power there safely *"housed,"* its linked circles radiating their shimmering energy for the free world, this time with a GE Vice President pointing it out as if probing the center of a cut-away womb. The ad shows the pregnant moment before the domestic birth of nuclear energy. At the popular level the icon is being born, this in the very summer that much news about the dangers of radiation fallout was entering mass consciousness.

The antiseptic white background, Atom Man's latex gloves and booties, and the housewife's dress seem to suggest nothing sexual. But the tumbling cherries, the long nozzle which the woman grips at Atom Man's fulcrum, his spread legs and her stance between them, his right hand beckoning to her crotch, his left hand poised behind her to push the male plug into the female socket—these all design a congeniality meant to eroticize for Americans the fun of nuclear power. The two figures are grinning uneasily, doubtless as embarrassed by their costumes as by their subliminal suggestiveness. The picture is of the moment before initiation, sexual or nuclear, when authority is pressing to overcome resistant or nervous reluctance from the innocent partner. As the accompanying text confirms, "working with the government, private companies have already begun to turn a major source of fear into a major source of fuel. . . . As we see it, this is progress in the American way" (5).

When Pollock painted this American's progress in his *Sounds in the Grass* series of late 1946, both he and the public attitude were much closer to the Bikini Atoll terror than to the housewife's delight at Atom Man plugging in her vacuum. Pollock was closer to the force of the Bikini Atoll circles, to an intuitive understanding of the way they could sunder all physical reality into the essential particles that remain at the end of entropy. But he was also trying to understand the force in the world positively. His was an art, he said himself, of "energy and motion made visible" (O'Connor and Thaw 253). Yes, and in his ambivalence he also painted the process of mind that he and the world public underwent following Los Alamos, Nagasaki, and Bikini.

The orb coming and going structurally played out this ambivalence. In painting these ambivalences as his content, Pollock showed entropic dissolution as well as enthalpic resolution, and, therefore, the process of mind coping with conflicting consequences. In painting this content, he used form to convey his emotion. He made form the extension of his content (as Robert Creeley and Charles Olson would proclaim it must be in 1950). *Shimmering Substance* was an apt painting for the onset of the era of deliberate speed.

Jackson Pollock's paintings are visual oxymorons. They reflect and inculcate a holding together of opposites that anticipated Earl Warren's progressive fifties politics and the oxymoron *he* chose for it, "deliberate speed." Pollock painted the condition of being between states, or being in both at once, or never letting go of either. Once you see him that way, then he is much more exact and much less abstract than the usual labels imply. He refused to settle into any one state. That is, he resisted both a single focus in his paintings and their interpreters' paraphrase. He insisted on the excluded middle that binary logic passes over. He juggled what was precisely neither here nor there, but up in the air.

For these reasons, Pollock's paintings were germane to their moment and continually contribute to the history of representation. He was a bounder who refused to leave representation behind, who found yet another way to straddle its edge. He rigorously hewed to standards while making art that seemed to duck them. He was inclusive rather than exclusive. He wanted to hold onto traditional form as well as reopen it to poplore.

"KEEP COOL, BUT CARE"

*We feel as if we had to repair a torn spider's web
with our fingers.*

— Ludwig Wittgenstein,
Philosophical Investigations

*The inert universe may have a quality we can call
logic. But logic is a human attribute after all; so
even at that it's a misnomer. What are real are the
cross-purposes.*

— Thomas Pynchon, *V.*

As far out on tightwires as Jackson Pollock, Jack Kerouac, Robert Frank, and Ornette Coleman pushed, times must have come when their sense of congeniality faltered. Somersaulting near the big top while crowds scarfed spun sugar and gaped at the seals below, these aerialists surely wondered if they performed for themselves. They eventually found audiences, but what sort? How interested, aware, or helpful could such crowds be? Ralph Ellison describes feeling this way in "The Little Man at Chehaw Station." You think no one knows what you are about, an early teacher told him, then you encounter the little man sitting behind the wood stove at a rural Alabama whistle stop. "There'll always be the little man whom you don't expect," she said, "and he'll know the *music,* and the *tradition,* and the standards of *musicianship* required for whatever you set out to perform!" (*Territory* 4).

The stove-warmer is unaccountably knowledgeable, a "vernacular music critic" (38). He measures the performance against his own uncodified experience, accepting or rejecting, correcting and proving the art. The little man behind the stove at Chehaw Station is Bakhtin's laughing chorus in Alabama guise. Depending on the art and the artist, confrontation with the vernacular critic may be a nightmare. But artists need the little man's high expectations to remind them of their own. The little man holds performers to their congenial point.

A tiny public has sometimes had to suffice. No matter how small it may be, however, its necessity shows in a story that the jazz singer Sylvia Sims has told about Lester Young. She complained to the saxophonist that club audiences drink, talk, everything but listen. "Lady Sims," Young replied, "if there is one guy in the whole house who is listening — and maybe he's in the *bathroom* — you've got an audience" (Balliett 237). Performers need that one critical consciousness behind the stove or in the stall who really attends, has learned the score out of school, and holds performers to their highest standards. When the house relaxes into enjoying the entertainment, it is the vernacular critic who jacks their response up a notch. The little men behind the stove or in the stall are less congenial to a performer's success than to the vernacular truth they share.

Sometimes this figurative standard bearer has quite actually honed performance. Important here is the little-known story that deserves to be famous of what brought down Ludwig Wittgenstein's confident performance in his *Tractatus Logico-Philosophicus* (1921/22). Wittgenstein recognized the tiny public for advanced philosophical work in the first paragraph of his preface. He noted that perhaps only "someone who has already had the thoughts that are expressed in it" would understand the *Tractatus*. Following publication and for complex reasons — including his certainty that he had solved the major questions of philosophy as well as despair that his solutions were insignificant — Wittgenstein retired from philosophy. He taught elementary school in rural Austria, gardened at a monastery, designed and built his sister's house in Vienna (a severe modern structure, whose beauty "is of the same simple and static kind that belongs to the sentences of the *Tractatus*" [von Wright 24]). This man who had written what was almost immediately recognized as the most important modern philosophical text did no philosophy for eight years. Then he returned to Cambridge in early 1929, again for involved reasons, submitted his book as a dissertation, received his Ph.D., and became a Fellow of Trinity College. Within a year he began to write an alternative philosophy that included his own critique of the *Tractatus*.

The *Tractatus* has remained the exemplar of modern philosophy. But the new philosophy culminated in a posthumous text titled *Philosophical Investigations* (1953), an exemplar of postmodern philosophy. Wittgenstein was the only philosopher to write the central texts of two succeeding philosophical movements, both persuasive, the second negating the first. His career is a parable of the achievement and crisis in modernism which generated the webbed tightwires of deliberately speeding culture.

Immediately upon his return to Cambridge and to philosophy, he entered into hard dialogue with the young philosopher Frank Ramsey (who having helped translate the *Tractatus* from its Austrian into English had also found and helped restore its author to academe). Ramsey's attention would have been smart and intense, surely competitive, but finally collegial. Wittgenstein called it "bourgeois."[1] Moreover, Wittgenstein also began defending his book's claims even more intensely against the onslaught of an outsider named Piero Sraffa. Sraffa was Wittgenstein's vernacular critic. As such, Sraffa's attention was skeptical and probing, professionally disinterested, and fundamentally commonsensible. Wittgenstein found it devastating.

Sraffa was aged 30, a decade younger than Wittgenstein, a young Italian economist whom Mussolini drove into exile (Nedo and Ranchetti 232). He settled in Cambridge to study with Keynes in 1929, the same year that Wittgenstein returned. Sraffa was passionately interested but not professionally trained in philosophy. (Likewise, when Wittgenstein wrote the *Tractatus,* he was an undergraduate himself, most experienced in mechanics and mathematics.) Wittgenstein and Sraffa ambled the public footpaths arguing about cases, logical multiplicity, and chiefly about the nature of propositions — which were the astringent building blocks of the *Tractatus,* both in its style and content. Wittgenstein had written and still believed that

> in a proposition there must be exactly as many distinguishable parts as in the situation that it represents. The two must possess the same logical . . . multiplicity. (*Tractatus* 4.04)[2]

This is a cardinal point in the *Tractatus* for its own sake and also, it has turned out, for modern conceptualization in general, of which the *Tractatus* is the most crystalline precipitate. For example, Wittgenstein's definition of a proposition precisely corresponds to T. S. Eliot's definition of an "objective correlative" which was for him the building block of poetry. Eliot's definition appeared in "Hamlet and His Problems," in 1919:

> The only way of expressing emotion in the form of art is by finding an "objective correlative"; in other words, a set of objects, a situation, a chain of events which shall be the formula of that *particular* emotion; such that when the external facts, which must terminate in sensory experience, are given, the emotion is immediately evoked. (*Selected Essays* 124–25)

Wittgenstein had finished the manuscript for the *Tractatus* in August 1918 — but had in hand the central component of the picture theory that expressed correlatives as early as September 1914. Therefore, Wittgenstein's formulation was both earlier and more elegant than Eliot's. In fact the relevant sections of the *Tractatus* and Wittgenstein's *Notebooks* leading up to it have the excitement and beauty of great poetry.

What both Wittgenstein and Eliot defined so similarly was fundamental to modern thought. Their shared premise was that "a common logical pattern" (4.014) governed, underlay, or acted the Archimedean fulcrum for reality as all people experienced it. This order of the world was its "sublime" condition, "the bottom of things" (§89), its case, which made all language and other forms of experience universally intelligible.[3] This logic contained the scaffolding for relations — between minds, images, arts, classes, and countries. Gottlob Frege, first in Jena, and Bertrand Russell, subsequently in Cambridge, had begun to isolate and express this logic mathematically, just as Ludwig Boltzmann had a few years earlier in Vienna found constants across physical states. Wittgenstein intended to study with Boltzmann (but did not because of Boltzmann's death). He had visited Frege first to discuss these issues, and later reported that the shy old man, "wiped the floor with me, and I felt very depressed" (McGuinness 83). But Frege also sent him to Russell, who cheered and encouraged him.

Russell was the linchpin here. While lecturing at Harvard in 1914, Russell had met the young philosophy student Thomas Stearns Eliot. Now that Eliot was married, resolved to live in London, and inclining from philosophy to poetry, Russell was acting both the intellectual mentor and intimate marriage counsellor. In his own London flat, Russell housed the poet and his first wife during the early months of their disastrous union. He interceded with Eliot's parents and took the bride to Torquay, supposedly to calm her nerves (Ronald Clark 311–13). Russell was partly at loose ends because Wittgenstein had begun to sap his confidence in his own work with logic. Russell was marking time now between the early, grueling work of his monumental logic and the later political pacificism for which Cambridge fired and England imprisoned him. When he was not dallying with the Eliots, Russell was writing "shilling shockers" about his serious work, all the while waiting for Wittgenstein to take "the next big step in philosophy" (McGuinness 130).

Socially and intellectually, Russell linked several central conceivers of a logical correlate for reality. Still, even without Russell's help, the idea darted right through turn of the century German, Austrian, and English thought, well beyond Wittgenstein and Eliot, Frege and Russell. While he was deeply involved in the writing of the *Tractatus,* during World War I, Wittgenstein absorbed Emerson's "History" (McGuinness 224). Emerson's first two sentences (written in 1840) precisely express the diffuse feeling that many others assumed for the next eighty years. Whatever the demand within philosophy to specify the shape of Emerson's "mind common to all," the concept of a correlate was an attempt to make rigorous the loose confidence about a rational world everywhere apparent in both the democratic and imperial theories of the day. Freud's theories, for instance, depend on a universally superior rationality. Sir James G. Frazer's *The Golden Bough* is a second instance.[4] And the long-dominant Cambridge School of anthropology and myth criticism which Frazer spawned, a third example, confidently assumed that the codes of human behavior were the same from Land's End to Kuala Lumpur. Like the early Wittgenstein, Frazer believed reality was similar in all cultures. He ignored or severely minimized contextual differences.

With her homespun prescience, George Eliot had diagnosed and predicted this hubris in *Middlemarch* (1871–72), her novel perched on the first cusp of modernism. Her central character, a dry fool named Mr. Casaubon, sought his life long a "Key to All Mythologies." He died unable to achieve it, but George Eliot's making an example of him was an insufficient prolepsis against what Wittgenstein later ruefully described as "This despotic demand" to locate essential form, what he termed "The hardness of the logical must" (§437; he is attacking his own early notebook here). Unfortunately, others as responsible for central and influential strains in modernism as Wittgenstein could also not avoid the despotic demand that Casaubon displayed. James G. Frazer, Sigmund Freud, Karl Marx, T. S. Eliot, Ezra Pound, W. B. Yeats, James Joyce, Heinrich Hertz, Gottlob Frege, Bertrand Russell, and the early Ludwig Wittgenstein of the *Tractatus* — all these and many more thought they had found Casaubon's Key. They tried to impose it on, or discover it underlying, or send it arcing over the rest of the world.

Thus the strong sense of a correlate to reality was diffuse when Ludwig Wittgenstein was a young man turning to the problems of philosophy from the problems of large kites and small airplanes. The "next big step" was to specify the systematic shape of logical reality, and to bind it into a seamless whole.[5] If someone could describe and circumscribe its properties specifically, there would be proximate proof that a logical ground of being existed, was rational, and would support the climate of thought that validated much else, including European colonialism and sexual politics. Wittgenstein, certainly, and Russell, probably, were concerned only with description, circumscription, and proof. But foul uses trailed their ideas.

Ludwig Wittgenstein's *Tractatus Logico-Philosophicus* sums up and crystallizes high modernism's early stage. His insights came to him in the period before the First World War. He found concrete ways to present those insights while he was on leave from combat during the war. He published the *Tractatus* soon after his release from prisoner-of-war internment. But he began to doubt these ideas as soon as he returned to their earnest discussion in the late twenties. By the thirties Wittgenstein was convinced the *Tractatus* was wrong and he had begun composing its critique.

What was Wittgenstein's major contribution in the *Tractatus*? How did it develop? And what brought it down?

Norman Malcolm has recorded Wittgenstein's account of the "origination of the central idea of the *Tractatus*."[6] During the First World War, in which Wittgenstein had enthusiastically enlisted on Austria's side, he saw a newspaper article which described an automobile accident by mapping it: "it occurred to Wittgenstein that this map was a proposition and that therein was revealed the essential nature of propositions — namely to *picture* reality" (*Memoir* 57). Wittgenstein himself referred to this insight in his notebook, late September 1914, at the beginning of the war. In fact, the key insights about correlative pictures and essential coherence came to him suddenly over nine days, and it is exciting to see the birth of this central modern idea.

On Sunday the 20th, he flays himself with questions and doubts, finally commanding, "Don't let yourself get overwhelmed with questions; just take it easy." After a night's sleep, on the 21st: "Now it suddenly seems to me in some sense clear that a property of a situation must always be internal." On the 24th: "The question how a correlation of relations is possible is identical with the problem of truth." And 25th: "For the latter is identical with the question how the correlation of situations is possible (one that signifies and one that is signified). It is only possible by means of the correlation of the components." On the 26th he wonders "What is the ground of our — certainly well founded — confidence that we shall be able to express any sense we like in our two-dimensional script?" And on the next day, the 27th, he has an important answer that is almost there: "A proposition can express its sense *only* by being the logical portrayal of it." He takes Monday off, then comes the breakthrough that pulls all this together on 29 September 1914. He recalls the generating event in his parenthesis:

> The general concept of the proposition carries with it a quite
> general concept of the co-ordination of proposition and situation:
> The solution to all my questions must be *extremely* simple! In the
> proposition a world is as it were put together experimentally. (As

when in the law-court in Paris a motor-car accident is represented
by means of dolls, etc.) This must yield the nature of truth straight
away.... It can be said that, while we are not certain of being able
to turn all situations into pictures on paper, still we are certain that
we can portray all *logical* properties of situations in a two-
dimensional script. (*Notebooks* 5–7)

This remarkably swift shoring up of certainty about the elegance of
signification and coherent essences allowed a major step in philosophy.
Wittgenstein brought the Platonic ideal out of the mind into some postu-
lated and describable space—logical space, a place that Wittgenstein could
map in his *Tractatus*. It was an extraordinary feat of concentration, of
holding all the possible permutations of reality in observable tandem and
establishing their formulaic configuration. It was as if he had achieved
Causaubon's Key, and underwritten the grounds for Eliot's objective
correlative.

Beyond their unequalled pure rigor, the importance of Wittgenstein's
clarification of propositions-as-pictures, as maps, or as correlatives is that
they support distant analysis despite the analyst's ignorance of a situation's
local contexts. Correlative maps assume the possibility of universal formal
description and provide a conceivably correct and fixed central discipline.
Wittgenstein's ringing first proposition in the *Tractatus* predicted that what
one understood correctly in Birmingham held equally in Berlin and Byzantium. To say "The world is all that is the case" ("Die Welt ist alles, was der
Fall ist") was to be sure one's local instance of logical space truly pictured all
the world.

Whether the map or the logical space it pictured was the major
achievement is perhaps moot. But they were to Wittgenstein dependently
related. When one went, both went. Not Russell nor G. E. Moore, nor
Frank Ramsey, nor any of the Dons brought them down, however. It was
Piero Sraffa—a stove warmer in the stations of philosophy—who tumbled
Wittgenstein's logical scaffold:

Sraffa made a gesture, familiar to Neapolitans as meaning something like disgust or contempt, of brushing the underneath of his
chin with an outward sweep of the finger-tips of one hand. And he
asked: 'What is the logical form of *that*?' Sraffa's example produced
in Wittgenstein the feeling that there was an absurdity in the
insistence that a proposition and what it describes must have the
same 'form'. This broke the hold on him of the conception that a

proposition must literally be a 'picture' of the reality it describes. (Malcolm, *Memoir* 58)

Thus it was a proverbial little man, a laughing chorus, a rude vernacular gesture that pulled the girder from modernism's most elegant and beautiful underpinning. The girder was the assumption of universally similar interpretation. In his later philosophy, Wittgenstein's concepts are held in common but not everyone is in the same commonality. Because of the laughing little man, and his own corroborating experience, Wittgenstein now saw that interpretation must be circumstantial.

Wittgenstein slowly went on, then, to accrete not a second philosophical system so much as an anti-system. It culminated in *Philosophical Investigations,* a distinctively postmodern volume. Wittgenstein had the *Investigations* published posthumously, unfinished, full of interruptions, cross-references, and clipped-in fragments. Why? Because the consequence of Sraffa's critique was that philosophy must be an activity rather than a solution, an improvisation rather than an achievement.

Philosophical Investigations therefore emphasized multiple rather than fixed form. In it Wittgenstein renounced analysis as uncovering some hidden, essential properties, for in the world as he now found it, nothing was hidden (§435). He denied penetration of phenomena as proper behavior (§90) for philosophers or anyone else, arguing instead for searching looks at everyday reality that left it alone, left it whole and intact as before analysis, for "Philosophy . . . leaves everything as it is" (§124).

Suddenly finding language and life orderly but hardly constant, Wittgenstein began writing metaphors of process to replace the paradigms of static essence that had populated the *Tractatus.* "Our language," he writes in the *Philosophical Investigations,* "can be seen as an ancient city: a maze of little streets and squares, of old and new houses, and of houses with additions from various periods, and this surrounded by a multitude of new boroughs with straight regular streets and uniform houses" (§18). This language maze gives nub and personality to thought, making it as irregular as reality. Projecting himself back into his earlier mind, he remembers the feeling of the *Tractatus* as "slippery ice where there is no friction and so in a certain sense the conditions are ideal, but also, just because of that, we are unable to walk. We want to walk: so we need *friction.* Back to the rough ground!" (§107).

Surely his most famous image of process is in the image of language as games leading to family resemblances:

And so the result of this contemplation is thus: we see a complicated net of similarities that cross and interweave.[7] Similarities great and small.

67. I can characterize these similarities no better than through the term "family resemblances," for so interweave and cross the various resemblances that persist between family members: build, features, color of eyes, gait, temperament, etc., etc. And I state: games comprise a family. (§66–67)

Relationships across groups and within groups are not based on logical correlates, *not* on some continual essence running through them. They are instead like the spinning of a thread—that paradigmatic vernacular activity—an activity persons perform on reality:

In spinning a thread we twist fibre on fibre. And the strength of the thread does not reside in the fact that some one fibre runs through its whole length, but in the overlapping of many fibres. (§67)

The net or web is no longer conceived whole and sufficient, as in the *Tractatus,*[8] but constantly created and recreated, performed piecemeal. Also, Wittgenstein shows that this constant recreation is the common way in the world, not a new or startling fact. The special case was when in the *Tractatus,* and in modernism in general, people supposed that they could wholly map reality.

The style itself changed in the *Philosophical Investigations.* From the astringent propositions of the *Tractatus,* in their epigrammatic High German, Wittgenstein moved to a personal hectoring and noodling dialogue. He was renouncing the esoteric argot of professional philosophy, calling the discipline home to everyday language. Without an ideal underlying form for philosophical speech to locate and emulate, everyday language is all there is. That's life in a world where the little men, the laughing chorus, rub their fingers outward across their stubble, scoff aloud at your pared propositions, and return you to the real, unmappable landscape. Everchanging, full of local cultural and material surprises to accompany its pleasing intimations of regularity, the landscape Wittgenstein described in 1953 constantly shames maps of clean, well-lighted, logical space—including his own in the *Tractatus* (§23).

To bequeath its coherent picture of logical space, the *Tractatus* deemed regular messiness beside the point. When he again incorporated everydayness in the *Philosophical Investigations,* Wittgenstein bequeathed an incoherent landscape. What chiefly impeded the second book's publication was Wittgenstein's attempt to do justice to the workaday world's rough means. A perfectionist aware of his difference from common people, yet admiring their fit in the world as they found it, Wittgenstein hoped to render a philosophy that likewise fitted rather than fought the world. He wanted for his thoughts and their arrangement, he wrote in the preface, his book's most protracted remark, "a natural order. . . without breaks." He wanted vernacular seamlessness. However — and this is at the center of what is important about his work published in the fifties — he said "Elegance is *not* what we are trying for" (*Blue* 19).

He created neither unconscious fit nor analytic elegance, but something else — a performed web. He found it impossible to weld the strengths of his ideas together. He soon lamed them if he forced them too far in any *one* direction, as he emphasized, against their inclination to multiple branching. That's why *Philosophical Investigations* traverses "a wide field of thought *criss-cross in every direction.*" Continually sketching points anew from different angles, Wittgenstein considered many of his remarks mangled ("mit Mängeln behaftet"). Consequently, he spent much of his time rejecting, cutting down, and rearranging his sketches "to be able to give the observer an image of the landscape." The continual rearrangement of points was the point, was the web, was the philosophy.

The apparently unstable skein of process in *Philosophical Investigations* is hardly lackadaisical, therefore, but cardinal. His performed web is important within philosophy, surely, but beyond it Wittgenstein's late form may be his most important achievement. It validates the broken-field running of contemporary culture. At the time he wrote the preface to *Philosophical Investigations,* in January 1945, he jotted in his notebook a feeling that conveys the quandary of culture trying to move past modernism: "It is as though I had lost my way and asked someone the way home. He says he will show me and walks with me along a nice smooth path. This suddenly stops. And now my friend tells me: 'All you have to do now is find your way home from here'" (*Culture* 46–47). For everyone in every shifting context, the way home is always different and it is always necessary to perform it anew.[9]

Just as his aim in the *Tractatus* was to picture the form of the world, so in *Philosophical Investigations* Wittgenstein does likewise. But this time around the pictures, plural, are of different, contemporary forms — manmade, personality insistent everywhere, infinitely adjusted and continually improvised, amazingly complex and echoic, robust but delicate. "We feel," he says, "as if we had to repair a torn spider's web with our fingers" (§106).

The web or net is an image that the early Wittgenstein had inherited from nineteenth-century thought as representing the fine lattice work of essential order. For the author of the *Tractatus* as for, say, the author of *Middlemarch,* the web is "the great mirror" (5.511) and "primary."[10] But the later Wittgenstein whose *Philosophical Investigations* precipitates the form of postmodern, contemporary, or deliberately speeding reality has had to replace an inherited web with his own torn surrogate: "*an* order . . . not *the* order" (§132). To some people the man-made, allover design is abhorrent and risibly inadequate. To others it is the more beautiful for its fragility and tentativeness, its insistence on standing alone. In any case, as the *Tractatus* was the crystalline precipitate of high modernism, so *Philosophical Investigations* performs an improvised shape for the deliberately speeding culture that has succeeded modernism.

The zigzag progress and criss-cross persistence of *Philosophical Investigations,* its quick sketches arranged and rearranged, the personality percolating all over its surface and diddling its every nuance — these are Robert Frank's and Jackson Pollock's hallmarks as much as Wittgenstein's. Several years before publication of *Philosophical Investigations,* Kerouac used the term *sketching* for his own attempts to represent a similarly jagged landscape. Wittgenstein's thorough reliance on everyday tools and rejection of professional argot, his direct address to the audience and supposition of dialogue are all parallel to techniques Nabokov, Ellison, Coleman, and Ginsberg favor. The attraction to coherent development in *Philosophical Investigations* ("thoughts should proceed from one to another in a natural order"), but refusal to cripple the parts for the whole, is the same integrity which produced short masterpieces like Coleman's "Congeniality" and long ones like Kerouac's *Visions of Cody.*

Probably none of these parallel characteristics is an *influence,* because Wittgenstein still remains formidable reading, even for philosophers, until one works oneself onto his perch and reaccustoms oneself to viewing the landscape from his angles. Little Richard's insistence on everyday language and the associative echoing of his blues form is *like* the late Wittgenstein, the multiple perspectives compacted in "Long Tall Sally" almost exactly so. But the singer of "Tutti Frutti" never spent one synapse worrying whether the world is all that is the case. Rather, Little Richard's songs, like Chuck Berry's and Charlie Parker's, were vernacular scoffings that validated the wider case of the *Philosophical Investigations.* An example at a more cunningly deliberate level (doubtless still without direct influence) would be

Jasper Johns's increasingly overt toying with the terms of representation. His process came to a culmination in such works as *Map* (1967–71); its misplaced sections and randomly stenciled place names laugh at the whole idea of an objective correlative. Johns, then, in the fifties and sixties was an artist profoundly parallel to Wittgenstein's writing. But at least one author demonstrably learned directly from Wittgenstein: Thomas Pynchon, particularly consciously in his first novel, *V.* (1963).

Pynchon accepts and further winds up the deliberately speeding aspects of the fifties. Pynchon's characters chase, cannot find, and must invent their parents. They wander deeply through African history and the Herero belief in a life-sustaining mother earth. They encounter genocide abroad and an inorganic world of plastic robotry at home. Still, some few of Pynchon's characters fend off sexism, betrayal, and self-mutilation to achieve provisional love and commitment. Like the culture he expresses, Pynchon's form is fragmented, his language is fast and heady, and his prospects poise on an interface between despair and optimism. *V.* is the perfect novel to demonstrate that the fifties was no nostalgic hole in history, but a time when historical force and human need coalesced to create discrete cultural codes for the contemporary epoch.

There are two fundamental plot concerns in *V.* They will not now nor ever proceed in the then-natural order which achieved modern hegemony in the nineteenth century, no matter how hard Pynchon or his readers push and twist, cut and rearrange them. The first words of the first chapter of *V.* initiate the contemporary plot line on "Christmas Eve, 1955." That's when Benny Profane joins Pig Bodine and other out-riding members of what they fondly call their Whole Sick Crew at a bar in Norfolk. Partly AWOL sailors (hence its nautical noun), partly avant-garde (hence its boasting self-diagnosis), the Whole Sick Crew comprises additionally a covey of painters, writers, musicians, singers, secretaries, one plastic surgeon and one meta-dentist variously on the verge of doing something, or more likely nothing, with their talents. Some of them, like Benny, yo-yo aimlessly from Norfolk to New York, Times Square to Grand Central, and vice versa—learning in their criss-crossing, says Benny, not a goddamn thing (454). Some, like the saxophonist McClintic Sphere, and the secretary Rachel Owlglass, are more ruminative in their flip-flopping than young Profane. Some others, like Herbert Stencil, are far too encased in what they have learned. Always at issue with all these layabouts is the shape of experience—as the name "Stencil" suggests.

Herbert Stencil links the Whole Sick Crew and its contemporary plot line to the second, historical plot curlicue. Herbert Stencil has devoted himself to finding a woman named V., whom he believes is likely his mother and whose idea blooms for him into an obsession about decay and decline. Herbert Stencil criss-crosses the western world repeatedly in fact and memory to find and reproject the clues about V. bequeathed him in his father's journal. The father, Sidney Stencil, sets up and the son Herbert continually restamps the idea that V., like Kurtz in Conrad's *Heart of Darkness,* is ineffably not so much evil as destructive, deliquescent, decadent. "There is more behind and inside V.," Sidney noted and Herbert memorably fulfilled, "than any of us had suspected. Not who, but what: what is she. God grant that I may never be called upon to write the answer, either here or in any official report" (53).

Pynchon spares Sidney this report, giving Herbert the calling. The historical plot scumbles some six snatches of V. between 1898, when she appears young and optimistic in Cairo as Victoria Wren, and 1943, when she dies on the island of Malta, cynical and dressed as a priest. All six appearances Pynchon marks by a special carved comb, which V. wears in her hair. All her incarnations except the last are Herbert Stencil's elaborations on tips from his father's journal or her other acquaintances. The younger Stencil's constantly repeating, constantly failing reconstruction is thus a parody of the modern mythic method of attempting to stencil the world with mythic patterns from the past.

The way Pynchon has Herbert reconstruct V. parodies modernism's vector. She proceeds from an enactment of virtù, defined as belief in "individual agency" (199), to "something entirely different, for which the young century had as yet no name" (410). If readers unscramble the chronology of her episodes, V. represents intention gone awry and cynical. Her career is imperialism finding its fate — eventual incapacity and disassembly by children who are constructing their own discrete dispensation. Stencil understands her career increasingly along the way as an attempt to repress her "dynamic uncertainty," like a ball on a roulette wheel unable "to come to rest anywhere inside plausible extremes" (256). If the tenor of the Whole Sick Crew has seemed to some readers experience unresolved, Stencil's tenor is experience overresolved. He cannot give up his patternings even when, especially when, he finds them misleading.[11] He has become encased in V.'s case. He illustrates the process of self-delusion, the hard logical must, that leads to thinking that all the world is as one's case is.

Pynchon's parody of modernism is, however, considerably more thoroughgoing than this tracing of the loose vector of Victoria Wren's life, or than Herbert Stencil's search within it for the one Key to his own life, or than that this search is in turn a parody of Joyce and Eliot's so-called "mythic method," or that it all depends on Wittgenstein's early mistaken logic. All the historical chapters are aggressively negative. Pynchon has organized them all around specific, celebrated texts. He shows all these modern actions—most of them high modern—to be foolish, negligent of consequences, or worse—misogynist, racist, and genocidal. *V.* is an activist novel. It resists and talks back. It makes definite points.

The two plot lines in *V.* illustrate the central problems of one lore cycle springing from the too-tightly pretzeled concerns of its predecessor. In the historical chapters that cover high modernism, Pynchon shows cultural cases deluding and confining their practitioners in Paris, Florence, South West Africa, and Malta. In his contemporary chapters, Pynchon shows how the extreme modern contraction propels the reality germinated within itself quite beyond the case, like a baby from the womb. Mondaugen rides out of Foppl's siege party. Paola escapes both Malta and the Whole Sick Crew in recommitting herself to Pappy Hod at the end of the novel.

Pynchon's ambivalence about both his plot lines is also instructive. He realizes the complex beauty of modern artifacts, but clearly shows a characteristic cruelty in their performance. He realizes the congeniality of new cultural forms, but does not pretend they have the resonance of a mature form. He is always appraising the conditions of maturity and renewal. Each of his first three novels has probed those conditions working at the end of the modern cycle and the beginning of his own cycle of deliberate speed.

All the novel's historical glimpses of modern life and culture are about siege. Instances of siege enact Pynchon's assessment of how modernity felt to moderns; how, feeling embattled, they withdrew into pure cases; why, having withdrawn, they systematized their shrunken space to export it abroad; how, profiting from distant cultures, they looked for Keys to all Mythologies that would justify their colonialism. The siege party at Foppl's farmhouse in South West Africa, the siege of feminine Malta, the children surrounding and dismantling the Bad Priest (V.'s final incarnation) within the siege of Malta, the brute knifing of Botticelli's Venus to lift her from her frame, the *Rape of the Chinese Virgins* in chapter fourteen—all these are continuations of the same principle. They are in Wittgenstein's terms sketches of the same landscape. They are versions of "the virgin who is tortured to death defending her purity against the invading Mongolians" (396). The virgin's imperiled purity is the major theme of prestigious high modernism from "The Waste Land" to Greenberg's *Art and Culture*.

When they did not have what Fausto emphasized as "plots" (319, 324) of Italian bombers besieging them, modernists invented Mongolian manqués. Or they fantasied Herero hordes overrunning their farms. Siege was so crucial to their self-definition that they invoked its presence far and wide, in their colonies, as in Africa, and in their capitols, as in Paris. In Pynchon's analysis, the quintessential modernist location is to be caught, besieged by actual or fantasied cretins or cretinized lore.

This squeeze, siege, choke or contraction happens at a certain stage of the lore cycle, when the once-rising lore passes its apogee and resists its descent. The squeeze shapes the lore group and confirms its identity on its way up. On its way down, the group celebrates images of the squeeze as its ennobling heritage, thereby prolonging its sense of identity. Thus, the fortress that houses the siege party in South West Africa in 1922 (chapter nine) has a casual "stained-glass window portraying an early Christian martyr being devoured by wild beasts" (237). The supposed inevitability of this idea is what Wittgenstein expressed in the *Tractatus*. When Fausto calls his island an "arena in quarantine" (322) or notes that he once wrote, "There is no more world but the island" (325) — his phrasing exemplifies the shrunken cases epitomized in the first sentence of the *Tractatus:* "Die Welt ist alles, was der Fall ist": "The world is all that is the case." The anxiety of Wittgenstein's initial proposition percolates through much of *V.*, not just the South West African chapter where it most notoriously appears.

Throughout the historical episodes, Pynchon jostled together several texts from the Renaissance and after (paintings and poems, political and philosophical monographs, novels and operas), showed how they shape and reflect behavior, and illustrated their contradictions. In these historical chapters Pynchon used modern texts as organizational centers. They are also more or less calm points of comparison, as when one character wryly notices, "We are not, any of us, in the Renaissance at all" (201). The panoply of Pynchon's attitudes flushes with his full ire, however, in *"V. in love"* (chapter fourteen) and in "Mondaugen's story" (chapter nine).

"V. in love" takes place in Paris during the dog days of July and August, 1913,[12] and revolves nominally around V.'s love for a young ballerina, Mélanie l'Heuremaudit. "V. in love" alludes freely to landmarks of modernism, from "Swann in Love," the third part of Proust's *Swann's Way* (1913), to the longing for rain that Pynchon's Parisian characters share with T. S. Eliot's wastelanders in his "Unreal City." Moreover, Mélanie's father had initiated her sexuality while "a small night bird had lit on the windowsill and watched them" (390). This is an echo of the nightingale in "The Waste

Land" who is changed into her state from Philomel, after King Tereu raped her, and sings forever in remembrance of his rude forcing.

That's the genetic tapestry, psychological and literary, before which V. and Mélanie play their affair. Its variety of weave shows it is modernism Pynchon mocks, not an individual author or event. All the action of the chapter's story is to this purpose. The two lovers fulfill their desire by languidly observing each other in mirrors — their audience is their own selves and doubles. The lovers hide away in claustrophobic encasement with only artificial enlargement — they have withdrawn into a simplified situation apparently without consequences. Their experimental decadence parallels the condensed political beliefs swirling around in the café-talk outside their room — "You are not real," says V. to Mélanie when she first meets her (404); "Your beliefs are non-human," says the dance's producer to a political organizer in a café, "You talk of people as if they were point-clusters or curves on a graph." "So they are," comes the dreamy response (405). And the dance's composer provides their whole story to Stencil, years later — "Perhaps he felt guilty about his chart of permutations and combinations. . . . His description of them is a well-composed and ageless still-life of love at one of its many extremes: V. on the pouf, watching Mélanie on the bed; Mélanie watching herself in the mirror; the mirror-image perhaps contemplating V. from time to time. No movement but a minimum friction" (409). This is a picture of an experiment, a peopled logical space. It shows the modern withdrawal from nub and contradiction, from the friction that allows people to walk in the real world, as Wittgenstein said, years later, about his own modern philosophy. Pynchon is building an elaborate play to show how in skewering others the agenda of prestigious high modernism skewered itself.

Taking ballet as a paradigm of modern artistic fusion, Pynchon scrutinizes here the *ballets russes,* with which associated a host of artists from Maurice Ravel to Henri Matisse, André Derain to Igor Stravinsky, Pablo Picasso to Jean Cocteau, Vaslav Nijinsky to Eric Satie. The necessary glue for these talents was Serge Diaghilev. His bridging of all the theatrical disciplines established his modern conception against that of classical ballet. "Perfect ballet can only be created," Diaghilev maintained, "by the very closest fusion of the three elements of dancing, painting, and music" (Haskell 196). His fusion rested in theory on a logic common among all the disciplines. In fact, however, the disarray of the *ballets russes* after Diaghilev's death in 1929 indicates that the unity was charismatic and imposed rather than essential. In "V. in love," Pynchon shows modernist collaborators negligently, irresponsibly in love with their own ideas — forcing them on in a single direction, just as Wittgenstein would later warn against, rather than letting them have their "natural inclination" to multiplicity (*Philosophical Investigations* vii).

Pynchon devotes the chapter to his version of the rehearsals and infamous opening night of *Le Sacre du Printemps (The Rite of Spring)*, renaming it *L'Enlèvement des Vierges Chinoises (Rape of the Chinese Virgins)* and giving much more than artistic reason for the opening-night audience's riot. The version in *V.* has music by Vladimir Porcépic (roughly Igor Stravinsky), choreography by Satin (roughly Vaslav Nijinsky), production by one M. Itague (roughly Diaghilev), the major patron being V. (for whom no reality corresponds). In Pynchon's *Rape of the Chinese Virgins*, fifteen-year-old Mélanie l'Heuremaudit (roughly Marie Piltz) danced Stravinsky's "chosen virgin," which phrase was probably the source for Pynchon's punning title.[13]

These approximations are characteristic of Pynchon's technique. He bases his characters on historical or textual allusions, but peppers them with contradictory details that frustrate any secure connection to their supposed correlative. Stravinsky did not share the taste Pynchon's Porcépic had for Black Mass ritual. Unlike Pynchon's Itague, aristocratic Diaghilev never tended bar at the Place Pigalle, never spat on Captain Dreyfus. Because everything depends on his contextual setting, Pynchon's attention to his local needs in *V.* disturb his larger connections to history. Nothing locks in place. Like those of his deliberately speeding peers, Pynchon's correlatives are subjective.

Despite the disturbed connections, throughout this chapter Pynchon counterpoints V.'s hothouse affair with Mélanie to the like collaboration of the modernists preparing for their ballet spectacle. Indeed — and this also is characteristic for Pynchon in *V.* — there is a full sense of collusion among all the elements of the episode. Young Mélanie's father had initiated her sexually, then abandoned her. Her mother, too, has left her to V., a self-absorbed woman, and more explicitly to these self-absorbed men. They see Mélanie as a gift from her father to them, a gift that mirrors the father's use of the girl, a gift that expresses the presence of his (and her) symbolic last name, l'Heuremaudit — cursed hour, evil epoch. Itague says "The girl functions as a mirror" reflecting back the "ghost" of her diddling father at everyone who looks her over (399). That's why they want her for *Rape of the Chinese Virgins*. She is the victim who shows her victimizer superimposed on her own blank image. Dancing the step and rhythm of their era, Mélanie is a concentration of the era's illness into a single symbol, a small case; not for naught is she "fétiche" (395) to her associates, "La Jarretière" (396) on the stage. Not for naught do Mongolians besiege her. Not for naught is her virgin purity only apparent.

Pynchon is collecting and compressing the fifties theme of derelict, decadent, corrupt authority. Befitting someone carried on the swell of a rising lore cycle, he goes further than any of his predecessors, further even than his teacher, Nabokov, whose theme of corrupting innocence he multiply extends. As one example, Humbert Humbert may have seemed a singular psychopath in *Lolita,* but Itague, Porcépic, Satin, and (their patron) V. work on Mélanie in concert. On Mélanie Pynchon is focusing much recent history and several psychosocial notions about colonial relations. The idea for choreographing her penetration on the pole Satin had gathered "from reading an account of an Indian massacre in America"; Itague habitually referred to the male dancers as "Mongolized fairies"; and Mélanie "was impaled at the crotch . . . and slowly raised by the entire male part of the company" (413). True, she leaves off the protective device that was to fit over and protect her crotch from the spear at the moment of *enlèvement,* but her failure was to ignore the line between art and reality. Perfect modernist victim, she died for being rather than pretending to be Itague's, Satin,'s, Porcépic's, and V.'s objective correlative:

> The conception depended on [Mélanie] continuing her dance while impaled, all movement restricted to one point in space, an elevated point, a focus, a climax. . . . La Jarretière's movements became more spastic, agonized: the expression on the normally dead face was one which would disturb for years the dreams of those in the front rows. Porcépic's music was now almost deafening: all tonal location had been lost, notes screamed out simultaneous and random like fragments of a bomb: winds, strings, brass and percussion were indistinguishable as blood ran down the pole, the impaled girl went limp, the last chord blasted out. (414)

Behind this performance stands the hubris and presumption of modernism at large, its thoughtless neglect of consequences, and its relation to colonialism. Pynchon makes no claim for a cause-and-effect relationship, either way, but clearly identifies one of the later Wittgensteinian "family resemblances" between the violence — tonal, rhythmic, and physical — of this team of international avant-gardists and the scenes elsewhere in the novel and world of like cruelty against similarly powerless men and women. Over and over, Pynchon's European white men use sexual imagery to describe and inscribe their dominance of women, men of color, and the landscape, too.

There are too many such scenes of rape and violence against women, ranging from the casual frolics of the Whole Sick Crew to the plastic surgery of Schoenmaker and on to the decadent sadism of Paris and South West Africa for any reader to think it is unconscious on Pynchon's part. It is a conscious part of his skewering of modernism and its remnants. In *L'Enlèvement des Vierges Chinoises,* Pynchon hoists modernism on its own petard, revealing its indulgent and irresponsible fetishism. It is a scene of excess and condemnation likely to occur only in a first novel, by a young man. Remarkably, however, Pynchon deepened similar vitriol a decade later in *Gravity's Rainbow.*

Meanwhile, he confirmed and further expanded it in chapter nine, "Mondaugen's Story," set in South West Africa in May of 1922, eight years after the Paris ballet. Herbert Stencil found one Kurt Mondaugen working in a defense plant on Long Island, heard his story over a beer, then "Stencilized" it to fit his needs. Kurt Mondaugen was an engineering student stationed in what has become Namibia, but was then South West Africa, a former German colony which South Africa was administering for the League of Nations after World War I, when Mondaugen arrived. Concerted Europe is to the natives there as the international collaborators were to Mélanie in the *Rape of the Chinese Virgins.*

Why was Mondaugen there? He was recording "sferics"—short for the atmospheric radio disturbances common on the short wave band and in telephone messages of the era. Ever since Heinrich Barkhausen named the whistling babble of the airwaves, calling it "atmospherics," while "listening in on telephone messages among the Allied forces" (230) during the war, Pynchon implies there had been effort to parse their grammar. Mondaugen is part of that supposed worldwide effort to hear what the universe is telling mankind.

What's special about Mondaugen's location? Depending on how you look at it, everything or nothing. He moves at the beginning of the chapter to the ongoing "siege party" of Foppl, a now-prosperous farmer. Originally Bavarian, Foppl had come to Africa as a trooper in General von Trotha's genocidal march through the country in 1904. Von Trotha annihilated eighty percent of the Herero population, as well as sizable portions of the Hottentots and Berg-Damaras (245). Pynchon singles this march out as instituting genocide for the twentieth century. It confirmed and depended on a fantasy of "Väterliche Züchtigung; fatherly chastisement, an inalienable right" (267), with the paternal colonialist's commensurate fear of retaliation on the flipside. As a result of this fear, at the first hint of native resurgence nearly two decades later, in this May of 1922, Foppl has gar-

nered all Europeans in the locality in his farmhouse. It is a fortress replete
with moat and turrets, and Foppl has clearly anticipated, even ensured, that
events would come to this pass. His party in this fortress is the essential case
of his life and, Pynchon indicates, of European colonialism. Barkhausen
and his atmospherics, von Trotha and his march, the politics and the
colonial cruelty in this chapter are all historically real. Foppl and his siege
party are Pynchon's extrapolation on the history.

Foppen means in vernacular German to trick or deceive gaily, having
the same root as the English verb to fob; also, there is a game Foppen und
Fangen, not unlike Capture the Flag, of taunting and imprisoning opponents.
With its diminutive l, "Foppl" is a bitter play on genocide as a game,
whipping and rape as delight. It mines more deeply the same lode Pynchon
pictured in "V. in love" of a theatrical ballet so concertedly self-involved and
cavalier with consequences that it killed its ballerina. Later, in Gravity's
Rainbow, he would dramatize similar elements in Weissmann's launching of
his lover in a rocket's nosecone. In the present chapter, Foppl is catching
into his special and shrunken worldview an assorted variety of Europeans—and much less fortunate Africans, too—fobbing onto them the
fantasies he long ago fobbed onto himself. Because his world is theirs
expressed extremely, the Europeans agree readily.

What were Foppl's fantasies, and how did he come by them? During
his march with von Trotha, Foppl fantasied he had experienced essential
reality. He and a colleague had just whipped and clubbed to death a
complaining Hottentot. Instead of the usual annoyance at futility, as when
a person slaps one mosquito in a swarm, Foppl felt something considerably
more:

> Things seemed all at once to fall into a pattern: a great cosmic
> fluttering in the blank, bright sky and each grain of sand, each
> cactus spine, each feather of the circling vulture above them and
> invisible molecule of heated air seemed to shift imperceptibly so
> that this black [Hottentot victim] and he, and he and every other
> black he would henceforth have to kill slid into alignment, assumed
> a set symmetry, a dancelike poise. (264)

This then is Wittgenstein's Case, not described in abstract space, but
experienced in the world.

Pynchon is showing its arbitrariness—the way it seemed to fall out
("was der Fall ist"). But Foppl convinced himself it was reality: "different
from the official language of. . . orders and directives, . . . different from
colonial policy, international finagling, hope of advancement within the

army or enrichment out of it" (264). Here, he thought, was the real, hidden, underlying case. Here was what the world *was:* it "had only to do with the destroyer and the destroyed, and the act which united them" (264). But Pynchon makes cumulatively clear it was neither independent nor underlying, rather it was that old matrix of convention and indulgence. It was the cluster of prejudice and need mistaken for essential reality that the deliberately speeding culture was trying to isolate and avoid.

Moreover, Pynchon is critiquing young Foppl's symmetry exactly the way the mature Wittgenstein undercut his own early masterpiece. Pynchon's green trooper fobbed off on himself as essential the very set symmetry that he needed to find. Had Wittgenstein lived to read *V.,* he could have glossed this passage with his §437:

> A wish seems already to know what will or would satisfy it; a proposition, a thought, what makes it true — even when that thing is not there at all! Whence this *determining* of what is not yet there? This despotic demand?

"Even when that thing is not there at all": "The ideal, as we [thought] of it, is unshakeable. Where does this idea come from?" Wittgenstein asked earlier, "It is like a pair of glasses on our nose through which we see whatever we look at. It never occurs to us to take them off" (§103). Foppl's experience of essential reality, its "dancelike poise," was a stripping away of the contextual complexity and consequences of acts, a will to find a space evidently unbound by emotional claims, foreordained, fundamental. Having in this way tricked himself, Foppl leads others in the modern European outpost to trick themselves similarly.

It is important that, until its end, "Mondaugen's Story" is not really Mondaugen's, but Foppl's. Rather, Mondaugen has been aurally and visually a voyeur, as the literal rendering of his name suggests: moon eyes. He attended to these dark events rhythmically, silently — "he had a gift of visual serendipity: a sense of timing, a perverse certainty about not whether but when to play the voyeur" (246). Foppl, mainly, but also others educate this young man in the genocidal colonialism they have thrived on during South West African history. Foppl's legends of the concentration camps, rapes, carnage, and forced concubinage that accompanied extreme power unchecked by conscience — these have made up the chapter's content.

How then does Mondaugen finally encounter a world real for him, and reclaim his own story? Asked from the abstract angle of *Deliberate Speed,* the question becomes, How can people involved in the terms of one lore cycle reject those terms and replace them with others? Pynchon answers these questions in the parable of Mondaugen claiming his own story. But first his case must be taken from him further, quite literally, quite wholly.

Enter Weissmann — White Man — an increasingly powerful and symbolically evil character in Pynchon's fiction. In *V.*, however, Weissmann is still at a Lieutenant's level. He is simply another guest of Foppl's who observes Mondaugen's scientific outpost with its receivers, home-made oscillograph, and antennae above his turret. Unlike the other guests absorbed in their make-up, their lace, and their aching gums, Weissmann also interests himself in the patterns Mondaugen believes may exist in the radio's "clicks, hooks, risers, nose-whistlers" (230).

Mondaugen has himself become interested in these sferics as possible messages from the universe. Although he has no idea what they might signify, he is a little loathe to look too closely. Weissmann, however, is a classic Pynchon paranoid. Suspecting Mondaugen may be a spy receiving messages from the English, Weissmann makes it his business to break the "code." That Pynchon never explains how Mondaugen's oscillograph converts clicks and nose-whistlers to text, German or otherwise, is merely one of the more obvious hints that this is all flapdoodle. From conception to conclusion, the whole scheme parodies the idea of analysis, of manipulating data to find a Key hidden within.

When Weissmann analyzes, what key does he find? He discovers the central creed of modern aesthetics:

> One night [Kurt Mondaugen] was awakened by a disheveled Weissmann, who could scarcely stand still for excitement. "Look, look," he cried, waving a sheet of paper under Mondaugen's slowly blinking eyes. Mondaugen read:
> DIGEWOELDTIMSTEALALENSWTASNDEURFUALRLIKST
> "So," he yawned.
> "It's your code. I've broken it. See: I remove every third letter and obtain: GODMEANTNUURK. This rearranged spells Kurt Mondaugen."
> "Well, then," Mondaugen snarled. "And who the hell told you you could read my mail."
> "The remainder of the message," Weissmann continued, "now reads: DIEWELTISTALLESWASDERFALLIST."
> "The world is all that the case is," Mondaugen said. "I've heard that somewhere before." A smile began to spread. "Weissmann, for

shame. Resign your commission, you're in the wrong line of work.
You'd make a fine engineer: you've been finagling." (278)

Weissmann's finagling has brought him through comic nonsense to the
thesis sentence of the *Tractatus* (1). Weissmann has found the Key by
following modern conventions, primarily a phony form of analysis with
neither rigor nor control; by a series of arbitrary operations tried at random
until something produced the desired result; and—not least—by scrubbing
personality from the text.

This scene is the climax of Pynchon's extensive parodying of modern
texts. It focuses on the *Tractatus* because the young Wittgenstein had
proudly boasted of having found, "on all essential points, the final solution
of the problems" (Preface); because its severe brevity represents all such
clean, well-lighted places; because its picture theory is the ground of the
modern objective correlative; because the objective correlative when
wholly expanded is the aesthetic arm of colonialism carried on by other
means; and because its concept of the case justifies the fatalism of *what is.*
That is, when Weissmann discovers that the universe is telling the murderous and self-destructive party at Foppl's that the world is as they are,
then their behavior seems to him justified. It is a message confirming for
those who need it their own prejudices and is in that way like Foppl's
discovery of "set symmetry."

Weissmann's discovery of the Key reenacts the modern withdrawal of
personality from the case, the modern search for a place beyond circumstantial culture and personality. When one compares Wittgenstein's *Notebooks, 1914–16* with the *Tractatus,* the lively excitement in the notebooks is
striking. Even more striking, however, is the elision of that emotion in the
curt final product. It is as if the excited hard work that the *Notebooks* and the
finagling toward clarity that Weissmann shows were suspect to moderns
because both betray the possibility that the found Key is a human imposition on the world rather than a genuine discovery of a world elsewhere, of a
"Logic" that can "take care of itself" (*Notebook* 2; *Tractatus* 5.473). One either
believes, as Weissmann excitedly does, that his analysis has uncovered
something true; or, when Weissmann fulfills its extremes, one sees the
entire ridiculousness of the process, as Mondaugen does. Immediately after
Weissmann's finagled confirmation that the world is in accord with their
besieged case Mondaugen proves for himself the opposite.

First he stumbled on the continuing decadent violence: Foppl whipping yet another Bondel, V. exchanging clothing with old Godolphin who
is singing a song from his imperialist youth while he, too, flicks the black.

Disgusted rather than fascinated by what he has peeped, Mondaugen this time gathers his records, sneaks out a French window, crosses the ravine, and trudges away while the other guests gather at the ramparts to croon his farewell, "their faces a Fasching-white." They are sure that he will not survive the black rampage beyond their walls that has driven them inside, they believe, to their behavior. Within a couple of miles Mondaugen meets a Bondel. Rather than slaughtering Mondaugen in revenge for the severed arm and lashed back which whites have given him, the African picks up the European, and together they ride the African's donkey toward the Atlantic, Mondaugen dozing "on and off, his cheek against the Bondel's scarred back. . . . Soon as they trotted along the Bondel began to sing. . . . The song was in Hottentot dialect, and Mondaugen couldn't understand it" (279). End of chapter, center of novel.

Foppl's case had led the Europeans to expect everywhere the same transparent language, everywhere a mutual slaughter between whites and blacks, and everywhere a death-hastening Fasching. Mondaugen found instead a song he could not understand, a hand to lift him, a scarred back to sleep on, and purposeful motion toward release. This Bondel's back conveys such a sense of differences that suddenly it even seems possible to escape the whole violation-revenge pattern. Considered completely rather than in isolated clusters, the world was *not* all what someone else's case was.

A voyeur by name and practice and, therefore, a stand-in for audiences of art, Mondaugen finally broke out of the case to which he had fallen, to which he was plotted. In *Gravity's Rainbow*, Pynchon will use Wittgenstein's "game" in this connection. He will speak of characters "quitting the *game*," meaning breaking out of the cases in which others have caught them. Two years prior to *V.*, in the book he had been writing since the mid-fifties, Joseph Heller had powerfully expressed this feeling: "Every victim was a culprit, every culprit a victim, and somebody had to stand up sometime to try to break the lousy chain of inherited habit that was imperiling them all" (414). Finally quitting Foppl's and Weissmann's game, Mondaugen made "Mondaugen's story" his own. His action is exemplary.

Mondaugen's independent action shows an alternative principle struggling with the modernist certainty of universal underlying order. Breaking out of the case to real help from the purported enemy, Mondaugen puts the lie to the governing idea within Foppl's fortress. Breaking out of that case, snuggling the Bondel's back, Mondaugen exemplifies the existence not of finagled logic, but of root cross-purposes.

☐ ☐ ☐ ☐ ☐

The consequences of cross-purposes emerge in Pynchon's "Epilogue, 1919." Alone of all the historical chapters, it is in a voice approximating Pynchon's own — not Stencil's impersonations, not Maijstral's confessions. Pynchon plays a conventional, omniscient narrator turning at last to face his readers, providing information that Herbert Stencil could not know.[14] Among much else, Pynchon affirms Sidney Stencil, the old Foreign Service spy, as a crafty and wise operator, a flexible man never frozen into dogma, stuck in no single case. To the contrary, Sidney Stencil believed each Situation to be "more mongrel than homogenous" because "it only existed in the minds of those who happened to be in on it at any specific moment" (189). For Sidney every Situation is "an N-Dimensional Mishmash" (470). Sidney's situational mishmash anticipates Wittgenstein's second philosophy, that of the *Philosophical Investigations* rather than the earlier, coeval *Tractatus*. Sidney's Situation gives comic expression of a serious principle. It contradicts the *Tractatus* and, therefore, Weissmann's finagling of that book's thesis.

Soft-shoe Sidney, Stencil's friends call him, because he worked them like a chorus line (189): Pynchon sets his critique of twentieth-century philosophy's most prestigious system in a vernacular metaphor of performance. Taking on the entire dream of independent purity in the *Tractatus,* and its mapping in objective correlatives, he ridicules it from the standpoint of a vaudeville routine. Sidney knew even then, in fin de siècle Florence, what Wittgenstein would come to in the *Philosophical Investigations:* "What are real," thought Sidney, "are the cross-purposes" (484). "The very nature of the investigation," wrote Wittgenstein in his preface to the *Philosophical Investigations,* "compels us to travel over a wide field of thought criss-cross in every direction."

The senior Stencil's metaphor underscores how much of Pynchon's fiction is spectacle or performance, conscious of an audience, scenic, based on theater and film. *V.* begins with Benny Profane noticing a street singer's impromptu performance. Meanwhile, in the street, a sailor sings a bawdy tune as he urinates in the tank of a '54 Packard Patrician, a small audience lending encouragement. This is a public novel. It is full of people acting, haranguing others, hanging out in groups, performing for others, wearing masks, changing costume. Pig is a guitar player, Slab a painter, V. a hardly typecast performer, Angel and Geronimo subway buskers. Roony Winsome and Ploy successfully play at failed suicide to the delight of audiences. Mélanie dances to her death to the horror of her audience and unthinking mentors. Sidney Stencil performs softshoe, his son Herbert does impersonations; Old Godolphin narrates his fantasy of an underground technicolor web so persuasively that he intrigues the foreign service into tentative suspension of disbelief. Metaphors of performance dominate the novel from the dance of the stars in Foppl's planetarium to Stencil's theory of the chorus line to Rachel's theory of love — "You have to con each other a little, Profane" (369). Roony Winsome spends his days recording sound effects — the equivalent of making random caries into cabals, turning random sounds and actions into performances. McClintic and Ruby (Paola) are both jazz performers — he in the polite, she in the raw sense of jazz. V.'s death is a performance (341–45); Fausto is seated in the "gods" — peering down from the roof into the cellar, where the children form the immediate audience. First the children become part of the performance, then Fausto joins it when he goes down to perform the sacrament of Extreme Unction.

Performance is a way out of cases. Performance obviates cases. There are always cross-purposes in performance that alter its outcome. Performance is always at least slightly different from its plan, map, or orchestration — as in Mélanie's death, as in Stencil's Situations. This unpredictability as clearly generated the performed web of V. as it necessitated Wittgenstein's hand-restored torn spiderweb (Spinnennetz) in Philosophical Investigations. Moreover, performance always implies an audience, willy-nilly giving space within its sphere to the corrective laughing chorus. Performers are people for Pynchon whose acting grounds abstract ideas. For instance, the personalities of the modernist collaborators of the Rape of the Chinese Virgins (Itague's anti-Semitism, Porcépic's black rites, Satin's drunkenness) and the madness of the initial performance are ways in which Pynchon deflates hauteur in modernism's high arts. They and their show are to Pynchon no more special than any other chorus line. They too are an N-dimensional mishmash. Theirs, too, is a net effort.

Sidney Stencil's cross-purposes are what change the case, move the Situation into its N-dimensions. Their chaos determines the form of Pynchon's fictions, the shape of Frank's The Americans, the improvised structure of Visions of Cody, the sound of Ornette Coleman's free jazz, and the "criss-cross" ("kreuz und quer") organization of everything philosophical Ludwig Wittgenstein wrote after the Tractatus. The existence of cross-purposes in any given Situation, rather than pat logic, is what provides the grist for those caught in it to break out. Sidney, then, proposes a flexible, shifting understanding of reality and its local cases. His son, Herbert, however, came to believe rather that "events seem to be ordered in an ominous logic" (449). Herbert's is an inflexible understanding of the case as inelastic and overdetermined.

The Stencils reenact the lore cycle. What begins as a loose insight, what Pynchon early on calls a "spur-of-the-moment tumescence" (142), fossilizes. What begins as an aid to understanding eventually impedes understanding. What brings the father close to a working relationship with what he needs to know drives the son on wild-goose chases to verify his principle rather than to bring him closer to the nature of reality. Pynchon knows that over time valuable insights become rituals, then rituals rigidify into institutions for their own sake. There is an obscenity in acting out a fairy tale, like Hänsel's and Gretel's, in the twentieth century—as Weissmann proves in *Gravity's Rainbow*. Ludwig Wittgenstein expressed this idea of ritual stench, or the ossifying of the lore cycle, in one of the earliest jottings he made for the *Philosophical Investigations* after returning to Cambridge. He noted in 1930:

> [*Philosophical Investigations*] has nothing to do with the progressive civilization of Europe and America.
>
> And while its spirit may be possible only in the surroundings of this civilization, they have different objectives.
>
> Everything ritualistic (everything that, as it were, smacks of the high priest) must be strictly avoided, because it immediately turns rotten.
>
> Of course a kiss is a ritual too and it isn't rotten, but ritual is permissible only to the extent that it is as genuine as a kiss.
> (*Culture* 8)

These kisses, these spur-of-the-moment tumescences, are characteristics of deliberately speeding culture. They exist at the outset of lore cycles.

Writing in *Partisan Review* in 1956, the poet John Hollander reviewed *Lolita* while it had still only appeared in its Olympia Press imprint in Paris. He nicely pointed out that "the most pervasive single device of style is the verbal diddle . . . it is a little like an extended trope on the pathetic fallacy, in which verbal hocus-pocus makes the obsessive object light up, in intellectual neon, everywhere" (559). The verbal diddle, the painted diddle, the riff as diddle, the characteristic splash of pigment, the tell-tale photographed gesture: everywhere in the fifties and after does one see the artistic need to daub surfaces with signature marks. From Bo Diddley's characteristic beat to Jasper Johns's obsessive variations on a motif, Little Richard's falsetto cry to Nabokov's puns, Miles Davis's spitting starts to Lee Friedlander's photographs of his shadow on all subjects — all these artists add their personality to their texts. They never want to withdraw it.

Hollander said *Lolita* lights up "everywhere." His remark transfers to literature the principle of Jackson Pollock's "allover" paintings. It is a reminder of the spread of charged vitality over all the apparent surfaces of the deliberately speeding arts. This is an important principle if only because it so interestingly differentiates deliberately speeding culture from modernism's intense focus on hidden abstractions behind, below, or above the evident surface of reality. Passing the bombed rubble of the English Club during the siege of Malta, Fausto Maijstral sees bared a lone flush-toilet, thinks, "What fine democracy in war. . . . Before they locked us out of their grand clubs. . . . But now even the most sacrosanct room of that temple is open to the public gaze" (333). As the times change, the preterite become privy even to the privy. This is a low joke revealing how the esoteric drift late in a lore cycle becomes exoteric early in the next. What was hidden comes into plain view.

Some modernists finagled their way to the place elsewhere. The early Wittgenstein confined his finagling to his notebook and simply stated his belief in the *Tractatus*. He assumed a logical space which his propositions described, but at the first book's end he declared a further domain which remained ineffable, even mystical ("das Mystiche," 6.522). To reach that place elsewhere, Wittgenstein provided a romantic image of a ladder. This was a characteristically stunning move, for after commanding commitment to the abstraction of logical space, Wittgenstein then commanded its transcendence ("muss diese Sätze überwinden") to see the world correctly. Anyone "who understands me eventually recognizes [my propositions] as nonsensical," he wrote, "when he has used them — as steps — to climb up beyond them. (He must, so to speak, throw away the ladder after he has climbed up it)" (6.54).

This was less the ironic ladder of Robert Frost's "Directive" (1947) than the earnest romantic ladder of his contemporary F. Scott Fitzgerald's in *The Great Gatsby* (1925):

> Out of the corner of his eye Gatsby saw that the blocks of the sidewalks really formed a ladder and mounted to a secret place above the trees — he could climb to it, if he climbed alone, and once there he could suck on the pap of life, gulp down the incomparable milk of wonder. (112)

Behind Gatsby, Fitzgerald's narrator seconds the feeling: "I was reminded of something," says Nick upon hearing Gatsby's story of the ladder to the secret place, "an elusive rhythm, a fragment of lost words, that I had heard somewhere a long time ago" (112). And behind Nick, is Fitzgerald—himself seeking that transcendent reality. But it remained for them all in turn, as for the early Wittgenstein, ineffable. They think they have heard the "fragment of lost words," but they cannot find them. These gestures by Fitzgerald and Wittgenstein, both with the same striking image, typify the modern withdrawal of personality from the world.

Coming late in their modern lore cycle, the common vernacular world is what Weissmann and the early Wittgenstein refused to proposition, as it were. But coming early in their deliberately speeding lore cycle the later Wittgenstein, Pynchon, and their colleagues continually court the common world. Every ascendant swing of the lore cycle champions its vernacular reality. There is a place elsewhere, agree these rising lores, but it is not a transcendent or privileged place. It is the place maturing modernism and other descending arcs of the lore cycle have tried to pass over, leave behind, withdraw from, and often define as dangerous. When the lore cycle turned during late modernism—Pynchon's three novels specify during the Second World War—the ascending sense of deliberate speed returned people to the vernacular understanding that the world elsewhere is this one. As Wittgenstein came to argue, after his later work abandoned transcendence, "Nothing is concealed. . . . Nothing is hidden" (§435).

The world elsewhere is this one. Instead of cases, this world has what Wittgenstein came to call *Lebensformen,* which his translators render as "forms of life."[15] Here Wittgenstein was referring to the age-old concept of lore, from which maturing modernism had wandered increasingly. Lore or *Lebensformen* are the shared gestures, assumptions, and judgments that people use when they perform the life of their community.

Language became Wittgenstein's means to describe the formal assumptions from which language stemmed and the life it enabled. Anyone can see that Wittgenstein ceaselessly scrutinized words in his later philosophy. More important, however, is how words and grammar for Wittgenstein cropped contingent on their particular humus. Language was philosophically important to him because its ways of existing revealed its circumstantial soil. His most telling expressions are often traditional folk metaphors—spinning and weaving fibers, also sowing and husbanding seed. "I believe," he wrote in his notebook at the end of the thirties, "that my originality (if that is the right word) is an originality belonging to the soil rather than to the seed. (Perhaps I have no seed of my own.) Sow a seed in my soil and it will grow differently than it would in any other soil" (*Culture* 36).

What grew in his soil was a sense of the sufficiency of these crude tools, the fitness of common language to the world's gravity and variety. He had in his early philosophy thought it necessary to provide a sophisticated alternative to common tools. In his later philosophy he was overwhelmed by the complexity of trying to reconstruct what had come naturally until self-consciousness paralyzed modern life. The spiderweb, the spun fiber, the growing seed: these folk metaphors that appeared in his second philosophy signaled his new reliance on the old vernacular.

He told his students in the transitional lectures published as *The Brown Book* that to imagine a language was to imagine a culture (134). This language, this culture, like the lore floating them both, like Topsy in Harriet Beecher Stowe's novel, just "grow'd." When her new mistress asks who or what made her, Topsy flashes back, "Don't think nobody never made me" (356). This reflexive, responsive level of human life is what Wittgenstein is probing when he probes language. He locates language within the unconscious gestures of human activity early in the *Philosophical Investigations:* "commanding, questioning, recounting, chatting, are as much a part of our natural history as walking, eating, drinking, playing" (§25). They are certainly the natural antecedents of philosophy.

No one body made Topsy, nor did any one body — neither philosopher nor king — make vernacular lore. Neither do members of other *Lebensformen* analyze their moves any better, or worse, than Topsy hers. The values and conditions of life to any group's members are as transparent as the air they breathe. They, too, just grew, responding to needs. They are, so to speak, a-responsible like the conditions of ecology developing in the push and shove of time.

Wittgenstein confirmed this idea well after the work on the *Philosophical Investigations* for which he had developed it. In fact, just a month before his death in 1951, Wittgenstein wrote that he conceived a *Lebensform* "as something that lies beyond being justified or unjustified; as it were, as something animal" (*On Certainty* §359). And then, on 19 April, less than a fortnight before he died, he wrote that

> the language-game is so to say something unpredictable. I mean: it is not based on grounds. It is not reasonable (or unreasonable).
> It is there — like our life. (*On Certainty* §559)

This striking statement has many consequences, among them that it is impossible to see one's lore so long as one resides purely in it. But how can that be if "nothing is hidden?"

To live purely in one *Lebensform* is to live in the textbook definition of literary "myth," which is "the absence of anomaly" (Holman and Harmon 317). Without anomalous conditions, everything would seem to be what the case of the myth is—the very idea he rejected when he repudiated the *Tractatus*. To see his *Lebensformen*, Wittgenstein therefore needs either some special condition that would critique normal life as had logical space in his first philosophy, or he needs some common perturbance that provides anomalous grain. He needs, finds, and probes these common anomalies. Indeed, his second philosophy is the great mid-century attending to common perturbance. Essential purity had been the mapped discovery of the *Tractatus;* perturbance and its consequences are the unmappable basis of his late philosophy.

The fortunate fall for Wittgenstein, as for deliberately speeding culture, is into anomaly or perturbation. Conflicting ethnicity, exhaustion of authority, a gathering youth culture, and new technological amplification all perturbed fifties life just as they provided the grounds for its understanding and new cycle. Their obviously anomalous cases besieged the privileged positions of modern life. Likewise, perturbance caused Wittgenstein all his busy sketching from alternate points of view, but it also made possible the seeing of one's case. The nature of the language game is that it is never pure, never everywhere the same. It exists purely only so long as its possessors do not think about it concretely. As soon as they are able to think of it, then it develops anomalies. If people can conceive their lore, it must have anomalous grain and texture overlapping it from another *Lebensform* participated in simultaneously.

It is simply there, like our life—until supposed impurities enter it. This can happen when a philosopher, like Ludwig Wittgenstein, imaginatively reenters the sphere of ball-playing. Or, when a black young man, like Ralph Ellison from Oklahoma City, or Richard Wright from Natchez, Mississippi, writes for Communist newspapers in New York City. When a trumpet player adds blue notes and syncopation to a sentimental movie melody, a painter drips over his canvas in quite separate stages, or a narrator palimpsests plot lines—when such lore-related activities overlap, then the assumptions of the first activity slip their transparency.

These overlapping cases color each other's air. Suspended in the circumstances of its own lore, a second group's values background the values of the first group. The added elements make not only themselves but all the air visible. That's why the "essential" logical space of the *Tractatus* was unessential and unnecessary. Wittgenstein replaced its Archimedean outside leverage with the internal leverage of mingled *Lebensformen*. He recognized that one *Lebensform* illustrated another, allowing people to see the forms that stand in the midst of their lives.[16] Wittgenstein's later philosophy shows why no one needed the place elsewhere that he had been so concerned to map, in his early philosophy, for modernism.

The hopes and fears of all the years are met in the lore people enact daily. Their performance continually invents and adjusts the values for their lore group. This everyday forming of life is neither intellectually superior nor inferior to the case invented in the petri dish of the philosopher or any other esoteric expert. But it is fuller, has been around longer; its fitness to the group's experience has been commanding a "wide and lasting attention" (Rourke 43), so has perforce a richer natural history. It is normative and makes no swollen claims for its invincibility. Moreover, it is good enough; it has sufficed. This world is what there is. Use it or lose it.

The strategy of recognizing the everyday world is regular at the onset of a lore cycle. Wittgenstein's maneuver, and Pynchon's, and Kerouac's and Frank's and Coleman's and Pollock's and Duchamp's, is for each the nudging along of a turning lore cycle. At such junctures, experts like them have the sense to seek value in the preterite common world. They catch up that way with what their predecessors abandoned.

That's why Pynchon keeps leaving the historical chapters and returning to his initial plot line about Benny Profane's Whole Sick Crew and their way of life in the mid-fifties. In fact, seeking value in the vernacular world is precisely what the opening pages startlingly enact both abstractly and specifically. They show the continual upwelling of spontaneous prankery. The sudden reappearance of repressed worlds and suppressed values defines the case that Benny Profane occupies during the fifties. All his streets have "fused into a single abstracted Street," but Pynchon chocks them with specific capers that are abstraction's opposite:

> East Main, a ghetto for Drunken Sailors nobody knew what to Do
> With, sprang on your nerves with all the abruptness of a normal
> night's dream turning to nightmare. Dog into wolf, light into
> twilight, emptiness into waiting presence, here were your underage
> Marine barfing in the street, barmaid with a ship's propeller
> tattooed on each buttock, one potential berserk studying the best
> technique for jumping through a plate glass window (when to
> scream Geronimo? before or after the glass breaks?), a drunken deck
> ape crying back in the alley because last time the SP's caught him

like this they put him in a strait jacket. Underfoot, now and again,
came vibration in the sidewalk from an SP streetlights away,
beating out a Hey Rube with his night stick. (10)

Repressed prankery is spilling over the Street's abstracted case right onto
your nerves, Reader, and everybody is scared.

The drunken deck ape whimpers in memory of the Shore Patrol. The
Shore Patrol himself walks this sideshow frantically sounding his Hey
Rube call like a Geiger counter at Bikini Atoll. He is whistling in the dark.
Hey Rube is a carnival expression, a secret sign among the cheats behind the
booths on the midway, that the victim (bumpkin, rube) is aware of their
con. It means the rube has discovered the trick clasps in the wood bottles
preventing their collapse no matter how viciously his baseball strikes their
pyramid. Hey Rube is a call to scatter before the rubes rise up to thrash their
scammers. Pynchon's Hey Rube, in a patrolman's mouth not a full page into
V., is his sign of a world erupting with vernacularity. What makes it erupt
are the cross-purposes of competing *Lebensformen.*

Pynchon records no situations in which the elements are pure. There
are always interfaces like the plate glass window here which the potential
berserk studies breaking, even down the most "abstracted" streets. There
are always events ready to cross over, dog into wolf, as here in this East
Main ghetto in Norfolk. This stirring of purities into mishmash is hardly
confined to ghettos, of course, as the unintended end of *Rape of the Chinese
Virgins,* Mondaugen's surprising breaking out of his siege party case, and
V.'s surprising altered incarnations themselves showed in all the historical
chapters. But this ghetto, in fact, is important. It is Pynchon's throwaway
representation of Thomas Kuhn's heap of facts that nobody knew what to
Do With when they were fitting data to paradigms.

These rejectamenta are here in Pynchon's case growing large enough
now to engender rude new principles of their own, barfing in corners and
pissing on Patricians. Nor are they alone in their ghetto. Obviously with
them are the police, who recognize the fragility of their control. For
Pynchon this condition is both a continual condition through any era for
individuals and a near rupture, a pregnant bulge in the historical hose of the
fifties. Pynchon's novels all show the alienation of individuals can grow
widespread enough at epochal junctures to pass a critical mass and spawn a
new lore cycle. *V.* begins with this scene of a whole culture on a fault line. It
ends with a glimpse of an earlier individual across the world finding that
fault line on his own. Sidney Stencil sailed on the last page into a quarter-
hour's waterspout off Malta and never came back. Emptiness turned sud-

denly into waiting presence and back again. The surface of the sea "showed nothing at all of what came to lie beneath, that quiet June day." With those final words, Pynchon emphasized the impulsive, accidental, cross-purposed world with which he began on the first page. In the summer of 1919 it was a fatal warning for Sidney Stencil and modernism. On Christmas Eve in 1955 it was a constant cultural condition.

The turning of the lore cycle makes practices apparent that persist subliminally at all times. Chief among these practices is the continual composition of gestures into patterns that hold territory for their composers. To hold territory in Pynchon's Street is to resist mastery from above — or from wherever it is that Shore Patrols derive — as well as resisting a lapse into impoverished cliché or the dreaded kitsch. Pynchon extends Ellison's idea of the vernacular rite into even less-privileged corners of ordinary life. Ellison's vernacular rites were blues and jazz performance, the Saturday juke dance carried to Harlem bars, the Sunday morning gospel, and the workaday week. Kerouac, too, explored the metaphorical possibilities of the jazz club as a surrogate religious sacrament. But Pynchon in *V.* repeatedly examines the moves and patterns common people make reflexively with merely rudimentary reinforcement. Pynchon's characters all juggle gestures.

Pynchon's people's games are much more like playing catch with yourself or pick-up with one other than like playing baseball. His players avoid recognizing their games' formal aspects — so they are more dialogic jousting than litany. They have more nervous twitches than contemplative developments — so they are more aggressive feinting than polite removal to symbolic distance. For all their quick passing and infra dig status, however, Pynchon's characters' rude gestures and truncated syllables still amount to a repertoire of moves even for those who use them unconsciously. They comprise micro strategies for encompassing and protecting preterite experience from incorporation into the patterns of others. They are the way people figure themselves for themselves. Their repertoire of gestures is the way people hold their own ground everyday.

There is an example in action from chapter six in *V.,* "In which Profane returns to street level." It is a tangled stringball of lore, but no more so than similar moments on nearly every page. Benny Profane, and two young Puerto Rican friends, Angel and Geronimo, are looking for fun on a Thursday night against the background in Little Italy, along Mulberry Street, of the Feast of San' Ercole dei Rinoceronti, which comes on the Ides of March. Such titles tease the neighborhood ethnic festivals of the City and the ancient proverbs behind them. Also in the background is an amateur band playing Giacomo Puccini's *Madame Butterfly* (the modern opera based on an American stageplay), its American Ensign and Japanese geisha to be rendered in Italian for the festival — "how was that," Pynchon asks, "for a tourist's confusion of tongues?" (140). Other apparently incidental details important to the setting include the mention of a TV western movie and a childhood do-good chum now studying to be a priest — from whom Angel and Geronimo poach aliases in their cony-catching games with three young Italian girls found at the wheel of fortune. Moreover, Profane sings to Lucille, one of the girls, a song he claims dates from the Great Depression. Lucille dislikes the song because it "doesn't have any beat" (141). Lucille would not appreciate such a square song because she is clearly named after the unattainable, uncontrollable, eponymous figure in Little Richard's rock song "Lucille," a song propelled by jackhammer drums and Penniman's manic treble runs. (Actually, Little Richard did not record it until the following January 16, but Pynchon is pleading poetic license with a lot of poplore here.) Angel and Geronimo also sing to the girls, presumably in Spanish. They ask Profane to talk to the girls in "Guinea," and he gives them two obscene syllables.

This N-dimensional mishmash of lore, then, updates the senior Stencil's Situation. Not only the international world of intrigue is complex and confusing. Every level has its mishmash practices. In concert, all this detail accumulates as the panoply of rites to which Pynchon is contributing his own sort of attention:

> "What do you guys do," Lucille said.
>
> I tell tall stories to girls I want to screw, Profane thought. He scratched his armpit. "Kill alligators," he said.
>
> "Wha."
>
> He told her about the alligators; Angel, who had a fertile imagination too, added detail, color. Together on the stoop they hammered together a myth. Because it wasn't born from fear of thunder, dreams, astonishment at how the crops kept dying after harvest and coming up again every spring, or anything else very permanent, only a temporary interest, a spur-of-the-moment tumescence, it was a myth rickety and transient as the bandstands and the sausage-pepper booths of Mulberry Street. (142)

Profane's practice is not the purist's folklore. Pynchon does not even say what Profane's tale is; certainly, no one will pass it into the oral tradition. It is immediately responsive, an improvisation to serve the spurs of Lucille's "Wha" and Benny's need. But it uses motifs that trace back to nineteenth-century almanacs—specifically to their Davy Crockett stories and Davy's pet alligator.[17] Davy became legendary for housebreaking the wilderness, including its scariest amphibians. Schlemihl Profane would by definition never domesticate anything. Instead, he finesses life with count-less inventions like this one on the spur of the moment—itself a wonder-fully exact phrase. In their fumbling way, Profane's inventions almost succeed; Lucille eventually lies down for him on a pool table ("Corner pockets, side pockets, and Lucille" [143]), but, before Profane can connect, a gang rumble intercedes and our schlemihl hides to watch. Profane exists in a novel, Crockett in legend.

Profane's practice is part of the everyday composition of experience, a failing strategy to encompass an eventfulness always too full to handle. Failures like Profane's, however, do succeed as moves to make up a life for their maker which neither high culture nor kitsch figure for him. They fail only relative to legend. Fabulous he is not, but Profane does successfully *make do*. His imagination runs in the channels of traditional lore that passes through print and out again, caught perhaps by almanac and newspaper writers, then reimagined at street level, rereleased orally, this time on Mulberry Street, in 1956, profanely. Benny hardly acts politically, but his maneuvering practice is a perfect example of the "antidiscipline" Michel de Certeau described as the "clandestine forms taken by the dispersed, tactical and makeshift creativity of groups or individuals already caught in the nets of 'discipline'" (xiv–xv). What the late French scholar de Certeau called discipline and antidiscipline, Pynchon in *Gravity's Rainbow* called the They-system and We-system.

The character in whose mouth Pynchon coined the term—a double agent—defines a They-system as "what They and Their hired psychiatrists call 'delusional systems.'" Just as in They-systems, "we don't have to worry about questions of real and unreal. They only talk out of expediency." A We-system, he continues, is "delusions about ourselves" (638). The charac-ters sufficiently self-aware to reach such insights are as few in fiction as in life. But they existed as early in Pynchon's work as *V.*, his first novel—in Paola and Fausto Maijstral, cynically in Eigenvalue the psychodontist and Schoenmaker the plastic surgeon, and more optimistically in Rachel Owlglass and McClintic Sphere.

Fiction would not seem full after modernism's example without such metacharacters, characters conscious of themselves as fictions. Yet it is characteristic of Pynchon, and others sharing in his deliberate speed, that the central characters in his novels be as regular as Benny Profane, Oedipa Maas, and Tyrone Slothrop, who hardly know what's happening to them but still compose their experience in practiced ways. They resist reflexively if not politically. They have much the same tender chutzpah as young Miles Davis daring to stand and blow his horn after Charlie Parker's solo on "Embraceable You." Like that youngest Miles Davis, Pynchon's characters perform a We-system more and less without knowing it. (The later Davis, like Jackson Pollock and Pynchon himself, is much more conscious of practicing resistance to orthodox high and clichéd low figures.)

In *V.* these characters resist the siege of contemporary life without a named theory to support their practice. These holding actions of the preterite against incorporation from above and below are the atoms of Pynchon's imagination — as they are of other deliberately speeding artists from Ginsberg to Pollock. As Little Richard and Chuck Berry compose barely liminal lore into forms that appear spanking new; as Pollock's compositions make a virtue of simultaneously embedding and projecting central cultural anxieties; as Robert Rauschenberg exhibits an erased de-Kooning painting, so too do Pynchon's characters stand on an interface between states always ready to turn inside out, zig or zag.

The character in the contemporary plot line of *V.* who raises this issue most fruitfully is McClintic Sphere. He is a jazz saxophonist who plays at a Bowery bar called the V-Note, which is the Whole Sick Crew's local. By virtue of his congenial celebrity for them, and his relationship with "Ruby" (who is an incognito incarnation of Paola), Sphere is a liminal member of the Crew. He shares their fumbling qualities, but he has more, also. He has a blues sense of reengagement, and though his aesthetic is more tentative than smooth it is never silly like Slab's. He deals with concerns larger than the cheese Danishes Slab incessantly paints. In the conventional narrative terms which Pynchon partly spoofs, Slab is a flat character and Sphere is fully rounded.

Sphere worries about moving from condition to condition, state to state, about starting over and the impulses that startle the change. He expresses these ideas in a medley of gospel motifs set in Tarbaby dialect, early computer slang, and fifties psychobabble jelled into lyrics for his band's signature tune, "Set/Reset:"

> Gwine cross de Jordan
> Ecclesiastically:
> Flop, flip, once I was hip,

> Flip, flop, now you're on top,
> Set-REset, why are we BEset
> With crazy and cool in the same molecule. . . . (293)

After admitting with Pynchon that Sphere is "no lyricist," the first thing to notice in these lines is that with them their author effectively catches the eclectic duffle of the period. For instance, they exactly anticipate argot and attitude in Dizzy Gillespie's memoir, *To BE or Not. . .to BOP* (1979). Just as cannily, they reflect the sense of "Howl" and the "Smart went crazy" feel in Allen Ginsberg's 1949 poem "Bop Lyrics" (*Collected Poems* 42). More importantly, Sphere's lines reflect a regular concern in the novel and era with the surprise of change, back and forth across a shifting, multiple dialectic with only rare — usually imaginary — rest in synthesis.

McClintic Sphere's music enacts the senior Stencil's, and the later Wittgenstein's, premise that reality is at bottom "cross-purposes" (484). Foreign Service agents, philosophers, jazz musicians, and novelists all express that conflict early in lore cycles. Late in lore cycles the dominant culture papers over the fundamental mishmash that once upon a time occasioned their rise. The fundamental mishmash implicitly backgrounds Profane's transient practices; it is quite explicitly what Sphere plays.

Here is Pynchon describing the sound of Sphere's group in the middle of the fifties, when both the musician and the reality he was representing were vulnerable and visible:

> Horn and alto together favored sixths and minor fourths and when this happened it was like a knife fight or tug of war: *the sound was consonant but as if cross-purposes were in the air.* The solos of McClintic Sphere were something else. There were people around, mostly those who wrote for Downbeat magazine or the liners of LP records, who seemed to feel he played disregarding chord changes completely. They talked a great deal about soul and the anti-intellectual and the rising rhythms of African nationalism. It was a new conception, they said, and some of them said: Bird Lives. (59–60, emphasis added)

In its cross-purposes, Sphere's music discovers the principle that the form of the novel warrants with its own consonant family resemblances and bastard discontinuities. Sphere's aesthetic is Pynchon's, as Pynchon's is late Wittgenstein's, and Wittgenstein's is the aesthetic of deliberate speed in a "kreuz und quer" (criss-cross) world.

In *V.,* this cross-purposed aesthetic achieved explicit mention chronologically first in Sidney Stencil's vaudeville metaphor, then in the eponymous winds that blew Fausto Maijstral through his multiple personalities just before and during the Second World War. Pynchon reiterates this aesthetic here during the fifties chapters when the Whole Sick Crew attend performances of Sphere's jazz. Readers discover it within the novel from the way Sphere forms his sound for his club audience and in the similar effect of the novel's bits blowing past them. Barreling down the city's avenues, the wind—like Sphere, its imitator; like Pynchon, its author—blows "the shavings, cutting oil, sludge of New York's lathe" (59) over them all, Sphere's and Pynchon's audiences alike. All this speeding flotsam is in deliberate emulation of the cross-purposes of the world: "Outside the wind had its own permanent gig. And was still blowing" (60).

Pynchon's evocation of the scene at the V-Note clearly emulates jazz writing of the fifties, down to the number of Sphere's reed (4½: Charlie Parker was said to use a 5 [Russell 9], and Ornette Coleman a 1 [Hentoff's notes to *Something Else!* OJC-163]), description of Sphere's embouchure, and send-up of the eccentricities of his sidemen, including the boy brought from the Ozarks to blow a "natural horn in F," a minimalist drummer, and a bass player who talked to his instrument. Even more specifically, the passage above refers to the remarks Martin Williams repeated in his liner notes for Ornette Coleman's *The Shape of Jazz to Come* (SD 1317), the album on which both "Lonely Woman" and "Congeniality" appeared. In his first paragraph, Williams cited Percy Heath and John Lewis, bass and piano players in the Modern Jazz Quartet, who since they first heard him in California had both been touting Coleman as Charlie Parker's heir, calling Coleman's music a "new approach" and a "new thing."

One of the earliest reviews of *V.*, by Stanley Edgar Hyman in the *New Leader*, called McClintic Sphere a "parody" of Ornette Coleman. In fact, however, if he is a parody he is much else besides. He is an affectionate rendering compacting details from Coleman and other jazz musicians, writers, and legends to create a complex tonal picture of a movement in avant-garde culture that bears the value of the novel—indeed, the value of deliberately speeding culture. Insofar as any character, idea, or complex carries Pynchon's meaning, McClintic Sphere does. As an African-American and an outsider (from Fort Worth, in his case), making a living performing for whites, Sphere is a man in the middle, conscious of the overlapping ways of life that make him up, and serve the world. He is eager to negotiate them all. For all his experience, he retains enthusiastic innocence enough to make tender remarks to friends, particularly to the woman he takes for a prostitute named Ruby. "We could make it," he tells her, recapitulating the concerns of a novel inheriting a soiled modern legacy, spelling out the anxieties of fifties culture in general from Beckett to Ellison and beyond, "it would be a fresh thing, clean, a beginning" (350).

Yet the sense of parody if not in Sphere, then in the remaining Whole Sick Crew, is inescapable, unstable, and has remained difficult for readers to place. A main reason for the invisible youth's return to street level in Ellison's novel ten years before *V.* had been that individuals of his sort in the underground were too scarce to sustain his mind's activity. But Pynchon claims in *V.* that just a few years later, by 1955 and 1956, there was a surplus of underground types. They erupted so quickly that the society did not know what to Do With them, and neither do Pynchon's gate-keeping critics know how To Read them.

Even among Pynchon specialists the author's attitude toward his underground remains undecided. This uncertainty stems partly from Pynchon's attraction to particular readers. His texts contain so much encyclopedic data that they attract readers with esoteric interests and knowledge. These readers assume that Pynchon is one of *them*—that anyone who knows about the Fashoda crisis *and* the Five Spot, about the history of the Bondelswaartz *and* the *ballets russes*, about the Mixolydian mode *and* mantissas, about entropy *and* T. S. Eliot all at the same time must disdain the string-smoking bounders and cads he writes about. (Too, string-smokers assume he is mocking the finicky esoterica of stamp-collecting, rocketry, and dodo devastation.)

Yes and no. It's hardly marginals that Pynchon disdains, but unthinking, unproductive people—be they central or edgy. Far worse by far than the Whole Sick Crew in *V.* are those empowered elites who do harm to others. In cornering and wasting resources, they let dwindle and dissipate the chances for social diversity and democracy that had once been so great at the outset of the industrial revolution and its attendant modern lore cycle.[18] Father Fairing eating—living on—the rats he has converted to Catholicism in New York sewers is the absurd example of this point (118–19). Systems devour their own resources.

This issue of Pynchon's relation to the underground and its poplore has therefore remained muddy all the intervening years since 1963. There are indeed many characters in the novels, not least in *V.,* some of them more or less sympathetic, who bristle at poplore and its initiates. Herbert Stencil, for one, describes the young painters and writers in the Whole Sick Crew as people engaged in "Romanticism in its furthest decadence; being only an exhausted impersonation of poverty, rebellion and artistic 'soul.'. . . Perhaps the only reason they survived, *Stencil reasoned,* was that they were not alone. God alone knew how many more there were with a hothouse sense of time, no knowledge of life, and at the mercy of Fortune" (56–57, emphasis added). That they existed is Pynchon's contribution; but how they existed is the younger Stencil's judgment, and he is no paragon of acuity. If he is partly disdaining them for being pests on the host culture, what is he to them (from whom he has been cadging lodging, drink, and food) but a pest on their pestilence? His life in its own way is at least as wasted as theirs. Although Pynchon here allows Herbert Stencil to mock the Whole Sick Crew, his assessment hardly constitutes the wholesale condemnation that it has seemed to some critics as they stewarded a comfortable acceptance of the book.

When people lack one's own experience, they seem to lack "knowledge of life." Stencil's birthdate synchronizes his life with the end of high modernism, and he looks askance on the younger Crew, much the way many in his and Clement Greenberg's generation looked askance at the kitschy proclivities of New York art. (Born in 1901, Herbert Stencil would have been eight years older than Greenberg.) But Pynchon comes out of this crew himself. The Whole Sick Crew is his own crowd, mingling his own Navy mates with his college friends. Their capers amount to a displaced account of life as it would have been for Richard Fariña, Mary Beal, David Shetzline, Earl Ganz, Jules Siegel, Pynchon and others from (and like) the Cornell crew had they lived in New York City in the mid-fifties instead of simply visiting it on holiday.[19] After Herbert Stencil's, the most scathing remarks about the Whole Sick Crew come from Dudley Eigenvalue, who considers these pretenders ephemeral. Dr. Eigenvalue collects dentures because "Teeth and metals endure" (298), theorizes his dotty psychodontia, and hopes to catch the attention of some future dental historian "in a footnote as Patron of the Arts, discreet physician to the neo-Jacobean school" (297).

Clearly, therefore, the risible judgments in *V.* of avant-garde life in New York are not Pynchon's, and not necessarily even his narrator's. When he has members of the Crew talk about their work, it is sometimes nonsense — as when Slab predicts his Partridge in the Pear Tree "will replace the Cross in western civilization" (282). This is exactly the sort of remark no artist of the Abstract Expressionist school, in particular, would make. Slab's cheese Danishes are Pynchon's compressed send-up of Andy Warhol's soup cans and Wayne Thiebaud's confections, of Tom Wesselmann's hoagies, Jasper Johns's ale cans, Edward Ruscha's Spam, and Claes Oldenburg's hamburgers and popsicles and BLTs — especially his *Danish Pastry* (1961). This smorgasbord is from the period of gestation for *V.* and Pynchon would have sampled it either in Manhattan or, in the cases of Thiebaud and Ruscha, in California. However, none of these painters thought about symbols as Slab did. None of these painters of the contemporary lore cycle hoped to substitute one symbol system for another so much as to obviate them with mad new proliferations.

For all this, Pynchon's send-ups remain ambiguous. Slab's Danishes, Roony Winsome's mock-serious recordings of gang warfare and other oddities of the fifties, even Mafia Winsome's Ayn Rand-like theory of Heroic Love are topics and concepts perilously close to Pynchon's own obsessions—to his daft songs and yo-yoing and filled-prophylactic water bombs. In mocking cheese Danishes he is mocking himself and his own crowd. But he is sensitive to these issues because in choosing to center emblems in his own art, in representing both historical events and contemporary trends, what matters is that the representations count. When one centers commonplace icons—as Duchamp did, as Rauschenberg and Johns and Warhol, Davis and Parker and Kerouac and Ginsberg, Brando and Dean and Kazan and Ray, and Pynchon did—then it matters all the more which icon. Looked at one way, the man who wants to elevate the letter "V" from a wedge shape, the shape of spread thighs, the painter's convention for foreshortening, and so on, to an icon for the entropy of modernism and more—this man has no business mocking Slab's snacks. Looked at from another angle, however, he has every reason to mock those Danishes because they make him nervous about his own representative efforts.

Representing reality in an era after Wittgenstein has annihilated his own early picture theory, after he himself has laughed at Eliot's objective correlative theory in "The Waste Land" and elsewhere, Pynchon is aware of the instability of all such portraits and landscapes. They mean different things to people in different *Lebensformen*. So also do his fifties characters mean different things to readers in their own varying contexts. The instability of Pynchon's reference is self-conscious and structural. Perhaps it is for this reason that he takes the cheese Danish's creator's name, "Slab" (who is one of many among the Whole Sick Crew with a single, rudimentary name) from an illustration early in the *Philosophical Investigations* (§2 ff.) of elementary and partial ("narrowly circumscribed" [§3]) language games that Wittgenstein shows are too "over-simple" to be real (§4).

At the same time, just as Wittgenstein was affectionate about those language games, choosing Augustine's theory (in §1 ff.), for instance, because it illustrated earlier naive commitments on his part, so too does Pynchon register his affection as an aspect of the Crew's capers and caprices. His affection and appreciation is why the term "parody" for the way he writes up both Slab and Sphere is too aggressive, "burlesque" too broad, "satire" too formal. Wittgenstein's terminology helps in understanding Pynchon: "The language games" Wittgenstein wrote, "are . . . set up as *objects of comparison* which are meant to throw light on the facts of our language by way not only of similarities, but also of dissimilarities" (§130). Pynchon likewise posits both the historical and contemporary chapters, the modern decadents and the contemporary Crew, as complex refracting sets. Each is what Wittgenstein called "a measuring-rod; not . . . a preconceived idea to which reality *must* correspond" (§131). Whatever term readers settle on, Pynchon's action is to amplify his audience's conflictual feelings about these meaningful louts, these living oxymorons. Like Wittgenstein, Pynchon is mixing the *Lebensformen.*

Certainly Pynchon scoffs at his own work as ruthlessly as at Roony and Slab, Esther and Mafia. Eigenvalue speaks interestingly to this issue. The Whole Sick Crew "produced nothing but talk," he says, "and at that not very good talk. A few like Slab actually did what they professed; turned out a tangible product. But again, what? Cheese Danishes. Or this technique for the sake of technique—Catatonic Expressionism. *Or parodies on what someone else has already done*" (297, emphasis added). Here Eigenvalue is hitting back at his author, at Pynchon, surely, because parodying the already-done is the heart of *his* method, particularly in the historical chapters of this his first novel. There are, nevertheless, plunging gradations between the scathings of modern decadence in "Mondaugen's Story" and "V. in love" and the burlesqued capers of the fifties chapters. Within these last there are, too, important differences between how he slights Slab and admires Sphere.

Slab's problem is that he is overly simple and partial: just as he would overly schematize it, Slab is a truncation of reality. Sphere, however, keeps escaping attempts to pin him down, and has done so continually since Hyman's review initially identified him with Coleman—without noticing that Pynchon named him in fact after Thelonious *Sphere* Monk. Pynchon admired and attended Coleman's performances, but Monk's excellence in the fifties was more assured. Thelonious Monk had been recording his own heralded compositions since 1947.[20] An acquaintance of the time says Pynchon referred to Monk as "God" (Siegel 170), and he was not alone. Drummer Art Blakey has pointed out that Monk's intensely personal attack preceded both Charlie Parker's and Dizzy Gillespie's (Feather 337–38). Indeed, Monk was also one of Coleman's models.[21]

Thelonious Sphere Monk and Ornette Coleman were two of the more interesting jazz composers of the fifties. Both figured in important sessions

in the mid- to late-fifties at a grungy club in the New York Bowery called
the Five Spot, which Pynchon has punned into the "V-Note." For the last
half of 1957, Thelonious Monk's Quartet played the Five Spot; Ornette
Coleman's Quartet played the club in 1959. Pynchon telescopes these two
sessions into one event in 1956 and their leaders into one musician, McClintic Sphere. Like Coleman, Sphere is a horn player from Fort Worth. Like
Coleman, whose record company paid his tuition at the Lenox School of
Jazz the summer before they sent him into the Five Spot for his landmark
gig, Sphere in *V.* spends time playing and mulling theory in Lenox. But
Pynchon named his character after Monk's middle name, and he gives him
the pianist's proclivity for odd titles. He also gives McClintic Sphere a
girlfriend to pine after named Ruby, based on Monk's famous tune, "Ruby,
My Dear."[22]

Ruby is a disguise in *V.* for Paola Maijstral, one of the novel's more
important characters and a link between the historical and contemporary
chapters. Paola inherited V.'s comb when the Maltese children dismembered her; as "Ruby," Paola carries on V.'s promiscuity (becoming a literal
prostitute). But it is Paola who also reverses this tendency at the end of the
novel with an earnest commitment of faithfulness to her husband, a sailor
named Pappy Hod. Although Benny Profane learns nothing from his
travels and experience, Paola learns plenty. In particular, she puts into
action the novel's creed, which she shapes with McClintic Sphere while
masquerading as his dear Ruby.

When Ruby confesses her identity and predicament to Sphere, the two
beat out a code for their times:

> The only way clear of the cool/crazy flipflop was obviously slow,
> frustrating and hard work. Love with your mouth shut, help
> without breaking your ass or publicizing it: keep cool, but care.
> (365–66)

This oxymoron, "keep cool, but care," is the difficult program the novel
follows.

This claim that "keep cool, but care" is the creed of *V.* cuts against the
grain of Pynchon's critics. From the first, they have been uneasy with the
direct complexity of Pynchon's imperative. Hyman's review, for instance,
inaugurated uneasy reception of Pynchon's imperatives by remarking pa-
renthetically, "(How treacherously [Sphere's motto] appears to resemble
Krishna's message to Arjuna in the *Bhagavad Gita:* Do your duty without
attachment)" (510). It took two years before Richard Kostelantz had found a
way to nestle Pynchon in with John Barth and Joseph Heller as novelists of

absurdity proposing a pointless world. His formulation took everyone off the hook of duty or intention. The point of such novelists, Kostelantz argued in what was to prove a comforting explanatory tag, "is That Life Doesn't Have Any Point."

As the early critics in their respective bailiwicks had received Jackson Pollock and Claes Oldenburg, Miles Davis and Coltrane, Rauschenberg and Johns as formalists without social content, so the accommodation to Pynchon and company proceeded similarly. Especially academia absorbed him as an artist whose social pictures are all parodies without an ethic. As it takes a while for nursing puppies to resnuggle and find their teats again after their bitch stands to growl or bark, so it takes critics and other gatekeepers time to settle in comfortably again after such disturbances as *V.* or Ornette Coleman's *Free Jazz* or Pollock's *Night Sounds.* No one should mistake any stage in this snuggling as the last. Comfort is a continual struggle when lore continues to cycle. Ten years later, when *Gravity's Rainbow* appeared, the supposed pointlessness of Pynchon became more difficult to push. If it was anything, that big novel was even less circumspect, even more youthful in its brash declaration. Its author was constantly and pointedly reminding readers that "Living within the System is like riding across the country in a bus driven by a maniac bent on suicide" (412). Pynchon angrily and inventively insisted that most people abandon themselves to that mad ride, trying to settle into their seats without a fuss.

In *V.* as throughout his work, Pynchon associates the counter principle of a vernacular caring for life and for passed-over people with jazz and ultimately with the blues ethic. Beyond Sphere and dark Paola (whose father referred to the Bantu as "brothers" [307]) this connection of persistent pointedness with the blues is clear from the other life-saving character in the novel, a "gargantuan Negro named Dahoud" (12). Dahoud saves a suicidal shipmate from jumping overboard early in the novel, scolding, "Don't you know . . . that life is the most precious possession you have?" (12). His caring for life and restraining its destruction is an infectious germ that even the lowlife Pig Bodine catches later when he comically restrains Roony Winsome's suicidal defenestration to the strains of Elvis Presley's "Don't Be Cruel." Pig repeats verbatim his former shipmate Dahoud's moral about life's preciousness (361). One does not disengage from society, Dahoud and the blues teach; one goes on with life. This exemplary Dahoud is doubtless named after jazz trumpeter Clifford Brown's famous fifties jazz composition, "Daahoud."[23] Life is the point.

Naturally enough in this novel where everything is open to skepticism, the creed "keep cool, but care" does not itself escape burlesque. For instance, the robot SHROUD tells it to Benny Profane as a "watchword" (369). What is this repetition but warning that technology routinizes charisma? Whether uttered by charismatic Sphere or by a routine robot, however, in a novel where most statements fail to hold, "keep cool, but care" has the virtue of telling the truth about itself: Pynchon clearly worked long and hard on *V.* Moreover, his journalism about Watts and contemporary Luddites shows that he tries to care coolly;[24] and his extraordinary privacy surely prohibits his publicizing himself. Trivializing and self-mocking as it may be for SHROUD to repeat Sphere's code, Pynchon significantly both includes that commentary and combats it. Assumptions shared with Sphere and Ruby are what drive Pynchon to describe the horrifics of European genocide in South West Africa, as well as watch the violent end of the ballet in chapter fourteen ("V. in love").

There is a further, hardly incidental link between Sphere and the historical chapters. The connection between the sferics Mondaugen records (and tries to decode) and the music Sphere makes is more than a pun. Although readers cannot hear Sphere's music they can imagine it from Pynchon's description and from their amalgamation of Thelonious Monk's and Ornette Coleman's playing in the fifties. Both sferics and Sphere's music are products of siege—cosmic and urban, respectively. They are both, in the coinage of Whitney Balliett, the "sound of surprise." After that, however, the family resemblance twists to reveal additional genes. Insofar as it is like Monk's and Coleman's, Sphere's jazz, though improvised, is highly practiced, disciplined, and regular beneath its initially apparent chaos. Sferics are random noise all the way down; they simply tease auditors, who feel a "logical must," to find authorized messages within them at whatever comical cost. Sphere's jazz works the other way. From admittedly disparate, unauthorized motifs speeding by, in his music Sphere deliberates his own logic. It is the opposite of finagling a phony message in random sound. Its construction is forthright and on the surface. It shows how to assemble a real life from flotsam.

McClintic Sphere's "keep cool, but care" is an oxymoron that translates Earl Warren's "deliberate speed." The two are synonymous phrases. Sphere's imperative is as important in Pynchon's novel as Warren's in the era. Sydney Stencil spoke about—and the novel has given readers—what the epilogue calls "fever dreams: the kind where one is given an impossibly complex problem to solve, and keeps chasing dead ends, following random promises, frustrated at every turn, until the fever breaks" (471), or the novel ends. In such a matrix of life or fiction, people can only cope through oxymoronic creeds that acknowledge, as the senior Stencil and McClintic Sphere and later Wittgenstein do, that life's cross-purposes disrupt seamless continuity and correlative representation. But for Pynchon as for many of his peers, to acknowledge the negation of those ideas does not mean flipping to an opposite pole. Rather, it means resisting the flip that leads to war as well as the flop that brings on a stark opposite: "no love, no hate, no worries, no excitement" (293). To negate *correlative* representation, for instance, is not to negate representation. Rather, it means that representation is more complex, more tonal and circumstantial, more interpretive and creative, sometimes concrete, sometimes vaporous, always elusive. The point comes and goes, as when a hand spins a fiber or a bard spins a yarn.

V.'s carved ivory comb is such a point. Throughout the historical chapters, Pynchon used it to indicate the continuity of its possessor despite the radical gaps in both her personality and story.[25] As her persistent trait, the comb distinguishes V. from apparently similar characters (Hedwig Vogelsang, for instance). The comb passed at V.'s death to Paola (342), thus confirming other family resemblances that Paola shares with V. She becomes a "balloon girl" (331), for instance, as was V. (67, 488). They have a mutual capacity to survive beyond situations, cases, doom. And they both adjust to their contexts, seeming to grow out of and express their determinants even while they surreptitiously heighten them. The comb depicts five British soldiers killed by Islamic followers of al-Mahdi during their fierce revolt against imperial control, which the British supported, 1881–85. Pynchon refuses to specify what the comb meant to its carvers, or to Victoria Wren when she bought it in Cairo, or to Paola. But clearly it must have served contrasting talismanic meanings for V., a colonial perpetrator, and Paola, a subject continually colonized whether in Malta or Harlem.

After Paola takes the comb at V.'s death in 1943, the comb goes out of the story to come back only when Paola hands it to her estranged husband Robert "Pappy" Hod, back in Malta again in 1956. It is her handsel that she will again be his wife when he returns: "I will sit home in Norfolk," she says, "faithful, and spin. Spin a yarn for your coming-home present" (443). Her decision reverses her promiscuous inheritance from V. She will no longer continue as the amoral victim of colonial policy. By choosing to play Penelope to Pappy Hod, vernacular yobbo nonpareil, Paola marks a passing from one way of being in the world to another. Paola passes from a modern imposition and preservation of cases to a contemporary survival of shifting cases.

Embracing the creed she and Sphere developed, she will coolly accept the discontinuity of her family's life — taught notably in her father Fausto's confessions; but she will also assert her continual caring for her husband. At the novel's end, more than ever, Paola is on that "enviable vantage" between young and old societies that her father proposed during the siege of Malta. As when she was five years old, Paola is still "creating a discrete world" (331). Like V., Paola is one who goes through states and remains confined by none of them. Unlike V., who continually commits herself to dominating whatever case she occupies, Paola's affinity for victims and her knowing scraps of all tongues (331) keeps her between states. V. survives states, in other words, by trying to impose her virtù on them. Paola survives like the invisible youth, by "running and dodging the forces of history instead of making a dominating stand" (*Invisible* 333); like Yossarian, who is a self-appointed expert at "evasive action" (*Catch-22* 51); like Rabbit, running through Updike's fifties; like the Beat caravansary; like Rojack, who in Mailer's sixties walks a high parapet between a suicidal jump toward the moon and a short hop to structural solidity, some thirty stories above wet Manhattan pavement, to prove he can keep in abeyance his besieging forces (*Dream* 223–25). They all succeed. All these deliberately speeding people support themselves by unorthodox concepts of who they are. It gives them, as it gives their culture, as it gave wartorn Paola, an enviable vantage. Passing from an entirely earnest and sober Paola to a wholly earnest but inebriated Pappy Hod, Paola's comb, that was V.'s comb, returns quite differently to the story.

This comb, then, is a curiously circumstantial trait, depending for its meaning on its contextual *use*. Pynchon has carefully borrowed the idea of the comb from its constant adornment of the mythic white goddess. Robert Graves claimed that the goddess was, among many others, the Virgin Mary and Robin Hood's maid Marian, the merry-maid that was the origin of *mermaid*. She was conventionally a beautiful woman always figured with a round mirror in addition to her comb and fish-tail. Traditionally she represented a love-goddess risen from the Sea. Aphrodite is one example of her lineage and Botticelli's *Birth of Venus* is her "exact icon." "Her mirror and comb," continues Graves, "stand for vanity and heartlessness" (395). In *V.*, however, Pynchon is both using and reversing Graves's confident universality.

V. is associated with Venus's vanity and heartlessness, surely, but Paola as certainly is not. When Pynchon mentions *The White Goddess* in introducing Veronica Wren, in the first paragraph of chapter three, he lumps it in the same phrase with *The Golden Bough*. Both these books suffer in contemporary perspective for insisting on a universality against the idea, in the words of Frazer's biographer, "of culture as the matrix, both conscious and unconscious, that gives meaning to social behavior and belief" (Ackerman 1). That local culture, the way it twists to its own ends what it palms from universality — that's what Paola and Pynchon emphasize in reversing the meaning of the comb she took from the modern woman V., from Graves, and from modern history.

Like his peers in fiction, folklore, anthropology, history — virtually every contemporary discipline — Pynchon brooks no Key to all Mythologies. He and Paola date that shift to the mid-fifties. That is the time when ambition in the arts could proceed with a different goal than analysis of phenomena down to a single unifying theory or proposition. The mid-fifties is when complementary truths and circumstantial meaning came to notch the most ambitious and self-conscious works as well as their vernacular kin.

What might it mean to say that meaning in *V.* is circumstantial, like meaning in the *Philosophical Investigations?* Because there is no one overarching common Case, but multiply shifting cases, a circumstantial *V.* would mean that there is no underlying key to the story — not even V. herself, as a woman. She has no stabler meaning than family resemblances. She signifies different purposes and affects in every surrounding. The repeated images and ideas in the novel, like entropy, the recurring color yellow, the code "keep cool, but care," and the terms "the Hothouse" and "the Street," would mean different things to interpreters in different cases. A circumstantial *V.* would mean that the standard sort of assertion about meaning in a novel, standard in the sense that it worked for eighteenth-, nineteenth-, and early twentieth-century fictions, would no longer work. This instability corroborates the conflicting feelings that readers have when they want to present a coherent statement about Pynchon.

It is very difficult to assert anything constant about the novel except its inconstancy. One instinctively feels that this apparently asserted inconstancy or chaos is wrong, however. That is, the skein that includes discontinuity also knots into itself intention and concern — caring that provides not unity but persistent meaning nevertheless: "*V.* is a novel that does not add up, but does mean" (Hite 50). Both perceptions are important, both necessary. When the deliberately speeding culture found its early conventional acceptance in reviews that suppressed its intentionality, claiming it was continually and characteristically pointless, Wittgenstein had already anticipated this misunderstanding at an important juncture in the *Philosophical Investigations*. He remarked:

> If someone wished to say: "There is something common to all these constructions — namely the disjunction of all their common properties" — I should reply: Now you are only playing with words. One might as well say: "Something runs through the whole thread — namely the continuous overlapping of those fibres." (§67)

He was speaking of his own propositions and their logic. But he might as well have been figuring Pollock, Frank, Coleman, Monk, Kerouac, O'Connor, and Pynchon. Wittgenstein is contemptuous here because it is commonsensical that overlapping and disjunction each depend on the other for either to be perceptible.

V. created a stir when it appeared in the early sixties because the relative weight of its apparent chaos seemed high, and because it set that chaos in the fifties, a time supposedly placid and controlled. As it has taken time to understand that the fifties era was bursting at the seams, so it has taken a while for readers to notice in *V.* its webbed family resemblances — the repetition of facts as well as the phrase "cross-purposes" characterizing Sidney Stencil's Situations in Cairo, Florence, and Malta in the historical chapters and McClintic Sphere's music in the novel's present. Every instance of a hothouse idea, each entropic unwinding of energy, every windblown piece of detritus, each incorrigibly selfish modernist, every gruesomely chauvinist male, every murderous colonialist, each analyst ridiculously turning a key in a mishmash, each parent/child relationship, every son or daughter seeking parentage — they all pile up family resemblances that counter the disjunction of the book. To the early readers who said that disjunction characterizes both V. and *V.*, one should reply: you were only searching for a key. One might as well say: "Something runs through the whole novel — namely the continuous reverberation of principles, ethics, and metaphors." These echoes throw readers back on the interface between assertion and confusion, meaning and nonsense. That interface is the split vantage that Fausto told Paola was enviable, but which feels painful and difficult in the practice of everyday life.

A circumstantial *V.* would mean that Pynchon agrees with the Wittgenstein of the *Philosophical Investigations*. There is no *Bild* of reality for either of them, no propositional one-to-one correspondence, no objective correlative. Nevertheless, there is meaning. *V.* generates a curious representation of the world as a place hovering between sense and nonsense, between order and disorder. It is just like a Pollock painting in that regard, just like

Robert Frank's narrative sequences in *The Americans*. It is like *Visions of Cody* more than *On the Road.*

Some, not much, of the topical content of *V.* is political: the Suez Crisis in the contemporary chapters, the nationalisms in the historical chapters converging on Florence, Foppl's siege party, and the café-talk in Paris. Of more lasting significance, and more substantially political, is Pynchon's representation of the emerging order that now seems real in the contemporary world because the science of chaos as well as painting and fiction and urban skylines today continually corroborate it. These are all circumstantial and echoic rather than rigid or truly anarchic. The shape of *V.*, in itself, is a complex representation of and for all its peers. *V.* structures an order that is not confining, that neither schematizes nor lays the world waste for an idea. It follows the maxim of the *Philosophical Investigations,* leaving "everything as it is" (§124). Its political achievement is that Pynchon wrote an aspiring volume without stenciling or damaging the world with his pattern. He manages ambitious intentions without being imperial. He manages no genocide, no holocaust, impales no dancers, but he is every bit as allusive, as wide-ranging, as sifting as the modern and nineteenth-century predecessors with whom he and his lore cycle compete.

Pynchon's stuttering form and style are knotted to his era's struggle to recreate itself with deliberate speed. Like his colleagues, some of whom he portrays within *V.,* he is trying to find a way to represent not so much the surface of his times as its principles, its turbulently grading ethics, its fragile coherence and performances of order. This is not to say that Pynchon's pictures of surfaces are not telling tableaus — from Profane dressing himself in *V.* (37) to the "bureaucratic smegma" sifting to precise layers on Slothrop's desk in *Gravity's Rainbow* (18). Rather, like Robert Frank who also makes odd and specific snaps of reality, or like Kerouac and Wittgenstein who sketched it obsessively from every angle, or like Ornette Coleman who can stun auditors with a delicate snatch of melody, it's not the snaps, sketches, or snatches so much as their arrangement that matters. The point is their mutual arrangement of the point.

□   □   □   □   □

. . . a repetition high and low of some prevailing form.
— Pynchon, *Gravity's Rainbow*

A decade after *V.,* in *Gravity's Rainbow* (1973), Pynchon would look back to the chaotic European Zone of the Second World War as the zero-ground, a closing but also an opening that allowed the contemporary epoch. Nothing in that account, however, contradicts his claim in *V.* that the mid-fifties was when it came together. "Christmas Eve on old East Main," 1955, has remained the time and place for him, as loosely for the rest of deliberately speeding culture, when all elements converged to reset the lore cycle. The starting conditions of that lore cycle are what *Deliberate Speed* has remarked.

The assumption throughout this chronicle has been congenial with Pynchon's—namely that putative high culture and low culture are not opposites. Rather, they enact mutual principles by different means. They do not grow out of each other by evolution or devolution so much as each tries to express their mutually underlying form. They stand in relation to each other as do urban jazz and rural blues, sometimes grabbing from each other but continuing in parallel play. They are found furthest apart late in lore cycles when high culture is straying into high-handed autonomy. At other much healthier times, they are congenial. At all times, to a greater and lesser extent, they have "a sympathetic magic, a repetition high and low of some prevailing form" (*Gravity's Rainbow* 232).

Mid-fifties consumers and the culture organizing them were becoming a consciously exploited concept on all sides, from industry to intellectuals. To point out the consumer's victimization—the way Benny Profane, for instance, "walked the aisles of a bright, gigantic supermarket, his only function to want" (37)—is to notice the bulk of the story. But there is also more. Much of the remainder is in the wave of alternative resistance Marcel Duchamp began to catch as early as the New York Armory show in 1917, when he displayed a men's urinal as a "Fountain." Signing his sculpture as "R. Mutt," Duchamp was already dogging the modernism he saw trying to flee its rude roots. He was reminding the art world of its resources. Many of the mates in Pynchon's Whole Sick Crew, like the rest of significant fifties culture, are afloat on this alternative wave.

Pynchon's character Fergus Mixolydian, for instance, is "the laziest living being in Nueva York." In that regard as in many others, he has the genes of Duchamp, said to have "died as phlegmatically as he had lived" (Alexandrian 89). Mixolydian imitates Duchamp right down to the "stall in the Penn Station men's room" that Pynchon says Mixolydian entered as a "ready-made" in an art exhibition (56). In calling to his colleagues to notice the ambiguous objects around them, Duchamp's idea was that artists, no less than everyone else, consume their era's objects. They can do no other. But perhaps like Ellison's invisible man they can change their attitude toward that consumption. All people are bound to the wheel of their time, but not obligated to its attitudes.

Not only Slab but everyone in that sense makes cheese Danishes. Duchamp chose urinals and stoppages and assemblages of George Washington and sugar cubes. Slab chose cheese Danishes. Paola chose Pappy Hod. Pynchon chose to admit that artists, like citizens, have to work with what is. He shows this near the beginning of *V.* with his elaborate variant on the poplore joke about the boy cursed with a golden screw where his navel should have been. The boy hates the screw and consults specialists for help in its removal. A voodoo doctor finally gives him a potion, which puts him into an involved dream, during which he is able to remove the cursed mark: "Delirious with joy, he leaps up out of bed, and his ass falls off" (40). This joke is a parable related to Sphere's creed, as well as to high modernism's doctoring of reality. Rejection of the given, however understandable, is likely to make things fall apart.

Resistant caring is what works: "help," argued Sphere, "without breaking your ass." And that involved "slow, frustrating and hard work" (365). Something of the same contradiction bothers some viewers, pleases others, but is in any case central to *Rebel without a Cause,* where delinquent Jim Stark (James Dean) ends up playing house with Judy (Natalie Wood) and Plato (Sal Mineo). When the police needlessly kill Plato, does that send Jim back over the edge into rebellion? No, it just makes him stand with his father at the film's finish — two men who now know the way of the world. Much of this film's dreamlike popularity derives from the delinquent's reconstruction of his father in a world where the authorities continue to bungle all assignments.

There was a strong need through the fifties for new rituals to replace the old. Sometimes this urge took the form of substituting urban spur-of-the-moment tumescences for old agrarian patterns, perhaps to kill alligators in the sewers rather than ride them up Niagaran cataracts. As with the playing house in adolescent games, in Elvis Presley's "Baby Let's Play House" (released April Fool's Day, 1955), and in *Rebel without a Cause,* sometimes the need was to warm up ancient practices that for whatever reasons had cooled beyond caring. Sometimes the fifties rituals were the ongoing patterns brought to the city from the country, like the ones Ellison hauled from Oklahoma and Alabama to Harlem, mingled with what he recorded there for the Federal Writer's Project, and used in *Invisible Man.* In 1938, at the corner of Lenox Avenue and 135th Street, he collected this full-blown whopper about Sweet-the-Monkey:

> Sweet could make hisself invisible. You don't believe it? Well here's
> how he done it. Sweet-the-monkey cut open a black cat and took

out its heart. Climbed a tree backwards and cursed God. After that
he could do anything. The white folks would wake up in the
morning and find their stuff gone. He cleaned out the stores. He
cleaned up the houses. Hell, he even cleaned out the dam bank! He
was the boldest *black* sonofabitch ever been down that way. And
couldn't nobody do nothing to him. Be-*cause* they couldn't never
see im when he done it. . . .

    The police would come up and say: "Come on Sweet" and he'd
say "You all want me?" and they'd put the handcuffs on im and start
leading im away. He'd go with em a little piece; sho, just like he was
going. Then all of a sudden he would turn hisself invisible and
disappear. The police wouldn't have nothing but the handcuffs. . . .
He won't let hisself be seen. (Levine 405–406)

From such lore of invisibility as Sweet's came the canniness of Trueblood
and Rinehart, Peter Wheatstraw and Sambo the laughing doll, came the
narrator his invisible self, came the Little Richard of "Tutti Frutti" and the
Chuck Berry of "Brown-Eyed Handsome Man" — all masked, all frisking
through formulaic rites, all refusing to let themselves be seen. "He didn't
need the money," said Ellison's informant, "Fact is, most of the time he
broke into places he wouldn't take nothing. Lots a times he just did it to
show 'em he could." Sweet, the proto-invisible man, enjoyed the practice of
his magic. And so did his audience.

    Sometimes these fifties performers and their audiences used the mini-
rites of everyday practice that people have always used to charm their space
and hold their ground. That is, they invented small equivalences for Sweet's
backward tree climb, the counting-out rhymes in children's games, the
opening and closing formulae of fairy tales, or the unmistakable ending
sounds of a symphony or hymn.[26]

    Between Nicholas Ray and James Dean, *Rebel without a Cause* devel-
oped a strong sense of ritual. Ray demanded it from the beginning. To
ritualize the film, he parted company with Irving Shulman, who scripted
many of the film's best scenes, because Shulman parried the dimensions of
"classical tragedy" Ray sought to give the film. Ray specifically wanted
Plato, at the end, to seek "shelter under [the planetarium's] great dome and
artificial sky . . . a gesture of anger and desperation that matched the kind of
thing I had heard," Ray maintained, "at Juvenile Hall" while researching the
topic (Koszarski 254). Ray tended to reach for the stars in these bloated
actions, but Dean worked in mumbles and stumbles, tics and nearsighted-
ness. Dean grounded Ray.

One of the ritual touches Dean added was the "Toreador" name-calling that turned the obligatory delinquents' knife fight into a California bullfight. Dean had long been interested in bullfighting ritual, and had presented a "matador's ritualistic preparations" as part of his Method training under Strasberg in New York (Garfield 95).

Whenever he can, Dean's character Jim Stark ritualizes action. During the film's opening sequence, 1 a.m. Easter morning, he seats his father on the police-station's shoeshine throne and pronounces him "King of the Ball." Even though the chicken-run of the cars over the cliff was unnecessary by the time they ran it—his jousting opponent had by then confessed friendship—they nevertheless went through with the event thinking to enjoy its choreography, its parallel kisses and palm wiping, its hair combing and cigarette smoking in slowdown as stylized as ready-set-go. They savored their gestures as much as any knight donning armor and hoisting himself on horseback to list for the maiden in Saturday matinees of yore. So much were they enjoying it that when Jim jumped laughing from his car at the last second, not knowing that Buzz had caught his jacket on the door handle and gone over the cliff with his horsepower, the death came as a shock. Jim took Judy's hand in a protracted gesture most viewers judge too postured, but which culminated the ritual and closed off the charmed space. The strut of the bullfight, the stylized chicken run, the hand-taking—these gestures and many more marked the phases of Jim Stark's courting behavior as he claimed his lass. Driving his prize home, Jim handed over her cosmetics case that he had found Easter morning at the police station. Now they had a compact between them.

Scenes of failed family compacts come next in the film, both in Jim's and Judy's homes. That's why Jim, Judy, and mock son Plato go through all the rituals of a young family buying, renovating, and decorating their new house. Earlier in the film Stark understood the gang's defense of the Dawson High School seal when he had walked on it; he hastened to apologize in all seriousness for his misstep. However overearnestly, this supposedly rebellious film generates rituals of its own to supplant the ones elders have failed to sustain meaningfully. And it shows especially the most reprobate delinquents desperate to sanctify and hold charmed turf, both actual and emotional.

Ray's wholly cinematic instincts not only translated intellectual action into visual dance, but in the process stylized gestures into small counting-out rhymes for the cinema. One example is when Jim sees his mother descending the stairs upside-down in her robe and pajamas. It is an odd sequence that only gradually comes clear as the audience realizes they are seeing this descent from the point of view of Jim lying on his back on the sofa. Jim puts his mother on her feet by sitting up, the image revolving south to north on the screen as he rises. The scene plays out Jim's desire to right his parents — which he achieves at the film's conclusion, when they all stand together.

Ray's magnification of tics into private ritual practices could bloat out of hand. When he was using tactless actors, his amplifications could be deft as a brick. Humphrey Bogart, playing Dix Steele in Ray's 1950 effort, *In a Lonely Place,* for instance, had a name as clichéd as Jim Stark's, but his straightforward delivery (as opposed to Dean's anxious murmur) emphasized as profundity such nonsense as "I was born when she kissed me, I died when she left me, I lived a few weeks while she loved me." In contrast to this oracular baloney, *Rebel without a Cause* is a diagnostic film for its epoch because Nicholas Ray encouraged Shulman, then Stewart Stern (who took over the writing), Dean, Sal Mineo, Jim Backus, Natalie Wood, and Dennis Hopper to diddle their performances with minute details that continually agitate their frames, stick in the memory, and militate against Bogart's forties sort of corniness.

Defending his own "30s and 40s" temperament, Andrew Sarris has descried Ray's "jittery mannerisms" (43) in *Rebel without a Cause.* But those jitters were the hooks that caught Ray's cult public even while they repelled viewers with wider intentions — precisely as such ritual charms are supposed to do. Beginning a story with "Once upon a time," a tale-teller renders normal reality inoperative. Turning a police station shoeshine stand into a throne, a thug into a toreador, Jim Stark is cursing what's shut out as well as charming what's closed in. Dean's and Brando's mumbling Method girds them against such tri-cornered enunciation as Bogart's, spreads out their spots of significance all across the screen and throughout the film, and links them with the verbal diddle that Nabokov rendered and that Flannery O'Connor learned from the repetitious double-talk of blues songs. Deliberately speeding art is often decentered like this. Like Pollock's canvases and Kerouac's Duluoz saga and Pynchon's long novels and Ornette Coleman's *Free Jazz* for eight improvisers playing pairs of four instruments, *Rebel without a Cause* was an allover construction, spread with stylized practices and ritual jitters all the way out to the edges.

Achieving this allover quality was no accident but an intentionally thorough change of the film's source. The germ of *Rebel without a Cause* was Robert Lindner's case study of a young psychopath named "Harold," published in 1944 as a book with the same name as the subsequent movie. Warner Brothers had bought the filmrights in 1946, cast Brando in the lead, then dropped the project when studio executives doubted the commercial vitality of teen melodrama. Then the fifties happened, the baby boom made itself felt, newsweeklies and tabloids played up juvenile delinquents, and Nick Ray started working on the script. Ray and his writers wholly transformed Lindner's academic account of adolescent rebellion, leaving only his title.

Rebel without a Cause, as a film, was thus not a popularization of high culture theory but a memorable compaction of free-floating fifties poplore. Lindner's "Harold" and Nick Ray's "Jim Stark" have nothing in common. Lindner's Harold is fluent if not eloquent, at least while in the hypnotic trances his therapist advocated. Dean's Stark emphasized distinctly wounded, emotional stuttering, which Ray certainly favored and encouraged. Lindner's Harold, indeed, all psychopaths according to his theory, are physiologically as well as psychologically "arhythmic" in their body systems, thus fundamentally unstable. Jim Stark was a fundamentally stable person irked by skewed mentors and outlandish peers. Lindner's delinquent was unstable in a stable society while Ray's rebel was stark in a flutteringly weak context. Lindner's logic was scholastic. Ray's cutting and editing were quirky and criss-cross, emphasizing Stark's shaky setting. Lindner's Harold had parents who tortured, beat, kicked, and yelled at him daily. Jim Stark had parents and a grandmother who coddled, spoiled, forgave, and bargained with him constantly. Lindner's Harold said, "My father always seemed rough. He always hollered at me. I guess I must have thought he might hurt my mother" (Lindner 207). Nick Ray's Jim Stark complains quite differently about the relationship between his mother and father: "She eats him alive and he takes it. . . . What a zoo. . . he always wants to be my pal. . . if he had guts to knock Mom cold maybe she'd be happy." Lindner's Harold could not live up to his parents' rigid expectations. Nick Ray's Jim Stark cannot make his parents live up to his own idealizations. His parents tell him not to be so idealistic; he says, "Just once, I want to do something right." Whereas Lindner's psychopath really wants to kill his father, and Jim Stark is accused by his mother of trying to strangle his father, in fact all Stark wants is to prop his father upright. Thus the movie finds its emotional apex when father and son stand up together at dawn, look each other in the eye, and the son introduces his new girlfriend.

This is heavy-handed imposition, but it is also diagnostic of the deliberately speeding generation. They would prop up fathers with clean new vernacular charms—"supplementary rites," Ellison called them (*Territory* 50). Such rites had to be spread jittery across their texts, Ellison had known, their participants had to see them as unimportant and belittle them, because of the association of rites with power and religion, which these sons and democrats were all eager to have as a personal but not an institutional condition. The need for rites goes on, as does lore (which is ritual's looser relative). But a vernacular rite must remain covertly related to its shy participants.

The jittery practices of deliberately speeding culture consort easily with the rapid oscillations of new life in the era. The material differences of consumer culture in the fifties brought people extraordinary mobility, of which hotrod and jet travel were only two of the more obvious signs. Like the rest of the art of this period, Pynchon images this mobility with shifting and unstable patterns. Like its main characters, Pynchon's novel constantly moves around three continents and back again. The Whole Sick Crew's goal-free yo-yoing alternates with the overly focused wild-goose chasing that Pynchon links to modern lives, like the younger Stencil's, and the intentional imposition of will which results in V.'s own decadent disassembly.

Pynchon's projection of instability in *V.* therefore serves at least three purposes. First, he is imaging the rattling speed of the era at the beginning of its lore cycle. Second, he is affirming these oscillations as more open and promising than the too-intentional behavior of V., Weissmann, Itague, and their modern models. Third, his mad movements are a second-level reflection of the earlier fifties art that he admires. He was in earnest when he wrote, as recently as 1984, that "one of the great American novels" is "*On the Road,* by Jack Kerouac" (*Slow Learner* 7).

Like Kerouac and Pollock, Pynchon and all of the deliberately speeding artists were thoroughly marinated in black culture. Pynchon's fondness for jazz is at least as clear as his reliance on European musics. He uses both as subjective correlatives for their participants' positions on form, sentimentality, romanticism, and much more. It is fruitless to argue that he preferred either African-American or European culture. Rather, he uses both as complex indices of characters' consciousnesses. During the writing of *V.,* and then again while he was constructing *Gravity's Rainbow* from many of the same impulses, European culture certainly came to represent "analysis and differentiation" to Pynchon. African culture, as embodied in the Hereros, came to indicate for him "unity and integration."[27] Like all American writers from Mark Twain and Henry James through Vladimir Nabokov and Joseph Heller, Pynchon understood how to butt these two cultures together to show each off (and up). It is hardly accidental that when European scientists injected truth serum in Tyrone Slothrop, Pynchon's most emblematic American, they discovered mingled among his deepest fantasies amalgamations of Charlie Parker and Malcolm X, the blues harmonica and *King Kong*.

The phrase "deliberate speed" comes from an activist decree. Earl Warren intended it to change American behavior. Similarly, the records and paintings, books and plays, films and poems that represent deliberately speeding culture are all zealous. Their push and pull neither take it nor make it easy. Nor do they despair. They are all hopeful that what seems outlandish at the time of writing will secure a place for itself in the world, for itself and for their congenial audience. Only toward the eighties, with Jasper Johns selling individual paintings for more than three million dollars, with Little Richard the constant *doyenne* of the talkshows, with personal media well past TV and tapes, with computers and compact disks replacing the typewriters and records of the period's exciting onset — only then was it apparent that the goals of the fifties were the givens of the present.

What had begun as an oppositional culture had become the operational present. Some of its members were sure to join whatever expanded canon survived into the next century. The most likely candidates were also those most surely addressing and reflecting deliberately speeding culture: Charlie Parker, Miles Davis, Thelonious Monk, and Ornette Coleman; Vladimir Nabokov, Ralph Ellison, Flannery O'Connor, Jack Kerouac, and Thomas Pynchon; Robert Frank; Allen Ginsberg and Frank O'Hara, and Charles Olson; Jackson Pollock, Robert Rauschenberg, and Jasper Johns; Little Richard and Chuck Berry among them.

High and low they repeated the prevailing forms of the deliberately speeding lore cycle. They assembled criss-cross patterns that occupied but never resolved the previously excluded middle. They were politically congenial to common people and vernacular culture but they loathed dogma. Because they sought and simultaneously spurned ritual, their result was a charming of everyday practices. Their improvisations came and went fleetingly, reflecting how practitioners make do. They accepted the commonplace and jittered it in deceptively slight gestures across their pages and canvases. Yet they did not eschew large ambition, nor the ambition to change people, nor the urge to figure reality. In all this they succeeded.

Who would have thought handmade webs would bear such weight?

NOTES

1. I cite Dr. Johnson's phrasing from the second edition (also 1765) of his eight-volume Shakespeare (28). F. R. Leavis used this phrasing—*deliberately* instead of the first edition's *deliberatively*—as the epigraph to his first chapter in *The Great Tradition* (9).

One MATERIAL DIFFERENCES

1. Written in 1942, the poem itself has seemed to fuel the hibernation thesis, except that its exhortation to surrender to "the land of living" and create its vernacular stories, art, and enhancements was precisely the creed the fifties did espouse. Frost's sort of out-of-favor modernism found fruition beginning in the fifties, as will become clear in chapters three and four below.

2. Carl Davidson popularized this term in talks he gave during the late sixties, although neither he nor his SDS mates may have coined it. Since it attempted to democratize energy consumption, the concept was galvanizing at the time. But because it ignores any complementary idea of stewardship for future generations, and is naively indiscriminate about sorts of energy, the "post-scarcity state" concept is too present-oriented. There can never be plenty of energy for the ideal future, which is a long time.

3. "Constance Rourke's Secret Reserve," my introduction to Constance Rourke's *American Humor*, glosses the historical context for this issue.

4. Frank photographed *The Americans* during 1955–56, but published the volume almost exactly like Nabokov published *Lolita,* first in Paris (1958) then a year later in the U.S., and for the similar reason that the land of Frank's topic only reluctantly admitted his apparently negative images of itself.

5. The full remark appears on a postcard Kerouac sent Robert Frank: "Dear Robert— That photo you sent me of a guy looking over his cow on the Platte River is to me a photo of a man recognizing his own mind's essence, no matter what." Frank printed the message on the page facing his photograph in *The Lines of My Hand.*

6. No word "Interstate" until 1968, says Webster's—but what then did I drive on when I

went north to college in 1962, marveling in the creamy concrete, the empty roads, the overpasses still unconnected and leading nowhere? Even the occasional finished cloverleaf, not yet populated, still had no giant high signs. To eat and sleep, one had to leave the superhighways and enter the small towns where the old boarding houses and motels were. They did not all have the same names, then.

7. See Ginsberg's account of this line in the *Original Draft Facsimile* (134–35).

Two   **DELIBERATE SPEED**

1. Earlier figures in this line would include the vaudeville and Ziegfield Follies comedian Bert Williams, as well as Louis Armstrong and Duke Ellington.

2. The fullest gathering of the primary material about Till is Stephen J. Whitfield's *A Death in the Delta: The Story of Emmett Till.*

3. The accounts of this event have reached mythic proportions. Their sanest recounting is in Garrow's opening pages, and in Branch, pp. 128–34. I have supplemented these versions with the oral accounts Raines collected.

4. Leonard Feather: Davis "was the first to make use of modal themes, a development later associated more closely with John Coltrane but actually going back to . . . when Coltrane was a sideman in Davis' group" (226). For a fuller, accessible explanation of this issue, see Martin Williams's "How Long Has This Been Going On?" in *Jazz in Its Time.*

5. These John tales are from Hurston pp. 74, 51–58, 75–78; her definition of *John* is useful:

> Jack or John (not John Henry) is the great human culture hero in Negro folk-lore. He is like Daniel in Jewish folk-lore, the wish-fulfillment hero of the race. The one who, nevertheless, or in spite of laughter, usually defeats Ole Massa, God and the Devil. Even when Massa seems to have him in a hopeless dilemma he wins out by a trick. Brer Rabbit, Jack (or John) and the Devil are continuations of the same thing. (253)

6. These lines conclude one version of the toast, "The Sinking of the *Titanic,*" from Abrahams's *Afro-American Folktales* (283). He gives several variants to the toast, and many like it, in *Deep Down in the Jungle.*

7. In an epigraph to *Word and Object,* Willard Van Orman Quine is responsible for making public James G. Miller's maxim that "Ontology recapitulates philology."

8. I wrote about characters breaking away from social patterns in American literature of the 1960s in "Breakaway," particularly pp. 300–306.

9. See particularly Houston Baker's extraordinary Chapter 3, "A Dream of American Form," in his *Blues, Ideology, and Afro-American Literature;* and Robert O'Meally, "*Invisible Man:* Black and Blue" in his *The Craft of Ralph Ellison* (Cambridge: Harvard University Press, 1980) 78–104.

10. The minstrel tradition in America is related to the vaudeville show but preceded and succeeded it. That is, during the period leading up to and following from the Civil War, the minstrel show achieved its enormous success. It came then to dominate the vaudeville show, which absorbed it. Because of this association, the two terms tend to merge, as in the label "vaudeville blues," which is a synonym for jazz or classic blues sung mostly by women with jazz combos or orchestras; these blues songs developed as part of the minstrel entertainment in vaudeville shows.

Before the growth of the vaudeville institution in America, however, there were black minstrel entertainments and skits. And the minstrel troupe persisted after the decline of the vaudeville tradition in the twentieth century. These minstrel troupes continued in ever more humble circumstances until they became the ragtag blues bands and medicine shows, roaming mostly across the South, that trained the rhythm 'n' blues and jazz performers of the fifties.

11. For the complexity of the minstrel show, see my essay, "Constance Rourke's Secret Reserve," and my bibliographical essay in the same volume. Roger Abrahams illustrates signifying in the tale-telling tradition in *Afro-American Folktales*. His definition:

> Signifying is one of those bedrock black terms that can be self-contradictory—that is, it comes to mean one thing and its opposite at the same time. . . . Signifying can refer, as it does in standard English, to the ability of a word or act to carry deep meanings to the surface. But when used in the black sense of the term, it draws on both the standard definition and the strategy of testing and even casting doubt on the ability to bear the conventional meanings. Signifying, then, becomes a stance toward life itself, in which the significance of a reported action cannot be interpreted as meaning only one thing, for it may convey many messages at the same time, even self-contradictory and self-defeating ones. (6)

A lengthy analysis of signifying is in Henry Louis Gates, Jr.'s full discussion of its contemporary use—"The Blackness of Blackness: A Critique of the Sign and the Signifying Monkey." For an incidental description of jazz signifying, see Ross Russell's description of Charlie Parker at the Parisien Ballroom (104).

12. Most widely available on Paul Oliver's collection *The Story of the Blues* (Columbia CG 30008). Chris Albertson has a minimal account of the session (179).

13. Enid Welsford lists the "grotesques of various kinds" whom the Graeco-Roman world recruited to function as fools: "hunchbacks, pygmies, dwarfs, negroes, living skeletons, caricatures of ordinary men and women, who are usually represented as bald, or idiotic or with an exaggerated phallus" (61).

Three   **OUT OF THE HOLE**

1. These lines doubtless lurk as a source for Ginsberg's opening line in "Howl," written four years later.

2. For Joan Crawford, see "Joan Rawshanks in the Fog," one of the most wonderful sections of *Visions of Cody*, pp. 275–90. For the Three Stooges, see pp. 300–6.

3. Baldwin wrote in his introductory notes to *Blues for Mister Charlie*, "the germ of the play [is] the case of Emmett Till" (5). Two of the stories in *Newsweek* appeared 12 September and 3 October 1955. The first identified the weight around Till's neck as a cotton-gin pulley, the second called it a fan; one looks through these stories today for a single detail that individualizes the picture, but it remains entirely in amber clichés: Till's mother, Mrs. Mamie Bradley, was a Chicago civil servant; the jury were mostly farmers, all white, all male; Carolyn Bryant, from whom Till bought his gum, was "an attractive, dark-haired mother of two"; the eulogy in Chicago included Christ's words: "For as much as ye have done unto one of these, my little ones, ye have also done unto me."

4. Black woman: Berry was originally calling "Maybellene" "Ida May," after the country song "Ida Red," a standard to which he had added his own touches; he changed the title at the behest of producer Leonard Chess. Berry insists that the new name was racially neutral, taken from a third-grade storybook cow named Maybellene (145). Berry's great pianist, Johnny Johnson, remembers the change differently: "we thought Maybellene was a joke y'know. Took the name off the hair cream bottle" (Lydon 9).

That Berry believed in his automotive symbolism is clear in his autobiography, where he mnemonically remembers scenes by the car that delivered him to the action. His first high school car was a beat-up 1934 V-8 Ford sedan (41) and he balances his being the first in his family to go to jail with being the first in his family to own a Cadillac (48). He drove a "seven-month-new red Ford station wagon" with his band from East St. Louis to Chicago for the "Maybellene" recording session (101).

5. An example of its use in the 1980s: "An athletic scholarship sent Mr. Jackson from Greenville to the University of Illinois, one of college football's Big Ten. 'The promised land,' says Jacqueline Jackson, sarcasm in her voice. 'Yeah, the promised land,' repeats her husband." (Joyce Purnick and Michael Oreskes, "Jesse Jackson Aims for the Mainstream," *New York Times Magazine*, 29 November 1987, 35.)

6. "First I was Prof. Eskew Reeder, then at Capitol I figured one name would add to the mystique. 'Is he Spanish?'" (Billy Miller 5).

7. White says that he left the Johnsons out of the biography because Penniman asked him to, saying they were "not important in his life" (phone conversation 11 July 1989).

8. David Evans suggests that "B. Brown" may be "Buster Brown, who came from near Macon and who recorded some blues hits in the 1950s. Brown played harmonica" (Letter 1).

9. See Billy Wright, *The Prince of the Blues* (Route 66 KIX 13). This part of Little Richard's education only surfaced when Penniman cooperated with biographer White, thirty-five years after the fact.

10. In addition to Constance Rourke's chapter on minstrelsy, "That Long-Tail'd Blue," for the minstrel tradition as it devolved into the twentieth century see Paul Oliver's chapter three, also called "The Long-tailed Blue: Songsters of the Road Shows" in *Songsters and Saints*.

11. "Good Golly, Miss Molly" written by Robert Blackwell and John Marascalco, courtesy of Jondora Music.

12. David Evans, letter to author, 1.

13. David Evans (77–78) and Jeff Todd Titon (114–15).

Four   **CONGENIALITY**

1. The term *poplore* has an embattled history too rococo to analyze here, though the merest summary is necessary. In 1950, in the magazine *American Mercury*, the folklorist Richard Dorson proposed the concept of "fakelore" to separate the proliferation of folklike material from authentic folklore. The effect was one more in the series of modern deracinations of popular culture. In the sixties, as a tactful answer to Dorson, Marshall Fishwick developed the term *poplore* to refer to urban culture which he thought was "as true to its environment as was folklore to an earlier one" (20). Richard Dorson counterattacked in his full-length defense of the folk-fake division in *Folklore and Fakelore* (1976). This dispute ripened for me after I naively thought I was coining the term *poplore* in a 1978 article on Bob Dylan. It turned out not to be my term, but I stand by its value.

2. "Silas Green from New Orleans" was an institution. Walker Evans had photographed posters for the Silas Green show in the thirties—see numbers 384 and 385 in his *Photographs for the Farm Security Administration, 1935–38.*

3. See Berry, Foose, and Jones. Melvin Lastie's father was Frank Lastie, who learned drums in the same New Orleans Colored Waifs Home that nurtured Louis Armstrong. He became a Grand Marshall of the funeral marches important to the jazz of the city, and he introduced drums to the city's storefront church services. His wife, Alice, sang. Their Ninth Ward home was a haven for musicians. Their three sons—Melvin, David, and Walter—all played professionally, and their daughter, Betty Ann, is a gospel singer. A. B. Spellman tells some of this story but has the Lastie name as "Lassiter."

4. This is Andreas Huyssen's useful term for cultural hostility. He has called "the great divide" the central problem for modern art especially at the end of the last century and the middle of this one. He need not have limited himself to modernism; what he is noticing is the natural resentment and aggression when an emergent loregroup is shouldering its way into the space of culture.

5. Jonson's judgment of Shakespeare's classical learning was prefixed to the first folio edition of his works, in 1623: "To the Memory of My Beloved, the Author Mr. William Shakespeare, And What He Hath Left Us"; it is in most poetry anthologies of the period. For Shakespeare's use of popular culture, see Cesar Barber. For Watteau, see Thomas Crow, *Painters and Public Life in Eighteenth-Century Paris,* Chapter II, "Fêtes Galantes and Fêtes Publiques," especially pp. 72–73. For the rise of early popular culture, see Peter Burke, *Popular Culture in Early Modern Europe.* For the separation of elite and popular cultures, especially see Burke, pp. 270–81; Burke persuasively calls this separation "the withdrawal of the upper classes."

6. I am thinking here of Great Dixter, an English half-timbered hall in Sussex, whose present structure dates from circa 1460, and whose original Manor is mentioned in the *Domesday Book* (1086).

7. I paraphrase here Webster's etymological root for *vernacular*—from the Latin *verna,* "slave born in his master's house." Houston A. Baker, Jr.'s epigraph cites this definition and reestablishes the etymological metaphor.

8. I use the term *public* in the sense that Thomas Crow has defined it in *Painters and Public Life in Eighteenth-Century Paris*: a public is "a commonality with a legitimate role to play in justifying artistic practice and setting value on the products of that practice. . . . A public appears, with a shape and a will, via the various claims made to represent it; and when sufficient numbers of an audience come to believe in one or another of these representations, the public can become an important art-historical actor" (5).

In that sense, Crow's *public* gives an urban name to what folklorists used to study as a *community* in rural settings. Both public and community act as small groups that cohere around their lore, or what Crow calls, partly for art-historical reasons, a "repertoire of signs" (17).

9. The question is, what sort of narrative? Jean-Francois Lyotard has described the attitude toward large narratives, *grands récits,* as diagnostic in discerning the advent of the postmodern moment. Crises have occurred in all modernism's legitimizing tales; they have all broken into unstable linguistic communities; postmodern people live in the vicinity of many of these small stories, partaking of them adventitiously (Owens 64). Frederic Jameson seconds this analysis in literary terms when he argues that modernism demanded commitment to the value systems of arch figures from D. H. Lawrence to Rilke and Hitchcock. He writes, "The crisis of modernism came, then, when it suddenly became clear that 'D. H. Lawrence' was not an absolute after all, not the final achieved figuration of the truth of the world, but only one art-language among others, only one shelf of works in a whole dizzying library" (113). Indeed, but that is also the crisis that occurs at the inauguration of every lore cycle.

10. These last three attributes are facets of Leslie Fiedler's, claims he made during his many lectures on popular culture during the 1970s. Also see his *The Inadvertent Epic,* 17.

11. The new public is composed of many smaller publics naturally not entirely in accord or synch with each other. There is an archness in Nabokov and his early public, as with Johns and *his* public, that is more tangential to than coextensive with the publics cuing on and emboldening Kerouac and Brando, Davis and Ray. Yet taken together, the deliberately speeding artists have similar large goals and more kinship with each other than with earlier groupings.

12. Henry Luce seems to have coined the term in *Life* magazine, 17 February 1941.

13. Both are reprinted in volume one of Greenberg's *Collected Essays,* but Greenberg left "Laocoon" out of *Art and Culture.* These brilliant distillations of modern values have attracted much commentary recently, some of the best by Thomas Crow, T. J. Clark, and Greenberg himself in *Modernism and Modernity,* eds. Buchloh et al., and in Diana Crane's *The Transformation of the Avant-Garde.* These provocative commentators generate much heat and commensurate light, but I have to argue with one point in Thomas Crow's particularly impressive essay, namely that Greenberg cites popular culture or kitsch as the force which determines the path

modernism took: "mass culture has determined the form high culture must assume. Mass culture is prior and determining; modernism is its effect" (221). This is what Crow, not Greenberg, believes.

Instead, Greenberg says, the move toward purification in painting began when all the modern arts tried to escape the dominance of *literature* as the preeminent art in the West. That is, sculpture, architecture, and painting tried to free themselves from the ideas and content that were important in literature. Because of the Protestant revolution and its antidecorative ethic, because of the portability and thrift of books following the invention of the printing press, literature rose in the West to a prominence that it does not have in other cultures. Consequently, the other Western arts compete with literature, so imitate its "ideas." He states this very clearly and bitterly: "painting and sculpture in the hands of the lesser talents — and this is what tells the story — become nothing more than the ghosts and 'stooges' of literature. All emphasis is taken away from the medium and transferred to subject matter" (*Essays* 1:25).

It is true that Greenberg in a much later essay, "Modernist Painting" (1965), repudiated this stance. There he argued that the purity of modern art derived rather from its drive to be true to its two-dimensionality, as opposed to the three-dimensionality which is "the province of sculpture," "and not so much . . . to exclude the representational or the 'literary'" (196). This essay, though, is particularly frustrating. It offers some of his clearest statements in programmatic language, then withdraws them at the end, saying, for instance, that modern painting is unusually self-critical and aware, and, later, that it was neither, but unconsciously following paths of least resistance (199). Finally, Greenberg repudiated this repudiation in the Vancouver Conference on Modernism in 1981 (Buchloh, Guilbaut, and Solkin 268).

In any case, it is not mass culture or popular culture or kitsch which is the determining force in Greenberg's concept of modernism. Rather, Greenberg's main determinant is an internecine squabble between the players in the drama of high culture, each competing to withdraw further and further into the rigor of the medium and the limits of the discipline.

14. Remember that less inflammatory commentators (as sympathetic to Marxist analysis as Greenberg) have found more accurate ways to describe this creation — from Dwight Macdonald's mildly demeaning "midcult" to Peter Burke's carefully neutral "chap-book culture . . . of the semi-literate, who had gone to school but not for long" to Mikhail Bakhtin's positive "laughing chorus" which judges the elite deficient.

15. Brendan Gill has reported: "Politically, Corbu [Le Corbusier: the crow] was not above flirting with Fascist notions, and during the Second World War he worked for a time with Pétain's puppet regime at Vichy" (104).

16. Which they would have read in Arthur Symons's *The Symbolist Movement* (1899, revised 1908), see Bush (19).

17. Heinz-Otto Peitgen and P. H. Richter's *The Beauty of Fractals: Images of Complex Dynamical Systems* stunningly confirms relevance for chaos science to the arts climate during the early deliberate speed period. Readers lacking sufficient mathematics can understand their preface, the beginnings of each of their sections, and the articles they commissioned by Mandelbrot, Eilenberger, and Franke. The relevance of the computer-generated graphics to paintings by Pollock and others will be immediately apparent. In their garish color choices and kaleidoscopic magnifications, one also sees a relationship between these techno-enthusiasts and the programmatic-poster style of Haight-Asbury, circa July 1967. Readers desiring a more patient technical introduction to the mathematics of chaos can begin with Hofstadter's *Scientific American* column, November 1981.

18. Two of the best studies of Frank compare his work to Walker Evans, who helped Frank win his Guggenheim and thus make the photos that became *The Americans* (Papageorge; Baier). Without doubt, Evans deeply affected Frank, and the younger photographer's compositions often allude to his great forebear. But he is of course more different than like his mentor.

Five   **THEY ALL JUGGLED MILK BOTTLES**

1. Merrill's Ouija experience "began in Stonington on August 23, 1955, with [his companion David Jackson's] wife, Doris Sewell Jackson" (Lehman and Berger 301).

2. The creation of consumers as a phenomenon beginning in the fifties was a topic of Chapter One, "Material Differences." The next step at the commercial level was parallel to the "Congeniality" of Chapter Four: artists created a community of purpose, entrepreneurs created a target audience. The electronic technology in both cases was able to surmount regional scarcities and unite isolated pockets of people into useful national collectivities. There may not have been enough people in any one area to make James Dean's mumbling momentum a major style, but when films and magazines united them all, across the nation, they constituted a cult, and Dean was a star. Likewise, Maine alone did not have a target audience of duck hunters and woods ramblers sufficient to compose a major sartorial style, but mail-order persistence uncovered enough closet Maine woods fantasists hunkered down in the megalopolis to turn L. L. Bean into a household word. From L. L. Bean to Banana Republic, Patagonia to Smith & Hawken, J. Crew to Williams-Sonoma, the art directors of the mail-order catalogues mushrooming since the fifties have discovered that selling clothes and tools and cobalt blue food processors is easier if they embed them in a way of life implying a cohesive community. I don't buy waterproof boots; I buy the lore and camaraderie of the Maine woods. I don't buy a spade; I buy an ecologically sound, organic ethic. This shaker-knit cotton top is less a sweater than a sunset clambake on Martha's Vineyard with wet-haired, round-cheeked college kids.

3. Of these, Riesman's understanding of loneliness would have the most generative staying power. The loneliness in mass society generated its internal critique and also invited the double use of the media from above and from below. To solve loneliness, macro-theorists prescribed compacting the populace from above into a manageable mass. From below, macro-activists tried to break the society into small groups that could behave like folk groups of old.

4. James E. B. Breslin gives another good example of such a proclamation and its simultaneous contradiction when he cites John Crow Ransom's remark in 1958 that "'the chances are not so bright now for poetries which are radically new,'. . .just at the time," Breslin goes on in his own voice, "when such poetries were beginning to appear — e.g., Allen Ginsberg's 'Howl' (1956), Frank O'Hara's *Meditations in an Emergency* (1957), Denise Levertov's *Here and Now* (1957) as well as Lowell's *Life Studies* (1959)" (22).

5. See Thoms's letter to *The Athenaeum*, 12 August 1846 (Dundes 4–6).

6. And it changed me, too, as a teenager growing up a Houston youth. My own interest in the deliberately speeding culture dates to a specific latenight dialogue between Mel Torme and Jack Teagarden about jazz. In retrospect, they seem entirely tame luminaries. However, to a twelve-year-old who had thought the airwaves consisted more or less of Hopalong Cassidy and the modulated voices of the Saturday opera, Torme and Teagarden opened secret gates. My radio then was a Sears Silvertone. It was small, beige-pink, monaural, had a circular dial, and tubes destined for multiple burn-out and replacement. Even with its buzz, broken knobs, and off-beam drift, I'd do anything to have it back again.

7. Some of the most hieroglyphic English Marxist sociology is devoted to accounting for this shift. With that caveat, here are some places to begin looking: Stuart Hall and T. Jefferson, eds., *Resistance Through Rituals*, London: Hutchinson, 1976. Also see Stuart Hall, "Culture, Media, and the Ideological Effect" in James Curran et al., *Mass Communication and Society*, Beverly Hills, Calif.: Sage, 1979. And Dick Hebdige, *Subculture: The Meaning of Style*, London: Methuen, 1979 — for my purposes, the best of the lot. A description of the robot-resistance change, based on the English terminology but quietly withdrawing agency from poplore and returning it to the avant-garde is in T. J. Crow's important article "Modernism and Mass Culture in the Visual Arts" (Buchloh, Guilbaut, and Solkin 215–64).

An accessible, even entertaining example of this theoretic strain in practice is Greil

Marcus's *Lipstick Traces: A Secret History of the Twentieth Century* (1989). Marcus's important book appeared after I had completed *Deliberate Speed*, so I was unable to incorporate his parallel perspective.

My concept of the lore cycle, which I described in the previous chapter and elaborate further in this one, developed partly in trying to understand this constant retitillation of exhausted totems into new fetishes. Whether mass culture absorbs or rehabilitates an external peasantry, whether society is falling from a golden era or ascending toward a better time are abstract issues both independent of and determinant of the lore cycle, which always has the specific grease and grain of style and argot, image and theme. Lore cycles intersect with the larger drifts of class and society most noticeably when an absorbed peasantry, an artisan class, or some other lore group makes a concerted move to log its values in canonical consciousness. Those are the epochal moments.

8. Men-in-aprons was a central anxiety throughout American culture in the mid-fifties. When the leaders of the Montgomery bus boycott were meeting to plan their meeting on the first day the buses had rolled without Negroes, some of the ministers were timidly trying to find ways to maintain anonymity before the public. E. D. Nixon rose to scold them: "'You ministers have lived off these wash-women [who were bearing the arrests while the men backed down like "little boys"] for the last hundred years and ain't never done nothing for them. . . . We've worn aprons all our lives,' he said, 'It's time to take the aprons off. . . . If we're gonna be mens, now's the time to be mens'" (Branch 136).

9. This popularity went on to become international, but it also was immediate and intense. Besides the throngs that jammed the Museum of Modern Art, the book reached positions 16 and 13 on the *Times* best-seller lists and sold 130,000 copies the two weeks *before* publication date (21 June 1955).

10. Susan Sontag has commented on the Steichen exhibit, naturally enough for some-one of her contemporary position, from an anti-Frazer angle:

> Five hundred and three photographs by two hundred and seventy-three photog-raphers from sixty-eight countries were supposed to converge — to prove that humanity is "one" and that human beings, for all their flaws and villainies, are attractive creatures. The people in the photographs were of all races, ages, classes, physical types. Many of them had exceptionally beautiful bodies; some had beautiful faces. As Whitman urged the readers of his poems to identify with him and with America, Steichen set up the show to make it possible for each viewer to identify with a great many of the people depicted and, potentially, with the subject of every photograph: citizens of World Photography all. (32)

By "universalizing the human condition, into joy," says Sontag, Steichen's exhibit "render[ed]· history and politics irrelevant" (33).

11. The Beats were aware of this connection to Whitman and the Twain era; Ginsberg cites this passage at the beginning of *The Fall of America* (1973).

12. See *Composed on the Tongue*, ed. Donald Allen, Bolinas, Calif.: Grey Fox Press, 1980.

13. Carl Solomon, to whom Allen Ginsberg had addressed "Howl," worked for Ace Books, a family firm specializing in drugstore paperbacks. They offered to publish *On the Road* as it was on the manuscript roll, plus his next two manuscripts. Kerouac was interested but ambivalent. His discovery of sketching in October 1951 absorbed him so much that: (1) he stopped thinking of *On the Road* as his final draft and (2) his revised versions were too extreme for a mass-market house to publish (Hunt, *Crooked Road* 119–20). Still, the roll manuscript had an autonomous life because of its vigor and Ginsberg's devotion to it. One way to understand *On the Road* is to see it as the ultimate poplore acceptable to a mainstream house in the fifties. The price for noticing a vernacular vitality that exceeded conventional carrying capacity was that it must finally be left out in the cold — as *Visions of Cody* was until 1972.

14. See my "Bibliographical Essay" in Rourke's *American Humor* (319–22).

15. In his short essay on *Ulysses,* Eliot singled out Joyce's greatest contribution as his mythical method. See "Ulysses, Order, and Myth."

16. A conveniently available version of this side is on *The Best of Count Basie* (MCA2-4050). Kerouac dates it incorrectly as 1938 (391). Schuller, in *The Swing Era,* puts it in "early 1939" (246).

17. *Partisan Review* went Beats-bashing every spring in the late fifties. John Hollander reviewed *Howl* in the Spring 1957 issue as "a dreadful little volume"; Norman Podhoretz elaborated this news the next year in his "The Know-Nothing Bohemians," *Partisan Review,* Spring 1958: 305–18; Diana Trilling weighed in with "The Other Night at Columbia: A Report from the Academy" in the Spring issue, 1959, 214–30. The Trilling piece is quite the most penetrating, but misapplies a feminist weariness of her husband's generation to their Beat offspring.

18. Gerald Nicosia points out this pun on *Adios* and compares the ending to Thoreau's conclusion of *Walden* (386–87).

19. Especially, *Nation* pieces on 7 April 1945, 1 February 1947, 24 January 1948, 19 February 1949 (all collected in Greenberg, *Essays* 2). Greenberg himself was contradictory on this point. The tenor of his argument was of course that advanced painting must move away from representation, and that Pollock was great to the extent that he did so. However, one of his most famous claims for Pollock, the one that got him in trouble with *Time,* appearing first in *Horizon* (October 1947, repr. *Essays* 2:160–70), had it that "Pollock's art is still an attempt to *cope with* urban life" (166). When I say that even the so-called pure artists were representing an attitude if not an object, I mean it the same way that Greenberg does when he tries to hide the idea in his euphemistic "cope with."

20. Prestige/Fantasy reissued the relevant quartet and initial Quintet sessions as *Green Haze* in 1976 (P24064). The history of Davis's growth on his own, of his tone, of his leadership, of his compositional skills, and as a soloist is available on the indispensable collection of all seventeen Miles Davis's sessions (94 performances) for Prestige from 1951 to 1956 as *Miles Davis: Chronicle* (P-012 [1980]; PCD-012-2 [1987]). Except for the sessions he did with Blue Note, some bootlegs, and the few jumping-the-gun sessions he had with Columbia at the end of 1955, *Chronicle* makes for a complete account of studio work during this significant period in his career.

21. Hodeir's chapter on Davis (116–36) remains an excellent introduction to Young's and Parker's influence on Davis's trumpet style.

22. One of the essential jazz albums is *Charlie Parker: The Very Best of Bird* (2WB 3198). It includes "Embraceable You," "Bird of Paradise" and many more in the 1946–47 years.

23. Diana Crane has a convenient list of "seven major styles" peaking successively in the New York art world of the last forty years — Abstract Expressionism, Pop, Minimalism, Figurative painting, Photorealism, Pattern painting, and Neo-Expressionism (2). Anyone can easily extend and subdivide these categories.

24. Rose's work is in Namuth's book, which she edited: *Pollock Painting.* Rosalind Krauss also has an important essay in *Pollock Painting,* "Reading Photographs as Text"; also see her earlier "Reading Jackson Pollock, Abstractly" collected in her *The Originality of the Avant-Garde and Other Modernist Myths.*

25. "Bikini," *Fortune,* December 1946, 158.

Six   **"KEEP COOL, BUT CARE"**

1. "Ramsey was a bourgeois thinker. I.e., he thought with the aim of clearing up the affairs of some particular community. He did not reflect on the essence of the state" (*Culture* 17 — this from Wittgenstein's notebook entry in 1931, the year following Ramsey's early death).

2. I refer to the propositions in *Tractatus* with their decimal numbers, and to the numbered sections of the *Philosophical Investigations* with the sign §.

3. Although the *Tractatus* remains a crystalline precipitate of modern thought, Wittgenstein was in this issue as in many others much more precise than his stablemates. The common logical pattern ("der logische Bau gemeinsam") was for him independent, like geometry, but not a priori or privileged, like the Ten Commandments.

4. Frazer and the early Wittgenstein shared assumptions, but the philosopher later developed a profound distaste for their shared governing confidence in progress. He voiced this aversion by attacking Frazer's distinction between the ritual-practicing simpletons he thought he studied and his civilized contemporaries: "Frazer is much more savage than most of his savages," said Wittgenstein, "for these savages will not be so far from any understanding of spiritual matters as an Englishman of the twentieth century. [Your Englishman's] explanations of the primitive observances are much cruder than the sense of the observances themselves" ("Remarks on 'The Golden Bough'" 34).

5. As early as 1913, in the move that had caused Russell's despairing turn away from disciplinary philosophy, Wittgenstein had pointed out that Russell's quite advanced formulation for archetypical judgments "omitted the binding factor, the element which would combine the disparate constituents into a significant whole, and make it impossible for a piece of nonsense — such as 'the table penholders the book' — to result from the formula" (Kenneth Blackwell, cited by Ronald Clark 206).

6. Although I nowhere else directly cite Norman Malcolm's *Nothing is Hidden*, his analysis of the *Philosophical Investigations* confirmed my sense of an epochal shift in mid-century thinking.

7. By using the word "network" where I have used "net," Miss Anscombe's standard translation slightly obscures an important conceptual aspect of Wittgenstein's idea. He is ringing changes on, and trying to reinstitute the fundamentally pre-modern idea of the *net*. Probably the best example of its profound resonance in English language literature is in George Eliot's *Middlemarch*, and J. Hillis Miller provides a telling examination of its uses there in his essay "Optic and Semiotic in *Middlemarch*." Wittgenstein uses both *Netz* (net) and *Spinnennetz* (spiderweb) in the *Philosophical Investigations*, but he does not use *Netzwerk* (network). See Kaal and McKinnon (351). In the *Tractatus*, Wittgenstein did use *Netzwerk*, correctly translated as "network," but it is a mistake to sustain that concept in the late philosophy.

8. At 5.511 he uses the image of a net to speak in a quasi-religious way about logic:

> How can the all-embracing, omnireflective logic use such quirky crotchets and contrivances? Only because they are all knotted in an infinitely fine network, *the great mirror*.

This net is "purely geometrical [and] all its properties can be given a priori" (6.35). And he is confident (at 6.341, 6.342) that man-made nets completely correspond to this essential net:

> What *does* characterize the picture is that it can be described *completely* by a particular net with a particular fineness.

In the *Philosophical Investigations*, he destroys both the a priori net and man's capacity to approximate anything very near it.

9. C.f. Pynchon's description of wartime despair in *Gravity's Rainbow*, and the need to appeal for help: "our scruffy obligatory little cry, our maximum reach outward — *praise be to God!* — for you to take back to your war-address, your war-identity, across the snow's footprints and tire tracks finally to the path you must create by yourself, alone in the dark. Whether you want it or not, whatever seas you have crossed, the way home . . ." (136).

10. George Eliot cites approvingly the French physiologist Marie François Xavier Bichat who showed that "living bodies . . . are not associations of organs which can be understood by studying them first apart, and then as it were federally; but must be regarded as

consisting of certain primary webs or tissue, out of which the various organs . . . are compacted" (Book II, Chap. 15, 101). George Eliot already saw the single web slipping, described it as multiple, and jostled it together with other powerful metaphors of process and flux.

11. In chapter eleven, Herbert hears of V.'s death, refuses to admit it, and chases all the way to Sweden false clues of other women whose names begin with "V."

12. The text is contradictory about the date. The second paragraph of the chapter specifies 24 July 1913 (392), but later the same day a small stage is illuminated by "uncertain August daylight" (395). A similar sort of uncertainty occurs at the beginning of the Epilogue, whose first word is "Winter," but which leaps to "June" by the second paragraph. In this latter instance, the Bantam paperback eliminated the reference to June, but the Harper Perennial Library, a photo offset of the Lippincott first edition, preserved the mistake in 1986. There are doubtless more of these vestigial remains of early drafts and such paltry gaffes as mentioning nine planets in the 1922 South West Africa chapter (239)—when in fact Pluto was not discovered until 1930.

13. Arnold Haskell is my major source for the details in this paragraph; David Cowart gives another interpretation.

14. The information that Herbert Stencil misses in this chapter is very important. The epilogue reveals, for instance, another meeting between his father, Sidney, and V.-as-Victoria that makes possible that she is indeed Herbert's mother. Until the epilogue, readers and Herbert alike must believe that he was conceived in April 1899, in Florence, and born in 1901. Herbert discovers no other plausible moment of conception. But that means that his mother carried him nearly two years in utero. For closely reading sleuths this might be another of V.'s weirdnesses, perhaps—like her metal feet, switch in her arm, clock eyeball, and jeweled navel. Or it might more likely mean that V. cannot really be Stencil's mother. But in the "Epilogue, 1919," Sidney Stencil remembers both their tryst in Florence (488) and her living with him in England "eighteen years ago" (489), hence in 1901, when Herbert Stencil was born. This English sojourn is more complex, however, because not only did he and Victoria live together, probably unmarried, but she was also cheating on him, as he sings in the Milkman song (466). Sidney chuckles at the notion that he is the father: "His father, ha" (489). Characteristically, Pynchon's apparent clearing up of irresolution has not, in fact, resolved ambiguity so much as further muddied the waters. He gives Herbert a likely mother, but throws doubt on his father. This is a gesture entirely characteristic of the deliberately speeding lore cycle.

15. The conventional translation of Lebensform as "form of life" is unsatisfactory because of the discriminatory adjectives "higher" and "lower" invariably associated with it. We speak of lower or higher forms of life, whereas Wittgenstein was attempting to find a neutral, flattening term, a way out of this very hierarchy. Consequently, I shall use the German word. It is a cognate less burdened with the English associations.

16. In this way, Wittgenstein was anticipating what folklorists and anthropologists would come to in the fifties when they stopped wondering if literate people could be a "folk," could be bound by deeper ties than formal institutions etch. Wittgenstein knew then what folklorists have acknowledged subsequently—that megapolitan groups are "separately literate, but communally aliterate" (Toelken 504). That is, urban people can read, are not illiterate peasants, nevertheless what really shapes them is not what they read, but the informal gestures and stories that they pass along outside of books. Well into the culture of deliberate speed, as we now are, it is difficult to recognize that urban lore was ever an issue; but it was, and hotly contested, too. As late as 1972, Richard Dorson, the dean of American folklorists, was asking in print "Is There a Folk in the City?" He answered "yes" only reluctantly, and with the proviso that city folk, like city mice, were closely related to country kin. Dorson thought their lore was remaindered from the rural past rather than something they were creating constantly anew. His article was a last assertion of the old idea.

17. Escaping rebellious French-Canadian soldiers in 1837, Davy rode his "great pet Alligator, 'Long Mississippi'" up Niagara Falls. The anonymous almanac writer narrating this

tale bragged that the feat excited a salute of five hundred double-barreled rifles from Uncle Sam's watching forces for "Colonel Crockett and his amphibious pet cataract navigator" (Dorson, *Davy* 12).

18. *Diversity:* c.f. *The Crying of Lot 49,* p. 136. This passage is a summing up for that novel, an important gloss on *V.* (especially "Set/Reset" and its "excluded middle" that Sphere would inhabit if he could), and an important point of departure for *Gravity's Rainbow,* whose Zone is just such an excluded middle, or interface as I am calling it here.

19. The novelist M. F. Beal has written that Richard Fariña introduced David Shetzline and her to Pynchon "in a jazz club in the Village called The Blue Note (?) [*sic*]. Ornette Coleman was playing. I only remember important details. We were all at Cornell at the same time, but Richard was the forward one of the lot, and made an effort to know people" (Letter to the author, 1 March 1973). *Gravity's Rainbow* is dedicated to Fariña; Beal and Shetzline are mentioned at pages 612 and 389 of that novel. Ganz and Siegel knew Pynchon at Cornell, as well as later, and have written about their acquaintance.

20. His first recordings were in 1944, with Coleman Hawkins, reissued on Milestone as *The Hawk Flies.*

21. One of Ornette Coleman's earliest pieces, from his first session, 22 May 1959, in Los Angeles, paid tribute with a Monk-derived melody, and with a title added later, "Monk and the Nun." Atlantic put it out first in 1971 on Atlantic 1588, then a decade later on *Twins* (SD 8810).

22. Recorded first in October 1947 for Blue Note, and reissued as BN-LA579-H2. There have been numerous recordings of the song by Monk and others. There are three takes, for instance, in the landmark boxed set, *Thelonious Monk: The Complete Riverside Recordings* (RCD-022-2). The one including John Coltrane shows "Ruby, My Dear" much as the Quartet must have been playing the song at the Five Spot during the sessions Pynchon depicts.

23. Brown composed "Daahoud" as early as 1953 (*Daahoud* MFCD 826), but Pynchon probably heard him play it in the period 1954–56, when Brown was touring with a now-legendary quintet that included Max Roach, Richie Powell (Bud Powell's younger brother), and sometimes Sonny Rollins. Nearly every recording of this group includes "Daahoud." Powell and Brown died in a car accident 26 June 1956 — confirming the truism that Pynchon's Dahoud proclaims in *V.*

24. See "A Journey into the Mind of Watts" and "Is It O.K. to Be a Luddite?" Pynchon's answer to the last question is, yes, indeed, and ends quoting Lord Byron's *"down with all kings but King Ludd!"* (41)

25. The carved ivory comb appears at 166, 200, 209, 342, 443 (linked with Kilroy), and 486.

26. Wittgenstein called attention to ending sounds in the *Philosophical Investigations:* "535. What happens when we learn to *feel* the ending of a church mode as an ending?"

27. Letter from Pynchon to Thomas F. Hirsch, 8 January 1969 (Seed 241).

WORKS CITED

Note: An earlier date in the following references is that of the first appearance of the work.

Abbott, Berenice. "It Has to Walk Alone." *Infinity.* (1951): 6–7, 14.
Abrahams, Roger, ed. *Afro-American Folk Tales: Stories from Black Traditions in the New World.* New York: Pantheon, 1985.
——. *Deep Down in the Jungle: Negro Narrative Folklore from the Streets of Philadelphia.* 2d ed. Hawthorne, New York: Aldine, 1970.
Ackerman, Robert. *J. G. Frazer: His Life and Work.* Cambridge: Cambridge University Press, 1987.
Agee, James, and Walker Evans. *Let Us Now Praise Famous Men.* 1941. New York: Houghton Mifflin, 1980.
Albertson, Chris. *Bessie.* New York: Stein and Day, 1974.
Alexandrian, Sarane. *Marcel Duchamp.* Translated by Alice Sachs. New York: Crown, 1977.
Anderson, Quentin. *The Imperial Self: An Essay in American Literary and Cultural History.* New York: Knopf, 1971.
Appel, Alfred, Jr. *Signs of Life.* New York: Knopf, 1983.
Art Directors Club Annual 34: Annual of Advertising and Editorial Art and Design. Edited by Alberto Paolo Gavasci. New York: Art Directors Club of New York, 1955.
Baier, Leslie. "Visions of Fascination and Despair: The Relationship Between Walker Evans and Robert Frank." *Art Journal* 41, no. 1 (1981): 55–63.
Baker, Houston A., Jr. *Blues, Ideology, and Afro-American Literature: A Vernacular Theory.* Chicago: University of Chicago Press, 1984.
Bakhtin, Mikhail. *Rabelais and His World.* Translated by Helene Iswolsky. 1968. Bloomington: Indiana University Press/Midland, 1984.
Baldwin, James. *Blues for Mister Charlie.* 1964. New York: Dell, 1980.

————. "Many Thousands Gone." *Partisan Review* November–December, 1951. Repr. in *Notes of a Native Son*. 1955. London, Corgi, 1974.

Balliett, Whitney. *American Musicians: Fifty-six Portraits in Jazz*. New York: Oxford University Press, 1986.

Barber, Cesar. *Shakespeare's Festive Comedies*. Princeton: Princeton University Press, 1959.

Barthes, Roland. *Writing Degree Zero* and *Elements of Semiology*. 1953 and 1964. Boston: Beacon Press, 1967.

Bell, Daniel. *The End of Ideology*. New York: Collier, 1962.

Berenson, Bernard. *Essays in Appreciation*. New York: Macmillan, 1958.

Berry, Chuck. *Chuck Berry: The Autobiography*. New York: Harmony, 1987.

Berry, Jason, Jonathan Foose, and Tad Jones. *Up from the Cradle of Jazz: New Orleans Music Since World War II*. Athens: University of Georgia Press, 1986.

Branch, Taylor. *Parting the Waters: America in the King Years 1954–63*. New York: Simon and Schuster, 1988.

Brautigan, Richard. *Trout Fishing in America*. New York: Delta, 1967.

Breslin, James E. B. *From Modern to Contemporary: American Poetry, 1945–1956*. Chicago: University of Chicago Press, 1984.

Brookman, Philip. Letter to the author. 8 July 1989.

Buchloh, Benjamin H. D., Serge Guilbaut, and David Solkin, eds. *Modernism and Modernity: The Vancouver Conference Papers*. Halifax: Press of the Nova Scotia College of Art and Design, 1983.

Burke, Peter. *Popular Culture in Early Modern Europe*. London: Temple Smith, 1978.

Bush, Ronald. *T. S. Eliot: A Study in Character and Style*. New York: Oxford University Press, 1984.

Chambers, Jack. *Milestones I: The Music and Times of Miles Davis to 1960*. Toronto: University of Toronto Press, 1983.

Chapple, Steve, and Reebee Garofalo. *Rock 'n' Roll Is Here to Pay: The History and Politics of the Music Industry*. Chicago: Nelson-Hall, 1980.

Clark, Ronald W. *The Life of Bertrand Russell*. New York: Knopf, 1976.

Clark, T. J. *The Painting of Modern Life: Paris in the Art of Manet and His Followers*. New York: Knopf, 1985.

Coleman, Ornette. *The Shape of Jazz to Come*. Liner notes by Martin Williams. Atlantic SD 1317. 1959.

Costello, Elvis. "Radio Radio." In *This Year's Model*. Columbia, JC 35331, 1978.

Cowart, David. *Thomas Pynchon: The Art of Allusion*. Carbondale: Southern Illinois University Press, 1980.

Crane, Diana. *The Transformation of the Avant-Garde: The New York Art World, 1940–1985*. Chicago: University of Chicago Press, 1987.

Crow, Thomas E. *Painters and Public Life in Eighteenth-Century Paris*. New Haven: Yale University Press, 1985.

Darnton, Robert. *The Great Cat Massacre, and Other Episodes in French Cultural History*. New York: Vintage, 1985.

de Certeau, Michel. *The Practice of Everyday Life*. Translated by Steven F. Rendall. Berkeley: University of California Press, 1984.

Dempsey, David. "The State of Business (1954) along Publisher's Row." *New York Times Book Review*, 2 January 1955, 23.

Dorson, Richard M. *Davy Crockett: American Comic Legend.* Selected and edited by Richard M. Dorson. With a foreword by Howard Mumford Jones. Rockland, N.Y.: Spiral Press, 1939.

——. "Folklore and Fakelore." *American Mercury* 70 (1950): 335–43.

——. *Folklore and Fakelore.* Cambridge: Harvard University Press, 1976.

——. "Is There a Folk in the City?" *Folklore: Selected Essays.* Bloomington: Indiana University Press, 1972.

Du Bois, W. E. B. *The Souls of Black Folk.* 1903. New York: Signet, 1982.

Dundes, Alan, ed. *The Study of Folklore.* Englewood Cliffs, N.J.: Prentice-Hall, 1965.

Dylan, Bob. *Lyrics 1962–1985.* New York: Knopf, 1985.

Eliot, George. *Middlemarch.* 1871/1872. Edited by Bert G. Hornback. New York: Norton, 1977.

Eliot, T. S. *Complete Poems and Plays: 1909–1950.* New York: Harcourt, Brace, 1952.

——. *Selected Essays.* New Edition. New York: Harcourt, Brace & World, 1960.

——. "Ulysses, Order, and Myth." *Dial* 70, no. 5 (1923): 480–83.

Ellison, Ralph. *Going to the Territory.* New York: Random House, 1986.

——. *Invisible Man.* 1952. New York: Random House, 1982.

——. *Shadow and Act.* 1964. New York: Vintage, 1972.

Esquerita [Eskew Reeder, Jr.]. *Esquerita.* 1959. Capitol, 1550791, 1984.

Evans, David. *Big Road Blues: Tradition and Creativity in the Folk Blues.* Berkeley: University of California Press, 1982.

——. Letter to the author. 30 January 1986.

Evans, Walker. *American Photographs.* New York: The Museum of Modern Art, 1938.

——. *Walker Evans: Photographs for the Farm Security Administration, 1935–1938.* New York: Da Capo, 1975.

Faulkner, William. *The Hamlet.* 1940. New York: Random House, 1964.

——. *The Sound and the Fury* and *As I Lay Dying.* 1929 and 1930. New York: Modern Library, 1946.

Feather, Leonard. *Encyclopedia of Jazz.* 1960. London: Quartet Books, 1978.

Fiedler, Leslie. "Come Back to the Raft Ag'in, Huck Honey!" In *An End to Innocence: Essays on Culture and Politics,* 142–51. Boston: Beacon Press, 1955.

——. *The Inadvertent Epic: From Uncle Tom's Cabin to Roots.* New York: Simon and Schuster/Touchstone, 1979.

Fishwick, Marshall. "Folklore, Fakelore, and Poplore." *Saturday Review.* 26 August 1967, 20–21, 43–44.

Fitzgerald, F. Scott. *The Great Gatsby.* 1925. New York: Scribner's, n.d.

——. *The Last Tycoon: An Unfinished Novel.* Edited by Edmund Wilson. New York: Scribner's, 1941.

Frank, Elizabeth. *Jackson Pollock.* New York: Abbeville Press, 1983.

Frank, Robert. *Les Américains.* Edited by Alain Bousquet. Paris: Robert Delpire, 1958.

——. *The Americans.* 1959. New York, Pantheon, 1986.

——. *The Lines of My Hand.* N.p., Lustrum Press, 1972.

——. *Robert Frank: New York to Nova Scotia.* Edited by Anne W. Tucker and Philip Brookman. Houston: Museum of Fine Arts, Houston, 1986.

Frank, Robert, and Walker Evans. "Walker Evans on Robert Frank / Robert Frank on

Walker Evans." *Still/3*. New Haven: Yale University. 1973. [The dialogue took place May, 1971].

Frazer, James G. *The Golden Bough: The Roots of Religion and Folklore*. 1890. New York: Avenel, 1981.

Freud, Sigmund. *The Interpretation of Dreams*. 1899. Translated by James Strachey. New York: Basic Books, 1955.

Fried, Michael. "Introduction." In *Three American Painters: Kenneth Noland, Jules Olitski, Frank Stella*. Fogg Art Museum/Garland Publishing Company, 1965.

Friedlander, Lee. *Self Portrait*. New York: Haywire Press, 1970.

Frost, Robert. *Complete Poems of Robert Frost*. New York: Holt, Rinehart and Winston, 1949.

Ganz, Earl. "Pynchon in Hiding." *Plum* 3 (1980): 5–20.

Garfield, David. *A Player's Place: The Story of the Actors Studio*. New York: Macmillan, 1980.

Garrow, David J. *Bearing the Cross: Martin Luther King, Jr., and the Southern Christian Leadership Conference*. New York: William Morrow, 1986.

Gates, Henry Louis, Jr. "The Blackness of Blackness: A Critique of the Sign and the Signifying Monkey." In *Black Literature and Literary Theory*, edited by Henry Louis Gates, Jr. New York: Methuen, 1984.

Gellatt, Roland. *The Fabulous Phonograph: 1877–1977*. New York: Macmillan, 1977.

Giddins, Gary. *Rhythm-a-ning: Jazz Tradition and Innovation in the '80s*. New York: Oxford University Press, 1985.

Gill, Brendan. "Corbu." *The New Yorker*, 9 May 1988, 103–9.

Gillespie, Dizzy, with Al Fraser. *To BE, or Not . . . to BOP: Memoirs*. Garden City: Doubleday, 1979.

Ginsberg, Allen. *As Ever: The Collected Correspondence of Allen Ginsberg and Neal Cassady*. Berkeley, Calif.: Creative Arts Book Company, 1977.

———. *Collected Poems: 1947–1980*. New York: Harper & Row, 1984.

———. *Composed on the Tongue*. Edited by Donald Allen. Bolinas, Calif.: Grey Fox Press, 1980.

———. *Howl: Original Draft Facsimile, Transcript & Variant Versions*. Edited by Barry Miles. New York: Harper & Row, 1986.

———. *Journals: Early Fifties Early Sixties*. Edited by Gordon Ball. New York: Grove, 1977.

———. "Robert Frank to 1985 — A Man." In *Robert Frank: New York to Nova Scotia*, edited by Anne W. Tucker and Philip Brookman, 74–76. Houston: Museum of Fine Arts, Houston, 1986.

Gleick, James. *Chaos: Making a New Science*. New York: Viking, 1987.

Graves, Robert. *The White Goddess: A Historical Grammar of Poetic Myth*. Amended and enlarged edition. London: Faber and Faber, 1961.

Greenberg, Clement. *Art and Culture: Critical Essays*. Boston: Beacon Press, 1961.

———. *Clement Greenberg: The Collected Essays and Criticism*. Vol. 1, *Perceptions and Judgments 1939–1944*. Edited by John O'Brian. Chicago: University of Chicago Press, 1986.

———. *Collected Essays and Criticism*. Vol. 2, *Arrogant Purpose, 1945–1949*. Edited by John O'Brian. Chicago: University of Chicago Press, 1986.

———. "Modernist Painting." *Art and Literature* 4 (1965): 193–201.

Guilbaut, Serge. *How New York Stole the Idea of Modern Art: Abstract Expressionism, Freedom, and the Cold War.* Translated by Arthur Goldhammer. Chicago: University of Chicago Press, 1983.

Hall, Donald. "The New Poetry." In *New World Writing,* no. 7. New York: New American Library, 1955.

Handy, W. C. *Father of the Blues: An Autobiography by W. C. Handy.* Edited by Arna Bontemps. 1941. New York: Collier, 1970.

Hansen, Haldore. "Charge-Account Prosperity." *The New Republic,* 22 August 1955, 11–12.

Haskell, Arnold. *Diaghileff: His Artistic and Private Life.* London: Gollancz, 1935.

Heller, Joseph. *Catch-22.* New York: Simon and Schuster, 1961.

Hite, Molly. *Ideas of Order in the Novels of Thomas Pynchon.* Columbus: Ohio State University Press, 1983.

Hodeir, André. *Jazz: Its Evolution and Essence.* Translated by David Noakes. New York: Grove, 1956.

Hodgson, Godfrey. *America in Our Time.* New York: Doubleday, 1976.

Hofstadter, Douglas R. "Metamagical Themas." *Scientific American* 245, no. 5 (1981): 23–43.

Hollander, John. "The Perilous Magic of Nymphets." *Partisan Review* 23 (1956): 557–60. Repr. in *On Contemporary Literature,* edited by Richard Kostelantz, 477–480. Freeport, New York: Books for Libraries Press, 1964.

Holman, C. Hugh, and William Harmon. *A Handbook to Literature.* 5th ed. New York: Macmillan, 1986.

Huie, William Bradford. "Approved Killing in Mississippi." *Look Magazine.* 24 January 1956.

Hunt, Timothy. *Kerouac's Crooked Road: Development of a Fiction.* Hamden, Conn.: Shoe String/Archon, 1981.

Hunt, Timothy. "The Composition of *On the Road.*" In *On the Road,* by Jack Kerouac, edited by Scott Donaldson, 465–84. New York: Viking-Penguin, 1979.

Hurston, Zora Neale. *Mules and Men.* 1935. Bloomington: Indiana University Press, 1978.

Hyman, Stanley Edgar. "American Negro Literature and the Folk Tradition." *Partisan Review* 25 (1958): 197–222. Repr. in *The Promised End,* 295–315. Cleveland: World, 1963.

———. "The Goddess and the Schlemihl." *New Leader* 46 (18 March 1963): 22–23. Repr. in *On Contemporary Literature,* edited by Richard Kostelantz, 506–10. Freeport, N.Y.: Books for Libraries Press, 1964.

Inge, William. *Four Plays.* 1958. New York: Grove, 1979.

James, Henry. *The Ambassadors.* 1903. Edited by S. P. Rosenbaum. New York: Norton, 1964.

———. *The American.* 1876–77. Boston: Riverside, 1962.

———. *Autobiography* (including, in one volume, *A Small Boy and Others, Notes of a Son and Brother,* and *The Middle Years.* 1913, 1914, 1917). Edited by Frederick W. Dupee. Princeton: Princeton University Press, 1983.

———. *Hawthorne.* In *Literary Criticism: Essays on Literature, American Writers, English*

270   DELIBERATE SPEED

Writers, edited by Leon Edel with Mark Wilson. New York: Library of America, 1984.

Jameson, Frederic. "'In the Destructive Element Immerse': Hans-Jürgen Syberberg and Cultural Revolution." *October* 17 (Summer, 1981): 99–118.

Johnson, Samuel. *Selections from Johnson on Shakespeare*. Edited by Bertrand H. Bronson with Jean M. O'Meara. New Haven: Yale University Press, 1986.

Joyce, James. *Finnegans Wake*. New York: Viking, 1939.

———. *Ulysses*. 1922. New York: Random House, 1961.

Kaal, Hans, and Alastair McKinnon, compilers. *Concordance to Wittgenstein's "Philosophische Untersuchungen."* Leiden, Netherlands: E. J. Brill, 1975.

Karmatz, F. N. "Television." *The New Republic* 133, no. 26 (1955): 21.

Kerouac, Jack. *Dr. Sax: Faust Part Three*. 1959. New York: Grove, 1975.

———. *On the Road*. [ms. 1951] 1957. New York: Signet, n.d. [Nineteenth Printing].

———. *The Town and the City*. New York: Grosset and Dunlap, 1950.

———. *Visions of Cody*. [ms. 1952] 1972. New York, McGraw-Hill, 1974.

Kerouac, Jack (Jean-Louis). "Jazz of the Beat Generation." *New World Writing*, no. 7, 7–16. New York: New American Library, 1955.

King, Martin Luther, Jr. *Stride Toward Freedom: The Montgomery Story*. New York: Harper & Row, 1958.

Kostelantz, Richard. "The Point Is That Life Doesn't Have Any Point." *New York Times Book Review*, 6 June 1965, 3, 28, 30.

Koszarski, Richard, ed. *Hollywood Directors, 1941–1976*. New York: Oxford University Press, 1977.

Krauss, Rosalind. *The Originality of the Avant-Garde and Other Modernist Myths*. Cambridge: MIT Press, 1986.

Kuhn, Thomas. *The Structure of Scientific Revolution*. Chicago: University of Chicago Press/Phoenix, 1964.

Leavis, F. R. *The Great Tradition*. 1948. London: Peregrine, 1983.

Lehman, David, and Charles Berger, eds. *James Merrill: Essays in Criticism*. Ithaca, N.Y.: Cornell University Press, 1983.

Levine, Lawrence W. *Black Culture and Black Consciousness: Afro-American Folk Thought from Slavery to Freedom*. New York: Oxford University Press, 1977.

Lhamon, W. T., Jr. "Break-and-Enter to Breakaway: Scotching Modernism in the Social Novel of the American Sixties." *Boundary 2* 3 (1975): 289–306.

———. "Constance Rourke's Secret Reserve." Introduction to *American Humor: A Study of the American Character*, by Constance Rourke, 1931. Tallahassee: Florida State University Press, 1985.

———. "Poplore and Bob Dylan." *Bennington Review*, no. 3 (December 1978): 22–29.

Lindner, Robert. *Rebel without a Cause*. New York: Grune & Stratton, 1944.

Luce, Henry R. "The American Century." *Life*, 17 February 1941, 61–65.

Lydon, Michael. *Rock Folk: Portraits from the Rock 'n' Roll Pantheon*. New York: Delta, 1973.

Mailer, Norman. *An American Dream*. New York: Dial, 1965.

———. *The Deer Park*. New York: Putnam, 1955.

———. *The White Negro: Superficial Reflections on the Hipster*. San Francisco: City Lights, 1957.

Malcolm, Norman. *Ludwig Wittgenstein: A Memoir.* 2d ed. Oxford: Oxford University Press, 1984.

———. *Nothing Is Hidden: Wittgenstein's Criticism of His Early Thought.* Oxford: Blackwell, 1986.

Manchester, William. *The Glory and the Dream.* New York, Bantam, 1975.

Marcus, Greil. *Lipstick Traces: A Secret History of the Twentieth Century.* Cambridge: Harvard University Press, 1989.

Marcuse, Herbert. *One-Dimensional Man.* 1964. Boston: Beacon Press, 1967.

McGuinness, Brian. *Wittgenstein: A Life. Young Ludwig 1889–1921.* London: Duckworth, 1988.

Merrill, James. *Divine Comedies.* New York: Atheneum, 1976.

Miller, Billy. "Esquerita! The Voola Is Back." *Kicks,* no. 3, n.d.: 4–8.

Miller, J. Hillis. "Optic and Semiotic in *Middlemarch.*" In *The Worlds of Victorian Fiction,* edited by Jerome H. Buckley, 125–45. Cambridge: Harvard University Press, 1975.

Mills, C. Wright. *The Power Elite.* New York: Oxford University Press, 1959.

Murray, Albert. *The Omni-Americans: New Perspectives on Black Experience and American Culture.* New York: Outerbridge and Dienstfrey, 1970.

———. *Stomping the Blues.* New York: McGraw-Hill, 1976.

Nabokov, Vladimir. *Lolita.* 1955/1958. New York: Berkley, 1977.

Naipaul, V. S. *The Enigma of Arrival.* New York, Viking, 1987.

Namuth, Hans. *Pollock Painting.* Edited by Barbara Rose. New York: Agrinde Publications, 1980.

Nedo, Michael, and Michele Ranchetti, eds. *Ludwig Wittgenstein: Sein Leben in Bildern und Texten.* Frankfurt am Main: Suhrkamp Verlag, 1983.

Newhall, Beaumont, ed. *Photography, Essays, and Images: Illustrated Readings in the History of Photography.* New York: Museum of Modern Art, 1980.

Nichols, Herbie. *The Third World.* [Recorded 1955–56]. Blue Note, BN-LA-485-H2, 1975.

Nicosia, Gerald. *Memory Babe: A Critical Biography of Jack Kerouac.* New York: Grove, 1983.

O'Connor, Flannery. *The Complete Stories of Flannery O'Connor.* New York: Farrar, Straus and Giroux, 1972.

———. *A Good Man Is Hard to Find.* 1955. Repr. in *The Complete Stories of Flannery O'Connor.* New York: Farrar, Straus and Giroux, 1972.

———. *The Habit of Being: Letters.* Edited by Sally Fitzgerald. New York: Vintage, 1980.

O'Connor, Francis Valentine, and Eugene Victor Thaw, eds. *Jackson Pollock: A Catalogue Raisonné of Paintings, Drawings, and Other Works.* Vol. 1, *Paintings, 1930–1947.* New Haven: Yale University Press, 1978.

O'Hara, Frank. *Jackson Pollock.* New York: George Braziller, 1959.

Oliver, Paul. *Songsters and Saints: Vocal Traditions on Race Records.* Cambridge: Cambridge University Press, 1984.

Oliver, Paul. *The Story of the Blues.* Columbia, CG 30008, n.d.

Olson, Charles. *The Maximus Poems.* New York: Jargon/Corinth, 1960.

———. "Projective Verse." 1950. In *The Poetics of the New American Poetry,* edited by Donald M. Allen and Warren Tallman. New York: Grove, 1973.

Opie, Iona, and Peter Opie. *The Oxford Dictionary of Nursery Rhymes.* London: Oxford University Press, 1951.

Owens, Craig. "The Discourse of Others: Feminists and Postmodernism." In *The Anti-Aesthetic: Essays on Postmodern Culture,* edited by Hal Foster, 57–82. Port Townsend, Wash.: Bay Press, 1983.

Packard, Vance. *The Hidden Persuaders.* New York: McKay, 1957.

Palmer, Robert. *Deep Blues.* New York: Penguin, 1982.

Papageorge, Tod. *Walker Evans and Robert Frank: An Essay on Influence.* New Haven: Yale University Art Gallery, 1981.

Patton, Charley. *Charley Patton: Founder of the Delta Blues.* Yazoo, L1020, n.d.

Peitgen, Heinz-Otto, and Peter H. Richter. *The Beauty of Fractals: Images of Complex Dynamical Systems.* New York: Springer-Verlag, 1986.

Perloff, Marjorie. *The Futurist Moment: Avant-Garde, Avant Guerre, and the Language of Rupture.* Chicago: University of Chicago Press, 1986.

Plath, Sylvia. *Ariel.* London: Faber and Faber, 1965.

Plessix, Francine du, and Cleve Gray. "Who Was Jackson Pollock: Interviews by Francine du Plessix and Cleve Gray." *Art in America* 55 (May–June 1967): 48–59.

Poirier, Richard. *The Renewal of Literature: Emersonian Reflections.* New York: Random House, 1987.

Potter, Jeffrey. *To a Violent Grave: An Oral Biography of Jackson Pollock.* New York: G.P. Putnam's Sons, 1985.

Pynchon, Thomas. *The Crying of Lot 49.* 1966. New York: Bantam, 1967.

———. *Gravity's Rainbow.* New York: Random House, 1973.

———. "Is It O.K. to Be a Luddite?" *New York Times Book Review,* 28 October 1984, 1, 40–41.

———. "A Journey into the Mind of Watts." *New York Times Magazine,* 12 June 1966, 34–35, 78, 80–82, 84.

———. *Slow Learner: Early Stories.* Boston: Little, Brown, 1984.

———. *V.* Philadelphia: Lippincott, 1963.

Quine, Willard Van Orman. *Word and Object.* New York: Wiley and MIT, 1960.

Raines, Howell. *My Soul Is Rested.* 1977. New York: Penguin, 1983.

Richman, Jonathan. *The Modern Lovers.* Home of the Hits, BZ-0050, 1976.

Riesman, David. *The Lonely Crowd.* New Haven: Yale University Press, 1950.

Riesman, David, and Nathan Glazer. "The Intellectuals and the Discontented Classes." *Partisan Review* 22 (1955): 47–72.

Robinson, Jo Ann Gibson. *The Montgomery Bus Boycott and the Women Who Started It: The Memoir of Jo Ann Gibson Robinson.* Edited, with a Foreword, by David J. Garrow. Knoxville: University of Tennessee Press, 1987.

Rose, Barbara. "Pollock's Studio: Interview with Lee Krasner." In *Pollock Painting,* edited by Barbara Rose. New York: Agrinde Publications, 1980.

Rosenberg, Harold. "The Parable of American Painting." In *The Tradition of the New,* 13–22. New York: Horizon Press, 1959.

Roth, Philip. *Portnoy's Complaint.* New York: Random House, 1969.

Rourke, Constance. *American Humor: A Study of the American Character.* 1931. Edited by W. T. Lhamon, Jr. Tallahassee: Florida State University Press, 1985.

Rubin, William. "Jackson Pollock and the Modern Tradition." Parts 1–4. *Artforum* 5

(February 1967): 14–22; (March 1967): 28–37; (April 1967): 18–31; (May 1967): 28–33.

Russell, Ross. *Bird Lives: The High Life and Hard Times of Charlie (Yardbird) Parker.* New York: Charterhouse, 1973.

Sackheim, Eric. *The Blues Line: A Collection of Blues Lyrics.* 1969. New York: Schirmer, 1975.

Sale, Kirkpatrick. *Power Shift: The Rise of the Southern Rim and Its Challenge to the Eastern Establishment.* New York, Vintage, 1976.

Sarris, Andrew. "The Acid Test of Auteurism." *The Village Voice,* 11–17 November 1981, 43.

Schuller, Gunther. *A Collection of the Compositions of Ornette Coleman.* New York: MJQ Music, 1961.

———. *The Swing Era: The Development of Jazz 1930–1945.* New York: Oxford University Press, 1989.

Schwartz, Bernard. *Super Chief: Earl Warren and His Supreme Court—A Judicial Biography.* New York: New York University Press, 1983.

Schwartz, Delmore. "Films—TV." *The New Republic,* 18 July 1955, 21.

Schwartz, Sanford. "Clement Greenberg—The Critic and His Artists." *The American Scholar.* 56 (1987): 535–45.

Seed, David. *The Fictional Labyrinths of Thomas Pynchon.* London: Macmillan, 1988.

Sekula, Allan. "The Traffic in Photographs." In *Modernism and Modernity,* edited by Benjamin H. D. Buchloh, Serge Guilbaut, and David Solkin. Halifax: Press of the Nova Scotia College of Art and Design, 1983.

Sidran, Ben. *Black Talk.* New York: Holt, Rinehart, Winston, 1971.

Siegel, Jules. "Who Is Thomas Pynchon. . . and Why Did He Take Off with My Wife?" *Playboy* (March 1977): 97, 122, 168–74.

Snow, C. P. *The Two Cultures.* Cambridge: Cambridge University Press, 1959.

Sontag, Susan. *On Photography.* New York: Farrar, Straus and Giroux, 1977

Spellman, A. B. *Black Music: Four Lives.* 1966. New York: Schocken, 1970.

Steichen, Edward. *The Family of Man.* New York: Simon and Schuster for the Museum of Modern Art, 1955.

Stevens, Wallace. *The Collected Poems of Wallace Stevens.* 1954. New York: Knopf, 1965.

Stowe, Harriet Beecher. *Uncle Tom's Cabin: or, Life among the Lowly.* 1852. New York: Penguin, 1981.

Tanner, Tony. *City of Words: American Fiction 1950–1970.* New York: Harper & Row, 1971.

Thoms, William. "Folklore." In *The Study of Folklore,* edited by Alan Dundes, 4–6. Englewood Cliffs, N.J.: Prentice Hall, 1965.

Thoreau, Henry David. *A Week on the Concord and Merrimack Rivers; Walden, or Life in the Woods; The Maine Woods; Cape Cod.* Edited by Robert F. Sayre. New York: The Library of America, 1985.

Titon, Jeff Todd. *Early Downhome Blues: A Musical and Cultural Analysis.* Urbana: University of Illinois Press, 1977.

Toelken, Barre. "The Folklore of Academe." In *The Study of American Folklore: An Introduction,* by Jan Harold Brunvand, 3d ed., 502–28. New York: Norton, 1986.

Toffler, Alvin. *The Third Wave.* New York: Morrow, 1980.

Tomkins, Calvin. *Off the Wall: Robert Rauschenberg and the Art World of Our Time.* Garden City, N.Y.: Doubleday, 1980.

Tucker, Anne W. "It's the Misinformation That's Important." In *Robert Frank: New York to Nova Scotia,* edited by Anne W. Tucker and Philip Brookman, 90–100. Houston: Museum of Fine Arts, Houston, 1986.

Updike, John. *Rabbit Run.* New York: Knopf, 1960.

Venturi, Robert. *Signs of Life: Symbols in the American City.* Exhibition Catalogue. Washington, D.C.: Smithsonian Institution, 1976.

von Wright, Georg Henrik. *Wittgenstein.* Oxford: Blackwell, 1982.

Washington, Booker T. *Up from Slavery.* 1901. Garden City, N.Y.: Doubleday, 1963.

Welsford, Enid. *The Fool: His Social and Literary History.* 1935. Gloucester, Mass.: Peter Smith, 1966.

White, Charles. *The Life and Times of Little Richard: The Quasar of Rock.* New York: Harmony, 1984.

White, G. Edward. *Earl Warren: A Public Life.* New York: Oxford University Press, 1982.

Whitfield, Stephen J. *A Death in the Delta: The Story of Emmett Till.* New York: The Free Press, 1988.

Williams, Martin. *Jazz in Its Time.* New York: Oxford University Press, 1989.

———. *Where's the Melody: A Listener's Introduction to Jazz.* New York: Minerva, 1966.

Williams, Raymond. *Television: Technology and Cultural Form.* New York: Schocken, 1975.

Williams, Tennessee. *Cat on a Hot Tin Roof.* 1955. New York: Signet, n.d. [Sixteenth Printing].

Wilson, John. *Jazz: The Transition Years, 1940–1960.* New York: Meredith, 1966.

Winner, Langdon. "Little Richard." In *The Rolling Stone Illustrated History of Rock 'n' Roll,* edited by Jim Miller. New York: Random House, 1976.

Wittgenstein, Ludwig. *The Blue and Brown Books: Preliminary Studies for the "Philosophical Investigations."* 1958. 2d ed. 1960. New York: Harper & Row, 1965.

———. *Culture and Value.* Edited by G. H. von Wright with Heikki Nyman. Translated by Peter Winch. 1977. Chicago: University of Chicago Press, 1980.

———. *Notebooks 1914–1916.* Edited by G. H. von Wright and G. E. M. Anscombe. Translated by G. E. M. Anscombe. 2d ed. Chicago: University of Chicago Press, 1979.

———. *On Certainty.* Edited by G. E. M. Anscombe and G. H. von Wright. Translated by Denis Paul and G. E. M. Anscombe. 1969. New York: Harper Torchbooks, 1972.

———. *Philosophical Investigations.* Translated by G. E. M. Anscombe. 1953. 3d ed. Oxford: Blackwell, 1963.

———. "Remarks on 'The Golden Bough.'" Translated by A. C. Miles and Rush Rhees. *The Human World,* no. 3 (May 1971): 28–41.

———. *Tractatus Logico-Philosophicus.* 1921/1922. New translation by D. F. Pears and B. F. McGuinness. London: Routledge & Kegan Paul, 1972.

Wright, Richard. *The Color Curtain: A Report on the Bandung Conference.* New York: World, 1956.

———. *Native Son.* New York: Harper, 1940.

———. *Uncle Tom's Children.* 1938. New York: Harper/Perennial, 1965.

Yeats, W. B. *The Collected Poems of W. B. Yeats.* New York: Macmillan, 1956.

INDEX